D1175079

The Enterprising Scot

The Enterprising Scot

INVESTORS IN THE AMERICAN WEST AFTER 1873

W. TURRENTINE JACKSON

Edinburgh University Press

EDINBURGH UNIVERSITY PUBLICATIONS
History, Philosophy and Economics
No. 22

EDINBURGH UNIVERSITY PRESS
22 George Square, Edinburgh 8
North America
Aldine Publishing Company
320 West Adams Street, Chicago 60606
Australia and New Zealand
Hodder & Stoughton Ltd
Africa, Oxford University Press
India, P. C. Manaktala & Sons Private Ltd
Far East, M. Graham Brash & Son
Printed in Great Britain by
ROBERT CUNNINGHAM AND SONS LTD
85224 001 5

Preface

Stinginess is the characteristic that most men immediately associate with the Scots. This viewpoint Wallace Notestein, in his study of the interplay of Scottish character and history, regards as a 'world myth' sponsored by the English and furthered by the Scots themselves. Few would deny, however, that the Scots have always been mighty men with money. Moreover, the Scots have a penchant for success, and late in the nineteenth century their aptitude for business investment, in particular, was widely recognized. It is not surprising that their reputation for shrewdness and thrift grew simultaneously with their managerial skill and insight.

This historical study of Scottish investment in the United States, chiefly in the trans-Mississippi West, presents evidence illustrating why the Scots, so recently in their long national history, gained a unique reputation as astute investors. Growth of this notion in America undoubtedly arose through contacts of United States citizens with the outstanding financial leaders of Scotland and with the managerial genius of that nation rather than with its rank and file. Scottish capitalists and industrialists in the forefront of investment activities possessed, and used, their financial resources to withstand adversity and periodic crises. The historian is forced to conclude that it was this 'staying power' and the tenacity of the Scots that, in the end, made possible their greatest financial triumphs in western America, as much or more so than the canniness demonstrated by the timing of their initial investments. Inevitably there were failures alongside successes, but the unfortunate ventures were usually sponsored by the inexperienced. Scotland's 'business aristocracy' was sagacious and determined as well as canny.

The Enterprising Scot traces Scottish interests in the western mining kingdom and the range cattle industry; in land promotions, including schemes of reclamation and colonization; in procuring and processing the products of the forest; and in growing and marketing the products of the soil. These undertakings in the expanding economy of the American frontier were made possible, for the most part, by the early profits from two basic types of Scottish investment: loans on real estate, chiefly in the farming communities of the western and southern states and territories; and from purchases of securities in the stock market, primarily those of the western railways.

This study is presented as a survey primarily to introduce a field of research of sufficient magnitude to justify further inquiry. As a historian concerned with the American West, I have attempted to integrate aspects of national and international economic and financial history with a narrative about the growth of an underdeveloped region. Western American historians will complain that the book lacks romance and human interest; economic historians will insist that the statistical data is inadequate and that the analysis and interpretation is minimal or faulty. The gulf between the research methodology of these two groups of historians is most difficult to bridge, but like the Scots, the author has the tenacity, if not the canniness, to attempt the job.

British imperial and United States historians have long written about the accomplishment of individual Scots in the American West during the late eighteenth and early nineteenth century, chiefly as explorers, navigators, and fur traders. They have long been vaguely aware of European influences in general, and Scottish in particular, in the economic development of the trans-Mississippi West during the last three or four decades of the nineteenth century. Only recently, however, have the source materials in Europe for this period become readily available to scholars from the United States, chiefly as a result of research fellowships overseas and programmes for the collection of western Americana in Europe, like that of the Bancroft Library of the University of California. All the new information suddenly made available will, in time, be assimilated, correlated, analysed, interpreted, and as a result the economic history of the American West will be built upon sounder foundations. The pages that follow represent a pioneering attempt to initiate an inquiry into the field, not to make a definitive statement on the subject.

The frame of reference for this study is the organization and operation of limited companies. Any statement made, or interpretation suggested, has validity only to the extent that the limited company is representative of the overseas investment of the Scottish people. Fortunately for historians, the legal requirement that all limited companies register their intentions, report periodically on their capital structure, and reveal the names of their shareholders has made possible a systematic inquiry into the public records. These official, albeit minimal, records of all limited companies involved in western American investments have been augmented in many cases by company reports and correspondence in Edinburgh and Dundee. No attempt has been made to locate records of firms individually owned or operated as partnerships nor has an effort been made to trace the business activities of Scots migrating to western America. Evidence is plentiful that Scots channelled money to the western United States by investing in limited companies outside of Scotland, chiefly in London, and Scottish funds in many other types of business organizations, such as the insurance companies, were likewise invested in that area. Although thorough investigations of all these factors are necessary to a definitive study of Scottish-American economic history, the collection of the information would, of necessity, be a haphazard process of seeking out manuscripts in wide-scattered libraries or in the hands of individuals. Generalizations from such fragmentary evidence will, in the end, of necessity be impressionistic, but coralled in a meaningful frame of reference such documentary material can throw additional light on the subject.

My research was launched in Scotland while serving as Fulbright lecturer at the University of Glasgow. Scholars, librarians, and businessmen demonstrated their interest in my inquiry by providing information or guiding me to other sources. Through the courtesy of the Registrar of Companies, I was given access to all the public records of the limited companies of Scotland with American interest. To two British scholars who have worked on aspects of Scottish-American investments I owe a particular debt of gratitude: W. H. Marwick and J. C. Gilbert.

Professor Herbert Heaton directed me to the most recent and authoritative information on the economic history of Britain and critically read the introduction. Leonard Arrington of Utah State University provided encouragement by his understanding and appreciation of my research project, and aided me by appraising an early draft of my manuscript.

Through the Bancroft Library's Program for the Collection of Western Americana in Europe, and a similar co-operative endeavour of the Library of Congress and the State Historical Society of Colorado, more extensive records of the Scottish companies have been made available on microfilm than I could obtain personally. My initial publication in this field, 'British Interests in the Range Cattle Industry', a monograph in the volume *When Grass Was King*, was facilitated by a grant-in-aid from the trustees of the Huntington Library for a period in residence at the library in San Marino. My greatest debt is to the Guggenheim Memorial Foundation for a fellowship that permitted me to obtain additional material at the Institute of Historical Research, University of London, and provided the time to write.

When the time came to select illustrations for my book, numerous research centres responded to my urgent plea for assistance.

The State Historical Society of Colorado and the Southwest Collection of Texas Technological College provided photographs of the range cattle industry. An outstanding collection of illustrations of copper mining operations in Arizona was located in the Arizona Pioneers' Historical Society Collections. At the Minnesota Historical Society, librarians made an intensive search to turn up illustrations of Scottish railroad and farming operations in that state. The Oregon Historical Society, the Oregon State Library, and Cronise Studio of Salem, Oregon all contributed either portraits of individuals or pictures of places important in the story of Scottish activity in the Northwest. A triumvirate of railway enthusiasts, George D. Abdill of Salem, Oregon, E. D. Culp of Salem, Oregon, and David L. Stearns of San Francisco produced extensive photographs of the Oregonian Railway from which I was able to choose a representative selection.

At the University of Edinburgh I am indebted to A. J. Youngson, Professor of Political Economy and Convener of the Edinburgh University Press Committee, and the members of that committee for their painstaking review of my manuscript prior to its acceptance for publication.

Mrs Lloyd L. Ingraham, my secretary, has made a significant contribution to the book by handling the extensive correspondence in the search of illustrations and with an overseas publisher, as well as reading the proofs with care.

W. TURRENTINE JACKSON
Davis, California, *April* 1967

Contents

List of Illustrations

ACKNOWLEDGMENTS

The publishers are grateful to the following individuals and organizations for permission to reproduce illustrations. Scottish American Investment Co., Ltd., Plates 1, 12, 20 and 21; Alliance Trust Co., Ltd., Plates 4, 5, and 29; Les T. Ordeman, The Oregon Journal, Portland, Oregon, Plate 3; Arizona Pioneers' Historical Society Library, Plates 17, 18 a, b, and 19 a, b; Minnesota Historical Society, Plates 6 and 25b; Library, State Historical Society of Colorado, Plates 13 and 14; Southwest Collection, Texas Technological College, Lubbock, Texas, Plates 9, 11, 15 and 16; Cronise Studio, Salem, Oregon, Plate 25a; George B. Abdill, Roseburg, Oregon, Plates 22, 23 and 24; Oregon Historical Society, Portland, Oregon, Plate 7; Oregon State Archives and Library, Salem, Oregon, Plate 8; Dundee Art Galleries, Plate 27; Edinburgh Room, Edinburgh Central Library, Plate 2; Mr Cremer, Edinburgh, Plate 28; Mr B. Lenman, Dundee, Plates 10 and 26.

TO BARBARA

In memory of our happy
and rewarding year in Scotland

Blackwood's Edinburgh Magazine
October 1884

There was a time when Scotland made a boast of her poverty. She was proud to be known as 'the land of brown heath and shaggy wood'. When her hillsides were left free to her hardy sons, she could look with Spartan contempt on the purse-proud Saxon with his meadows and his cotton factories. But the spirit of the age at length proved too much for the self-denying Scot. . . . He threw himself with characteristic energy and single-mindedness into every new venture that turned up . . . wherever money was to be made the proverbial Scotchman had not long to be looked for. . . . In the course of the first half of the present century Scotland was changed from one of the poorest to one of the most prosperous countries in Europe.

Introduction

At the beginning of the nineteenth century Britain was in the midst of the transition from an agricultural and commercial economy to that of an industrial nation. Machine production led to a substantial rise in the economic output for the international market and a corresponding increase in foreign trade. The production of goods rose much more rapidly than population and laid the foundations for a substantial rise in the standard of living and for the accumulation of investment capital. Professor J.D. Chambers has suggested that the great period of industrialization, when Britain became 'the workshop of the World', was between 1820 and 1880, or more specifically from the financial crisis of 1825 to the impact of the Great Depression of 1873. Britain was not only the pioneer in the world industrial revolution, but also the unchallenged leader in the world economy during these years. British economic supremacy did not come to an end in the last quarter of the century but underwent a transition whereby that nation became the world's banker and trader, and a vigorous competitor with other industrial nations of the world whom she had assisted in gaining economic maturity.[1]

In fact, migration of capital abroad had been a distinctive feature of British business and finance throughout the nineteenth century. Britain had secured her place as the leading creditor nation of the world by 1815, a place she was to occupy without question for a century. Although funds were needed for the industrialization of Britain, capital required for the industry of the geographically small nation was much less than that needed for large underdeveloped areas of the world like the United States. Another factor drawing investment capital overseas was the comparatively higher earnings on investments there. The steadily increasing funds available for export to the United States and elsewhere represented not only the savings of British people amassed over many generations, but the exceptional profits from industrial production and overseas trade that had developed in the early decades of the nineteenth century.[2]

After 1815, the flow of British capital to America was continuous but, according to C.K. Hobson, in some years the stream became a rushing torrent and in others it virtually dried up. Prior to the American Civil War, investment was an individual matter with investors seeking out and purchasing likely looking securities in the United States, usually upon the advice of their banker and counsellor. This capital went largely into banks, into bond issues floated by various states for public works, and to a lesser extent into private companies engaged in business. Optimum conditions for investment prevailed at mid-century, and English investors, heavily laden with idle capital, were searching for suitable investment fields in the United States. California gold discoveries in 1848 precipitated a rapid movement of capital to the Pacific coast.[3] The economic dislocation caused by the Civil War in the United States forced a temporary curtailment in British investment, but confidence in America's economic future came back rapidly after 1865. Securities of states were no longer favoured, but those of the federal government and the railroads that were rapidly expanding the transportation network more than replaced them. Railroad stocks became a universal family investment. These were generally considered 'investment securities' as opposed to speculative holdings, a type which J. H. Clapham asserted 'a country lawyer might not question if found among the inherited capital of a maiden lady'.[4] By 1869, when the first transcontinental line was completed across the American West, foreigners, the overwhelming majority British, were thought to have nearly £300,000,000 invested in the United States.[5]

Although expansion was the continuing and distinctive characteristic of nineteenth-century British economy, the economic cycle fluctuated violently at times. The years 1870–3 were characterized by prosperity and the rapid expansion of investment. British export capital rose from £28 million in 1870 to £76 million in 1872, but tapered off to £63 million in 1873. Late in the summer of that year, a sharp economic downturn developed in continental Europe, spread rapidly to Great Britain, then to the United States. The seven-year period, 1874–80, was characterized by a decline in British overseas investment. The annual flow of 1874 was only £49·5 million and the 1875 figure was virtually cut in half again. British investors had become as cautious as they had once been daring. Many withdrew their capital abroad either by direct sale or by failure to reinvest their holdings upon redemption.

By 1880 the pessimism and uncertainty created by the Panic of 1873 and the following recession had been dispelled sufficiently to permit a revival in the export of British capital. The trend was upward to 1890, although there were some relapses, the most pronounced occurring in 1883 and 1885. In 1890 the export of capital reached £85·6 million, exceeding the previous peak of 1872 for the first time. There was also a noticeable shift in geographic distribution of overseas lending in the 1880s. While commitments in continental Europe declined relatively, more investments were now being made within the Empire, notably in Australia, South Africa, and Canada, and in South America as well as in the United States.[6] The end of the decade, according to Hobson, witnessed 'a collapse in Argentina, followed by a crisis in Australia, and soon afterwards by a crash in America'.[7] Foreign investment fell off by more than a third in 1891, but the impetus gained during the years 1888–90 was not exhausted. The world-wide financial upheaval led to a panic in the United States by 1893 comparable in many ways to that of 1873. When prosperity returned in 1895–6, British capital did not again find a sizeable outlet in the United States. Industrial development had greatly expanded in that country during the two decades between panics, and domestic investment capital had become available for meeting attractive demands. In fact, the flow of overseas capital had reversed and many United States capitalists were purchasing American railway securities held by Europeans. American capital began to make an appearance in Europe, as well as in Canada, and Central and South America.

In spite of the periodic fluctuations in the amount of British foreign investment and the ever-changing emphasis on various geographic areas, one fact remains outstanding: the total of foreign investments had risen from about £800 million in 1871 to about £3,500 million in 1913. Sometimes less than half of this amount was lent within the Empire, and large sums were invested in Argentina and Brazil, and particularly in the United States, just prior to World War I.[8]

REGISTRATION, INCORPORATION AND REGULATION

Essential to an understanding of the role of the Scots in the economic development of the American West is an explanation of the nature and legal status of companies engaged in joint stock enterprise, as well as the procedures whereby they were launched and later supervised. Although much of the capital leaving Great Britain was handled by individual investors or directed by large investment banking houses, the joint stock company registered in London or Edinburgh provided a suitable vehicle for investors seeking economic opportunities overseas. British overseas trading companies were the first to utilize the principles of joint stock enterprise. At the beginning of the nineteenth century, however, English law virtually prohibited joint stock organizations for manufacturing and general investment purposes. Incorporation of a business could be achieved only through a formal application for a charter from the Crown or for a special act of Parliament.

The procedure was expensive, time-consuming, and by no means certain of success. In 1844, an act for the 'registration, incorporation, and regulation' of joint stock companies was passed by Parliament. Incorporation became a right and registration a routine procedure.

The most cumbersome feature of the new standardized system involved the details of 'provisional registration' in the initial stages of promotion and 'complete registration' after capital was raised but before business began. A proposed company's first act was to record its name, address, and objectives with the Registrar of Joint Stock Companies. Prospectuses were to be filed. Each director had to accept his appointment in writing and take at least one share of stock. In this way he assumed legal liability, as yet still unlimited. A Winding-Up Act was soon passed summarizing the legal steps for terminating business. These first statutes applied only in England. The need was by no means so great in Scotland, where legal restrictions on corporate enterprise were less binding, and business associations, in corporate form, were recognized under the common law.[9]

Many individuals of wealth, unable to enter business as active partners because of age, sex, or training had no means of investing a portion of their wealth in productive enterprises without risking all their possessions, on occasion involving the savings of a lifetime. Businessmen with limited capital and unlimited initiative complained that capital and enterprise were divorced. Limited liability was earnestly desired so that the investor would be obligated only for the nominal value of the shares in a company to which he subscribed. In case of financial disaster, no further levies could be made on his resources. The concern of men of wealth was not sufficient to win the cause, but 'in all this babel of opinion... among the merchant princes and the captains of industry, the humble voice of the small capitalists was not quite unheard'.[10] Under popular pressure, the government sponsored the Limited Liability Act of 1855 for companies, provided one-fourth of the nominal capital was subscribed at the time of registration, fifteen per cent paid up, and the word 'Limited' added to the company name. This new law constituted a change of first magnitude in the business history of Britain. Professor Jenks has suggested 'The Stock Exchange joined the House of Commons as an institution upon which the common hopes and fears of the enfranchised classes centered.'[11]

The Limited Liability Act of 1855 was repealed the following year and a more detailed Joint Stock Companies Act substituted. Any seven persons could form a limited liability public company. They were required to file a 'Memorandum of Association' with the Companies Registration Office stating the name of the proposed company, its purpose, and nominal capitalization. Subsequently, a second document known as the 'Articles of Association', including rules for the company, was to be filed. If the incorporators did not plan to solicit funds from the public, and if their shareholders were limited to twenty individuals, the company was designated a 'private' company. Those advertising for funds, through prospectuses, were known as 'public' companies. Minority rights were protected in the public companies so that one-fifth of the stockholders, holding as much as twenty per cent of the stock, could request an inspection by accountants of the Board of Trade.[12]

In 1862, a Companies Act was passed to consolidate all regulations relative to the registration, limited liability, and winding-up of business enterprises. An annual summary statement of capital structure and number of shares outstanding was required of every Company including the number of shares applied for since the commencement of the company, the amount of calls on each share, funds received on calls, calls unpaid, and the number and par value of the shares forfeited. In addition, a list of stockholders had to be filed annually, showing the number of shares held by each individual, his address and occupation, and the number of shares he had bought or sold during the year, with dates of the transactions. A limited liability company was still required to use the word 'Limited' at the end of its corporate name so that investors and creditors would know the directors and stockholders were not personally liable for business debts. Registered companies were also required to hold regular meetings of stockholders, appoint auditors to examine accounting records and report their findings to stockholders, and publish annually an audited balance sheet at the time stockholders convened. For purposes of uniformity, its provisions were applicable to Scotland as well as to England.[13]

Tradesmen and workingmen had argued that they had the *right* to some means of investment for their savings that would be safeguarded, and the Christian Socialists had taken up their cause. As Professor Chambers has suggested, 'The pressure had come, not from industry or the professional money market, but from reformist organizations and above all from the small provincial investors who were numerous and strong enough to press their claim to a share in the profits of enterprise over which they had neither the power nor the wish to exercise control.'[14]

Freed from the onus of assuming unlimited risk, men of wealth, particularly the landed proprietor who was inexperienced in commercial business, released their savings for the first time. In addition, a new source of investment funds, savings of the middle-income classes and the workingmen, became available. Numerous small shareholders pooled their resources in limited liability companies and their collective investment proved significant to the British economy. The way was thus prepared for the modern era of British investment. Between the Acts of 1856 and 1862 almost 2,500 limited liability companies were incorporated and within the next four years an additional 3,000 were registered, but of the last group one-third failed to engage in business.

This development coincided with the close of the American Civil War and a sudden and exceptional demand for development of the resources of the American West. The lure of this field ready for exploitation, coupled with the relative novelty of limited liability, help to explain the boom in British overseas investment in the United States, 1870–3. Here also lies a partial explanation of the period of unrestrained speculation in railroad, mining, and cattle shares that was a part of the investment picture in these years.

THE SCOTTISH ECONOMY AND OVERSEAS INVESTOR

Scotland and Scotsmen were significant factors not only in the tremendous economic growth of Great Britain in the nineteenth century but they also played a vital role in the migration of capital overseas. The pattern of Scottish foreign investments, as distinct from that of the English, has several distinguishing characteristics. For example, the Scots were somewhat slower and less aggressive than their English cousins in turning to foreign fields prior to 1870. A sporadic beginning was made in 1837 with the formation of the Illinois Investment Company. Within three years at least three additional middle western enterprises, the North American Investment Company (1839), Michigan Investment Company (1839), and the Galena Investment Company (1840), were launched by Aberdeen financiers who risked £120,000. Three of these companies sent home annual dividends of from twelve to fifteen per cent; only one, the Galena Investment Company, a lead mining venture, failed to become a profitable concern.[15] In these years the bulk of Scottish capital, much smaller than English reserves, was needed at home. Capital that was released by the partial liquidation and transformation of cotton enterprises in mid-century was used for the expanding jute manufacturies replacing the linen industry of Dundee. Soon tremendous capital demands were made for development of the metallurgical industry with its various branches of coal mining, smelting, forging, and shipbuilding. As the primary emphasis upon cotton textiles in the southwest of Scotland gave way to the 'heavy industries', a very large percentage of the country's investment capital was absorbed.[16]

When Scottish capital began to flow abroad in small but significant amounts during the late 1860s, the process took two main forms: establishment of productive enterprises in foreign lands, sometimes as subsidiaries of firms at home; and the direct investment of capital in land, mines, and securities of railway corporations registered abroad. Companies in the first category were usually concerned with exploitation of natural resources, such as minerals to provide supplies for Scottish manufacturers. The Glasgow Port Washington Iron and Coal Company, Limited, acquired nine hundred acres in Ohio expecting to develop mineral resources.[17] Another example of Scottish investment in overseas manufacturing enterprises to exploit natural resources is provided by Dundee investors, who financed the ultimately dangerous competitors in jute manufacture in India. The first jute spinning machinery was erected near Calcutta in 1855. By 1873 three Scottish-sponsored jute manufacturing companies had been formed whose capital was about one-third of that invested in Indian jute.

In the 1870s real estate was attracting far more Scottish capital than the subsoil mineral deposits. In addition to outright purchase of acreage and the promotion of schemes of immigration, there were investments in land mortgages, and outright buying and leasing of land to obtain range for cattle operations. Although the Scots sponsored some single-purpose ventures, they did not take advantage of the limited liability legislation to form this type of business endeavour with anything comparable to the enthusiasm of the English. However, they did follow the English lead in supporting construction of new railroads in the United States. As the account of Scottish investment in the United States, particularly in the western states in the last half of the nineteenth century, is revealed in the pages that follow, readers will understand that investments here were but one, albeit an important one, of worldwide Scottish investments. For example, a similar pattern will be found in Australasia where Scots were heavily committed to real estate, mining, and railways.[18]

The great drawback to individual and single company action was the difficulty of obtaining enough accurate information about a borrowing company or the general economic and political conditions of the area in which there was a desire to do business. The bondholder entrusted his money to a foreign corporation entirely at his own risk. In periods of crisis, foreign loans and investments were invariably harder hit than domestic. British bondholders in many instances became increasingly conservative, and American businessmen and financiers complained that they obstructed plans for industrial and commercial expansion. The growing insecurity of investment abroad reached a climax in 1868 when an indignant public opinion in Britain demanded creation of the Association of Foreign Bondholders. The idea behind the Association was to place responsibility upon the British banker who sold foreign bonds. Moreover, by means of financial boycott the Association could threaten any government or corporation refusing to honour its obligations. American railroads were making wholesale claims on British capital and much of the work of the Association was concerned with the sale of these securities in Britain and the regimentation of voting power of purchasers.[19] Nevertheless, financial manipulations and periodic depressions kept the investing public increasingly concerned and cautious about new American ventures. The Association, a temporary agency established on the basis of retaliation, was far from satisfactory. A permanent, legalized form of business investment directed by British citizens was sought to give counsel in the initial stages of security selection.

Prior to the early 1870s, informal co-operative investments were undertaken in England when the landed classes sought the advice of lawyers and businessmen. Men of money and comparative leisure formed alliances with men knowledgeable in finance for joint investments. In Scotland men who had made fortunes in commerce and industry but who had limited understanding of investment depended upon the counsel of a financial agent residing in London or Edinburgh. Co-operative joint ventures were rare.[20] Moreover, the landed class did not play an important role in the historical evolution of the investment trust in Scotland as in England. The first Scottish investment trusts, located in Dundee, were sponsored by manufacturers and merchants who had become wealthy from nineteenth-century industrialization. They served not only as trust directors but also were among the heaviest purchasers of certificates.

With the investment trust, the burden of responsibility could be shifted from the individual investor to a group of experienced financiers. Trust company directors assumed an obligation for purchase and sale of securities, and for periodic shifting of investment funds. Thus the trust provided two desperately needed functions: expert advice and management of investment capital coupled with a wide diversification of securities. This more satisfactory procedure in exporting capital with a reasonable guarantee of security and profit did not evolve until Britain had been the world's leading creditor for over forty years.

A case can be made for the selection of 1873 as the beginning date for the modern period of Scottish overseas investment. The severe economic crisis of that year in the United States temporarily depressed many securities in the stock market, particularly those of the overcapitalized railroads. Scots seized this opportune moment to enter the American investment field. The significance of this development in the total British investment picture has been illustrated by the statistical calculations of C. K. Hobson. In the early 1870s the flow of capital away from Britain was greater than the return from overseas holdings. This was partially explained by the diminishing income from United States investments during the depression. In a reinterpretation of the figures, C. R. Fay suggests also that 'after the crisis had broken out, Great Britain could not, or did not choose to, bring resources home. Perhaps she, too, was picking up properties cheaply in America at this point.'[21] As evidence in subsequent chapters will prove, this was certainly true of the Scots. Need for money to reorganize the railways of western America was acute. Moreover, as Scotland entered the 'Great Depression', that struck with unusual severity in agriculture, the booming production of American grain belts could not be disregarded. Loans were being sought far and wide to push the 'Farmer's Frontier' westward; interest rates were unusually high on land loans to farmers, in some localities four times as great as in Scotland. Capital was continuously required for the expanding western economy after 1873. For at least half a century, the Scot found an outlet and a reward for his capital and enterprise in the United States.

Chapter One

The Scot Discovers the American West as a Field for Investment

Throughout the nineteenth century, the United States, particularly those states and territories west of the Mississippi River, constituted an underdeveloped area. The procurement of development capital was imperative. In addition to capital accumulated by the national output of material goods, the available supply was increased by funds brought to the United States by immigrants and by the inflow of foreign capital seeking a higher rate of return than was generally available in Europe. As the credit of the nation and its states improved, the future development of the tremendous natural resources of the nation was assured, and more and more capital came in for permanent investment. In the earliest years of the century money was invested in land, government bonds, or stock in the two United States Banks, and to a lesser extent in canals and manufacturing establishments. In the 1820s European banking houses began to establish branches in the United States. A large amount of foreign capital was invested in state government bonds, issued so freely in the early thirties; but when many of the states collapsed financially during the Panic of 1837 the inflow of capital quickly ceased. Even so, American railway securities were being dealt with on the London Exchange in the 1840s. As the flow of capital increased into the United States in the 1850s most of it went into railroads. The greatest portion of this capital, as suggested earlier, came from Great Britain, but France and Holland also contributed significant amounts. The amount of foreign investment in the United States can only be surmised, but scholars have estimated the total at $200 million by 1850 and twice that in 1860.[1]

The mounting inflow of capital attained large proportions in the period from the close of the Civil War up to the Panic of 1873, at which time the total foreign capital in the United States had risen to an estimated $1·5 billion. Most of this was still invested in railroads and government bonds. Although there was some withdrawal during the depression of the 1870s, leaving an overall slight reduction in foreign capital in the United States, some influential syndicates in England, and especially in Scotland, adopted investment policies running counter to the general trend. In short order the general inflow of capital was resumed and by 1890 the total had risen to twice what it had been in 1873. The last decade of the century brought with it monetary uncertainties and another depression that led to a resumption of withdrawals; but this was followed by an abounding prosperity, which induced further inflow of capital that was not checked until the outbreak of the world war in 1914. At this point, foreign capitalists had between $5 and $7 billion invested.[2]

EDINBURGH AND AMERICAN INVESTMENT

Edinburgh was not only the political and social capital of Scotland in the 1870s but a financial centre as well. Many successful industrialists, merchants, and professional men resided here, and the owners of estates in the Highlands usually conducted their business affairs in this city. Therefore, it is not surprising that the first Scottish companies taking advantage of the Companies Acts of 1856 and 1862 to invest in the United States were launched in Edinburgh. Within sixteen months, 1873–4, two were registered: one destined to concentrate on stock market securities, the other on mortgages on real estate. These enterprises, the Scottish-American Investment Company, Limited, and the Scottish-American Mortgage Company, Limited, were pioneers.

On 14 March 1873, William J. Menzies, an astute lawyer and financier of Edinburgh, assembled nine of his associates to consider establishment of a company to invest Scottish money in the United States. Son of a University of Edinburgh professor, Menzies, then thirty-nine, had been educated in both Scotland and Germany. In 1858 he had become a Writer to the Signet and at the same time became engaged in the business of advising investors, an activity that took him to the United States in 1864, 1867, and 1872.[3] On the last trip, New York and Chicago bankers convinced him that an investment company, channelling gold to the United States, could make immediate profits.[4] On his return, he drew up a preliminary draft of a prospectus, written in glowing terms, that he asked his friends to examine:

> The growth of America in population, resources, and wealth, is too well known to require any statement.... The wonderful fertility of the virgin soil, the multitude and variety of its productions and manufactures, the rapid development of its railroad system,... and the enormous immigration taking place in America, all combine to the development of almost illimitable resources and the creation of material wealth.

> The population of the United States is now larger than that of the British Isles, and besides natural increase, receives by immigration an additional half-a-million annually; its territory is twenty-eight times as large, and the legitimate requirements of the country in developing its resources afford ample opportunities for employing capital profitably, that for many years to come the demand must be greater than the supply, and the rate of interest therefore high.[5]

None of the group had greater enthusiasm for the venture than the Edinburgh publisher, Thomas Nelson. His father, who set up as a local bookseller in 1798, had died when Thomas was a seventeen-year-old student in the High School; Thomas then entered the business along with his brother William. Specializing in school books, maps, and atlases, and developing a department of juvenile literature, the firm soon acquired a distinctive reputation. Nelson visited the United States several times in connection with the establishment of a New York branch of his firm. He was a great admirer of American institutions and enterprise and took a deep interest in the American Civil War.[6] Nelson, who was 'the richest and most influential of the coterie who gathered round the board', was described by an associate as 'small in stature, physically rather weak', but 'mentally a giant'.[7]

As finally organized, the Scottish-American Investment Company, Limited, had a Board of Directors composed of Menzies as managing director; Nelson; Edward L. I. Blyth, civil engineer; J. Dick Peddie, architect; Alexander Hamilton, Writer to the Signet; A. R. Duncan, advocate; and John Cowan, paper-maker.[8] Cowan was a wealthy and influential Liberal politician, an intimate of Gladstone.[9] Edward Blyth, a large, handsome individual who had made a fortune in civil engineering, was reputed to be 'almost as well known in Edinburgh as Sir Walter Scott's monument'.[10]

As was the custom of the time, businessmen gave dignity to their joint stock enterprises by securing the services of a member of the landed aristocracy in their councils. Sir George Warrender, Baronet, of Lochend, Dunbar, proprietor of large estates adjoining the southern boundary of Edinburgh, officer in a Highland regiment and captain in the Coldstream Guards, was prevailed upon to become chairman of the Board.[11] Warrender, 'a shrewd, keen man of business', was known to be 'purse proud', but at a board meeting 'if a shareholder proved unruly, or was unduly prosy, Sir George could snuff him out in a very polite and decided way'.[12]

Nominal capital of the Scottish-American Investment Company was £1,000,000, divided into 100,000 shares of £10. Only half the shares were immediately subscribed, and £2 was called on each.[13] Plans were made to invest in the securities of American railways by making direct purchases in the stock market through New York agents. The Scottish investing public was promised that no more than one-tenth of the company capital would be invested in any single enterprise.[14] Initial investments of $50,000 were made in each of eleven mid-western and far-western American railroads.[15]

The time was ripe to move into the investment field in the United States. Civil War currency, known as *greenbacks*, although depreciated in value, was legal tender, and Scottish gold would bring a premium in the money market. The United States was expected to resume specie payments in two or three years and every dollar invested in currency would then be worth a dollar in gold, thereby representing a considerable capital gain. During July 1873 the managing director was sent to the United States to be on hand at the time when an anticipated money stringency would precipitate a drop in the value of securities. A panic which developed on the Vienna Bourse in May forced many European investors to unload their securities on Wall Street and withdraw from the American market. All gold which the Scots sent to New York was bringing a fifteen per cent premium. When the panic commenced in New York upon the failure of Jay Cooke and Company on 18 September 1873, Menzies, having large deposits in the bank, was able to purchase many first-class securities at ridiculously low prices before his funds were exhausted. By the year's end, the Scottish company had invested £436,917. John S. Kennedy and Company had given valuable advice during the financial panic and this firm became the official New York representative of the Scottish company.

The crisis had developed as a result of the overproduction of agricultural and manufacturing products and an overexpansion of the railway network. With the fall in prices for farm crops, the purchasing power of farmers diminished along with shipments on the railroads. When rail construction was forced to stop, railroad securities, particularly those of a speculative nature, rapidly toppled in value. Railroad bonds and stocks with adequate security behind them were likewise pulled down, and it was these that the Scottish capitalists sought out, knowing full well that in time their value would rise again.

As originally conceived, the company planned not only to invest in securities but to loan money on real estate. Menzies had been authorized, while in the United States, to select an advisory board in New York for this purpose and to establish lending agencies in Chicago and Toledo. After visiting Cincinnati, Chicago, and St Louis, he was satisfied that dealing in railroad securities was preferable to purchasing mortgages on real estate. In his opinion the land mortgage business would require an extensive organization of American agencies. Farms would have to be inspected, the average loan would be small, and considerable trouble would be experienced in collection. Although he had reservations about the mortgage business in general, if the company was to enter the field he preferred that they start in urban areas rather than in rural. Stockholders engaged in a thoughtful discussion at the first annual meeting, but on the basis of Menzies' recommendations voted to confine their activities to stocks and bonds.[16]

For the next six years the company was continuously engaged in expanding capital and reaping handsome profits. An extraordinary meeting in 1875 doubled the authorized capital to £2,000,000.[17] The practice of declaring ten per cent annual dividends became a habit. A reserve fund was systematically accumulated until it reached £90,000 by 1879.

On 14 January 1875, the United States Congress passed a law to resume specie payments at the beginning of 1879, after a lapse of a four-year transitional period. This legislation led to a mad scramble to obtain stocks. New York bankers made large stock purchases of first-class securities, whereupon the market value rose to such high values that the Scots refused to buy. The Scottish-American Investment Company found itself with large balances of unused capital, so Menzies hurried to the United States, and upon the advice of John S. Kennedy and Company decided to make real estate loans through a native company. The two men toured the West and agreed that land values were not as inflated on the Pacific coast, where payments were still made in specie, as in the Midwest. The Edinburgh Board approved a plan to lend money on West Coast real estate, as a temporary measure, and selected a San Francisco agent.[18] The venture into the mortgage business, though small, also proved profitable.

In 1877 the United States experienced a depression in business. Sir George Warrender explained to Scottish stockholders that the issuance of paper money in the Civil War period had led to an inflation in the value of real estate and labour wages. Now the recession had come. Moreover, American business had been upset by a series of railroad strikes and by the political conflict that followed the Hayes-Tilden presidential campaign. The business community was also suffering from anxiety over the new craze for the free coinage of silver sponsored by inflationists from the West.[19] When the United States returned to a hard money, or specie basis in January 1879, it was apparent that when the securities of the Scottish company fell due, or were sold, a permanent profit would be recorded through payments in a greatly appreci-

1. *Thomas Nelson, Director of the Scottish-American Investment Company, Limited, Edinburgh*

2. *Bowhead, Edinburgh, about 1870*

ated dollar. Thus a premium was gained when the gold was converted into paper money for investment, and when repaid there would be a conversion profit.[20]

Over one-third of the initial shareholders in the Scottish-American Investment Company belonged to one of three occupational groups: first in number were record keepers in banks and law offices–clerks, cashiers, actuaries, and accountants; secondly, lawyers, almost as numerous; and finally, merchants and tradesmen. Next in line were the professional people–doctors, ministers, and teachers. Close behind came manufacturers, bankers, and Army and Navy officers. Those interested in land were noticeably absent–only nineteen investors out of 433. The small number of shares held by eight farmers, half of this group, would not indicate that they belonged to the 'aristocracy'. Six men registered as gentlemen and four as landed proprietors. Sir George Warrender appears to have been the only peer with a financial stake in the company. Virtually every known occupation was represented.

When the number of shares issued by the company was doubled in 1875, the number of shareholders increased from 433 to 506. This is conclusive evidence that most of the original shareholders seized the opportunity to increase the size of their holdings. No evidence of speculation in shares was apparent. At the decade's close there was no noticeable increase in the number of investors holding large blocks of shares. On the contrary, the most significant change was the ever-increasing participation by small investors. There was the same continuing pattern of occupation groups investing.[21]

News that Scottish gold was available for American investments travelled fast. Within a year following the registration of the Scottish-American Investment Company, two Chicagoans, Henry I. Sheldon, a solicitor, and Daniel H. Hale, a Dearborn Street banker, were seeking untapped resources in the Scottish capital.[22] Funds were desperately needed to rebuild the Windy City following the great fire of 1871. With a population estimated at 400,000, Chicago, third largest city in the United States, was reconstructing its business district and incorporating large tracts of land to the south and west of its limits. The demand for loans on real estate there and in the farming communities of the State of Illinois was great. Minimum interest rate was eight per cent, while in Pennsylvania and New York money loaned on land brought only six per cent.[23]

Hale and Sheldon found James Duncan Smith, solicitor before Supreme Courts of Scotland, an interested party to their proposals. Together they registered the Scottish-American Mortgage Company, Limited, on 24 July 1874, to receive Scottish money on loan for fixed periods and to lend it, together with the paid-in company capital, on the security of real estate in the United States.[24] Smith, as managing director in Scotland, was to secure the cash and transfer it to Sheldon, managing director in America, who was to make loans with the approval of Hale, general agent, and an Advisory Board in the Commercial National Bank and First National Bank of Chicago.[25] As a symbol of the joint enterprise the company had two plaques, one of the Scottish Lion and the other of the United States flag, cut into the entry way of the Edinburgh headquarters. Plans were made to incorporate both in a company seal.[26]

Joining the two managing directors on the original Board were three well-to-do merchants: William Lowson and Robert Mackenzie of Dundee, and Alexander Thompson of Edinburgh. In addition, Thomas J. Gordon, Writer to the Signet, and Charles W. Cowan, paper manufacturer, signed the Memorandum of Association. Cowan, a well-known politician, who had ousted Lord Macaulay as Edinburgh's representative in Parliament, was an elder brother of John Cowan, one of the incorporators of the recently-established Scottish-American Investment Company. Chairman of the mortgage company's Board was John Guthrie Smith, Sheriff of Aberdeen and Kincardine.[27]

Authorized capital was £1,000,000 divided into £10 shares. The initial issue was 50,000 shares upon which £2 was to be paid-up. Emphasis was to be on borrowing through debentures, which were limited to the amount of uncalled capital. Interest rate in Scotland was four or five per cent. As the chairman explained to the stockholders, 'It does not require a very intimate knowledge of finances to understand that, if we can borrow in this country at 4½ and 5 per cent and advance in Chicago at 8 per cent there is a substantial profit... any schoolboy could tell that'.[28] In addition, it was now generally recognized throughout Scotland that there was the likely prospect of profit in the money market.

Although the Scottish-American Mortgage Company and the Scottish-American Investment Company had chosen different types of business activity, their capital structure and financial history display remarkable similarities. Their respective managing directors, both legal men, made initial investments after an extensive American tour. There was less 'big money' behind the Scottish-American Mortgage Company. However, landed proprietors demonstrated more interest in the mortgage business. Even so, the basic capital and leadership largely came from merchants and manufacturers from Dundee.[29] In November 1876, when the Scottish-American Mortgage Company increased its capital to £750,000, by the issuance of additional shares, thus enlarging its borrowing power to £600,000, the Dundee influence remained strong.[30] Among the ten largest shareholders, two were Americans, four were Dundee merchants, and of the remaining four from Edinburgh, two were directors. As a group, the shareholders followed the same occupations as those of the Scottish-American Investment Company. Merchants and shopkeepers, clerks and stockbrokers, and the lawyers were most numerous. Manufacturers were next in number followed by ministers, doctors, schoolteachers, engineers, and some farmers.[31]

The first loans were not made until 15 October 1874. A conservative procedure was followed. No advance was greater than fifty per cent of the appraised value of any property taken as security and each loan had to be approved by agents in both countries, the American Advisory Board, and the directors in Edinburgh. The initial dividend of nine per cent received by Scottish shareholders steadily increased each year until twelve and one-half per cent was paid on the fourth year of operation.[32]

By 1879 the State of Illinois was no longer a satisfactory field for mortgage investment, for the community had become so prosperous the interest rate had dropped to six per cent. After a tour of the American Midwest, J. Duncan Smith reported with favour upon Iowa; southern Minnesota farm lands were also a good investment, but he warned the company to avoid the lake and pine country to the north. In Iowa and Minnesota eight per cent interest, a thing of the past in Illinois, could be secured.[33] The company was concentrating its investment in the northern Plains of the trans-Mississippi West at the decade's close. Loans in Kansas and Missouri were handled by Underwood and Clark Company of Kansas City. Iowa and Nebraska operations were under its jurisdiction for a few months, but soon the Muscatine Mortgage Company controlled that business. Local agents were secured in Sleepy Eye, Minnesota; Yankton and Sioux Falls, South Dakota; and Fargo, North Dakota.[34]

Towards the close of the decade, two additional Edinburgh companies were registered to invest in the United States: the American Mortgage Company of Scotland, Limited, in 1877, and the Edinburgh American Land Mortgage Company, Limited, in 1878. Little is known of the early history of the first company. The directors made loans in Missouri, Iowa, and Dakota in the Midwest, in Oregon and Washington in the Northwest, and in Georgia, Alabama, and Mississippi in the South.[35] After an initial dividend of five per cent, shareholders' income was reduced to only three per cent and a reorganization became necessary. Although the dividend record was good in the 1880s, the £2 shares were quoted on the Stock Exchange at only 34s. in 1886.[36]

Chief promoter of the Edinburgh American Land Mortgage Company, Limited, was John Paton of Messrs Jesup, Paton and Company, New York bankers who were to become general agents in the United States. A distinguished American Advisory Board, composed of Chicagoans, was established to consult with Paton: John Crerar, vice-president of the Chicago and Alton Railroad; George Straut, president of the St Louis, Jacksonville, and Chicago Railroad; and William Mitchell, a retired merchant.[37] Paton was joined in signing the Memorandum of Association by Alexander O. Cowan, yet another member of the paper manufacturing family in Penicuik; James Muirhead, professor of Civil Law in the University of Edinburgh; James Stormonth Darling, Writer to Signet; John McLaren, advocate and Sheriff of Chancery; and William Wood, a chartered accountant, who was named managing director.[38] Darling was the eldest son of the owner of a Highland estate in Angus known as Lednathie.[39] Shortly after registration, a search was initiated for some lord or 'gentleman of high position' to become chairman of the Board. When no one was immediately available, John McLaren, soon to be raised to the peerage, was chosen to head his associates.[40]

Advertisements in the newspapers of Scotland's four leading cities–Edinburgh, Glasgow, Dundee, and Aberdeen–attracted a flow of funds for investment. Meanwhile, detailed instructions to general agents and the Advisory Board in the United States were drawn up. No loans were to be made for less than $500; any loan over $5,000 was to be referred to Edinburgh for action. Improved farm loans were the preferred security, at eight or eight and one-half per cent interest. Limited amounts could be lent on city property, but only if the annual rent was fifteen per cent of the loan asked and the property was insured to cover the loan and interest. No more than forty per cent of the appraised evaluation of any property was to be lent and all expenses in securing the loan were to be paid by the borrower. The Advisory Board in Chicago was to employ a solicitor to examine titles, and he was to be responsible to the company for their validity. Each loan was to receive final approval by the managing director in Scotland.[41]

New York agents travelled throughout Illinois, Iowa, and Minnesota seeking reputable loaning agencies. Francis Smith, with headquarters in Indianapolis, was authorized to represent the company in Indiana.[42] The Board approved sizeable loans in Kansas and Nebraska. *The Edinburgh Courant* reported, however, that the company was encountering some difficulty in placing loans at eight and eight and one-half per cent interest, and the directors were forced to channel accumulated capital into railway bonds and municipal securities, at least on a temporary basis.[43] Four Iowa mortgages were found to be forgeries, so the Board resolved to send one of its members to the United States on an inspection tour. He was authorized to call for documents and information from the general and local agents everywhere and to examine all properties mortgaged. Apparently he was reassured concerning the reliability of the company's representatives.[44]

Shareholders were soon disappointed in the comparatively meagre returns on their investment and company officers were in disagreement as to the investment policy most likely to produce greater profits. In short order one fact was more apparent than any other. Mortgage and investment companies launched in the 1880s could not hope for the profits accruing to those begun during the favourable exchange conditions and the slowly rising business cycle of the 1870s.

By 1880 these four Scottish companies had invested approximately £2,250,000 in the United States. The bulk of this money, probably £1,700,000, had been borrowed. The Scottish-American Investment Company was the most heavily capitalized with its £1,350,000. The two newer companies had time to raise only £100,000 each. Practically all of the Scottish-American Mortgage Company's £700,000 was lent on real estate, and the Pacific Coast holdings of the Scottish-American Investment Company increased the total Scottish investment in land mortgages to £1,000,000. An equal amount, or perhaps slightly higher, had been put into stocks and bonds, with eighty per cent of the capital in issues of western railroad companies.

THE INVESTMENT TRUSTS OF DUNDEE

Dundee capitalists shared with those of Edinburgh an early interest in the United States as an area for investment. Emphasis in Dundee, however, was in the trust arrangement for investments, rather than in utilizing limited liability to organize joint stock companies with extensive borrowing powers. In the 1870s Dundee was designated the 'home of the investment trust movement'. The man primarily responsible for this reputation was Robert Fleming, a bookkeeper to Messrs Edward Baxter and Son, a Dundee textile firm that had built a family fortune in factory production of linen. Fleming went to work for the business at thirteen, and by the time he was twenty-one had been chosen private clerk for the senior member of the firm, Edward Baxter. The Baxters held extensive American securities. Robert Fleming was tutored in investment procedures by Edward Baxter and given the responsibility, in time, for the management of his American holdings. In 1870 he was sent to the United States as agent for Baxter and returned to Dundee greatly impressed with the potentiality of the United States as a region for Scottish investment.[45] Like William J. Menzies of Edinburgh, he came to appreciate the fact that the American *greenback* would soon rise in value.

Dundee had tremendous reserve funds seeking an outlet. As early as 1830, linen manufacturers learned that jute fibre could be treated and made into yarn and cloth by a slight adaptation of the machines used in the flax industry. Many uses were found for jute products, particularly in making inexpensive cloth bags, and the jute manufacturers found world-wide markets. More and more capital went into the textile trade, and the exceptional prosperity of the 1860s earned fortunes for 'the juteocracy' of Scotland. The last period of heavy investment in that industry came in 1873. After that, Dundee had capital reserves for investment elsewhere. As the rising competition from Indian jute mills near Calcutta, which were near the raw materials and a plentiful labour supply, coincided with a return of prosperity in the United States, Dundee financial circles transferred their investment interest. By 1880 that city had become a centre for investment in business across the Atlantic.[46]

The First Issue of the Scottish American Investment Trust was made available to investors in July 1873. Robert Fleming, company secretary, secured the services of four well-known Dundee businessmen as trustees. Although the earliest plans called for an initial issue of £150,000 in £100 certificates guaranteeing six per cent annual interest, public confidence in these men was so great that the company's bankers were flooded with applications; the first prospectus was immediately withdrawn, the amount of the issue doubled, and still it was oversubscribed. According to the original agreement, all investments were to be realized in 1883 and the profits distributed. Just before the Panic of 1873, Fleming and his associates made a Second Issue of £100 trust certificates, amounting to £400,000. This arrangement was made for twenty years, rather than ten. With market prices low, the time was favourable for investment and this issue soon accumulated greater reserves than the first. A Third Issue, amounting to £400,000, was arranged in 1875, bringing the capital controlled by the Fleming associates to £1,000,000.[47]

Just as the investment of the £300,000 in the First Trust had been completed, panic developed on the New York Stock Exchange and the value of securities tumbled. This was particularly true of railroad stocks and bonds which were the dominant type of investment made by the Scots.[48] In the midst of the panic, all interest coupons on the company's bonds were paid. The market value of its securities showed, *in toto*, an increase, and certificate holders of the Trust received their promised six per cent. No greater tribute could have been paid to the managerial skill of Fleming. Ten years later he jokingly remarked that in the company's cable code, the word conveying the message that all coupons due during a given month had been paid, was 'miraculous'.

By 1879 the trustees could report: 'The Scottish American Investment Trusts were never in so prosperous a condition as they are at the present time'. If an attempt had been made to buy the securities held by the companies in the stock market, they would have cost £350,000 more than the £1,000,000 of company capital. The Fleming companies had a combined reserve fund of a quarter of a million pounds sterling. The annual net revenue had been between eight and nine per cent.[49] This was a remarkable financial record in a period of economic depression.

The original trust deeds issued by Fleming and his associates had been modelled on those of the Foreign and Colonial Government Trusts, first launched in Britain in 1868. Lord Westbury, Lord Chancellor of England, had prepared the trust agreement. No question arose for a decade, until the Master of the Rolls insisted that such associations be registered as joint stock enterprises under the Companies Acts of 1862 and 1867; otherwise they would be illegal. The English Trust whose status had been questioned elected to appeal to the House of Lords. Meanwhile, injunctions had been issued restricting its operation. To avoid such a legal tangle, trustees of the Scottish American Investment Trusts proposed that each issue be registered as a limited company. The reorganization proposal was accepted by the certificate holders in March 1879. No time limit on the trust companies' existence remained. Assurances were given investors that no advantage would be taken of the limited liability of the shareholders to borrow through debentures.[50]

Upon registration as limited companies, the Dundee trusts announced the names of their shareholders for the first time. Of the 385 shareholders in the first Company, more than half had less than £400 invested. Among the heaviest investors, those with £3,000 or more at stake, the majority were merchants and manufacturers. Only a limited number of shareholders' occupations were revealed in the official list of 1879, but the greatest number of those providing this information were likewise merchants and manufacturers. The pattern was the same as that found in the Edinburgh companies in these years, with the possible exception of more merchant influence in Dundee and fewer lawyers, clerks and accountants than in the Scottish capital. In both financial centres, however, these groups led the procession of investors, followed by engineers, doctors, schoolteachers, military men, farmers, dyers and bleachers, bankers, shipowners, grocers, and tax collectors.[51]

A second group of Dundee trust companies primarily concerned with United States investments had their beginnings in the land mortgage business. The first field of operation was in the Pacific Northwest. William Reid, at the time vice-consul of the United States in Dundee, promoted the Oregon and Washington Trust Investment Company, Limited, registered on 16 October 1873.

During the Civil War, jute fabric, used for sandbags, was shipped in large quantities from Dundee. Ready payment was not always forthcoming, so mortgages on land were occasionally accepted as security. These mortgages produced a high rate of interest, from seven to eight per cent, and the Scots thus learned that capital needed in the United States for land development would bring much greater returns than in Scotland. With this information in circulation, Reid had little difficulty in gaining support for his project from Dundee capitalists.[52] He particularly recommended Oregon and Washington Territory as a frontier area where the acute need of capital would keep interest rates high.

Twenty-five men of Dundee and vicinity, most of them successful jute manufacturers, signed the Memorandum of Association. The original Board included Thomas Bell and William Lowson, merchants; James Neish, solicitor; Thomas Couper, shipowner; Thomas H. Cox, manufacturer; and John Leng, newspaper publisher.[53] Cox had also been one of the original trustees of the Scottish American Investment Trusts. Leng, proprietor and editor of the *Dundee Advertiser* since 1851, was a well-known pioneer in the field of journalism and a member of Parliament. He had served as chairman of the Dundee, Perth, and London Shipping Company, Limited.[54] Lowson was a director of the Scottish-American Mortgage Company of Edinburgh. These men prevailed upon the Earl of Airlie to chair the Board; Reid was to act as secretary. The authorized capital was £150,000, but the original issue was for only one-third of the shares.[55]

A three-year agreement was made with Alonzo G. Cook, Vancouver attorney, as American agent and manager to investigate and report on proposals for loans. He subscribed to three hundred £10 shares in the company. Cook was to receive two-thirds of the usual commission paid by borrowers on getting their loan, one-third to go to the company. In addition, the company agreed to pay his office rent, legal charges, and one-half per cent of the interest payments collected on each loan. A detailed list of instructions was drawn up by the directors for the guidance of Cook, and a local Board was to be established in Oregon. Loans on farm lands in the Willamette Valley were preferred. No applications were to be received along Puget Sound north of Seattle, farther east than Cascade City, or south of Roseburg. Lands were to be occupied and within ten miles of a navigable river or a railway, or within ten miles of a town of 800 inhabitants or more. Applications for loans on town property were to be received only in Portland, Salem, Albany, Vancouver, Olympia, Walla Walla, Astoria, and Seattle. No loans were to be made on wharfs, warehouses, grain stores, factories, sawmills, woollen mills, tanneries, or oil works. No proposals were to be entertained on timber lands; each farm had to be one-third cleared and under cultivation. In estimating the value of lands, no consideration was to be given to coal, iron or other mineral deposits, but based exclusively on agricultural value. No loan was to be made in excess of one-third the valuation of the property, and borrowers had to produce receipts for taxes when paying their annual interest.[56] If such rules were adhered to, the Scots were taking very little risk with their money.

When Cook arrived in Portland from Scotland, he reported that the Pacific Northwest was prosperous in spite of the Panic of 1873. The immediate call for loans totalled £25,000, or all the company's initial capital. The prevalent mortgage loan rates were twelve to thirteen per cent. Interest in the Scottish venture ran high in Oregon, and former governor Addison C. Gibbs, Chief Justice E. D. Shattuck, and John McCracken, a leading merchant, joined the local Board.[57] Shattuck was an early organizer of the Republican Party in Oregon and had been a member of the Oregon House of Representatives. Gibbs, formerly a New York lawyer, came to Oregon as the director of the Umpqua Townsite and Colonization Land Company. He was associated with Jesse Applegate in real estate promotions in southern Oregon in the 1850s and carried the mail between Yoncalla and Scottsburg. Moving to Portland in 1858, he continued the dual interest in Republican politics and real estate promotions. McCracken, also a pioneer of the 1850s, had been elected a lieutenant colonel in the state militia.[58]

In Dundee, the directors voted to issue the remaining authorized capital, £100,000. Unlike the Scottish American Trusts, this venture was always a limited liability company. Moreover, from the very first the practice of borrowing investment funds through debentures had been followed. Apparently no difficulty was found in securing funds for two years at five per cent, four and a half years at five and one-half per cent, and from five to seven years at six per cent.[59]

The company subscribed to the Portland weekly *Oregonian* and the *Bulletin*, and soon the directors were agitated over the extent and boldness of the advertising by the local Board. Cook was notified that 'having in regard the interests of both the shareholders and debenture holders of the Company it is the wish of the directors to establish a thoroughly safe rather than a very extensive business and hence they do not wish the Local Board to hold out attractions to borrowers by *continued* advertising for loans in the Oregon newspapers having no doubt that the advantages offered by the Company will be fully appreciated'.[60]

Reid, who had served as secretary of the company during the first year, was sent to Oregon on a tour of inspection in 1874. The directors commended him 'to the courteous consideration of the Local Board in Portland,...to the Governors of the State of Oregon and Washington Territory, and to the various public officials therein, and to the other public and private corporations of Oregon and Washington believing that a free interchange of views through Mr Reid may be of mutual benefit to the Company and to the State and Territory in which the operations are to be conducted'. Reid soon resolved to remain in Oregon and was named a member of the local Board. When Cook resigned, ostensibly for health reasons, Reid became general manager in America.[61]

The new secretary of the Oregon and Washington Trust Investment Company in Dundee was William Mackenzie, destined to have a brilliant career in Scottish financial circles. A native of Dumfriesshire, he was the eldest son of a distinguished minister of the Free Church who was the author of a *History of Scotland*. Educated at Dunfermline, young Mackenzie entered business in Dundee and was an original member of the Dundee Stock Exchange. Years later, he admitted that when he became secretary of the company, he could manage to keep a cash book and balance it with accuracy, but that he had not yet grasped the secrets of double entry bookkeeping and knew nothing of company law or management. He had never seen a mortgage contract.[62]

In Portland, Reid worked aggressively to secure loans. The home office was bombarded with requests for modifications of the original company rules to take advantage of numerous offers. The Dundee capitalists restrained him in every instance and he grew restless in the yoke. In the Oregon press, advertisements three columns wide and a foot long announced:

MONEY TO LOAN
by the
OREGON and WASHINGTON
TRUST INVESTMENT COMPANY
TO FARMERS AND LANDOWNERS
Of Oregon and Washington Territory!
Do You want to borrow Money?
–either–

To Buy more Land for yourselves or your Sons?
To Build new Houses or Barns or to Fence?
To clear off Brush Land, underdrain or otherwise improve your Farms?
To change your present Mortgage and get a new one to be re-paid each Fall from the profits of your Farm by yearly instalment payments, so as to give you three to ten years to pay up your Mortgage easily? OR FOR ANY OTHER PURPOSE?

IF YOU DO,
Write
WILLIAM REID, PORTLAND[63]

The bulk of Scottish money in this company had been loaned to farmers, but funds had also been advanced on town lots, chiefly in Portland. The usual annual interest rate paid by borrowers was twelve per cent and the Scottish Board refused any below eleven per cent. The first annual dividend to stockholders had been six per cent, but the next year it was raised to seven.[64] The Scots worked out a most conservative policy. For example, the company had a scheme, previously unknown in Oregon, whereby periodic repayments of capital could be made, in addition to annual interest, rather than making a lump-sum payment of the entire amount borrowed at the end of the loan period. Following this practice, the company was partially protected against depreciation, and security for the loans was correspondingly increased. The directors, in addition, limited their debentures to the amount of uncalled capital even though they legally could have borrowed more.[65]

William Reid's annual salary was $2,150, out of which he paid office rent and clerical salaries. He pressed the Dundee Board for a more favourable financial arrangement soon after arrival in Oregon, presenting an alternative bid to work for a California company. Although the Scots were impressed by 'the very handsome' offer, they informed Reid, 'the remuneration is certainly much greater than this company can afford to give or than, as Mr Reid is aware, was ever contemplated at the time of its formation'. They agreed not to stand in the way of a better opportunity, but expected him not to jeopardize the interests of their company, on whose behalf he went to Oregon, by a sudden departure for a more lucrative position.[66] Reid finally decided to keep his connection with the Oregon and Washington Trust Investment Company, but to form a savings bank under his own guidance, aided but not dominated by Scottish capital.

Authorized capital of the Oregon and Washington Mortgage

Bank was £60,000. This Portland bank was to be modelled on California savings banks first begun in 1858, but numbering twenty-six in 1876, that earned twelve per cent dividends by investing their capital in real estate mortgages. Money borrowed for fixed periods in Oregon and Scotland was also to be lent on the security of land mortgages.[67] Two-fifths of the capital for this bank was raised in Oregon before its registration in Edinburgh. The remainder came from Dundee. There were two Boards, one in Portland and one in Dundee. Some members of the Board in Scotland were also directors in the Oregon and Washington Investment Company. There was an interrelationship between the two companies, but the management was in no sense identical.[68] The investment company advanced funds to construct a three-story building on First Street in Portland, one-half to be occupied by the Savings Bank and the other by the Trust Investment Company. One of the faces decorating the façade above the door was reported to be that of the Earl of Airlie.

While Reid was preparing to start his savings bank in Portland, Oregon, the directors of the Oregon and Washington Trust Investment Company were considering the extension of their operations outside Oregon and Washington. John Leng was sent to the United States to check on their investments in the Northwest, and was instructed to study the propriety of entering the mortgage business elsewhere in the United States.[69]

Upon Leng's return in 1876, the directors and some leading shareholders of the Oregon and Washington Trust Investment Company decided to form a new company, the Dundee Mortgage and Trust Investment Company, Limited. The object of the new company was like the old: although mortgages over real estate were to be the favoured class of investments, the company included a provision authorizing purchases of preferred stock in railway and related securities. Legal permission was granted to do business anywhere in the United States or her territories and in the British Dominions and Colonies.[70] The Dundee Mortgage Company began operations on a much larger scale than its predecessor. Original plans called for an authorized capital of £500,000. The public issue was oversubscribed three times. The directors then voted to sell 15,000 rather than 10,000 shares, raising the subscribed capital to £300,000. By 1878, another 10,000 shares were issued at a premium of 5s.[71]

The company's general agent in the United States was Messrs Jesup, Paton and Company of New York, also agents for the Edinburgh American Land Mortgage Company. The Illinois Trust and Savings Bank became Chicago representatives, and before the end of the year Messrs Balfour, Guthrie and Company of San

Francisco were to lend in California. These three cities represented the earliest centres of investment. While the company sought agents to place land loans, funds were temporarily invested in the securities of the Central Pacific and Union Pacific railroads.

Upon Leng's recommendation, Francis Smith of Indianapolis, already working for Edinburgh's Scottish-American Mortgage Company, was appointed an agent, and lending operations were extended into Indiana. Soon Messrs Underwood and Clark were advancing money for the company in Kansas, Missouri, and Iowa. During the first year the Board debated the advisability of lending money in Canada. The Earl of Airlie expressed reservations because of the difficulty in finding experienced agents. In the end he agreed that funds might be advanced in Ontario at eight to nine per cent, but a boycott was issued temporarily against sparsely-settled Manitoba where, in the opinion of cautious Scots, the productiveness of the soil was yet to be proved.[72]

The directors of the Dundee Mortgage Company were plagued by the problems of monetary inflation in the United States. Agitation for silver coinage was so strong at the close of 1877, and the policy of Congress so uncertain, that local agents were instructed not to make any additional loans until the pattern of silver legislation was determined. This situation lasted until the United States Congress passed the Bland-Allison Act. The limitations on monthly silver purchases of the Secretary of the Treasury imposed by this law were sufficient to dispel Scottish fears of inflation. The Scots had been prepared to include a clause in their loan agreements demanding payments in gold, or the equivalent, but American agents assured them they would be placed in a poor competitive position.[73]

Several of the loan agencies used extensive advertising campaigns among farmers of the United States. For example, Francis Smith posted advertisements in many Indiana hamlets proclaiming:

THE ONLY WAY
for
FARMERS
to
GET OUT OF DEBT
and
KEEP THEIR FARMS

Is by Funding all of their Debts...and paying a small part of the principal each year.
Scarcely any farmer can control a sufficient sum of money at one time to pay off the whole of his mortgage when due.

> Nearly all good men could pay some part of their debt each year, if they had the opportunity....
> As I offer liberal terms, I insist upon the best security which applicants can give.
> Write!...
> NO LIFE INSURANCE REQUIRED. NO DELAY....[74]

Simultaneously John Paton, who supervised all American agents, told the Scottish shareholders in 1878 that every applicant for a loan had to swear to the value of the security offered, and was criminally liable for false statements. The land was then appraised by two valuators. Their findings were checked by agents of the Dundee Mortgage Company, and all documents forwarded to local Boards in Chicago or Indianapolis. When everything was in order, including security of title, the documents were sent to Dundee, and the money was shipped from there to the lending agent in the United States.[75]

This company paid dividends starting with six per cent in 1877 and reaching ten per cent in 1879. As part of a programme of self-education Mackenzie decided to visit the United States. In New York he was impressed with John Paton's knowledge of the American economic scene. Travelling west, he also met William Reid for the first time and was convinced that he was far less reliable than Paton.[76]

Another favourite enterprise launched by the Dundee capitalists first associated in the Oregon and Washington Trust Investment Company was the Dundee Land Investment Company, Limited. Under the chairmanship of the Earl of Airlie and with William Mackenzie as secretary, this was an organized speculation in land, registered in September 1878. Lowson and Leng were on the Board. According to its prospectus, the company was to 'purchase, lease, or acquire', then 'hold, improve, manage and sell' real property of every description and tenure situated in the United States or the Dominion of Canada. Operations of this character were not included in the legalized activities of the Dundee Mortgage and Trust Company. Just as that company had been registered to expand the geographic area of operation, the new one gave a wider latitude to business activities.[77] The authorized capital of £250,000 was handled in the usual way.

The directors employed William Smith, farmer of Stone-o'-Morphie near Montrose, to examine the tracts of American land recommended by Paton.[78] Smith was instructed to buy some lands immediately productive of rent to meet current expenses of the company and justify a three or four per cent dividend. This was to maintain the company's prestige in financial circles. Uncultivated tracts in good agricultural areas were to be selected with the idea of inducing Scottish emigrants to purchase acreage on the instalment plan. The company proposed to break ground, erect essential farm buildings, and build necessary roads in joint enterprises with individual Scottish settlers. Smith was authorized also to buy a few lots in the neighbourhood of new western towns. Consideration was to be given to the immediate purchase of sections of land between those of the railway land grants.[79]

From the United States, Smith sent back favourable reports on Indiana, Wisconsin, and the Texas Panhandle. Jesup, Paton and Company urged investments in Missouri, Iowa, Wisconsin, and Minnesota. Nearly ten thousand acres of land were purchased in northwest Iowa counties–Pocohontas, Emmet, O'Brien, Sioux, and Lyon–at prices ranging from $2·30 to $3·65 an acre. A group migration of Scottish farmers was planned. Wisconsin timber lands were secured from the Milwaukee, Lake Shore, and Western Railroad. An agent of the Wisconsin Valley Railroad Company also sold the Scots 15,707 acres of land in Oconto County, near Green Bay, at $1·00 an acre. Profits from the resale were to be divided among the railroad, Jesup, Paton and Company, and the Dundee Land Investment Company.[80]

In Minnesota, the Scots purchased two town sites along the line of the Minnesota Southern Railroad. Streets and sidewalks were graded, a small hotel and grain elevator constructed. The new communities were named Airlie and Dundee. The St Paul *Pioneer Express* revealed these developments in an article, 'A New Rome Founded / The Town of Airlie, at Clear Lake, Nobles County / on the Southern Minnesota Railroad Extension'.[81] Soon the Scots learned that the St Paul and Sioux City Railroad was establishing a rival town site within two miles of Airlie. Under the circumstances, the company elevator and small inn, destined to become a farm house, were sold to the Minnesota Southern. Partial payment was taken in 400 acres of agricultural land, and the site of Airlie moved out to Pipestone County. The Scottish directors also decided on a similar honour for William Lowson. His residence of Balthayock in Scotland was deemed an unsatisfactory name because Americans could not pronounce it, so Graybank, his former residence, was substituted.[82]

A land agent of the Central Pacific Railroad interested the Dundee capitalists in a 1,760 acre tract near the site of Willows, in Glenn County, California. Jesup, Paton and Company supervised investment in Kansas City real estate. These American agents advised against increasing agricultural property held in Iowa and were opposed to entering either rural Kansas or Texas.

When it was realized that an extension of the Chicago, Milwaukee, and St Paul Railroad was to be constructed in northwestern Iowa, the temporary ban on agricultural lands there was quickly raised. Messrs Drummond and Brothers of Montreal were authorized to invest an initial $15,000 in Manitoba lands in anticipation of the construction of the Canadian Pacific railroad. Later interest was expressed in town lots in Winnipeg. Through William Reid, money was invested in the Portland business district, but directors of the Land Investment Company refused to purchase shares in his South Portland Real Estate Association to develop the outskirts of the town.[83]

Only occasionally did the Scots refuse an offer. The Platte Land Company, which planned to buy 300,000 acres of dry land in Colorado from the Kansas Pacific and Denver Railroad and then build an irrigation canal to turn the area into farm sites, was deemed too speculative an undertaking. Nor were they interested in ranching. As early as 1879, they declined an opportunity to purchase the Osage Ranch on the St Charles River in Colorado.[84]

Since 1875, the Oregon and Washington Trust Investment Company had been increasingly successful. Meanwhile the Scottish directors had grown weary of bickering constantly with William Reid. Several complained that his business policies were not sufficiently conservative, and all were agreed that he was antagonized by advice. Arrangements were made to send Robert Connel, trained in the Clydesdale Bank, to Oregon as joint manager with Reid. Upon Connel's arrival, Reid asked permission of the Board to realize on his capital, since his new colleague had not been expected to become a stockholder. Because Reid felt his money could be more profitably spent elsewhere, the Scots accepted his request. From this time forward there was a deterioration in the relations with Reid, now secretary of the Chamber of Commerce of Portland.[85]

But Reid's antagonism did not affect Scottish confidence in Oregon as a field for investment. The state's population had increased from 80,161 in 1868 to an estimated 160,000 in 1878. During the decade Portland had grown from a village of 6,717 to a town of 20,000. By 1878 Oregon annually shipped 176,000 tons of wheat, the major portion of which went to Great Britain. Canned salmon, exported for the first time in 1871, had increased from 30,000 to 345,000 cases annually. Canneries erected on both sides of the Columbia River had an income of over three million dollars. Statistics on foreign trade, ocean and river steamboat traffic, railroad construction, and agricultural production revealed a rapidly expanding economy.[86] Real estate had become so valuable along

3. *One of the masks decorating the Oregon & Washington Trust Investment Company building, Portland, Oregon. Possibly the Earl of Airlie. The façade is shown overleaf, plate 4* (see p.28)

SAVINGS BANK

the Willamette Valley that the Scots preferred to lend on lands in the Puyallup and Rogue River valleys in anticipation of a great increase on land values there.

In October 1878 the Scottish financial world was shocked by the failure of the City of Glasgow Bank. The Oregon and Washington Trust Investment Company called home most of its cash reserves in the United States. The reserve fund had been invested in British bank stocks, greatly depreciated by the scare following a major bank failure, and the company elected to sell the securities at a loss to its reserve fund. Moreover, the harvest of 1878 in Oregon was comparatively poor, and a few farmers had failed to pay the interest on their mortgages. Nevertheless, lending was resumed at the year's close. Neither panic at home nor a poor harvest abroad kept the company from making profits justifying a ten per cent dividend.[87]

During December 1879 the Oregon and Washington Trust Investment Company was amalgamated with the Dundee Mortgage Company. Both companies were paying annual dividends of ten per cent; they had the same Board of Directors; they were engaged in identical enterprise. Thus the land mortgage business in the Pacific Northwest was merged with that elsewhere in the west.[88] At the first annual meeting of the Dundee Mortgage and Trust Investment Company following the amalgamation, the Earl of Airlie casually announced that the usual dividend of ten per cent would be paid. The reserve fund amounted to nearly thirty per cent of the capital called up.

In 1880 the company sent John McCullock, a thirty-seven-year-old farm manager, to the United States as Superintendent of Agencies and Inspector of Loans. McCullock had extensive experience in agricultural arbitrations, in the preparation and revisal of leases, and had been a regular contributor to the *North British Agriculturist*, especially on subjects of dairy and farm management. On eight occasions his essays had won a medal awarded by the Highland and Agricultural Society. He had also served as director and vice-president of the Scottish Chamber of Agriculture.[89] The Earl of Airlie admitted the company had every reason to be satisfied with its agents in the United States, but the volume of business now justified a field officer working solely for the Scots, someone in whom they would have complete confidence.[90] John Leng, in acknowledging his re-election to the Board, reminded the shareholders that they had entrusted him with the administration of £700,000. He noted, however, 'This company will contrast very favourably with that of some institutions in the United States, managed entirely by Americans, and chiefly administering American funds.'[91]

Mackenzie, who had initiated the successful merger, was just launching his programme of amalgamations. In 1881 he became secretary of his fourth Dundee company, the Oregon and Washington Savings Bank, and immediately issued a proposal for its consolidation with the Dundee Mortgage and Trust Investment Company. Mackenzie was moving rapidly and far in the construction of the financial empire to become known as the Alliance Trust. In 1881 Robert Fleming of the Scottish-American Investment Trusts, became a director in Mackenzie's Dundee Mortgage Company, thus providing a connecting link among all Dundee men interested in United States investments. It was a tightly-knit and prosperous little group.

The Mackenzie companies were administering between £800,000 and £900,000, either furnished by the shareholders or on loan from the Scottish public. The Fleming trusts were capitalized at £1,100,000, so the total stake of these Dundee enterprises in the United States by 1880 was approximately £2,000,000. Coupled with Edinburgh's slightly greater investment, the Scots had transferred at least £4,150,000 to the United States. This sum can be accounted for in enterprises registered under the Limited Liability Acts, but the actual movement of Scottish capital was probably far greater.

The phenomenal financial success of the mortgage and investment companies was noted by the *Scottish Banking and Insurance Magazine*, which usually assumed the role of watchdog for the small investor. With these young companies averaging nine and one-half per cent dividends and accumulating reserves during a period of general depression in the United States, the publication announced that their annual reports were sound and suggested that since the price of shares had not gone too high, the investing public would be well advised to investigate.[92]

Foreign investments were far more profitable between 1870 and 1880 than investments in Britain. To meet competition from the United States and Germany, Britain was forced to lower the prices for her industrial products during the 1870s. Simultaneously with the lowering of profits from the export trade, events of the general depression, particularly in the United States, served as a stimulus to send capital abroad where the income would be greater. Of all foreign investments, those of the United States were the most rewarding. The return on United States government bonds was 7·5 per cent, while the average return on all other foreign government bonds was 4·4 per cent. The return from United States railroads was 9·3 per cent, while the return on all foreign rails was 6·72 per cent. Both were greater than income from British lines.[93] If annual profits from the land mortgage business in the United

States were included with those from stocks and bonds, the pre-eminence of the United States as a field for British investment would stand out even more sharply.

In retrospect on the decade and in predicting the future, *The Economist* remarked:

> Looking back to the close of the Civil War, with the redundant paper circulation and consequent inflation of values, we have seen the United States, as it were, first taking breath, then suffering from the inevitable decline in values–a shrinkage the most trying and severe within the memory of living men–until at last a return to specie payments, involuntarily brought about, is accepted by general consent as the bottom or hard pan from which to take a new departure, and on which to build future prosperity....
>
> Since January [1879] the general movement, with occasional exceptions, has been all in one direction–the direction of increasing business, rising values, and substantial progress;...the country generally is preparing itself for one of those onward movements that may astonish themselves as well as others....
>
> While, therefore, we are alive to the sudden changes that overtake American enterprise, and for which all due allowance must be made, we are inclined to believe that the return to American prosperity may exercise a solid and beneficial influence on British trade.[94]

The Great Decade of Scottish-American Investment

The decade of the 1870s was a period of experiment for Scottish investors in the American West. Experience indicated that limited company organization was ideal for mortgage and investment enterprises, making possible unusually large dividends for shareholders who could borrow cheap and lend high. The basic principles upon which investment trusts had been formed also appeared to be justified. The tremendous financial success of the earliest syndicates–Scottish-American Investment Company and Scottish-American Mortgage Company of Edinburgh; the Mackenzie companies and Fleming trusts of Dundee–prompted eight or nine other groups of capitalists to try to emulate their success. Some companies proposed modifications in capital structure and methods of finance and investment that they hoped would make their ventures even more lucrative. The established companies, flushed with prosperity, moved into the single-purpose field–in mining, cattle, land promotions and railroad construction–on the principle that success breeds success. Newcomers to the mortgage and investment fields, and oldtimers engaged in new ventures, combined to produce the great decade of Scottish-American investment. Never before or since was there such a rapid increase in the flow of capital from Scotland to the United States. Nor was there ever a period of equal length in which the financiers encountered so many varied problems with success and failure alternating so rapidly.

MORTGAGE COMPANIES OF EDINBURGH AND GLASGOW

The great success of the Scottish-American Mortgage Company in Indiana, Minnesota, Iowa, Dakota, Kansas, and far-away California, where over a thousand small loans, averaging from $300 to $600, were placed at seven and eight per cent, gave the Scots too sanguine a view of the agricultural situation in the Great West in 1880.[1] This outlook was strengthened by contrasting conditions in the United States with the dismal fortune that had overtaken the agriculturalists of Scotland. Henry I. Sheldon, managing director in the United States, had to explain to the Scots that it was a mistake to think, as some did, that the country lying west of the Mississippi was limitless and inexhaustible. One could reach a point in western America where the rains did not come, where irrigation was essential to produce crops, and where the farmer needed, in addition to ploughs and horses, 'ditches, and canals; ponds and reservoirs'. Loans placed in the Great Plains area had to be carefully supervised, and Thomas F. Binnie of Glasgow was named a 'special inspector' of the company for this purpose.[2]

By exercising caution in spreading its lending operations, the company continued to conduct a most successful business. Annual profits increased so that shareholders received a two and one-half per cent bonus for 1880 in addition to their customary ten per cent annual dividend. Conditions were to justify a similar annual return for the remainder of the decade. Another issue of twenty-five thousand shares in 1881 raised the company's capital to the authorized £1,000,000.[3] In this year, the directors decided that the southern and southwestern states, where interest rates were nine and ten per cent, provided an inviting field for the employment of capital, and new agencies were opened in Dallas and San Antonio, Texas, and Montgomery, Alabama.[4] The number of loans increased from twenty-five hundred to thirty-eight hundred the following year; the average loan reached a new high of $850; interest rates varied from seven to ten per cent. The company's reserve fund was £100,000 in 1883, equal to one-half the paid-up capital. Agencies opened in the southern states and Texas had proved most satisfactory.[5] In the southern states, the Scots insisted that loans not be made to farmers dependent upon cotton alone, and with the exception of a few carefully placed loans on wheat farms in North Dakota and Minnesota, no money was ever advanced on any tract depending upon a single crop.

Each year's business appeared better than the last. By 1884 fourteen agencies were operating. New offices had been established in Waco and Austin, Texas, with the latter operated by 'a gentleman from Glasgow'. Numerous South Dakota loans were made by the Yankton and Sioux Falls agencies among Norwegian, Swedish, Danish, and German farmers.[6] The company chairman reiterated the fact that 'a principle in our administration is to see that the business is properly spread and yet confined to districts judiciously selected, that, as regards climate and soil, are likely soon to fill up with a prosperous population'. Speaking of 1885, he reported: 'This year we have opened no new agencies, but we have now a very substantial hold upon Texas, which, I feel persuaded, is going to be a great State, and the business in which continues to be both very remunerative and altogether satisfactory.'[7]

The Edinburgh American Land Mortgage Company likewise had loans on real estate placed throughout Minnesota, Iowa, Indiana, Nebraska, Kansas and Missouri at the beginning of the decade. Working through their general agents, Jesup, Paton and Company, these investors continually encountered difficulty in making land loans, and approximately twenty per cent of their funds had to be placed in railroad, municipal, and school bonds. The initial annual dividend of seven per cent could be raised to only seven and one-half per cent in 1882, and there it remained for the next ten years.[8]

Highly dissatisfied with the result, the directors concentrated their efforts in rooting out the causes. A basic factor was competition from other leading agencies which were able to make loans directly from Scotland and not wait for approval from New York. Moreover, many local agents were unwilling to divide their commission with Jesup, Paton and Company as general agents. This New York firm finally agreed to terminate the business relationship with the Scots but continued to draw a commission on loans already made until the principal had been paid. All new loans were to be made directly through local agents, supervised by an inspector of agencies sent from Scotland.[9]

Later in 1883 this inspector reported that the land in Minnesota, Iowa, and Dakota was heavily mortgaged and the competition destructive. In his opinion, northern Minnesota was too dependent upon the fluctuations in wheat production and prices; the Fargo 'boom' was speculative and he advised that all lending there cease. Farther west, the soil was too poor for the farmers; east of the Mississippi the interest rate was too low. The one remaining area for making profitable loans was the South. The inspector told the directors that if they intended to go into the southern states the time had come. The cream of the upper Middle West was lost by delay. The Scottish-American Mortgage Company and the Dundee companies had already started lending in South Carolina, Mississippi, Louisiana, and Texas in 1881 and the situation would soon be the same in that section. Agents in San Antonio and Dallas promised loans at ten per cent on the agricultural lands along the Brazos and Colorado rivers, and Texas was declared to be the most desirable place to make loans in the Southwest.[10]

Local agents in Sleepy Eye, Sioux Falls, Yankton, Dallas and Memphis, already working for the Scottish-American Mortgage Company, requested certification and the advancement of cash by the Edinburgh American Land Mortgage Company. The available funds were concentrated in Iowa and Texas, and agents elsewhere had to wait. In 1884, there was a sudden reversal of policy when a decision was made to avoid the southern states, but in February

1886, Francis Smith and Company was again allowed to lend money on plantations in the Mississippi Valley from its Vicksburg headquarters. Later in the year an Alabama agent was named who agreed to limit loans to one-third the appraised value of agricultural property, guaranteed an eight per cent annual interest, and subscribed to four thousand shares in the Edinburgh American Land Mortgage Company.[11]

Between 1882 and 1884 five Scottish mortgage companies, with either Edinburgh or Glasgow headquarters, were registered in hopes of earning profits comparable to the two pioneering enterprises that had entered the United States field in the 1870s. In 1882 Carson and Waters, chartered accountants of Glasgow, promoted the organization of the Scottish Mortgage and Land Investment Company of New Mexico, Limited, with an authorized capital of £200,000. Glaswegians signing the Memorandum of Association announced their intention to lend money on real estate and, should the occasion warrant, to hold and improve land by fencing, draining, or irrigating.[12] Within the year a local Advisory Board was selected in Las Vegas, New Mexico.[13] No dividend was paid until 1884 when a seven per cent annual return was declared.[14] Throughout the 1880s the directors had approximately £100,000 to lend, with twenty per cent representing share capital and eighty per cent debentures. Between 1886 and 1888 a single dividend of eight per cent was paid. This land and mortgage company, the only one initiated in Glasgow in the 1880s, soon passed into the control of well-known Edinburgh capitalitss. Colin J. Mackenzie was elected chairman and Sir George Warrender had subscribed to a large block of shares.[15]

William Reid, well known in Dundee for his promotions in the Pacific Northwest but whose good-will in that Scottish community was rapidly diminishing, prevailed upon, in 1883, another group of wealthy Scots to organize the Oregon Mortgage Company, Limited, with Edinburgh headquarters. The company prospectus announced a nominal capital of £500,000 in £5 shares. The first issue was to be 20,000 shares, with not more than £1 called on each share.[16] The promoters planned to lend money on mortgages in Oregon, the territories of Washington, Montana, and Idaho, and in British Columbia. Oregon lands were declared to be as favourable for farming as those of southern France. According to the promoters, the state's population had doubled in twelve years and the region was destined to remain a popular field for emigrants. Wheat exports had increased tenfold in a decade and the Northern Pacific, a transcontinental railroad now near completion, was certain to bring additional prosperity. Eight per cent of the tillable soil in the Greater Northwest remained the property of the United States government; much of the remainder was controlled by the railroads; both wanted settlers. The current interest rate in Oregon was nine per cent. The Scots announced that Reid, managing director of the Oregon and Washington Mortgage Savings Bank of Portland and president of the First National Bank of Salem, Oregon, had been secured as agent. This banker had already placed $6,500,000 in farm loans.[17]

Reid and his 'Oregon friends' agreed to take 2,000 shares, to be held as long as he was company representative. The new company proposed to pay Reid a commission of one and one-half per cent on farm land loans. For loans on city property he was to receive one and one-fourth per cent the first year and one per cent on payments for each of the remaining years of the loan. Since the Oregon Mortgage Company planned to divide its loans equally between city and rural property and the city loans would be larger and less trouble, the directors had asked for this more favourable arrangement. This agreement was similar to the one Reid had with the Dundee Mortgage and Trust Investment Company. The agent was instructed to limit single loans to $10,000 and not to concentrate too heavily in Portland.[18]

Scarcely had the Memorandum of Association been signed, when Reid became heavily involved with the Oregonian Railway and disaster appeared imminent.[19] As Dundee investors lost faith in his judgment, he pressed their Edinburgh neighbours for more funds. In November 1883, he cabled '183 loans for $300,000 rejected. Urge Oregon Mortgage Company and [Edinburgh] American Mortgage Company to supply more funds. Dundee Mortgage Company loaning everywhere. Serious consequences if more funds not sent.' The directors shortly requested that he not be so speedy, that he write rather than cable. They rejected his requests to lend money on unimproved lands sold by the Northern Pacific and insisted that loans should not exceed thirty per cent of appraised value and that no money was to be advanced on farms more than ten miles from a railway station. Their misunderstanding became so acute that Reid informed the directors that they knew little of conditions in the United States. At this point 'the Secretary was directed to mention to Mr Reid that the Directors were much dissatisfied with the tone of his letter...and to express a hope that in the future he would keep in view that the Board expected to be addressed in respectful and measured terms'.[20]

In the summer of 1884 James Tait, a director, went to Oregon to consult with Reid about irregularities in the transmission of mortgages, to inquire about his failure to pay for his shares, and to discuss with others the advisability of lending on city property.

Upon Tait's return he reported complete confidence in the Pacific Northwest, but misgivings about Reid. The upshot was the termination of the company's agreement with the Oregonian and the appointment of Robert Livingstone, an Edinburgh solicitor, to go to Portland to take over the business.[21] Soon this company was spreading out geographically as the others had done. In 1885 the directors started lending in Dakota and Minnesota.[22]

Early in 1884 Francis Smith, who had for some years done business with the Scots either from Indianapolis or Vicksburg headquarters, made an agreement with a new Edinburgh syndicate headed by Holmes Ivory, Writer to the Signet, out of which developed the United States Mortgage Company of Scotland, Limited. The company was registered in March 1884, with a capital of £1,000,000. Smith was given a five-year contract as sole agent and general manager in the United States and a seat on the Board of Directors in exchange for subscribing to four thousand £5 shares in the limited company.[23]

The following month the directors drafted general instructions for the manager. Advances were to be made only on improved, cultivated, and saleable land to the extent of fifty per cent of its appraised value. Loans were to range in size from $400 to $10,000 with those above $1,000 being approved in Edinburgh. A maximum of ten years was to be allowed to repay the larger loans. The company expected a minimum of eight per cent a year on each loan made. Smith was held responsible for investigating the background of every applicant, and was to undertake the lending, collecting, and remitting of funds to the Scot's bankers. The manager was also to supervise all properties held in foreclosure and to bear all expenses connected with the realization on properties foreclosed. In cases where loans were made on the cotton crop, no more than $15 was to be advanced for each four-hundred-pound bale and the total must never exceed $2,500. Cotton loans were only to be granted when the company had a first mortgage on the land.[24]

Smith was soon empowered to name local agents throughout the United States. At his request, loans on city property were also approved up to one-third the appraised value. Seventy per cent of the initial loans were made on cotton lands in the south, the remainder on real estate in Indianapolis, earlier headquarters of Smith's firm. In December 1884, Smith announced the removal of his office from Vicksburg to San Antonio and requested approval of loans on Texas property as high as $40,000. The directors urged caution and expressed a preference for cotton lands over cattle.[25]

By 1885 loans were scattered through five southern states and the chairman notified stockholders 'In our investments, more than four-fifths in number and value are repayable in *installments* extending from 3 to 10 years. This is a valuable and a peculiar feature of our company. Few foreign mortgage companies have such an arrangement. Its importance, especially in agricultural loans, is easily seen.'[26] In 1886 the United States Mortgage Company of Scotland paid its first dividend, seven and one-half per cent.[27] Soon Smith moved headquarters for a fourth time, to Memphis, and formed a partnership, Francis Smith and Caldwell. After an inspection tour of the properties in the southern and southwestern states, John Dick Peddie, Scottish director, approved of the local management and proposed that company shares be increased to create a borrowing power of £200,000.[28]

James Tait, director of both the American Mortgage Company of Scotland and the Oregon Mortgage Company, promoted the American Trust and Agency Company, Limited, in 1884. Thomas Lawson of Neosho, Missouri, a well-known land and cattle evaluator, and Leverett B. Sidway, a Chicago real-estate broker, both of whom had worked with other Scottish capitalists in the formation of land and cattle companies in the American West, were the company representatives in the United States. Although capitalized at £100,000, this Edinburgh promotion was comparatively small with only twenty-five per cent of that amount subscribed and only a fraction paid up. By 1889 the company had to wind-up.[29]

Britishers also became interested in Florida real estate during the 1880s. The Scottish press described Florida south of the St John's River as the finest area in the world for growing oranges, pineapples, lemons, and guava. Here also was America's choicest truck soil and most sublime climate. A great migration of health-seekers, sun-lovers, cold-haters, vegetable-growers, and orange-raisers was reportedly heading for Orlando, Florida.[30] The state was presented as a 'European Sanitorium' and Scottish tourists were advised to spend their holiday in this 'Queen of Winter Homes' rather than in the 'cholera-infested continental countries'. The state population of approximately 270,000 in 1880 was estimated four years later at half a million.[31] Europeans were urged to move while lands were still at prairie prices and before the Americans took up all the property. Promotional literature suggested:

> In its residential and agricultural capacity Florida possesses the means of sustaining a larger population than any other State in the Union.... To the valetudinarian, to the emigrant, to the father of families [*sic*], and to the investor willing to embark in Florida lands, that State presents a strong claim for prior consideration, while to land and mortgage companies she exhibits a remunerative, ample, and virgin field.[32]

In October 1884 the Florida Mortgage and Investment Company, Limited, was formed to purchase lands from the Florida Land and Improvement Company of Philadelphia and to invest money in mortgages on freehold property. The company also had the power to improve, cultivate and resell any property that might become its possession through foreclosure. Capitalized at £500,000, the first issue of £5 shares was limited to £150,000, with only £1 called-up.[33]

The public proved reticent and had to be reassured about the project and urged to invest. Florida was said to have special advantages for the mortgage business because of the economic diversification including industries, market gardening, and fruit growing. Five acres of land in Florida for any one of these businesses was considered equal to one hundred acres in the best of the grain-producing states of the Northwest. The state was as large as England and Wales combined, and first class mortgages were said to bring ten to fifteen per cent.[34]

In February 1885 a Scottish inspector reported that an extensive tract of land purchased by the company at Sarasota Bay included thirty-five hundred acres of sawgrass which, when drained, would make some of the best sugar beet and vegetable land in the State. This section of Florida was virtually cut off by lack of transportation, but railroads were being constructed south of Tampa toward Charlotte Harbor and promised to open up the region.[35]

The land proved of little value, however. The company was unable to meet interest on debentures in November 1888, so the shareholders in an extraordinary general meeting voted to wind-up voluntarily, and shortly thereafter the Scottish courts approved this action under judicial supervision. For the next five years little progress was made toward settling the company's affairs. In 1890 its assets were nothing more than the arrears on capital calls, loans on a few mortgages, and the property in Florida. The Manatee and Sarasota Railway and Drainage Company was given deeds to land, with the approval of all concerned, in the hope that the swampy areas could be drained sufficiently to build a railroad and thereby improve the value of the Scottish-owned lands in and around the town of Sarasota. The liquidator was unable to dispose of any of the property for cash and asked to be relieved of his responsibility in 1905.[36] The excitement over Florida's potentialities had cost the Scottish investors at least £150,000.

Scottish enthusiasm for lending money on real estate in the United States, so prevalent between 1881 and 1884, was slack during the next five years. Available funds were invested in previously established companies rather than in the formation of new ones. Registration records reveal that only two small mortgage companies were begun between 1885 and 1890. The Edinburgh Lombard Investment Company, Limited, capitalized at £250,000, but with no more than £30,000 paid-up by shareholders, placed many loans in the Midwest through James L. Lombard of Kansas City, Missouri. This company included many prominent manufacturers of New England on its list of shareholders.[37] The Scottish and Trans-Atlantic Mortgage Company, Limited, organized by merchants in Selkirk and Galashiels, proposed to borrow money from the Scottish public and lend funds in Texas. The two Texas promoters, land agents from Waco, upon their return home were unable to come to a satisfactory business arrangement with the shareholders, and by 1894 the project was given up.[38]

The shifting position of mortgage investment companies first became apparent in 1883, when shares of the formidable Scottish-American Mortgage Company dropped from £3 8s. to £3 6s. 6d.[39] In 1884 the shares of this company went down ten shillings more, and by then the market value had declined fifteen per cent. Shares in smaller companies dropped from two to five shillings a share. The aggregate depreciation on shares of all the mortgage companies listed on the Edinburgh Stock List in 1884 was approximately £100,000.[40] This loss was temporary, and as has been noted, the splendid dividend record of the oldest company was unimpaired. Directors could not have been too disturbed, for the established companies, like Scottish-American Mortgage and Edinburgh American Land Mortgage, approved agencies in new areas and increased the volume of loans. On the other hand, newer companies such as the Scottish Mortgage and Investment Company of New Mexico and the United States Mortgage Company, were delayed several years in initiating dividends. Others like the Oregon Mortgage Company had a slow start. Available evidence suggested that land and mortgage companies launched after 1880 could not hope for the success of the earlier ventures in the United States. Moreover, it appeared unwise to concentrate loaning operations in a single area, such as Oregon, New Mexico, or Florida. Companies that survived long enough to realize the desirability of geographic diversity spread into other areas and sought the leadership and advice of experienced investors in Edinburgh and Dundee.

Professor Allan Bogue, a careful student of the land mortgage business in the American West, has demonstrated how money loaned on the security of agricultural lands in the newly-opened regions of the western states returned a handsome rate of interest.

Moreover, the security in land, if wisely selected, had a tendency to appreciate in value, so if foreclosure became necessary the mortgage company was not likely to experience loss. Some United States mortgage companies obtained a maximum return of sixteen to seventeen per cent in the mid-1870s, but of course this income had to be divided between the eastern investor and the western mortgage agency.[41] The earliest Scottish mortgage companies undoubtedly earned a comparable amount, if not more, because money borrowed through debentures could be obtained at a lower rate of interest in Scotland than in the eastern United States. As a result of increasing competition among both domestic and foreign mortgage companies in the early 1880s there was a decline in the interest rate obtained in the northern Plains. This development largely explains the decision of the Edinburgh mortgage companies to experiment with loaning in the Far Northwest, the South and Southwest. Once a successful Scottish company moved into a new area, the rest followed close behind and the effects of competition were again felt.

The success of any investor in the mortgage business largely depended upon a clear understanding of the nature of land titles in the United States and the peculiarities of land laws in the western states and territories. The efficiency and caution of the agent who was responsible for gathering applications for loans and making recommendations to the investing company often meant the difference in success and failure. Scottish companies tried to supervise local agents by employing well-known firms in the eastern United States to oversee these western representatives, by establishing basic principles to be followed in making loans, and by sending out company directors on periodic inspection trips. Constant surveillance was necessary to make certain that the agent was adhering to the basic regulations, and that the borrower did not destroy the value of the land, the investor's only security, or fail to pay his taxes.

Western farmers, of course, complained at the high interest rates for borrowed money. Professor Bogue contends, however, that the investor from the eastern United States was no more avaricious than the local money lenders in the West.[42] The same generalization undoubtedly applies to the Scottish investor. Moreover, it should be noted that these mortgages were not an indication of financial distress when they were made, even though in time some became a symbol of blasted hopes. Mortgage agents did advertise vigorously to attract borrowers both in the 1870s and 1880s, but the Scots were unusually conservative in this practice and constantly urged their representatives to exercise caution. Agrarians also complained that the mortgage companies exerted undue financial pressure because they coveted the borrowers' real estate. The investor in the eastern United States, and certainly those from abroad, were not nearly as likely to be interested in the farmer's land as the lender in the West, because the problems of absentee administration increased in direct proportion to the distance to be bridged between the land and the investor's home. The Scottish mortgage companies undoubtedly made a significant contribution to the business by experimenting with various methods of repayment of loans in instalments.

THE AMERICAN RAILWAY MARKET

The initial success of the Scottish-American Investment Company had been so great in the 1870s that the directors agreed that their phenomenal prosperity and profits from buying and selling American railway stocks could not continue. As opportunities occurred in 1880, they realized on the securities quoted at a premium and reinvested the proceeds in bonds at a lower rate of interest. The premiums that might have shrunk were thus converted into capital. The exceptional income in 1880 justified an increase in the annual dividend from ten to twelve and one-half per cent. The chairman felt the record proved the wisdom of concentrating on the stock exchange rather than upon mortgages over real estate.[43] In 1881 the income from investments was again the highest of any year in the company's history. Shareholders received an annual dividend of fifteen per cent. Subscribed capital of the company was now increased to £1,700,000. The directors observed the tremendous amount of railway construction in the United States, agreed that the system was rapidly overexpanding and that collapse was inevitable. The Scots planned to cushion the shock by increasing bond holdings.[44]

The prosperity of the Scottish-American Investment Company in these years was itself a tribute to the managing ability of its promoters and directors, because the market for railway securities was generally depressed and there were several financial tragedies between 1880 and 1883. The Philadelphia and Reading, 'less a railroad carrying coal, but more a coal company operating a railroad to carry its product', went into the hands of the receivers in May 1880. This development precipitated a depreciation in the majority of American railway securities. The railroad directors apparently had made the mistake of raising money to buy their coal fields by borrowing rather than issuing share capital. When reverses came in 1877–8, they further complicated the company's position by trying to side-step an essential reorganization of finances.[45] The *Scottish Banking and Insurance Magazine* concluded 'Great discrimination in the choice of Trans-atlantic investments, and the discouragement of shareholders' committees to manage bondholders' interests may perhaps be held to sum up the lesson of this latest American financial scandal.'[46]

By the end of 1881 the financial press wrote of 'the long continuance of depression in the New York railway market'. The contractors of many new lines in the West were unable to float the shares and bonds of their enterprises either in the United States or Europe, and they were forced to sell securities of well-established lines to raise construction funds. The volume of these forced sales depressed prices of the best of railroad securities. The 'railway wars' between competing lines and syndicates and the 'dearness of money' in the United States only aggravated the situation.[47] During this year 7,000 miles of lines were constructed and between 8,000 and 9,000 miles had been projected for 1882. Yet a careful enumeration of the 'paying and non-paying lines' revealed that half the capital invested in United States railroads earned no return and less than one out of four lines paid dividends.[48] In 1882 *The Statist* observed:

> The depression in the American Railway Market has lasted much longer than anybody was prepared to expect; and, in consequence, there is a growing feeling in this country that it is unwise to have anything to do with American railway property, that the savings of investors are at the mercy of unscrupulous and reckless operators, who never hesitate when an opportunity offers to enrich themselves at the expense of those who put their money in American railway enterprises...we think that the discredit of American railway enterprises is being carried entirely too far, and we would advise investors to pause and study the matter carefully before they throw away their property at a time like the present....[49]

The fluctuation in the value of railroad securities reflected not so much the value or earning capacity of any particular line but rather the manipulations of the stocks and bonds on the market by men like Jay Gould. Starting in 1877–8 Gould and his business associate Russell Sage had bought up a network of bankrupt lines that ran from the west end of Lake Erie to St Louis and the Missouri River. These were strung together in a 'system' and their low purchase prices made it possible for them to be operated at a profit during 1880. The following year Gould's competitors organized to force down the value of his holdings on the stock exchange. Wabash preferred stock quickly dropped from ninety-eight to fifty and when British investors were frightened out early in 1882, it went below twenty-seven. The Wabash system experienced financial collapse. In the next raid on railroad shares, Gould played the role of aggressor, and the Louisville and Nashville, the leading railroad of the southern United States, was the victim. In 1880 this line had launched an extensive programme of expansion, buying up all stray bits of railroad within its reach. Tremendous outlays of capital were needed to put these lines in order, to build connecting links, and to provide additional rolling stock. Recognizing its vulnerable position, Gould brought it to the brink of insolvency by stock market pressure. Shares that had been selling at 106 were halved within a few months. Then Gould bought up sufficient shares to force his way into the directorate and incorporate the Louisville and Nashville into his 'system'. By 1883 British investors could buy stock in this 'Pennsylvania of the South' at forty.[50]

After a steady deterioration in its financial affairs for three years the Denver and Rio Grande Railway collapsed during 1883.[51] The Gould interests had taken advantage of its weakness and driven down the stocks on the exchange. British investors lost heavily in this enterprise, for the stocks had been 'puffed and glorified' as rising investments until some 'unlucky fools' who bought them at 113 were let down by the run that dropped them to 18. When Jay Gould started buying up the shares in this company, the *New York Herald* expressed surprise that he would buy up a road which 'has nothing but two streaks of iron rust and the right of way through snow-filled cañons and plains whose only productions are sage-brush and Indians, a few borrowed locomotives and cars that serve to annoy the jackrabbits along the 1,000 or more miles of road'.[52]

The general depreciation in stocks during 1883 was sufficient to be described as 'The American Railway Collapse'. An examination of the sixty leading securities revealed that all but two had experienced severe declines. The stocks of companies associated with Henry Villard, particularly the Oregon and Transcontinental, had suffered the sharpest drop, but the Central Pacific had also fallen sufficiently to cause the British to lose faith in this early favourite. All of the 'Granger Roads', including the St Paul and Omaha, the Milwaukee and St Paul, and the St Paul and Minneapolis, witnessed a lessening of the market value of their stocks, while all increased in earning power. The Gould lines of the Southwest, such as the Missouri Pacific and the Missouri, Kansas, and Texas, had a lot of the inflated value, or 'watered stock' squeezed out of them. The so-called Trunk Lines running from Chicago to New York or the eastern seaboard were not in the difficult position of the far-flung systems west of the Mississippi River, but there had been some decline in the value of their stocks. Total loss of capital in the sixty leading railroad securities was estimated by one

5. *'Dundee Reid', promoter of the Oregon & Washington Trust Investment Company*

6. *Locomotive of the St Paul and Sioux City Railroad*

analyst as high as $242,648,314 for the single year 1883. If this fact were not appalling enough, the twenty-five more speculative railroad securities were estimated to have declined in value $357,564,515 from the highest quotation during 1881. Although the British participated in a 'dead loss of seventy millions sterling', they were comforted in knowing that they did not bear the brunt.[53] Other analysts estimated that the losses and temporary decline in the railway market might reach as high as £150,000,000.[54]

The editor of *The Edinburgh Courant* attempted an explanation for his readers:

> Wall Street knocks about shares by millions and tens of millions. It is not only the largest stock market in the world, but it is the most daring and most restless. The gigantic operators at the head of it can turn or twist it almost as they please. If they combined in one direction they could wreck property or 'boom' it up to double its value just as they found it convenient. But happily, or unhappily, they do not often combine. Their normal condition is a state of war, and when they put forth their strength it is a war of giants.... In English finance the ruling idea is investment.... But in America it is the speculators who rule the market, and the investors who are the fringe upon it. Last year [1883] in Wall Street was a famine year; brokers had to give up champagne and go back again to lager beer, business was so bad; nevertheless, there were sold during the twelve months something more than 96 million shares of one kind or another. In 1882 the total sales had amounted to 113,720,665 shares....

To the puzzled foreign observers who witnessed the fall in New York Central stock between 1881 and 1883 while its net earnings were greater than at any time in history, he pointed out the tremendous funds being spent to crush the West Shore and Buffalo line, a potential competitor. The Scots who had 'dabbled' in American securities and 'been burned' had too often, in his opinion, concluded illogically that the stocks were to blame rather than the men who manipulated them.[55] Although conclusive evidence is not available, the Scots in all probability incurred about fifteen per cent of the total British loss in 1882 and 1883. The great bulk of this money had been invested directly by individuals in the American railroad corporations' securities, and not through Scottish managed investment companies and trusts.

In contrast, the financial position of the Scottish-American Investment Company was so solid that these events through 1883 had little effect. The customary fifteen per cent annual dividend was paid. The reserve fund now totalled £250,000 while the paid-in capital was only £340,000. Shares on the stock exchange increased from £4 4s. to £4 7s. 6d. in value, a gain of £29,750.[56]

The only departure from established policy was a decision to invest reserve funds in land promotional companies.[57] Menzies, the managing director, and his associates had already raised capital to float single-purpose companies in mining, cattle, and timber business, but they had never invested Scottish-American Investment Company funds in such projects. In 1883 the investment company obtained stock in the Canada North-West Land Company which had the right to a half interest in all the town sites located in the North-west Territory of Canada between Brandon, Manitoba, and the British Columbia border. In Regina, capital of the territory, the Scottish-American Investment Company was restricted to a one-fourth interest in the town site, since the Canadian government took half, leaving the remaining half for equal division between the railroad and land interests. Within the first two months, the sale of various town sites brought in $800,000, and the Scots received their fourth. The land company claimed two and a half million acres of land in southern Manitoba. Within a single year, however, there was a great shrinkage in land values and the directors voted not to place funds from the reserve in such speculative ventures again.[58] When the shareholders met in 1884, Menzies was bitterly criticized and a minority of the investors insisted that he should devote his full time as managing director to the investment company and give up side-line promotions.[59] The following year the directors were again criticized for placing funds in the Canadian Lumbering and Timber Company. Concerted pressure from shareholders was placed upon the directors to avoid use of any investment company funds in other companies with which they were connected.[60]

The slowly falling market for American railway securities was thought to have reached rock bottom in 1883. The periodic rallying of prices during the last three years had always been of brief duration. *The Economist* was convinced that there would be another sharp crisis before the market turned upward again. The causes were thought to be the same as those in 1873, which, reduced to simple terms, were excessive railroad construction, the tremendous disproportion between the supply of securities and the buying power of investors, the loss of confidence in railway management due to 'vicious financing', and the 'unscrupulous action of official speculative cliques'. Although quotations on the stock market for 1884 were near the low point of 1879, the depreciation was not nearly so great as in 1873–5 when one hundred and fifty-seven railroads defaulted on their bonded debt of eleven millions sterling. However, two-thirds of the stocks on the New York

Exchange were on the non-dividend paying list. Financial journals warned against further investments in the Northern Pacific and its Oregon lines and in the Gould system in the Southwest. Both were thought to be 'enormous, almost chaotic, systems, with great liabilities which form an increasing heavy burden to the capitalists'. Gould's Wabash, St Louis and Pacific, an attempt to combine thirty companies with 3,500 miles of lines in six states, was proving too much for his strength. The Texas and Pacific seemed to be 'following in the wake of the Wabash, and between them they might bring the Missouri Pacific down'. The editor of *The Economist* was convinced that the weaker elements in the transportation pattern were apt to be eliminated or transformed shortly and then the sounder securities would show a marked appreciation.[61]

In August 1884 the Wabash, St Louis and Pacific Railroad announced a reorganization scheme whereby the *general* mortgage bondholders were to bear the brunt of previous losses. This proposal was described in Britain as a 'swindle' in which unidentified 'prior liens' in the United States were to be protected at the expense of the British bond and shareholders.[62] Investors were also warned that the New York Central, in whose stock four to five thousand British families had invested an estimated ten millions sterling, was heavily overcapitalized and would have difficulty in meeting regional competition.[63]

To strengthen British control over American investments, plans were laid in 1884 for the organization of the English Association of American Bond and Shareholders. The registration of shareholders by American corporations was not a legal requirement, and many Britishers, failing to register, had previously left the management entirely in the hands of American operators by default. Railway shares came to Britain from the United States in ten-share certificates usually matched by an equivalent in bonds, both in the names of large arbitrage dealers. These certificates then passed from hand to hand without transfers being made and registered. Actual owners at a given time were unknown, and the danger of fraudulent circulation was very great. According to this new proposal, a central registration office was to be established for purposes of record and inquiry. A small advisory council, experienced in railway matters and competent to take judicial action, was also to be organized. If this association was properly supported, no longer would Britishers be unable to raise their voices when company elections occurred or new policies were adopted. Ultimately the association hoped to get legislative action limiting the powers possessed by most American railway Boards to issue shares and bonds, to borrow money, and to dispose of the entire property as it saw fit without consulting the stockholders. It also aimed at additional publicity, the publication of annual accounts in a clear and uniform shape, keeping capital and revenue accounts separate, and at having these reports distributed in time for each investor to have an opportunity to be heard.[64] British shareholders in the New York, Ontario, and Western immediately made their influence felt through this organization, and the Wabash investors followed suit. Their action came a little late.

The year of 1884 had been tragic for most investors, particularly in the railroad security field. After summarizing the declining market values of the shares in the Louisville and Nashville, Pennsylvania and Ohio, St Paul, New York Central, Denver and Rio Grande, Wabash, Reading, Erie, Oregon and California, and in the Ohio and Mississippi, an analyst writing for *Blackwood's* suggested 'Americans were supposed to be in the dirt at the end of 1883, when they were found to have shrunk 150 millions sterling in two years, but last year they contrived to drop another 50 millions sterling or more.' In bitterness, the Scot suggested 'As for American railways, they were the veritable lamp of Aladdin. They had only to shed their fertilizing light on the boundless prairies and it would blossom as the rose in dividends.'[65] In 1865 there had not been an American railway stock or bond officially known in London, yet twenty years later British investment in railroads had been so great that their collapse had resulted in a depression throughout the United Kingdom.

> The depression we now suffer from is the slowly gathering result of causes which have been in operation for at least ten years.... No one will say there has ever been within historical memory a depression at once so severe and so widespread as the present. Not a single section of the community is exempt from it and though happily the working class has been so far less affected in proportion than any other, it may be only a matter of a few months when depression shall pass into far-reaching destitution. The hard gripe of genteel poverty is already keenly felt in homes which still offer a fair and smiling face to the world; and where a few years ago the serenity of opulence reigned, anxiety and care are now eating into daily life.... A default on the bonds of some little-known railway in the Far West may have an easily traceable effect on the whole circle of our commerce.[66]

At the annual shareholders' meeting, in March 1885, directors of the Scottish-American Investment Company finally had to admit the development of a serious depression in the American stock market. Interest on investments was £14,000 less than in 1883 and in some cases payments had not been met on bonds. Although the annual dividend of fifteen per cent was maintained for 1884, there was a discussion about the advisability of lowering it. Following this meeting the price of the company shares dropped for the first time in years.[67] Each share was soon quoted at ten shillings less.[68]

Rumours circulated that the directors were sacrificing first-rate interest-paying bonds to purchase speculative stocks in order to keep up annual dividends. The price of shares dropped until the total depreciation was approximately £125,000, and at least one investor, who had bought heavily, urged the directors to make a complete statement about the affairs of the company.[69] Once this was done public confidence in the syndicate and its directors returned, new buyers came forward, and the market began to rise.

The annual dividend for 1885 was cut to twelve and one-half per cent. Great difficulty had been found in securing worthwhile investments so the directors had refused to realize on their sound and high-priced securities for purposes of reinvestment. However, the book value of the bonds and stocks had increased, and with the reserves each share in the Scottish-American Investment Company was worth £4, or twice the capital called-up.[70] At the close of the year, the company had investments amounting to £1,767,000, of which 93·6 per cent were in the United States.[71] An analysis of the holdings revealed that £1,112,493, representing the bulk of these funds, was in railroad bonds and securities, £296,076 in mortgages over real estate, and the remainder in small investments, chiefly municipal bonds in the United States, Manitoba, and Ontario.[72]

At the close of 1885 the average price of American railway securities advanced rapidly, the New York Exchange was full of rumours, and excitement was intense as more and more shares were exchanged. The stock market rise was partially the result of improvement in trade and, in particular, of the agreement among the owners of the Trunk Lines to terminate their suicidal rate-war. Throughout 1884 and 1885 competition had been so keen that some lines carried goods below the cost of transportation and, in a desperate attempt to meet capital charges, cut operating costs. Although employees were dismissed in droves, the lines still could not operate at a profit. Workers were not re-employed when the rate agreements were reached, and for a short while larger net earnings were obtained without increasing staff. However, *The Economist* warned that this first rise in security prices might be speculative and urged investors to use caution and discrimination to avoid becoming involved in a serious relapse.[73] By July 1886 most financial observers admitted that the return of prosperity to the railroads appeared certain. Not only had rate differences been adjusted and some labour disputes settled, but good harvests of cotton and grain were predicted. Materials such as rails and rolling stock were also comparatively cheap and the money market was freer than it had been in three years.[74] The Scottish-American Investment Company participated in the prosperity. In 1888 the annual dividend was raised to thirteen per cent and two years later it was again fifteen per cent. Total investments now reached £1,961,000.[75]

In 1888 the securities of eighty-two American railway companies were quoted on the London Official List with a nominal capital of nearly four hundred and fifty millions sterling, whereas in 1867 securities of only ten such companies had been listed, amounting to seventy-eight millions. Of the total investment in 1888, forty-six millions was represented by sterling bonds, held almost exclusively by British investors. In spite of some defaults, purchasers had received an average return on their money of five per cent. Dollar bonds totalling one hundred and seventy-five millions, were held largely in the United States rather than in Britain. American railroad shares, valued at £228,000,000, had earned on the whole slightly more than one per cent. These were held by Britishers in limited quantities. Although it was impossible to determine the stake of the British in terms of exact figures, the nation had certainly produced a large bulk of the capital to finance the American rail network.[76]

Railway securities from the United States were still being brought over in the names of arbitrage dealers who had no interest in them after they arrived. The following figures were published on securities offered to the public by the larger London houses between 1879 and 1889:

Baring Brothers	£24,552,400
Morgan and Company	9,610,000
Speyer Brothers	6,192,000
Morton, Rose and Company	5,159,997
smaller companies	23,923,000
	£69,437,397

This by no means represented the total investment, because the great financial houses had, through the years, introduced large amounts of stocks and bonds without a public issue.[77] Through these London houses individual Scots made extensive investments but the Scottish-American Investment Company bought directly through its agents in New York.

Concerned about the situation, the English Association of American Bond and Shareholders reported that Britishers had largely concentrated their American railroad investments in twenty companies. Out of these, fifteen companies paid no dividend at all on an investment of $639,000,000, an estimated three-fourths of which was held in Britain. Britishers had received an estimated 2·82 per cent on their total investment in American rails. As evidence of the ineptitude of British investors who selected railway securities on their own volition, the Association reiterated that only five of the twenty railroads most actively dealt in on the London market had paid dividends, while there were three hundred dividend-paying railroad securities available in the United States. *The Statist* was convinced

> There seems to be very little doubt that at least $400,000,000 of non-dividend paying American Shares are floating about in this country on blank transfer endorsements, none being registered in the names of the real owners. We constantly hear complaints made of mismanagement of American Railways; but it is futile for holders to be constantly crying out when they have the remedy in their own hands, and will not use it.[78]

The journal's crusade on behalf of united action by British investors through a permanent English Association of American Bond and Shareholders soon failed, so it urged the arbitrage dealers to provide for registration and to secure the country's voting power in the hands of trusted representatives so its authority could be felt. Shareholders' committees for each major railroad were particularly needed to work with the great banking houses. All these proposals seemed to fall on deaf ears.

The problems and minimum profits of the individual investor in American railway securities, particularly in England, only emphasized the excellent management of the Scottish-American Investment Company during the 1880s. The Scots who invested in the company came through these crises unscathed. Those who bought directly from arbitrage dealers held shares that possibly depreciated as much as £2,000,000 at the market's lowest point, but it is doubtful that more than a fifth of this amount was actually lost by investors forced to sell.

NEW EDINBURGH TRUSTS

After fourteen years of operation as the only Edinburgh company exclusively interested in stock market securities, the Scottish-American Investment Company witnessed the rise of competitors after 1887. Several directors and leading stockholders in the United States Mortgage Company of Scotland decided to launch a new venture, the Scottish Investment Trust Company, Limited, in July 1887, with a nominal capital of £500,000 in £10 shares. At an early meeting of the directors three committees were formed to specialize in handling investments: one to deal with insurance companies, government bonds, and banks; a second, with railways and investment companies; and a third, with all other types of investments.[79] There was no intention to concentrate on railroad investments nor was there a desire to limit the field of operations to the United States. As initial investments, the directors purchased shares in the Scottish-American Investment Company, the Scottish-American Mortgage Company, the Dundee Mortgage and Trust Investment Company, and the Australian Land and Finance Company. They also invested in Argentine government bonds, South American as well as North American railroad securities, and in shares of submarine cable, telephone and telegraph, and shipping companies. Later gas, coal, tea, and insurance companies were added.[80]

The Scottish Investment Trust Company invested £375,000 during its first year, having raised the funds by issuing equal amounts of preferred, deferred, and debenture stock among 403 proprietors. Between 1888 and 1890 the company earned annual dividends of six per cent and at the end of this period the subscribed capital had been doubled.[81] The success of this company prompted the same capitalists to launch the Second Scottish Investment Trust Company, Limited, in 1889, with a similar capital structure and investment programme.[82]

Robert Fleming, who had been responsible for the Scottish investment trusts in Dundee, had subsequently moved to London and organized the Investment Trust Corporation in that financial centre. In 1889 he returned to Scotland to organize an Edinburgh investment trust, in conjunction with John Guild, of the Scottish American Trust Companies of Dundee. Their British Investment Trust, Limited, was capitalized at £1,000,000.

A new form of capital structure was introduced to Scotland. After subscription, each share was to be divided, with three-fifths representing preferred stock and two-fifths deferred. The preferred stock was entitled to a cumulative dividend of four per cent a year. After a reserve fund had been established, the surplus profits were to go to the deferred shares up to eight per cent, and all income thereafter was to be divided equally between the two classes of securities but with a maximum of five per cent to be paid on preferred shares. The company also planned to issue debenture stock equal to the amount of *subscribed*, rather than paid-up capital and pay four per cent interest on this borrowed money. All shares were issued at a premium of 10s.

According to the prospectus, the high price of investment trust stocks on the market was sufficient evidence of their success and the esteem with which they were held by the investing public.

Like the pioneer trusts, the British Investment Trust expected to spread the share and debenture capital over a large number of securities, with not more than one-twentieth of the total invested in any one company. A considerable portion of the capital was to be placed in United States railroad bonds. The directors agreed, however, that no investment would be made in a company with unlimited liability. Moreover, funds would be invested in a company with limited but uncalled liability only with the unanimous consent of the directors. Such caution was essential because this trust was borrowing money equal to its paid-up capital and not the difference between the amount subscribed and paid-up. On the original Board, Fleming and Guild were associated with John Cowan, an Edinburgh Writer to the Signet, whose family had made a fortune in paper milling, R. D. Balfour, a London stockbroker, George Dunlop and J. P. Wright, Writers to the Signet and members of well-known legal firms of the Scottish capital, and Mitchell Thompson, later to be raised to the peerage and become Postmaster General.[83]

Confidence in the ability of these men prompted the public to subscribe £600,000 immediately, and the directors were hard pressed to find suitable investments rapidly enough. Although they followed the precedent of other trust companies in not indicating details of their investment at the time, company records now reveal that the greater part of the money was placed in the United States and the bulk of that in railroad mortgage bonds. Into this type of security alone they put £735,824. Of secondary interest were investments in Brazil, Mexico, and the Argentine, where railway and government bonds were purchased, particularly those of the Mexican National Railway.[84] During the first year, the company paid a five per cent dividend on preferred shares and eight per cent on the deferred. Thus the purchaser of each share before conversion into the two categories received approximately six per cent. World conditions were unsatisfactory in 1889 with Brazil in a state of revolution, a depression in Argentina, and a money stringency in the United States, but Cowan, the chairman of the British Investment Trust, insisted

> the arrangement of capital is such that it is not necessary to strive after very high rates to have fair results. If present funds are invested at an average 5 per cent net, the company can pay 8 per cent on the deferred and have a good surplus.[85]

This was possible because so much Scottish capital had been borrowed through debentures.

The Edinburgh Investment Trust, Limited, was also established early in 1889 with an authorized capital of £1,000,000. Three hundred thousand pounds was allotted in £10 shares and immediately converted into £180,000 preferred stock ranking first for a cumulative dividend of four and one-half per cent, and £120,000 deferred stock, taking all the surplus earnings. Power was also granted to the company to issue debenture stock up to two-thirds of the subscribed capital. Thus the basic arrangement of its capital was similar to that of the British Investment Trust, a scheme which had been worked out over the years to produce the greatest possible return on the deferred shares. All shares in the new company were issued at a premium of 10s. The available money had been distributed over 209 investments, but the effectiveness of the investment programme of the directors had been given no real test by the close of the decade.[86]

'Considering how heavily the dice are loaded in favour of the shareholder as against the debenture holder, it has often been a puzzle how the Edinburgh Companies have been able to keep down their dividends so well', observed the *Courant* in 1884. In the Scottish capital, where dividends of five or six per cent had been the height of shareholders' ambition, distributions of ten and twelve per cent by the Scottish-American Mortgage and Scottish-American Investment companies had caused quite a 'flutter'. In many quarters their organization and success were too easily mistaken for financial genius, according to the editor, while in reality the generosity of debenture holders had more to do with it. These loans had produced big profits because debenture holders were willing to take a smaller slice and give the big slice to shareholders. The newspaper suggested that it was 'an amusing sort of partnership when looked into'. For example, if the shareholders of a company subscribed only half of their authorized capital and borrowed the remaining half at four and one-half per cent, and then lent it in the United States at an average of nine per cent, they could make between thirteen and fourteen per cent each year. If they did not legally limit the borrowing power to the amount of unpaid capital, they could make as high as fifty per cent annual returns. Payments of less only indicated poor management, bad debts, payment of excessive commissions, or the desire to build up a large reserve fund. According to the editor, these companies enjoyed too large a margin of profit from the difference in their borrowing and lending rates, a margin that was inevitably contracting year by year as money became more plentiful in comparatively new countries, like the United States, where their financial operations were carried on.[87]

The following characteristics of Scottish capital sent abroad by the investment and mortgage companies were apparent. Less than one-fourth of the capital in the companies was actually owned by the shareholders who took the risk of the business and the lion's share of profits. The remaining three-fourths was furnished by parties who accepted a mere fraction of the profits. As the company became more prosperous, the interest rate for loans dropped and the shareholders' income was augmented. Secondly, although the channels of investment were varied and geographically scattered, neither the shareholders nor the debenture holders knew where their funds were located or how they were administered. Finally, the continuous and increasing efflux of capital abroad, particularly to the United States, was creating a dearth of money at home. Some observers thought the financiers took too much for granted when they assumed the overabundance of Scottish capital would never again be needed within the country.[88]

Although the Scottish mortgage and investment companies appeared sufficient to meet the demands, so many new undertakings appeared between 1887 and 1890 that the directors experienced difficulty in purchasing proper investments. Within three years the Scottish Investment Trust Company, the Second Scottish Investment Trust Company, the British Investment Trust, the Edinburgh Investment Trust, and the Alliance Trust Company of Dundee had come into existence in Scotland. These were launched so rapidly, one right on the heels of the last, that all could not make a favourable beginning. *The Economist* noted that there had developed a 'ring' of trust directors who were undoubtedly well qualified to direct trust companies, but it was doubted that they could act efficiently for several of them at the same time. The numerous trust companies, having to a large extent the same guidance, attempted to purchase the same securities and thus drove prices up against themselves. Later, when they decided to sell, they inadvertently conspired to push down quotations to their mutual disadvantage.[89] The first Scottish mortgage and investment companies continued their great prosperity throughout the eighties, the new mortgage companies begun then had to be content with lesser profits, and the investment trusts registered at the decade's close had insufficient time to prove their soundness.

DUNDEE, AN INVESTMENT CAPITAL IN SCOTLAND

Although several mortgage and security investment companies were started in Edinburgh in the 1880s, no similar registrations were made in Dundee. Investments were made through the earlier Dundee companies that concentrated on consolidating their financial position. The Mackenzie enterprises were brought together into a single organization known as the Alliance Trust Company, Limited. The Scottish American Investment Trusts proved beyond a doubt the soundness of investment trust principles, yet their earnings were comparatively small because they invested only the funds of their certificate holders, being unwilling to borrow as did most limited companies. Although the resources of the town were far less than those of Edinburgh and Glasgow, such a large percentage of its capital was placed abroad that the community gained an international reputation as a centre of Scottish investment. Throughout the decade, western America remained the favourite field for Dundee's overseas investment.

By 1882 the mortgage business of Dundee was controlled by the Dundee Mortgage and Trust Investment Company.[90] Although this company was not legally restricted in the geographic area of its operations, the larger part of its business was conducted in North America. Apart from a few loans in New South Wales, the rest was placed in western Canada or the United States.[91] In comparison with other British mortgage companies, the Dundee enterprise had a very simple organization. Its agencies were less numerous and far flung; its directors confined lending to six offices directed by men well known in Scotland. Like the Edinburgh groups, the company had appointed a single superintendent of agencies and inspector of loans to travel among these local agencies and report directly to the Scottish Board.[92] The balance sheets of the company for 1880–1 revealed that 650 loans, amounting to $1,262,759, had been made through William Reid in Portland, at annual interest from nine to fourteen per cent. Elsewhere interest rates on the company's mortgages were from eight to twelve per cent.[93]

The company's prosperity reached an all-time high in 1882. Real estate taken by foreclosure was nominal and income justified a shilling bonus on each share in addition to the traditional ten per cent dividend. Company assets were twice the uncalled capital, so that lenders had little cause for anxiety.[94] During the year the Scottish company severed relations with Reid and sought another Portland agent. Mackenzie, who had always had difficulties with Reid, discovered that the agent had, from time to time, debited his accounts with the mortgage company for sums paid out in connection with the Scottish-financed Oregonian Railway.[95] Although Reid later appeared in Dundee and made an explanation at least partially acceptable to the directors, his business connections in Dundee were damaged beyond repair.[96]

By 1883 the company was forced to make adjustments because of the depression in the United States, which was characterized by declining prices for agricultural products. Mortgage payments were in arrears and there was difficulty experienced in placing new loans. In spite of adverse conditions, the Dundee Mortgage Company paid dividends and added to its reserve fund.[97] The next three years were difficult. The directors elected to place reserve funds in stocks and bonds, chiefly of the railroads, when mortgage loans became difficult to procure. Shortly thereafter the collapse in railroad securities of 1884 led to a temporary depreciation, but by 1886 the tide had turned and the railroad bonds could be sold at a profit. The agricultural depression was so widespread and severe in 1884 that the directors compared conditions with 1873, and prices for the farmer's land and products did not recover as rapidly as the stock market. As the agricultural depression continued, the company was forced to take over unwelcomed real estate. The company's splendid financial reputation was unimpaired because of its large reserves and the maintenance of annual dividends.[98]

The report to the shareholders of the Dundee Mortgage Company in April 1888 emphasized the steadily declining interest rate the company had to pay on borrowed money through the years. More funds were available at three and three-fourths per cent than could be employed. The company enjoyed an excellent credit because of the exceptional security for debenture holders. Annual net revenue was two and a half times the interest charges on borrowed funds, and of the thirty-one mortgage and investment companies in Britain only one exceeded this proportion. The only discouraging development was the increase in real estate taken by foreclosure. The chairman remarked:

> We regret foreclosures very much, and do all we can to avoid them by giving delinquent borrowers every reasonable facility and leniency. Perhaps it might be better for us in a mere money point of view if we dealt more sharply with them, but we do not wish to give the Company a name for hard dealing, but rather to deserve and retain the friendship of the people amongst whom we are doing business. When we are compelled to take real estate it is our aim to sell it quickly, and to seek nothing out of it but our principal, interest, and expenses. In ordinary circumstances this policy commands ready sales, but at present farming lands are not easily sold, and it is sometimes necessary in America–just as at home–to wait until a customer turns up.[99]

Given the opportunity to speak, several shareholders objected to the brevity of the annual report, to the amount of real estate that had to be taken over, and to operating expenses that appeared excessive. Under questioning, Mackenzie revealed significant details concerning the company's method of operation. Foreclosed properties represented only five and one-half per cent of the total mortgages. Less than thirty foreclosures had been made during the year out of the 2,000 mortgages held. Eighty per cent of these foreclosures occurred in the Portland and Montreal agencies on loans made eight to ten years previously. The company had originally advanced between forty and fifty per cent on the foreclosed properties but had received, in most cases, from eight to ten per cent interest on the loans for many years. Although some farms had run down, most could be sold for the amount of the original loan. Expenses, including taxes, had amounted to twenty-seven per cent of the gross profits. The secretary explained that in some states taxes were three per cent on the assessed value of the real estate. American agents received from ten to twenty per cent on the interest collected. Expenses appeared high also because, contrary to British practice, in the United States the agent rather than the borrower often paid the expense of making and collecting the loan and this expenditure was included in the annual account.[100] By 1889 the Dundee Mortgage Company held mortgages and liens over real estate amounting to £829,427.[101]

Real estate speculations in western America were being handled in 1880 by the Dundee Land Investment Company, one of the 'Mackenzie group'. Although investors had originally been told that dividends in this company would be much slower coming, by 1881 a bonus of five per cent was paid in addition to the customary five per cent dividend. On the death of the Earl of Airlie, in September 1881, William Lowson had become company chairman.[102]

With the assistance of Jesup, Paton and Company, the Scots continued to purchase Wisconsin timberlands from railroads and sell the acreage at a profit. Through Drummond Brothers they invested $50,000 in town lots in Winnipeg and Emerson, and purchased a major interest in the town site of Odanah on the Little Saskatchewan River, hoping it would become a major centre on the Canadian Pacific Railroad. Several office buildings were acquired in Kansas City through Underwood, Clark and Company. Investments in the cattle kingdom were made by purchasing securities in established companies. In 1881 most of their investments were still being placed through Reid, who purchased buildings in downtown Portland, as well as real estate in new residential developments and in the neighbourhood of the proposed Portland depot of the Oregonian Railroad. Soon £10,000 was invested in downtown real estate in Denver, and then the company started purchasing acreage in the Colorado coal fields in Boulder County.[103]

In 1881 the Colorado Mortgage and Investment Company of London, interested in purchasing the 250,000-acre Chavez Land

Grant in New Mexico, asked the Dundee capitalists if they would share in the £100,000 investment. The original grant to Ignacio Chavez and others had been made in 1768 by Pedro Fermindo de Mendinueta, governor of the Spanish province. The right of the governor to dispose of the royal domain in this fashion was well established, and in the Treaty of Guadalupe Hidalgo the claims to such land grants were fully recognized and protected. In December 1874 the surveyor general of New Mexico notified Congress that the Chavez Land Grant was genuine and legal and recommended its confirmation. Four years later it was surveyed and the plat and field notes filed. No sooner had the two Scottish companies completed their purchase than squatters on the land began to dispute the title. Directors of the Dundee Land Investment Company proposed fencing the land and placing a tenant interested in raising sheep upon it. More important, they sought congressional action validating their claim and instituted action in the federal courts to remove the squatters.[104] This was but the beginning of a long struggle to protect their investment.

Drummond Brothers also had 100,000 acres of Canadian Pacific lands to market in Scotland in 1881. William J. Menzies of Edinburgh suggested that Dundee investors subscribe sufficient funds for the recently organized Scottish American Land Company, Limited, to make the purchase. The upshot was the formation of a joint company known as the Scottish Canadian Land Company, Limited, to take over this Canadian Pacific grant. The Scottish American Land Company and the Dundee Land Investment Company were to sponsor the new promotion, each putting up $125,000.[105]

Land purchases were also made in Minnehaha and Moody counties in southeastern Dakota Territory. Town lots in Fargo and in nearby Fergus Falls, Minnesota, were bought for speculative purposes. The Dundee Land Investment Company made an agreement with the Chicago, Milwaukee, and St Paul Railroad to build the town of Scotston in Dakota Territory. The Scottish company was to receive the town site for $1,200 provided they built a railroad station and a grain elevator in 1881 and a suitable hotel and store the following year. Once this was done, any profits from the sale of town lots belonged to the Scots. Early in 1882 several tracts of Arkansas pine lands including at least 50,000 acres were procured through railroad corporations, and the Dundee company went into another joint speculation with Menzies in the Arkansas Lumber and Land Company, Limited.[106]

Suddenly in 1882 the directors of the Dundee Land Investment Company decided to reconstitute the company to permit investments in stocks and bonds and loans on mortgages over real estate. The new company, registered in April, possessed a similar capital structure as the former company, with £500,000 authorized and £250,000 subscribed in £10 shares, and £75,000 paid-up. The Board of Directors of the land company were joined by Robert Fleming, who was to assist in the transfer from real estate to mortgages and securities. Between 1881 and 1886 he was on the directorate of all five of Dundee's mortgage and investment companies.

Fleming introduced a change of policy tending toward conservatism. The extensive speculations in land were curtailed and the directors used their new powers to invest in land mortgages, railroad bonds, and other securities such as Western Union stock. Orders had been given to dispose of the Company's real estate in the cities of Portland, Winnipeg, and Kansas City when favourable terms were presented.[107] An Iowa cattle farm was sold at a loss and the directors agreed to sell the shares held in the Kansas City Cattle Company, the Arkansas Valley Land and Cattle Company, and the Powder River Cattle Company. Because the range cattle business was booming at this time, they received a premium on most of these shares. The Canadian River Cattle Company of Texas, in which they had invested, was in the process of being absorbed by the Hansford Cattle Company. An exchange of shares was agreed upon, but as soon as the transfer was made the investment company sold out. The directors were also trying to sell their holdings in northwestern Canada, and finally Menzies agreed to give them their half of the cash invested in the Scottish Canadian Land Company. For the time being, the Colorado coal lands were held.[108]

In short order the difficulties to be encountered by any Scottish company owning real estate in the United States were acutely apparent, and many investors were congratulating themselves on the wisdom and timing in shifting the nature of the company's operation. During 1883 information arrived in Dundee that acreage purchased in Kentucky and Tennessee proved upon survey to be less than that paid for. There were three hundred squatter claims on the verge of being validated on the company lands in Arkansas. Moreover, the title to 2,500 acres of land in that state appeared to be invalid. The directors voted to turn the whole problem of the lands in these three states over to John M. Judah, a new partner of Francis Smith. In time the vendors agreed to take back all the properties and pay the company ten per cent on the purchase price to avoid a suit for damages. The directors refused the proposal unless the payment also included the company's expenditures in improving the lands. Tremendous effort

7. *Chief Justice Erasmus Shattuck* (see p.25)

8. Governor Addison C. Gibbs (see p.25)

was exerted to procure the $75,000 involved. When this failed Judah was instructed to sell the land at $1·75 an acre but to take $1·25 rather than miss a sale. The directors also dutifully paid-up the capital calls in the ill-fated American Lumber Company, but just before its collapse the shares were transferred to Mackenzie, Leng, and Andrew Whitton, another director, to avoid unfavourable publicity for the investment company. Liquidation of real estate and cattle company shares continued throughout 1883.[109] The directors, bitterly criticized at this time, waived all remuneration for their services during the year, and Lowson, the chairman, retired from the Board. John Leng assumed the chairmanship. Because of the numerous legal difficulties, the directors agreed to engage in no more lumber ventures and to avoid outright land ownership. In spite of their wishes in the matter, it was difficult to sell property in the United States in 1883. Fleming remarked 'without entering into the merit and demerit of land investments it must be very evident to shareholders that they are not a form of investment that can be relied upon to produce regular annual profits, nor are they a suitable medium for investments for a company with a heavy debenture debt'. In 1884 Leng resigned his seat on the Board and two new appointees submitted their resignations after serving less than a year. Fleming had emerged as chief policy-maker within a period of three years.[110]

As presiding officer of the annual meeting of 1885, he apologized for the legacy of the land company and counselled patience:

> When I see the results of other American Land Companies formed at the same time as this, I feel thankful, and I am sure shareholders who have watched events must feel thankful, that the Directors had the courage to abandon the business for which the old Company was formed, and to resolve to have no land investments unless in mortgages at a good rate of interest, and with ample margin of security.

One shareholder, a Scottish farmer, complained 'I have been here for several years, and have always been told the same story, that the Company has earned a dividend, but that nothing can be paid.' After similar remarks Mackenzie was goaded to comment 'The Dundee Land Investment Company paid a dividend every year of its existence except the first.' To which Fleming responded

> I think the mistake was in paying the dividends they did. (Hear, hear.) If they had contented themselves with 5 per cent they might have kept it up. But with booming times in America, which enabled them to sell portions of their real estate and to realise profits, they paid away all these profits, so that when times changed, as they have changed,... there are no profits.[111]

The editor of *The Edinburgh Courant* noted in this year that although Aberdeen was a 'paradise of stockbrokers' and had long been the leading provincial town for speculative enterprise, Dundee was taking its place. He observed further:

> Dundee is a striking example of the incongruity there often is between business success and success in speculation. Wealth in Dundee has on the whole been easily made. Money taken out of business has been put into American railways, ranches, copper mines, and foreign trading companies. . . . Dundee has committed itself to investments more or less speculative, and nearly all outside the range of its proper business, to the extent of nearly five millions sterling. Of that it has actually paid up over three millions, and remains liable for a million and three quarters more. On the uncalled liability it has borrowed to the extent of over a million and a half. The ten principal companies carry on their business abroad–all, with one exception, in America.

The editor inquired whether a manufacturing centre could safely drain itself of such a large quantity of funds needed to maintain its factories and working people. Dundee had lying abroad between nine and ten times the value of every building and every foot of ground the burgh contained. The total income of its inhabitants was estimated at a million and a half pounds sterling each year, and its savings not over a quarter of a million. Thus, it had spent on 'financial recreations' in foreign lands the savings of at least twenty years.[112]

The Dundee Investment Company paid a five per cent dividend in 1885, the first in three years. By now the bulk of its money was in land mortgages. Among notable loans of the year was a £5,000 investment in Lord George Campbell's syndicate that loaned $350,000 to Charles Goodnight, the Texas cattleman, for five years at ten per cent on the security of the Palo Duro Cattle Ranch.[113] With the return of prosperity in the United States in 1886, company income was almost double that of the previous year. Most of the office buildings in Kansas City and Portland were sold at a profit. Just as the company began to prosper, Fleming resigned from the directorship to devote his entire energies to promotion in London.[114]

The largest block of real estate in company hands, the Chavez Land Grant, still remained a source of difficulty. Financial support was given Colorado lawyers who sought a special act of Congress confirming the grant. If successful, the legal advisers were to have an option to purchase the property for $180,000. Some squatters' claims were being purchased to avoid suit. In May 1886 the federal district court in Bernalillo County, New Mexico, upheld the company lawyers' request to quiet title of various occupants on the estate, some of whom claimed to be heirs of the first grantee. Once the lands were secured by this court action, the directors agreed with the Colorado Mortgage and Investment Company to lease the land for an annual rent of four cents an acre or to sell it at seventy-five cents an acre if an opportunity appeared.

Under instructions from the Commissioner of the General Land Office, George W. Julian, the surveyor general of New Mexico, re-examined the Chavez grant and declared it invalid in 1886. This decision directly contradicted the earlier 1882 ruling of the Secretary of the Interior. Once again the lawyers instituted action to hold the claim. The Scots finally resolved to enter into contract with Omado Chavez to rent the area for $1. He agreed to put a sheepherder at each of the valuable springs to protect the water supply for flocks, and to build corrals that would become the property of the company at the lease's termination in 1888. Meanwhile the company sought legislative action protecting its grant against the action of the General Land Office.[115]

By 1888, the Dundee Investment Company had been transformed from a real estate investment enterprise into a mortgage company, with four times as much money in land loans as in stock market securities. Capital returns from real estate were minimal because most of the property had been sold. A block of business buildings on the principal street of Winnipeg, still held, returned eight per cent interest. Between 1883 and 1888, the reserve fund had been increased from £2,500 to £24,000. As company credit improved, the interest rate demanded by those making debenture loans declined.[116]

At the shareholders' meetings of 1887 the directors of both the Dundee Mortgage Company and the Dundee Investment Company proposed to unite the two companies. After approval of the shareholders, the directors began preliminary discussions, with Mackenzie, the joint secretary, as a guiding voice. The Alliance Trust Company was incorporated for the purpose of amalgamation on 21 April 1888. Chief stumbling block in the way of the proposed union was the real estate held by the Dundee Investment Company. At the 1889 annual meeting of the Dundee Mortgage Company, John Guild, the chairman, reminded shareholders that the directors of the two companies were identical with the exception of himself. He added further

> Two years ago at our annual meeting the subject was brought up, but I thought it was at any rate premature, and that it would be better to wait till the Investment Coy. had brought themselves more into a position like our own. The kind of business they do now is the very same as ours, and through

> the same agents, so that the only difficulty in the way of amalgamation is the amount of money they have sunk in property. The comparative value of the assets of the two Companies could only be ascertained by a thorough investigation.

Shareholders' committees were elected at each company's annual meeting to assist directors in working out the details.[117]

The Alliance Trust Company had an authorized capital of £2,000,000 of which £1,100,000 was subscribed. In July 1889 it was announced that 90,000 ordinary shares had been issued, with 70,000 going to the mortgage company and 20,000 to the investment company. This represented a transfer of mortgage company shares into the Alliance Trust at par, while the 25,000 shares in the investment company had been reduced to 20,000, or twenty per cent. Moreover, shareholders of the investment company had paid-up £3 on each share which was lowered to £2, similar to shares of the mortgage company. Thus, £75,000 in the Dundee Investment Company became £40,000 in the capital account of the Alliance Trust. This reduction was partially cushioned, for, in addition, each shareholder in the investment company was to receive in cash 5s. 6d. a share. Preference shares of the mortgage company were also exchanged at par for similar shares in the Alliance Trust Company, amounting to £200,000. The new company began its business in a position of unusual strength because the paid-up capital, other than the preference shares, was £220,000 while the reserve fund stood at £155,000. The company was empowered to issue debentures up to £720,000 and the privilege had already been exercised by borrowing £705,000. Shareholders approved the amalgamation in October 1889, and an interim dividend was declared at the rate of ten per cent per annum.[118]

In 1890 the company had 948 shareholders and 1,316 debenture holders whose funds were dispersed over 2,245 loans on first mortgage. Affairs got off to a good start. The first year's revenue made possible a ten per cent dividend and an addition to the reserve fund, increasing it to £170,000. Although the Alliance Trust was primarily a land mortgage company, only 86·90 per cent of its funds were so invested because of the practice of placing the sizeable reserves into securities such as United States railroad, county, and municipal bonds.[119]

Years later William Mackenzie took credit for initiating the merger and for the persistence necessary to make the Alliance Trust a reality.

> In our consolidated Company we contain five previous corporations, each of which in its day and generation was known and dealt in. The policy of amalgamation has proved an

entire success,... It also enhanced our status, for the public no longer talked with some degree of mistiness of one of Mackenzie's Companies, but always of the great Alliance Company.[120]

One land mortgage company of Dundee outside the Mackenzie group was the Western and Hawaiian Investment Company, Limited, registered in October 1883. This company, with interests in western America, was an outgrowth of the Hawaiian Investment and Agency Company, established in 1880 to make mortgage loans in the Hawaiian Islands. In the beginning, capital was only £20,000 with £1 called on 20,000 shares of £5. After two years of operation, the directors reported that the unavoidable delay in transmitting funds to the Pacific Islands meant that shareholders' capital had been invested for only a seven-month period.[121] Although they continued to have confidence in the Islands as a safe field for investments, the directors by the following year wanted authority to do business elsewhere.[122] Thus, the new company was formed to extend operations into the United States and Canada. There was no increase in capital. Funds were borrowed to the extent of the uncalled share capital so that by 1885 debentures amounted to approximately £80,000. At the same time the company adopted a policy of gradually withdrawing funds from the Hawaiian Islands because rates of interest there had become unremunerative. In June 1885 £80,000 was invested in Hawaii; in June 1889 only £48,000 remained.[123] From the first, the company's policies were unofficially guided by the men who built the Alliance Trust Company, and soon it was to come within this financial circle.

The three Scottish American Investment Trusts (from their beginning in the 1870s) were under one management, with John Guild serving as chairman and Robert Fleming as secretary. They were known as the 'Fleming companies', interested in stocks and bonds in contrast to Mackenzie's group of land and mortgage companies. At the time of their official registration in 1879, the First Company held over fifty different securities, primarily bonds of railroads that had an average of twenty years to run before maturity. The current market value of their holdings was £143 for each £100 certificate held by members of the trust.[124]

Capital in all three companies was of one class–ordinary. During the prosperity years, 1881 and 1882, the trustees adopted a policy of selling bonds with a short currency when they could be marketed at a premium, even though they brought in a high interest rate. Funds received were reinvested in bonds of a much longer duration at a lower interest. Thus, in times of prosperity the rise in value of securities was capitalized and future company income assured for a longer period of time.[125]

At the annual meeting of 1883, Guild reminded shareholders that the original trust agreement would have come to a close at this session had they not elected to reorganize and officially register the trusts in 1879. The trustees' original plan for investing in American railway bonds had earned more than the seven per cent expected annually. Although profits had proved even greater in other American investment trusts, this company had followed a sound, conservative policy whereby there was no borrowed money and no risk beyond the subscription. The original £300,000 invested was then worth £464,686 on the market.[126]

The trustees were gravely concerned about the unsettled New York stock market of 1883, when only the very best securities maintained their value. As has been mentioned, the unprecedented fall in railroad stocks created a state of mild panic among speculators in the United States, but the Scottish American Investment Trusts were fortunate in holding no railroad shares but only bonds. As the general depression of 1884 developed, the trustees were somewhat smug about not being liable for calls upon unpaid capital and having no borrowed money. The business crisis had virtually no effect upon the income of these trusts.[127]

After summarizing the company's investment policies in 1886, the chairman announced that the average date at which the First Company's investments became payable was June 1913, or twenty-seven years later. He also stated:

> I advert to these facts again thus fully, and bring them clearly before you at this time, in consequence of reading an article lately in the London *Economist* on American railway investments, calling attention to the steady appreciable increase in the market value of bonds for some years, and to the fact that many buyers of these bonds appear to forget that in the fulness of time, instead of money which they lay out on bonds at a high premium they will receive back their face value only, and that in strictness they ought to lay by a certain portion of the interest each half-year to meet the shrinkage on the principal–a thing that very few people ever think of doing, though it is a vital point when the yield from investments are in question. This is just what we have all along recognized and acted upon,...[128]

Throughout the decade there had been a steady pushing forward of the maturity date on the company's securities, an increase in the market value of its bonds, and in 1888 a dividend increase from eight to eight and one-fourth per cent was possible.

The two sister companies, the Second and Third Scottish American Investment Trusts, had much the same experiences during the decade. Because of the advantageous time of its beginning, the Second Company continued the most prosperous. For 1880 and 1881 it paid eight per cent and as early as 1883 was able to increase its dividend to eight and one-fourth per cent. The Third Company, on the other hand, paid smaller dividends than the First, distributing seven and one-half per cent from 1881 to 1887 and seven and three-fourths per cent after 1888. Although it had been launched too late to gain the advantages of buying during the Panic of 1873, the trustees had built up a reserve fund by 1891 comparable to that of the First Company.[129]

Each year Fleming's financial interests took him more often to London. In 1890 he asked the trustees of the three Scottish American Investment Trusts of Dundee to relieve him of the secretaryship. Arrangements were made for him to continue as advising secretary to these trusts that had been his first venture in the field of investment finance. In 1900 Fleming opened a London office that became eventually Robert Fleming and Company, an agency offering to various investment trusts the advantages of co-operative management, purchasing, and underwriting of financial activities. All the Dundee investment companies used his firm as London representative, and through the years his financial influence was tremendous. In 1927-8 he served as director on five investment trusts that controlled £25·4 million. Through membership of these Boards, he had personal contact with six directors who sat on the Boards of thirty-nine other companies. Additional power was exerted through Robert Fleming and Company's advice to twelve trusts supervising £19·7 million. The Scot was thus able to influence fifty-six trusts that together controlled £114·8 million.[130] To the end of his career, Fleming's primary interest was in the United States. This meant crossing the Atlantic one hundred and twenty-eight times in the fifty years of his active career. In the end he claimed that Scottish capital made possible the building of the American railway network many years earlier than otherwise would have been possible, and that in periods of great agricultural depression, the Scots had underwritten the American farmer and given him more time and greater opportunity to recoup his losses than his fellow citizens in the eastern financial centres.[131]

There had thus developed in Dundee, as in Edinburgh, two basic types of investment in the United States: the land mortgage business that was supervised by a syndicate under Mackenzie's leadership, and operations on the stock and bond market in which Fleming was a specialist. The success of the Scots was temporarily halted by the depression of 1884, for one analyst estimated that the securities of the mortgage and investment companies of Dundee had depreciated £400,000.[132] Outright losses were imminent on some purchases of the land companies. The Scots appeared somewhat impatient when their real estate failed to produce income and they undoubtedly sacrificed potential capital gains over a period of time for immediate dividends. Their anxiety was increased by the widespread problems over alien land ownership. All these difficulties were transitory, prosperity soon returned, and the Dundee mortgage and investment companies earned a large percentage of the money that their shareholders risked in many single-purpose ventures in the expanding economy of western America.

Chapter Three

The Scottish Cattle Company Boom[1]

Scots engaged in expanding the operations of their land and mortgage companies along the Pacific Slope, in the northern prairie states, and in the agricultural regions of the South and Southwest, developed during the 1880s a simultaneous interest in the range cattle industry of the Great Plains. The western march of American farmers had either halted at, or passed over, this vast grassland because its arid climate, the absence of trees, and the unfamiliar soil made it unsuited for the agricultural methods used in the East. Their reluctance to occupy this unfamiliar and inhospitable environment provided a unique opportunity for another group of westerners–the cattlemen. The cattle industry had its beginnings in Texas in the years following the close of the American Civil War, when returning Confederate veterans seeking a new occupation began to round up the wild longhorns in the southern tip of that state and drive them to northern markets. Animals could be purchased for $3 or $4 a head, driven north, and sold in the upper Mississippi Valley, where livestock had been depleted by the war for $40. Specific south-north cattle trails were developed eadling to the railheads of the various lines laying rails from east to west on to the Great Plains. For example, one of the earliest trails terminated at Sedalia on the Missouri Pacific. When the Kansas Pacific built farther west, cattle were driven along the Chisholm trail, first to Abilene and later to Ellsworth, Kansas. Construction of the Santa Fe railroad still farther west into the Plains led to the establishment of the shorter Western trail terminating at Dodge City. From these various cow towns cattle were shipped to eastern packing centres and markets.

Soon the cattlemen realized that the scrawny Texas animals would bring more on the market if they were held on northern ranges for fattening before being shipped to the markets. Other ranchers were interested in improving the breed of stock. Within a short span of fifteen years the range cattle industry had expanded into an area half the size of Europe. Conditions on the Great Plains suggested that cattlemen were destined to make fabulous profits. Much of the land carpeted with grass was free to use, cattle could be bought at a low price and sold for a high one, and the market appeared unlimited. A rancher staking out a claim along one bank of a stream secured as much of the river or creek as he pre-empted, or purchased, and what was recognized as a 'range right' to all the land running back to the 'divide', or highland, separating his stream from the one lying beyond. Cowboys were employed to ride the line along the borders of cattlemen's ranches and periodically to round-up the cattle, brand the new-born calves, and select the yearlings to be shipped to market.[2]

When United States agents of Scottish 'syndicates' broached the subject of investment in American cattle ranching in 1878, Britons had only romantic notions about the business. Stories about huge herds of 'wild cattle' in Texas, the long drives to the northern grasslands, and the round-ups were vaguely known, but usually dismissed as fiction about faraway places. Yet earlier reports from some of these syndicate agents about America's vastness, economic potential, and lucrative investments, once thought to be highly exaggerated and romantic, had proved realistic enough to produce sizeable dividends. So the canny Scot began to seek every shred of information on the western range cattle industry.

Interest in cattle raising on the American plains was greatly stimulated by a sudden upswing in the volume of livestock imported from the United States. For many years Britain had depended upon heavy imports of livestock to feed her rapidly increasing population. Disease ravaged both the herds at home and those on the European continent in the 1860s, prices for beef soared because of the short supply, and the hungry British turned to the United States for relief.[3] Between 1877 and 1879 the export of beef on the hoof from the United States increased almost three fold, and over sixty per cent of the shipments went to Great Britain.[4] At the same time, oceangoing vessels were outfitted with refrigeration to protect fresh beef in transit and to eliminate the necessity for its immediate sale and distribution upon arrival, regardless of demand and price. As a result, the average tonnage of fresh beef imported into Britain for each year, 1878–80, was over fifteen times as great as it had been in 1876. The United States provided eighty per cent of this supply. In short order a multi-million dollar business had emerged.[5] The volume of importation, of course, wrought havoc with English and Scottish stock raisers, and the agricultural classes were distressed. Even so, the increased importation made beef plentiful and consumers rejoiced in the reduction of prices. Everywhere people were talking of the new cattle trade: in Parliament, over the tea tables of the aristocracy, and in the market place. Near riots occurred in Liverpool and Dublin when the masses eagerly attempted to purchase the cheap meat.[6]

In the spring of 1877, *The Scotsman* of Edinburgh sent James Macdonald, an expert on animal husbandry, to the United States on a tour to investigate the cattle industry as it affected the homeland. His chief conclusion was that the threat was not immediate because range cattle beef did not have the quality of domestic animals. Once the range herds were improved by selective breeding and a quality beef produced, the inevitable mass importation would lead to disaster for British stock raisers.[7] Macdonald's report only increased the excitement. The British government established a Royal Commission on Agriculture in 1879 to investigate the range cattle industry in the American West. The commissioners noted in their report that the region labelled 'The Great American Desert' in British schoolbooks was now stocked with tens of thousands of cattle. In glowing terms they told of ranges covered with '*self-made hay*' free for the taking by the owners of adjacent streams of water. By controlling the water, the cattlemen made the adjoining lands of little value, worth not more than twelve and a half cents an acre, and no farmer was likely to pay the government price of $1·25 an acre for arid land. Competition for the time being was thus eliminated. The commissioners observed 'It is generally acknowledged that the average profit of the stockowner has been for years fully 33 per cent. No doubt this is the most remunerative branch of American farming, but to secure the greatest return a large amount of money must be employed.' The report concluded 'With regard to cattle, for the present the American stockman in the West is possessed of singular advantages; land for nothing and abundance of it.'[8]

While the Royal Commission was conducting its investigation, the Earl of Airlie, chairman of the Scottish-American Mortgage Company, also toured the West and upon his return in 1881 issued a warning to Scottish agriculturalists not to migrate to the United States without sufficient capital. Should one elect to go, pastoral farming would prove more profitable than cultivation of the soil. 'It was not uncommon for a cattle breeder to clear 80 or even 100 per cent on his capital', Airlie reported, but such early profits led to competition and a well-managed ranch could only earn from 25 to 30 per cent a year. The Scottish nobleman pointed out that the business of cattle breeding required more capital than arable farming, but the larger the operation the greater the profits.[9] While the established Scottish investment syndicates pondered his observations, vendors had already approached financiers in both Edinburgh and Dundee about cattle investments. An attempt to interest the Dundee Land Investment Company in a Colorado ranch on the St Charles River had failed in 1879. Promoters were more successful in London where the Anglo-American Cattle Company, Limited, was registered in May 1879.[10] The Colorado Mortgage and Investment Company of London registered the Colorado Ranche Company, Limited, in December 1879, to operate a property known as the Osage Ranch.[11] These initial English companies were undercapitalized and quickly came to a bad end.

BOOM OF 1880 TO 1882

At the close of 1880, Frank L. Underwood, who had placed numerous land loans in Iowa, Kansas, and Missouri for the Scottish-American Mortgage Company, convinced capitalists associated with that company that profits could be made in the ranching business. J. Duncan Smith, manager of the mortgage company, was among the first to be convinced, and he prevailed upon several of its directors to register the Prairie Cattle Company, Limited, on 30 December 1880, capitalized at £200,000. Shareholders were lured into the project by a prospectus stating that United States cattle companies were making from twenty-five to forty per cent annual profits, and, in some instances, as high as fifty per cent.[12]

At the outset a contract was made with Underwood, Clark and Company whereby the profits were first to be applied to a ten per cent annual dividend on all paid-up capital. Any annual balances were to be used to repay shareholders a sum equal to the capital contributed. As soon as all investment capital had been returned and all indebtedness liquidated, the Kansas City firm, acting in the meanwhile as American agents without salary or commission, became entitled to three-eighths of the whole assets of the company as compensation for its services.[13] These agents received unlimited authority from the Scots to purchase land and cattle and soon they were purchasing range rights and herds along the Cimarron River in northeastern New Mexico, on the Canadian River in the Texas Panhandle, and in southeastern Colorado. Company representatives expanded so rapidly the first year that ranchers in the Southwest got the impression that the Prairie Company was preparing to own 'all outdoors'. Then in 1881-2 land purchases were made to obtain 'a more scientific frontier', or, in plain language, to make their properties as compact and secure as possible. In all, the company already held 117,000 acres.[14]

Shareholders who had paid up £4 on each £10 share they had purchased were notified at the first annual meeting that the experiment had proved an immediate success. Profits were equal to twenty-six per cent on the paid-up capital. A ten per cent annual dividend was declared, together with a bonus of 9s. 6d. per share, both free of income tax. Success justified an increase in company capital from £200,000 to £500,000 by the creation of 30,000 new shares. Of these, 25,000 were sold at par to the original shareholders on a ratio related to their initial investment. The second year of the Prairie Company's operation was more successful than the first and the directors recommended payment of the usual ten per cent dividend and an increase of the bonus to 17s a share.[15] It is not surprising, therefore, that the Prairie Cattle Company made a tremendous impression in Scottish business circles.[16] John Clay, who was among the most successful Scots engaged in the cattle business in the United States, later recalled:

> The financial officers of that conservative old city [Edinburgh] had found a new mine to exploit. The drawing rooms buzzed with the stories of this last of the bonanzas, staid old gentlemen who scarcely knew the difference betwixt a steer and a heifer discussed it over their port and nuts. Mr Underwood, a banker in Kansas City, the promoter, was a little tin god and Mr J. Duncan Smith was his prophet.[17]

After promoting the Prairie Cattle Company in Edinburgh, the energetic Underwood went to Dundee where he started the Texas Land and Cattle Company, registered in December 1881, with an authorized capital of £240,000. Several capitalists associated with the successful Dundee investment and mortgage companies signed the Memorandum of Association and invested heavily in the cattle company, but the management of the Texas Company was not dominated by these pioneer Dundee enterprises to the extent that the Scottish-American Mortgage Company controlled the Prairie Cattle Company. The Kansas City promoters held fully-paid deferred shares worth £30,000 as a security for an agreement whereby they were entitled to one-half of the surplus profits *each year* after the payment of a ten per cent dividend on the ordinary shares. The Americans had driven a hard bargain whereby they would share in the profits immediately without waiting for the return of investment capital to shareholders, as in the case of the Prairie. Under the terms of the agreement, they were certain to push for the distribution of maximum surplus each year. Underwood joined the Board of the Texas Company while his partner, W. A. Clark, of Iowa, sat on the directorate of the Prairie.[18]

The Texas Company purchased from Mifflin Kennedy the Los Laureles Ranch in Nueces County, in the southern tip of Texas, consisting of 236,000 acres, and agreed to buy any adjoining acreage he could obtain for not more than $2 an acre. Herds on the ranch were estimated at 50,000 but the Scots wisely insisted on a count before the final payment was made, and the vendor agreed to a return of $9·75 for every head less than the estimate. The south Texas property was useful as a breeding ground, but in 1882 the company leased two ranges which were needed for additional grazing and fattening. One of these was in the Texas Panhandle along the Canadian, Washita, and Sweetwater rivers; the second was acreage held by the Kansas City Cattle Company that had originally leased reservation lands in the Indian Territory through the Cherokee Live Stock Association.[19] This expansion necessitated an increase in authorized company capital from £240,000 to £630,000.[20] The initial annual dividend of the company was fifteen per cent so the Kansas City promoters immediately received five per cent on the paid-up capital.

The success of the Texas Land and Cattle Company encouraged Dundee capitalists to seek additional ranch properties in Texas. The Matador Land and Cattle Company, Limited, registered in December 1882, purchased approximately 100,000 acres of 'selected watered lands' and a herd of cattle, guaranteed to be 40,000 head from two Texans, Alfred M. Britton and Henry Campbell. The purchased acreage was so arranged that a range of 1,500,000 acres was secured, described in the prospectus as all of Motley County, half of Dickens and Cottle, and one-third of Floyd counties; the price was $1,250,000. The distinctive feature of this cattle company was the continuing interest of the vendors in its finance and management. Only $500,000 was paid in cash, the remainder in stocks and debenture bonds. Campbell was employed by the Scots as ranch superintendent and Britton as manager on salaries. Should the annual profits average twenty per cent for each of the first five years, amounting to the return of the capital investment, the ranch management was to be entitled to seven per cent of future profits. The Matador Company was capitalized at £400,000, with £6 called up on each £10 share, a total of £240,000. The company issued debentures for £160,000, the amount of uncalled capital. Robert Fleming, on the Board of both the Texas and Matador companies, hastened to Texas and instituted large scale purchases to secure the Matador range. Within four months the company had 60,000 head of cattle and 303,264 acres of freehold land guaranteeing ranging privileges over 1,800,000 acres. Fleming's rapid expansion was timely and fortunate for the company. The average cost of the Matador's land was $1·68 an acre; the ink was scarcely dry on the sales contracts when the Texas legislature passed a law setting a minimum price of $2·00 an acre on all unwatered lands sold directly either to companies or individuals. Acreage on water fronts commanded a higher price. As often happened, the race to increase the company's acreage and herds had cost more than the initial company capital, so 10,000 additional shares were issued, with original shareholders having a first option to purchase, bringing the company capital to £500,000.[21]

The third Texas cattle company launched in Dundee simultaneously with the Matador was the Hansford Land and Cattle Company, Limited, capitalized at £210,000. Its ranches were located along the Canadian River in the north-central portion of the Texas Panhandle. A distinctive feature of this company was the directors' decision to consider only the income from cattle sales as profit, crediting nothing for the uncertain increase in the herd. On the basis of this conservative method of bookkeeping the company earned a six per cent dividend in 1882.[22]

In Edinburgh the directors of the Scottish-American Investment Company were eager to follow the lead of the Scottish-American Mortgage Company in entering the cattle business, particularly after the announcement of the initial dividend of the Prairie Company. They dispatched John Clay, a sub-commissioner of the Royal Agricultural Commission, to California as inspector of ranch properties recommended by the company's agents, Faulkner, Bell and Company of San Francisco. He reported favourably on the Chowchilla ranch in Merced and Fresno counties of the San Joaquin River Valley. In November 1881, while in California on a trip round the world, William J. Menzies decided to return to Edinburgh with an option on the 94,000-acre property. Back in Scotland, the California Pastoral and Agricultural Company, Limited, was organized to purchase the ranch, in which Faulkner, Bell and Company had a one-third interest, with the remainder owned by the Bank of Nevada, at that time controlled by James C. Flood and William S. O'Brien, Nevada silver kings. The capital of the company was £250,000, with ten thousand £10 shares entitled to a preferential dividend of seven per cent and the remainder in ordinary stock. The directorate included the chief policy-makers of the Scottish-American Investment Company.[23] In January 1883 the company declared a ten per cent dividend on ordinary shares after meeting the fixed payment on preference shares.[24]

In July 1882 Clay was instructed to go to Wyoming and inspect the Seventy-one Quarter Circle Ranch along the Sweetwater River just above the Devil's Gate, owned by John T. Stewart of Council Bluffs, Iowa. This property was located in a centre of ranching activity between the Green and Ferris mountains, along the boundary line of Sweetwater and Carbon counties. Upon Clay's favourable report, the Wyoming Cattle Ranche Company,

Limited, was registered in August 1882, with an authorized capital of £200,000. The American vendors retained a 'deferred interest' in the company, which allowed them, after the shareholders had received a twelve and one-half per cent cumulative annual dividend, plus the repayment of their investment, three-eighths of the remaining assets, provided the herd on the ranch totalled 50,000 at the time of sale. The prospectus revealed that $400,000 had been paid for the property, and in glowing terms it praised Wyoming as a bonanza cattle territory and the vendor Stewart as a painstaking breeder whose cattle brought the highest prices. It also noted the initial financial success of the Prairie and Texas companies.[25]

The Menzies group in Edinburgh organized a third Scottish-American ranch company in 1882, known as the Western American Cattle Company, located for thirty-five miles along the Belle Fourche River, the north branch of the Cheyenne River, in Wyoming and western South Dakota. In this instance, three vendors who owned the VVV ranch had travelled to Scotland seeking purchasers and had employed the services of Gordon, Pringle, Dallas and Company to assist in the search. Thomas J. Gordon was a director of the Prairie Cattle Company. According to the first proposals the American owners were to be retained as managers of the property. The financial agreement was contingent upon a favourable report by Clay and Pringle after inspection. Clay was impressed with the potentiality of the ranch but Pringle presented an unsatisfactory report on his return to Scotland, questioning the representations made by the vendors concerning the size and increase of the herd and expressing doubt concerning the competence of their management. As a result the Western American Cattle Company did not complete the purchase and the money subscribed for shares was refunded.[26] The American vendors were not willing to let the project die. In January 1883 a meeting was held in Edinburgh to organize Western Ranches, Limited, to take over the same property. The deferred shares provided for in the earlier company, that represented a potential annual return of £10,000 for the founder-vendors, were replaced in the new set-up with £12,000 in shares, on which they might earn annual dividends of £1,200 to £1,800. The vendors were no longer responsible for the management, so the Scottish directors reserved the right to deduct ten per cent from their dividends to help compensate company agents and ranch superintendents in America. Pringle was to be sent from Scotland as superintendent; Clay served as agent in Chicago. The Scots had learned that the American owners of this Dakota-Wyoming property were in serious financial straits, partially owing to the expense they had incurred

9. *H. H. Campbell's house, yard, and general setting in background* (see p.78)

10. Princes Street, Dundee, showing the Baxter Brothers textile firm, about 1914

in forming and floating the former Western American Cattle Company, and the Scots had driven a hard bargain that was to prove very lucrative.[27]

In addition to the three companies sponsored by the established capitalists of the Scottish-American Investment Company, the Missouri Land and Livestock Company, Limited was launched in 1882. The primary objective of this company was to buy large blocks of agricultural lands, subdivide it into suitable farms, and sell these to agriculturalists, many of them Scottish immigrants. Through a Chicago agent the company obtained 165,000 acres of land in Jasper, Newton and McDonald counties, in the southwestern corner of Missouri, from the St Louis and San Francisco Railroad Company at $1·50 an acre. Within a year the Scots had sold approximately 10,000 acres at an average price of $4·88 an acre. The St Louis and San Francisco Railroad, eager to capitalize on its remaining scattered acreage in Missouri, offered the company all its lands in Christian, Greene, Lawrence, Stone and Polk counties, believed to be 175,000 acres, again at $1·50 an acre. To make this purchase company capital had to be increased to £150,000.[28] Shareholders were informed that during the first year six per cent of the original land purchase had been sold and that the total price realized was twenty per cent of the original investment. In Jasper County the company had already recouped its entire investment and had two-thirds of the acreage left.[29] Operations on its Sandyford ranch, just begun, were to concentrate on the raising of bulls for the western cattle ranges by using Polled Angus bulls to breed with high-grade Shorthorn and Hereford heifers. The directors considered profits from land sales sufficient to justify a ten per cent dividend.[30]

A fifth prospectus, that of the American Cattle Company, Limited, circulated in Edinburgh in 1882. The promoters proposed the purchase of the Niobrara Home Cattle Ranch in Nebraska, with a range of 1,500 square miles extending from east to west thirty miles and north to south fifty miles on both sides of the Niobrara River. No evidence has been found that this company was ever floated, so perhaps the project was too tenuous for even the most gullible.[31]

Scottish interest in the western range cattle industry was not confined to those companies registered in Edinburgh and Dundee. London financiers were just as excited about the business as those in the northern communities. Edinburgh firms often had both English and Scottish shareholders. Many Scottish businessmen also purchased sizeable blocks of shares in English enterprises. Because of such interrelated interests it is difficult to identify one cattle company as being Scottish and another English. In 1882 the knowledge and experience of the Scots in cattle raising was in great demand by London capitalists. For example, the Cattle Ranche and Land Company, domiciled in London, was owned largely in Scotland. Chief promoter was Rufus Hatch who had secured sizeable 'range rights' in western Kansas, the Indian Territory, the Texas Panhandle, and 'No Man's Land' north of the Panhandle. His London agent was Webster, Hoare and Company. John Clay received a fee for an inspection together with the promise of a bonus in company shares if the promotion was successful. The company also had a distinguished American Board composed of Hatch, Clay, Senator John P. Jones of Nevada, and James B. Houston, president of the Pacific Mail Steamship Company.[32] Another London company, largely sponsored by Scots in 1882, was the Western Land and Cattle Company, Limited. W.R. Green, the Texas manager of the Prairie Company, called the attention of Mitchell and Baxter, Edinburgh solicitors, to the availability of the IOI and VI ranches along the Cimarron. The Scottish firm became agents for the property, with the understanding that its sale would be promoted in London because of the saturation of the Scottish market.[33]

Dundee financiers, Andrew Whitton and William G. Thompson, sat on the Board of Directors of the Arkansas Valley Land and Cattle Company, Limited, capitalized at £250,000, to acquire the Holly Sullivan Ranch in Colorado, which stretched along the north bank of the Arkansas River for thirty miles.[34] The same type of representation prevailed in the Powder River Cattle Company, Limited, capitalized at £300,000, to take over Moreton Frewen's 76 Ranch along the Powder and Crazy Woman rivers in Johnson County, Wyoming Territory. Whitton also sat on this Board along with John Leng.[35] A fifth English company promoted in connection with the range cattle industry was the Maxwell Cattle Company, Limited, that held a lease on the Maxwell Land Grant in New Mexico and Colorado for thirty-eight years. The British public was invited to buy eight per cent first mortgage bonds of £100 to raise funds to stock the estate of one and three-quarter million acres.[36] J. Guthrie Smith of Edinburgh sat on the distinguished Board of managing trustees for the British bondholders.[37] Certainly the fact that Scots either promoted or sat on the Board of Directors of every cattle company registered in London during 1882 attests both to their interest and success in this line of endeavour.

Ten major British-American cattle companies had been incorporated during 1882. Capitalization of the smallest, Western Land and Cattle, was £115,000; that of the largest, the Matador in Texas, £400,000. The total subscribed capital of these cattle companies was approximately £2,200,000. Approximately seventy per cent of the subscribed capital had been called up to purchase land and cattle in western America, amounting to nearly £1,600,000. When capital investment of the earliest Scottish companies, the Prairie Company and the Texas Land and Cattle Company, up to 1882 is included, the staggering total reaches £3,100,000 subscribed and over £2,000,000 expended within a three-year period.[38]

The steps by which the Scots invested their capital in the range cattle industry had already formed a pattern destined to be used by companies incorporated during the rest of the decade. In the first place, news about an available and likely property was usually obtained through a banking or investment company in the United States already representing a Scottish firm. Occasionally information was secured by a Scotsman sent on a tour of investigation, or the vendor turned up in Edinburgh, Dundee, or London, seeking capital. If the prospect appeared good, the second step was to organize a joint stock company, issue a prospectus, file necessary financial records, and raise money. Meanwhile, a reliable inspector was dispatched to examine the ranch property, and until his report was received the final negotiations with the vendors and the incorporation of the company were held in abeyance. If the report proved favourable, the selected ranch or range was purchased, including the herd, and the 'cattle king' who had sold it was often retained as manager, at least for a while. Sometimes the financial house which proposed the transaction was requested to organize an 'American Board' to advise the Scottish directors.

Detailed financial arrangements varied. In the beginning, American promoters often demanded an annual share in the profits. Soon it was the custom for them to have only a 'deferred interest' which was not recognized until after the payment of specified annual dividends to the shareholders and upon the return of their original capital. In this manner the British hoped to guarantee the continuing interest of the vendor. Occasionally there was a proviso that he could not dispose of his shares for a definite period of years. Some vendor-managers worked without salary until such time as they could share in the company's profits. Thus the interest of the Scottish investors was intertwined with that of the American vendors and managers. In short, the Scots, in general, thought they had been shrewd in drawing up financial arrangements with the Yankees.

The rapid formation of the cattle ranch companies did not pass unnoticed by the financial press. *The Economist* pointed out that most American cattle companies issued a prospectus dwelling on the success of the Prairie. The Texas, Cattle Ranche, and Western Land and Cattle companies had also announced high initial dividends. The public was ill-advised, according to the editor, to assume that such profits could continue, for the dividends had been justified only by placing an inflated evaluation on the stock. Competition in the industry was certain to lower the value of cattle.[39] The editor of the *Scottish Banking and Insurance Magazine* agreed that the sudden competition among the cattle companies had temporarily driven up the price, but the level could not continue because the herds were increasing in size and the market for meat could not be expanded.[40] A correspondent of this magazine pointed out three basic dangers in the range cattle business. In the first place, most of the stockmen were squatters on the land, who had purchased only narrow strips along the waterways, and the range was being used at the sufferance of the United States government. Already the Laramie, Wyoming *Boomerang* was reporting that the Secretary of the Interior had instructed United States attorneys to see that fences enclosing the public domain come down. A second danger was the possible severe winter climate when stock would have to find shelter behind bluffs and in valleys. An unusually dry summer and autumn, or a range fire, could destroy the fodder and further aggravate the situation. The third danger was the haphazard 'tally' or 'book count' used in Western America for calculating on paper the size of the calf crop and thereby increasing the herd each year without exact information. The only certain way to know the correct number was to gather the cattle and rebrand, but that was time-consuming and expensive. The fact that there were cases where ranchers at the time of sale refused to guarantee the delivery of more than seventy five per cent of the stock estimated by book count was ominous.[41] When agitated critics insisted that the financial press was too pessimistic, editors reprinted the reports of auditors of the Prairie Cattle Company and the Western Land and Cattle Company urging caution in dividend distributions until the business had been tested by further experience.[42] While the financial press displayed a characteristic conservatism, the Scottish newspapers, such as *The Edinburgh Courant*, published editorials and feature stories attempting to satisfy public interest. The recurring themes were the vastness and cheapness of western lands, the enormous profits in raising cattle on the open range, and the eagerness of the railroads on the northern plains to dispose of their land grants at bargain prices.[43]

The most impressive characteristic of Scottish investment in the range cattle industry was the speed with which it was made. The Scots appear to have abandoned their usual care and deliberation in placing such quantities of money in a single line of endeavour. The concentration of capital available for investment in the east of Scotland may explain why American overseas investment centred there in the 1870s, but the presence of a large capital reserve is not a completely satisfactory explanation for their precipitate action in cattle ranch promotions between 1880 and 1882. Perhaps the answer can be found in the fact that in their homeland Scots for generations had specialized in animal husbandry. When the possibility of raising cattle on such a large scale in the American West was presented to them, their imagination was quickly captured and their excitement seems in many instances to have overcome their usual good judgment and caution. Rumours also circulated that the strategic land controlling the running water, thus guaranteeing range rights, was limited and only those who seized the opportunity quickly would be rewarded. Many of the cattle companies were overcapitalized and soon contributed to the general overexpansion of the range cattle industry. Meanwhile, the Scottish role in the western cattle trade became the most widely publicized of all their economic activities in the United States.

OVERCAPITALIZATION AND OVEREXPANSION

By 1883 the Prairie Cattle Company had consolidated the acreage on its three divisions. Publicity concerning the vastness of its domain brought to the attention of many United States citizens the extent to which Scottish capitalists had invested in the range cattle industry. The Arkansas Division of the company extended from the Arkansas River on the north to the Colorado-New Mexico boundary on the south, a distance of seventy miles; and from a north-south line ten miles west of La Junta, on the Atchison, Topeka and Santa Fe Railroad, it extended east a distance of fifty miles. The total acreage was 2,240,000, or 3,500 square miles. The cattle, valued at $25 a head, were worth $1,705,000. The Cimarron Division stretched from the Colorado-New Mexico boundary southward to the southern boundary of Mora County, a distance of eighty-four miles; and from a north-south line from Sierra Grande on the west to the Texas state line on the east, a distance of forty-eight miles. The area was larger than that of the Arkansas Division–4,032 square miles–and the cattle were evaluated at $1,445,000. The Canadian Division was located in Potter and Oldham counties of Texas with the southern boundary on the Canadian River and extending northward for twenty-five miles. The western boundary ran through the town of Tascosa; the range extended sixteen miles eastward. This smallest holding of the Prairie Cattle Company embraced only 400 square miles. The empire in America was valued at $4,416,484.[44]

Shareholders were already expressing criticism of the directors' management. Many looked askance upon the herd statistics indicating that either the natural increase was not what was predicted or the 'book count' of the herd at the time of purchase was in excess of actual numbers. At the same time a committee of inspection reported that the company's ranges were over stocked, that yearly increase in the herds would have to be marketed or a fattening range in Montana purchased.[45] Many investors found the company's connection with Underwood, Clark and Company distasteful and complained that at the rate bonuses were being paid a settlement with Underwood would not be due for thirteen years. The American promoters suggested a proposal whereby their contingent interest could be liquidated by transferring to them the property and herds along the Canadian River in the Texas Panhandle. Underwood and his partners would pay a bonus to the Scots of £30,000, but expected a rebate if they could secure a leasehold of 200,000 acres in the Indian Territory, to where some of the cattle on the crowded ranges could be transferred.[46] The proposition was accepted by the directors but not without dissension and resignations. Shareholders were warned by the financial press against agreeing to the arrangement. Shares dropped from £9 to £8 10s. Leading shareholders drafted a substitute scheme for a financial settlement and an extraordinary meeting was called. At this point the directors withdrew the original Underwood proposal and announced that the financial arrangements would remain unchanged.[47] The suggestion that the company might obtain 'range rights' in the Indian Territory had raised questions about the nature of land tenure in the United States. Shareholders were told that, in Colorado and New Mexico, aliens could hold land by deed if, as a corporation, they declared the place of business and the name of an agent upon whom legal papers could be served. In Texas, a British subject held lands under the same terms a Texan enjoyed in Great Britain. The British Naturalization Act of 1870 made it possible for an alien to hold property in Britain, so Scots had the rights of native citizens to lands in Texas.[48] In 1883 the directors recommended a regular ten per cent dividend plus a bonus of 10s. equal to twenty and one-half per cent on paid-up capital; £9,000 was placed in reserve. When the shareholders assembled, they voted to divide the £9,000 reserve by declaring another five per cent dividend, thereby hastening the termination of the Underwood contract. At the same time, the minority was criticizing the directors for issuing overoptimistic reports and paying excessive dividends.[49] Prairie shares dropped to £8. 'Why', asked the editor of *The Edinburgh Courant* 'should what is still the best and foremost of all the companies have set the rest such a bad example in steadily and irresistibly losing ground as an investment?' In his opinion, public confidence had been shaken by an obvious lack of policy in Edinburgh.[50]

Other Edinburgh companies continued operations during 1883 with varying degrees of success. The Missouri Land and Livestock Company continued its policy of buying large tracts of land at $1·50 an acre and selling it for over three times its cost. A pamphlet praising the company's farm lands was distributed wholesale, with five thousand copies circulated among prospective emigrants in Scotland, ten thousand distributed in the United States, and four thousand copies, translated into German, were sent to central Europe. At this time, the cattle raising experiment remained a sideline.[51] Among the companies sponsored by the Scottish-American Investment Company, the California Pastoral and Agricultural Company had already come upon hard times as a result of drought in the San Joaquin Valley and the realization that the herds purchased on the basis of book count were short.[52] The Wyoming Cattle Ranche Company was likewise the victim of book count and the Scots had decided upon legal action against John T. Stewart the vendor when the calf brand was only thirty per cent of the number he had guaranteed.[53] The future of Western Ranches appeared more promising because the company had bought its small herd by actual count and had spent the year building it up. The *Courant* suggested the Prairie Company and Western Ranches should work out a scheme of co-operation: 'The one has precisely what the other wants,' he pointed out, 'and it might be safer for them to deal together than to try new ventures with the Heathen Chinee of the Far West.' The Prairie Company could secure a splendid feeding range and Western Ranches obtain a share in the yearlings the Prairie was forced to market.[54]

In Dundee, the Matador Land and Cattle Company declared an eight per cent dividend for 1883, one of the smallest announced, while the Texas Company was distributing twelve and one-half per cent. At the same time, the Matador shares were worth more on the market. Shares in this company had risen slowly since its inception because of confidence in the management both in Scotland and Texas and the fact that the calf crop was larger than anyone had predicted.[55] The Texas Land and Cattle Company was victimized by the Underwood syndicate, which pressed for the highest possible annual dividend in order to obtain its one-half interest in everything above ten per cent. Critics thought the company had not earned more than eight per cent. Moreover, the American promoters had delayed in making the herd count guaranteed at the time of purchase. The Texas Company claimed to have 63,000 head on the Laureles Ranch in Texas, but once the round-up was made, the management admitted that about one-third of them were 'so wild that no human being dare handle them'. The *Courant* thought Underwood had 'about as much right to sell them as he had to sell a herd of buffaloes in the Rocky Mountains'. Some of the thirteen- and fourteen-year-olds, if they came into the market, would come 'as redwood, and not as beef'. The directors of the company were trying to raise an additional £20,000 on debenture, but Scottish investors were warned against it.[56]

Scottish enthusiasm for additional cattle ranch investments had begun to wane by 1883. The Dickey brothers, who had large herds in the Indian Territory and on the Little Missouri River in South Dakota, Wyoming and Montana, were among the many who came to Edinburgh expecting to launch a new company only to be disappointed.[57] Glasgow and Aberdeen promoters attempted to get into the business belatedly through the sponsorship of the Deer Trail Land and Cattle Company, Limited, which had an option on lands due east of Denver, Colorado, but the investment capital was not forthcoming.[58] The only major Scottish-American cattle company floated in this year was the Swan Land and Cattle Company, Limited, capitalized at £600,000 to purchase the lands and herds of Alexander H. Swan and his partner, Joseph Frank, in southeastern Wyoming along the waters of the Laramie, Chug and Sybille. This domain in Laramie, Albany, and Carbon counties extended one hundred and thirty miles from east to west and the north-south breadth increased from forty-two miles on the eastern end to one hundred miles on the west. The Scots paid $2,387,675 for the property. In short order the company was purchasing additional lands and cattle, and the authorized capital had to be increased to £750,000. Swan and his partner subscribed for a one-sixth interest and he was named manager for a term of five years. Although the initial dividend of nine per cent appeared small alongside the Prairie's twenty-six per cent, Swan shares brought a premium on the stock market. This was largely explained by the exceptional confidence in Swan's management, as expressed by the Scottish press, and thoroughness of the reports prepared by the company secretary, Finlay Dun.[59]

In London there was no evidence of diminishing resources for investment in the range cattle industry, or of a slackening of financiers' interest as there was in Scotland. Among the enterprises was the Dakota Stock and Grazing Company, Limited, with £250,000 authorized capital, which purchased the Hat Creek Ranch, controlling a range of 640 square miles along the Cheyenne and Hat Creek rivers in Nebraska, Dakota, and Wyoming. The acreage was a part of the Sioux Indian Reservation opened to cattlemen in 1876. Richard Frewen, brother of Moreton, was named manager for five years on a profit-sharing basis.[60] The Nevada Land and Cattle Company, Limited, secured ranch lands in Humboldt and Elko counties, Nevada, about thirty miles north of the Central Pacific Railroad route along the Humboldt River.[61] The Kansas and New Mexico Cattle and Land Company, Limited, purchased a ranch of one thousand acres in Sedgwick County, Kansas, and additional range and water rights from the Atchison, Topeka and Santa Fe Railway.[62] The Sand Creek Land and Cattle Company, Limited, obtained a ranch in Carbon County, Wyoming, with headquarters at the junction of Sand Creek and the North Platte River.[63] Two companies promoted in London in 1883 got off to an exceptionally bad start. The Rocking Chair Ranche, Limited, in which Lord Tweedmouth was the principal investor, discovered that its Texas herds listed at 12,000 on the books amounted to 2,500 and that the investment of shareholders had disappeared.[64] The United States Cattle Ranche Company, Limited, organized to take over range properties on the Republican River, where Colorado, Kansas, and Nebraska joined, found it necessary to make a financial reorganization before the year was over.[65] Most of these London companies of 1883 appeared to be ephemeral from their inception. Scottish promoters who had been prevalent in England the year before were not nearly so active and the business was, for the most part, dominated by titled Englishmen and retired Army and Navy officers.

The six English and two Scottish companies–Swan and Western Ranches–registered in 1883 had a total authorized capital of approximately £2,100,000. Capital invested was slightly less than that of 1882. Percentage of cash paid-up in these companies was reduced from almost seventy per cent of the previous year to less than forty-five per cent, a total of about £860,000. The size of these undertakings was becoming smaller, for only the Swan could match the larger enterprises started in 1880–2. While Scottish companies had invested more money than the English in the three previous years, London promotions in 1883 were, in capital outlay, equal to if not greater than the Scottish. Total British investment had now reached £5,200,000 subscribed capital with approximately £2,860,000 paid-up. Scots alone had obligated themselves for approximately £2,750,000 through companies registered in Scotland, in addition to their investment in London ventures, conservatively estimated at £500,000. These figures by no means indicate the total financial stake of the British in the range cattle industry. Some of the older companies had increased their capital during the year. There were also many investors who formed a partnership, or private company with limited liability, that did not seek investment capital from the public. These enterprises do

TABLE 1. Comparative statement of cattle companies' balance-sheets for year 1838

	cattle and horses	land in fee-simple acres	cost of land per acre $	calves	sales numbers	sales realised per head $
Prairie	129,243	139,450	2.83	28,207	21,448	25
Texas	98,729	352,000	1.63	19,337 *1,106	7,856 *500	34.54 *35.35
Matador	76,600	374,717	1.62	20,844	4,816	30
Hansford	37,900	110,620	not paid	6,044	4,052	28.15
Arkansas	24,032	17,420	17.92	3,555	3,168	39.35
Cattle Ranche	28,471	nominal		4,461	4,109	35.18
Powder River	49,113	nominal		9,824	5,366	36.17
Western	31,039	70,359	2.49	6,197	4,217	31.58
Swan	109,800	6,037		19,334	8,363	40.40

* Horses and mules.

The above statement has been carefully compiled from the reports and accounts of the companies. Dundee, 12 March 1884.

not appear in listings of the London or Edinburgh stock exchanges nor is their history recorded in financial year-books. However, they were required, as foreign companies, to register in some western states and territories. In Wyoming alone this type of company had invested close to £1,000,000.[66]

The rush into the cattle business had been so rapid that there had not been time for an overall appraisal of the field for investment. As noted, the financial press early expressed alarm at the remarkably high dividends paid by the land and cattle companies in face of imperfect data, and by writing up the value of their cattle to the high, but fluctuating, market prices. These concerns were, in general, branded as being overhasty in dividing such profits. In an attempt to present the evidence, the *Scottish Banking and Insurance Magazine* published an elaborate comparative statement of the larger companies' balance sheets for 1883. All the Dundee enterprises were included and the larger limited companies of Edinburgh and London (see Table 1 above).[67]

In February 1884 *The Economist* noted that there was still a great demand for securities of the cattle companies in spite of the fact that almost three times as many of their shares had declined in value as had advanced in the last year. Even so, securities of

valuation of stock per head in balance-sheet $	American expenses per head s. d.	debenture or preferred capital paid up £	ordinary capital paid up £	dividend per cent on ordinary capital	reserve or balance forward £	ordinary shares paid £
13.88	4 10	223,240	250,000	20½†	10,413	5
15.10	4 2	207,170	240,000	12½†	3,376	5
20.30	2 6	160,000	240,000	8†	2,618	6
25.09	3 7	none	209,740	6	647	5
27.00	5 2	113,524	125,000	10	1,634	5
25.50	5 3	100,000	100,000	10	4,532	5
28.00	4 0	100,000	176,000	6	32,698‡	4¼
25.66	5 8	80,200	80,200	15	42,740‡	5
24.43	2 8	225,666	374,180	9	5,295	6

† The profits of the first three companies are subject to deferred interests.

‡ These reserves have been created by the re-valuation of the cattle.

ten of the sixteen companies prominently traded on the market were selling at a premium (see Table 2 of market values on p. 92).[68] The editors offered this evidence 'that a well-managed American cattle and land, or ranche, undertaking can be conducted profitably by a British joint stock company'. However, the earliest companies that bought their estates and livestock before competition had driven up prices in the American West had a distinct advantage.

Success of the cattle companies between 1880 and 1883 was largely determined by the continuous rise in prices for livestock. However, by the autumn of 1883 there was a decided slump in the market and those selling animals late in the year were disappointed in the prices received. Meanwhile, the export of cattle from the United States, after consistently increasing every year since 1875, fell off sharply in 1882. This was partially explained by the fact that American cattle had become too expensive for the British market and had thereby lost their comparative advantage in competition with the home supply. Another factor was the continuing demand for superior herds to stock new ranches being purchased in the West by the numerous cattle companies, thus reducing those available for export.[69]

TABLE 2. Market value of cattle company shares

	paid up per share	*market prices* Feb. 1884	Feb. 1883	*movement on twelve months*
Arkansas	5	$5\frac{3}{4}$	$4\frac{3}{4}$	+1
Cattle Ranche, preference	5	$4\frac{7}{8}$	$5\frac{1}{2}$	$-\frac{5}{8}$
Colorado Ranche	100			
Dakota	5			
Hansford	5	$4\frac{3}{4}$	$4\frac{3}{4}$	
Maxwell, 8% Mortgage	100			
Matador	6	7	$6\frac{3}{8}$	$+\frac{5}{8}$
Missouri	3	$3\frac{3}{8}$		
Nevada	$2\frac{1}{2}$			
Powder River, ordinary	$4\frac{1}{4}$	$3\frac{3}{4}$	$4\frac{3}{8}$	$-\frac{5}{8}$
Powder River, preference	10	$11\frac{3}{4}$	11	$+\frac{3}{4}$
Prairie, 1st Issue	5	$7\frac{1}{16}$	$9\frac{3}{4}$	$-2\frac{11}{16}$
Prairie, 2nd Issue	5	$7\frac{1}{8}$	$9\frac{3}{4}$	$-2\frac{5}{8}$
Prairie, 3rd Issue	5	$7\frac{1}{4}$	$9\frac{1}{2}$	$-2\frac{1}{4}$
Swan	6	7		
Texas	5	$6\frac{1}{2}$	7	$-\frac{1}{2}$
United States	5			
Western Land	5	$6\frac{1}{4}$	$7\frac{1}{4}$	-1
Western Land, preference	5	$4\frac{1}{4}$	7	$-2\frac{3}{4}$
Western Ranches	5	$4\frac{1}{2}$		

Of more immediate concern than cattle prices and international trade were the problems associated with management and financial administration. Serious conflicts had developed over the business arrangements made by the Scots whereby American vendors participated in profit-sharing schemes and retained a deferred interest in the enterprise. The British press pictured the vendors as men demanding tribute and determined to influence company policy along the lines of their interests. With this goading, Scottish investors clamoured for termination of the agreements, but without any sacrifice. The vendors, on the other hand, insisted that they were entitled to share company profits because they had guided the Scots to this lucrative field for investment. The problems of long-distance management were also quickly apparent. Local ranch managers complained that they were hamstrung by the directorate in Edinburgh or Dundee. Conflicting policies at home and abroad led to mistakes in the handling and marketing of cattle. In time, companies that had dispatched managers from the Scottish homeland found relations between the local management and the directors more harmonious. Little could be done about the mistakes made in initial purchases of land and cattle. Where possible, the practice of securing uncertain range rights was curtailed in favour of outright purchases of land. More attention was being given to counting the herd to make certain their number and to obtain some indication as to the size of the calf crop upon which the success of the business depended. In many cases, however, these changes came too late, and some Scots realized that they were to pay for their folly.

MOUNTING PROBLEMS

By 1884, evidence was beginning to mount that all was not right in the western American Cattle Kingdom. Prices received for cattle continued to decline. During the year some chronic problems approached a critical stage. The Prairie Cattle Company continued the struggle to establish harmony within the management and among its shareholders and to arrive at a satisfactory termination of business connections with the American vendors.[70] At an extraordinary meeting called to vote on a commutation scheme, bitter disagreement broke out prior to adjournment. A signatory of the original Memorandum of Association accused Guthrie Smith, chairman of the Board, of being more concerned with Underwood's interests than with the Scots'. Smith declared the proxies held by this group invalid, and this action led to an uprising of the rank and file shareholders to prevent the commutation scheme from being approved. The upshot of this conflict was the retirement of Guthrie Smith as chairman of the Board.[71] Resignations of three more Board members were soon announced.[72] The Scottish shareholders took the position that no settlement with the Underwood syndicate should be made until the cattle count was verified.[73] Meanwhile Prairie Company shares dropped to £6 10s.[74] In December 1884 a cash settlement was finally made with the Americans, following a land survey and cattle count, but not without vigorous dissent. The Prairie shares then moved up rapidly on the market.[75]

Other Scottish companies also had difficulties. The Texas Company, still plagued with the question of herd count, resolved to admit the shortage in 1884. The prevailing themes of the annual report were low prices and the shortage of calves.[76] The Wyoming Cattle Ranche continued to seek justice from John T. Stewart, who had overestimated the size of the herd he had sold them in 1882. The Nebraska Supreme Court ruled that the vendor must make a cash settlement with the Scots for the shortages. The sum agreed upon amounted to approximately one-third of the actual loss.[77] For the first time the Missouri Land and Live Stock Company was experiencing difficulty in disposing of its lands.[78]

TABLE 3. Comparative statement of cattle companies' balance–sheets for year 1884

	total herd	*land in fee-simple — acres*	*cost of land per acre $*	*land leased — acres*	*rent of land leased — cents per acre*	*calves 1884*	*sales numbers*	*sales realised per head $*
Prairie	125,516	164,396	2.56			26,481	10,399	29.95
Texas	102,635	388,174	1.64	496,480	2 to 6	14,986	8,779	29.06
Matador	94,017	419,176	1.62	253,167	8	24,136	8,587	23.60
Swan	121,211	563,876	1.59			21,428	9,286	40.67
Hansford	39,090	76,110	1.30	175,428	2¾	7,000	4,562	28.65
Cattle Ranche	31,989	nominal		153,607	2½	4,223	1,613	32.22
Western	35,998	76,523	3.61			7,262	4,762	35.15
Arkansas	27,877	17,420	18.27 D			3,234	1,695	29.15
Powder River	54,629	nominal				9,187	4,301	35.01

The profits of the first three companies are subject to deferred interests (Prairie Co. since commuted)

D. Meadow-lands producing hay for sale.

The above statement has been carefully compiled from the reports and accounts of the companies, and in most cases checked by the officials.

The Swan Land and Cattle Company continued its programme of expansion throughout 1884, and no major difficulty appeared on the horizon. In fact, everything revealed about the enterprise inspired confidence, and no one questioned the ability or success of the American management.[79] Although the Matador Company's directors complained about low cattle prices and excessive rail charges. *The Statist* insisted 'From its birth, the Matador has been a solid property, carefully and wisely administered.'[80]

Superiority of the Scottish over the English cattle companies as investments was already apparent. The largest Scottish companies, the Prairie and Swan, paid their ten per cent dividends. Several other Edinburgh companies had earned from five to seven per cent, and the energetic Dundee companies were paying either six or seven per cent (see Table 3 above). The forerunner of them all, the Prairie, had returned to its investors seventy-seven and three-eighths per cent of the original share capital within four seasons. Only the California Pastoral was in an embarrassing position, and this was primarily due to climatic factors, although a count had now disclosed that the herds were indeed short. Al-

valuation cattle per head in balance-sheet $	American expenses per head* s. d.	debenture or preferred capital paid up £	ordinary capital paid up £	dividend per cent on ordinary capital	reserve or balance forward £	ordinary shares paid £
13.86	5 9	244,970	250,000	10	12,795	5
14.87	4 4	240,000	240,000	6	1,806	5
17.50	3 3 A	200,000	280,000	6	2,184	6
25.00	3 0	279,876	424,310	10	4,918	6
24.13	3 11	none	209,740	7	3,242	5
26.62	4 4	110,600	100,000	nil	18,047 B	5
26.30	6 7 C	133,100	100,000	15	48,441 B	5
28.33	6 1	119,814	125,000	nil	10,013 B	5
28.00	5 10	100,000	199,921	3	39,699	5

A. These expenses are for eleven months only.
B. These reserves have been created by a re-valuation of the cattle.
C. Includes outlays on improvements.

American expenses includes rents of lands leased.

though ordinary shares had received nothing for two years, the obligation to preferred shareholders had been met, and the company's position was far from desperate. From the viewpoint of financial success, the London companies were in no way comparable to the Scottish concerns, with the exception of the Western Land and Cattle Company, and, temporarily at least, the Nevada Land and Cattle Company and the New United States Cattle Ranche Company. The Western Land and Cattle Company, which declared a fifteen per cent dividend, was Scottish promoted and managed, and largely Scottish owned, so the English could not claim exclusive credit for its success. Shareholders of the Maxwell Company, likewise registered in London, looked to the Scottish trustees to see that the interest was paid on their bonds. On the other hand, Scots received a large percentage of the blame for the financial loss in the Cattle Ranche and Land Company. In the case of this company, 'range rights' that had been acquired in the Indian Territory were illegally held and had to be forfeited, herds proved to be smaller than the estimate at the time of sale, the calf crop was far less than expected, and money received from cattle sales did not pay the running expenses on the range and the London office. Rufus Hatch, the vendor, assumed the role of villain in the eyes of Scottish investors; in turn, he stormed about the inadequacy of the management and forced the resignation of the ranch superintendent.[81] While Dundee residents were on the directorate of the Arkansas Valley Land and Cattle Company and the Powder River Cattle Company, there is no evidence that they had a determining voice in policy. Where English capitalists acted alone, with Scottish directors included chiefly for prestige as in these two companies and the Dakota Stock and Grazing Company, they were already facing dissolutions or reorganizations.

In addition to chronic problems associated with long-distance management and contractual obligations, along with the increasing anxiety over small calf crops, there were two unexpected difficulties related to cattle disease. The British Parliament had voted as early as 1879 to prohibit importation of American cattle except under the most stringent regulations, including slaughter of animals at the port of entry within ten days. This regulation was justified because of the infection of cattle in some sections of the eastern United States with pleuro-pneumonia. After their recent struggle to eradicate the disease, the British could not agree to accept cattle from the western ranges and exclude those from the states east of the Mississippi because of the vagaries of diverse state quarantine legislation.[82] The *Courant* thought the more restrictions placed on United States cattle by Europeans, the sooner the cattlemen would unite, do something to eradicate the disease, and urge national legislation.[83]

Rather than lose the important British market, cattlemen on the northern plains evolved a plan to ship their animals to Duluth, Minnesota, then over the Canadian Railways to Montreal, where they would be loaded on British steamers. In July 1884 a deputation headed by Moreton Frewen of the Wyoming Stock Growers Association went to England and requested the Privy Council to relax the terms of the Contagious Diseases Act to permit importation over the Great Lakes route through Canada. Permission was not only refused, but the two governments pondered whether stricter regulations along the Canadian frontier might be necessary. The Canadian government declined the right of passage through its territory or the use of its ports where native cattle were shipped. There the proposal ended, and western cattlemen, although not completely shut out of the British market, found the trade in live animals greatly reduced.[84]

The ranch business was further upset by another problem of disease – the 'Texas fever', which infected most animals coming

11. *Matador steers gathered at the company ranch near Channing, Texas*
12. (overleaf) *Page of a Minute Book of the Scottish-American Investment Company at the time when the formation of the company was being discussed*

At Edinburgh, within No. 22 Hill Street
14th March 1873.

Present.
Thomas Nelson, Esquire
Edward Blyth Esquire
Kenneth Mackenzie Esquire
J. Dick Peddie, Esquire
A. T. Niven, Esquire
A. A. Cowan, Esquire
J. H. Robertson, Esquire
J. A. Jamieson, Esquire
A. R. Duncan, Esquire
and
W. J. Menzies, Esquire

Mr Menzies stated that he had called this Meeting with the view of considering whether it might not be desirable to form a Company to afford the means of investing money in America, and that the idea of forming such a Company had occured to him while travelling in America last Autumn, and that he had talked over the matter with the leading men in New York and Chicago who all highly approved of the idea, and thought that any such Company was likely to be very successful. He read letters which he had received from Mr J. S. Kennedy of New York, Mr Paton, Agent of the Bank of British North America in New York, Mr Robert Rigg Reid and others, and he further laid before the Meeting the proof of a Prospectus which he had prepared and which he had sent out to friends in America for their opinion.

Mr Menzies further stated that since he had called this Meeting, he had ascertained that several leading gentlemen were contemplating a similar scheme and that he had seen them upon the subject that morning.

The idea of forming such a company was highly approved of by the Meeting, and it was agreed that

a

from the southern part of that state. The malady was transmitted by cattle tick to which Texas herds had developed an immunity, but whose bite infected animals on the central and northern ranges. The problem began with the first 'long drives' and, one by one, each territory and state passed quarantine and inspection laws to protect its herds. Fearful of pleuro-pneumonia from the east and Texas fever from the south, the northwestern associations waged an active campaign during 1883–4 for legal protection on a national scale. Texas cattle companies, many of them Scottish-owned, interpreted all this furore as deliberate discrimination. A national cattle convention in Chicago, dominated by Wyoming stockgrowers, appointed a committee in 1883 to urge national regulations against disease. Southerners took action the following year in St Louis in an attempt to keep the herds moving north to the fattening ranges. Congress was memorialized to establish a national cattle trail from the Red River in the south to the Canadian boundary, by allocating a strip of the public domain from three to six miles wide which would run for the entire distance.[85]

The route desired would run through the Indian Territory, then due west through 'No Man's Land' north of the Texas Panhandle, and turn northward again through eastern Colorado and Wyoming. Agricultural areas of Kansas and Nebraska would no longer be forced to wage a relentless fight against cattle transit. The majority of Texas ranchers, except those in the Panhandle, favoured the trail, but the cattlemen in Wyoming and Montana in general opposed it. They feared both the spread of disease and the overstocking of the range. Bitterest opposition was, of course, found among those ranchers working in the Indian Territory and 'No Man's Land', or the Neutral Strip, where the trail was to pass. Three of the southern organizations, the Cherokee Strip Live Stock Association, the Panhandle Association, and Western Kansas Live Stock Association, took action to protect their members. Local ranchers organized war parties to intercept the herds and force them back to southern Texas. British ranches concerned, particularly the Cattle Ranche and Land Company, actively participated in these demonstrations. The United States government intervened, however, and ordered that the herds go through, with the protection of the Army, if necessary. Southern cattle roamed through the Texas Panhandle and the Indian Territory, spreading Texas fever. More important, the cattle industry had been temporarily torn asunder on the issue.[86]

Another phase of the British investors' problem of 1884 was concerned with the land tenure question, which will be discussed as a unit in the next chapter.

The disappointing records of the Anglo-American cattle companies did not stop similar enterprises from being organized in London in 1884. Part of the responsibility can be placed at the door of land and cattle brokers, such as Tait, Denman and Company. Tait wrote a pamphlet on *The Cattle Fields of the Far West,* insisting that in this year of general economic depression the land and cattle companies were in the best shape of all enterprise. Investors were told that the cattle trade just could not be overdone; that fears of overproduction were groundless. This type of investment was absolutely safe for the English–no risk, no disease, impervious to panics. This propaganda tract also suggested that the shares of these companies were beyond the speculative influence of the stock exchanges.[87] Among the London companies launched in 1884 was the American Pastoral Company, Limited, capitalized at £400,000 to take over the LX Ranch in the Panhandle of Texas from two Bostonians. William G. Thompson and Andrew Whitton, already on the Board of the Arkansas Valley Land and Cattle Company, joined James W. Barclay and his London associates on the Board. Their American agents were the Colorado Mortgage and Investment Company of Denver, and plans called for a dual operation of ranching and the sale of agricultural lands to settlers.[88] The Espuela Land and Cattle Company capitalized at £500,000, took over the Spur Ranch in Texas largely owned by Chicago capitalists but with Fort Worth headquarters. This company had difficulty in marketing its shares and was not floated until April 1885. Scots of Aberdeen invested in the industry through this company because of their confidence in Robert Burnett, a director of the Caledonian Railways and the land surveyor of Aberdeen, who sat on the directorate of the cattle company.[89] The Cedar Valley Land and Cattle Company, Limited, a third Texas venture, raised £120,000 to acquire the T Anchor Ranch that was surrounded by British neighbours in the Panhandle.[90] The Carrizozo Cattle Ranch Company, Limited, also took over a ranching operation in Lincoln County, New Mexico, in this year.[91]

The attractiveness of Texas led to the promotion of a grand scheme known as the Consolidated Land and Cattle Company, Limited, to consolidate seven ranches and herds, consisting of 100,000 acres of freehold land and 75,500 branded cattle. The lands were located on both sides of the Double Mountain Fork of the Brazos River for sixty miles and on both sides of the Salt Fork for thirty miles. Water privileges gave the proposed company control of three thousand square miles of land north of Colorado City, shipping centre on the Texas and Pacific Railroad. A distinguished Board, headed by Lord Thurlow, included three Scots:

the Earl of Strathmore, the Earl of Mar and Kellie, and Lord Lovat of Inverness-shire. Before shares were placed on the market an investigation into the validity of land titles had to be made. Some irregularities must have been discovered, for the enterprise did not last long enough to be listed in the *Stock Exchange Year-Book*.[92] The attempt to float this company indicated that the British were still able to plan on a grand scale where investments in the range cattle industry were concerned. Another promotion that went awry in 1884 was the Cattle Ranche and Freehold Land Company of Texas, Limited. Two years later its name was changed to the Cameron Freehold Land and Investment Company Limited, the authorized capital was doubled, and its field of activity soon shifted to Mexico.[93]

During 1885 the Cresswell Ranche and Cattle Company of Edinburgh purchased another Texas property known as the Bar C Ranch along the Canadian River. The Scots now had sufficient experience to demand that herds be purchased on the basis of actual count; prior to its completion the cattle had to go through the hard winter of 1884–5 on the southern Plains and less than fifty per cent of the estimated herd was found. The initial capital needed by the company could therefore be reduced.[94] One company registered by London financiers in 1885, the Chama Cattle Company that was to take over the lease on a Spanish land grant in Rio Arriba County, New Mexico, was stillborn.[95]

As late as 1886, Alexander Swan and Joseph Frank sponsored the Wyoming Hereford Cattle and Land Association, Limited, in London, to sell £100,000 six per cent first mortgage debentures. As security, subscribers had claims on the freehold property of the Wyoming Hereford Association. Swan and his associates sought capital to stock their pasture with fine Hereford cattle brought from England. Colin J. Mackenzie, chairman of the Swan Land and Cattle Company, was one of the trustees for the English debenture holders.[96]

Citizens of Leith, Greenock, and Glasgow attempted to join their Edinburgh, Dundee, and Aberdeen neighbours in the American cattle industry in a small way between 1884 and 1886. A Leith family registered the Montana Sheep and Cattle Company, Limited, to take over a ranch in Custer County, Montana. Residents in the east of Scotland, chiefly from Newport, Haddington, and Falkirk, invested in this modest venture that was a financial disaster.[97] The Chalk Buttes Ranche and Cattle Company, Limited was organized in Greenock to take over a nearby ranch in eastern Montana.[98] In 1886 Glaswegians floated the Deervale Ranche Company, Limited, to underwrite a property in Menard County, Texas.[99] Each of these concerns was capitalized at less than £10,000 and managed by inexperienced men. As late as 1887 there were two newcomers to the ranching business in western America: the Denver Ranching Company, Limited, and the Rio Arriba Land and Cattle Company, Limited.[100]

By way of summary, it should be noted that capitalists in both England and Scotland moved with greater caution in making investments in the range cattle industry after 1883. The only Scottish companies started were of a sporadic nature with small amounts of money invested by men of limited business experience. London continued to support a few, new, heavily-capitalized companies, but even here proposals from American vendors that would have been deemed golden opportunities between 1881 and 1883 were now rejected as being too risky. This change in attitude was a reaction to the known difficulties of some of the older companies.

The six new companies started in 1884 were capitalized at over £1,400,000, the two registered in 1885 added £350,000 to the investment, those of 1886 another £120,000. In all, these companies had slightly more than £400,000 paid-up during the year. These totals may be too conservative, for at least two, and possibly three, of the companies promoted between 1884 and 1886 that appear to have collapsed before final registration may have had time to invest, and lose, some money. At any rate, at least £1,900,000 was added to the total subscribed capital in the British-American cattle companies. Thirty-three such limited companies had registered in Great Britain between 1880 and 1888 with a capital structure of more than £7,400,000. Of this amount, approximately £4,000,000 had actually been paid-up by British shareholders and transferred to the United States. It is also likely that another £2,000,000 was used by them from borrowed sources. One scholar has estimated that the aggregate paid-up capitalization of thirteen British land and livestock companies in Texas alone was £5,000,000.[101] In addition to the companies registered in London and Edinburgh, the British loaned money to hardpressed American ranchers on an individual basis and also invested in cattle corporations incorporated in the United States. The British may well have had as much as £9,000,000, or $45,000,000, invested in the American cattle business in the 1880s.

Chapter Four

Alien Land Tenure and Legislation

Exploitation of the public domain became a subject of popular debate and controversy in the United States during the 1880s. There was a steady growth of indignation over the excessively large land holdings acquired by corporate interests, in particular the railroads and the cattle companies. Timber merchants and cattle barons were exposed for their fraudulent, illegal, or at best, questionable, methods whereby they had obtained ownership or control of vast acreage. The Commissioners of the General Land Office called attention to their social sins by dramatic action and publicity, and the President issued decrees against their exploitive practices. All corporations engaged in questionable land acquisition practices were in trouble, but the greatest resentment was reserved, quite naturally, for foreigners. Scottish companies engaged in cattle raising, timber cutting, and mining were all involved in the acquisition of land. The land investment companies also took over large blocks of land from the railroads, anticipating later sales to settlers. The Scottish mortgage companies were occasionally obliged to foreclose and thus came into possession of real estate.

No group appeared as defiant of the land laws of the United States enacted for the benefit of actual settlers as the cattlemen. They purchased alternate sections of land from the railroads that had been acquired as part of the rail construction grants and then proceeded to fence both their section and adjoining ones belonging to the federal government, as one huge block. They acquired acreage along the water courses, shutting off others, thereby attaining 'range rights' to all the land back from the stream to the divide separating their range from that provided by a neighbouring stream. By devious methods the cattlemen had also managed to obtain leases on large sections of the reservations established by the government for Indian tribes.

Roger V. Clements has suggested that the controversy over alien ownership of land reached a crisis chiefly because Plains farmers suffering from many afflictions of domestic origin were seeking a scapegoat for their problems. In some areas railroad transportation for agricultural surpluses was inadequate; elsewhere the railroads had a monopoly and engaged in exploitive activity. Marketing was not only difficult and expensive but also monopolistically controlled. In addition, there were troubles traced to the environment, chiefly the absence of timber and the lack of water between the Missouri River and Rocky Mountains. Perhaps more important was the widespread belief that the available land was giving out, and every farmer struggling to make a living was sensitive to any development that made it more difficult for him to hold the land he had or that destroyed his hope of obtaining better land. Britishers who acquired land in the West had thus antagonized 'the homesteader, the democrat, and the American'.[1]

The public became aware of the extensive nature of foreign land holdings when various periodicals began publishing the names of corporations listing the amount of acreage each held. In May 1882 the United States Senate passed a resolution inquiring into the entries on the public lands by the Earl of Dunraven and the Estes Park Company, the Arkansas Valley Land and Cattle Company, Faulkner, Bell and Company in California, and others. For more than a decade indignation had been expressed in Colorado over Lord Dunraven's extensive holdings in Estes Park and the intimidation of American settlers by his agents in order to silence them about the questionable nature of his claims.

In response to the Senate resolution, Henry M. Teller, Secretary of the Interior, forwarded a report to the Senate from the Commissioner of the General Land Office, complaining of the multiplicity and complexity of the land laws and the difficulties of enforcement, and accusing both the Arkansas Valley Land and Cattle Company and the California Redwood Company of fraud. He compiled a list of foreigners' land holdings in the United States, including twenty-nine companies and individuals owning 20,000,000 acres.[2]

While the Senate resolution was under discussion, Tait, Denman and Company of Edinburgh, Cattle Ranche and Land Brokers, had requested that the Secretary of the Interior reveal the intent of Congress. The Congressional inquiry was causing considerable anxiety among the Scottish companies, and although consular officials had assured the Scots no law of a retroactive nature would be passed, trade in lands was at a standstill. The Scots had invested $25,000,000 in lands. Rumours circulated that Senator George F. Edmunds had introduced a bill to limit foreign holdings to thirty square miles, and many of the Scottish companies had twenty times that. Were their rights to be menaced?

Senator Charles H. Van Wyck of Nebraska read this letter to his senatorial colleagues, suggesting that the question had been honestly and justly presented by the Scots, and concluded 'It is due the American people that some action be taken at once, and it is due to foreigners who are relying upon the honesty of the American character that some steps should be taken at once.'[3] The United States Secretary of the Interior replied to Tait, Denman and Company in September, explaining that the public lands of the United States were not generally subject to direct purchase, especially in the states and territories west of the Mississippi River. Title could be lawfully acquired only by actual settlers who cultivated and improved the land, and then only in limited quantities. Claims to land under the settlement and improvement laws were not re-assignable and any contract made for the transfer or sale of the land prior to the completion of the residence and improvement requirements, specified by the law, were invalid. Possession, occupation, or enclosure was insufficient evidence of right, title, or claims to a larger quantity of land than that authorized by the land settlement laws. The Secretary concluded:

> ...It is contrary to national policy, and would be antagonistic to the sentiments of the country, to permit the appropriation of public land in large quantities, by individuals or corporations, whether native or foreign. It is not, in my opinion, probable that the restrictions upon the alienation of lands of the public domain will be so removed as to allow the acquisition of title beyond existing limitations.[4]

Scottish investors thus received a clear-cut answer to their inquiry.

The cattlemen were first challenged over their acquisition of land leases in the Indian Territory. Although the Indians had a distinct and clear claim to their reservation, they possessed no right to dispose of it to an outsider. After unsuccessful attempts on the part of individuals and companies to lease the Cherokee Strip for grazing, the Cherokee Live Stock Association was formed in 1882 and succeeded in renting the whole strip of 6,000,000 acres for $100,000 a year. Annual payments were made by individual ranchers allied with the association in proportion to the number of acres held. Holdings varied from one to three thousand acres, and annual payment was approximately two and one-half cents an acre. Once a block of land was obtained it was usually fenced. After obtaining the use of the Cherokee Strip, cattlemen then secured range rights to about four-fifths of the Cheyenne and Arapaho reservations, an estimated 3,000,000 acres, for $60,000. Many southwestern ranchers and domestic cattle companies, having secured these questionable leases in the Indian Territory transferred them to foreign-owned companies.[5] An example has been given in the case of the T-5 range in the Cherokee Strip that the Texas Land and Cattle Company took over from the Kansas City Cattle Company.

In Texas, where the state controlled its public lands, the liberality of the laws had appeared so attractive to foreign cattle companies between 1880 and 1882 that legislation had to be passed periodically to raise the cost of land and to regulate rental of alternate sections of land belonging to the school fund. Texas laws also prohibited fencing private lands that enclosed state lands, and the effect had been to compel those making use of public lands to pay rent on them; otherwise the fences would have to come down.[6] As settlers moved into western Dakota, Nebraska, and Kansas, and into eastern Colorado, a tempest developed when they came upon the fences strung by cattlemen. The large size of the British concerns brought most of the wrath down on alien heads. The Prairie Land and Cattle Company and the Arkansas Valley Land and Cattle Company, as examples, were said to have fenced a million acres in Colorado. Not only were settlers aggrieved but smaller ranchers complained that they were denied access to the Arkansas River. Although Americans were far more involved in illegal fencing operations than aliens, it was the latter who received the publicity.[7]

During President Chester A. Arthur's administration numerous bills and resolutions came before Congress that purported to investigate or check foreign acquisitions. When no legislation resulted, both Republicans and Democrats included a plank in their platform during the Presidential election of 1884 calling for a curb upon alien land holdings. The Democratic Handbook contained a list of foreign holdings to bolster the party's demand for restriction.[8] James G. Blaine, the Republican candidate, with his slogan of 'America for Americans', was more feared than Grover Cleveland. In discussing the political contest, the British press suggested that if the Republican candidate were elected he was certain to propose legislation restricting the right of aliens to hold land. Britishers were again advised that the safest lands for foreigners to buy were the railroad land grants. These were the only lands cattlemen could acquire in large sections. Some United States cattle company vendors had obtained large acreages by having all of the cowboys in their ranch outfit file claims, as *bona fide* settlers, under the homestead, desert, and timber land laws. Once these lands had been consolidated, the promoting cattlemen took over. Many of them had hurriedly got British companies to purchase their land holdings. Now that the spirit, if not the letter, of the law was found to have been broken, these vendors from the United States were out of the picture.[9]

Shortly after his election, President Cleveland ordered the cattlemen to withdraw their herds from the Cheyenne-Arapaho reservation in the Indian Territory. A deputation of cattlemen requested the President to delay enforcement of this proclamation. They received an absolute refusal of a time extension. The President reminded ranchers that less than 400,000 acres of the original 4,250,000 acres set apart for these two Indian tribes were still in their hands and this was considered a basic cause of Indian disturbances in the Southwest.[10] The same decree was later applied to the Cherokee Strip.

Bradstreet's had already reported the Department of the Interior's concern over the practice of fencing in sections of the public domain alternating with land otherwise acquired. As early as April plans were being made to issue a proclamation directing attention to the law and calling for the removal of the fences. If this was not done within a prescribed time, the fences were to be destroyed by the Army. 'It will be interesting,' the American journal suggested, 'to note the outcome of this attempt to determine whether the Government and settlers, or whether the cattle companies are in charge.'[11]

President Cleveland issued this proclamation against unlawful enclosure in August. Since national policy demanded that the public domain be reserved for occupancy of actual settlers, and Congress had passed a law, on 25 February 1885, against the unlawful enclosure of public lands in any state or territory that prevented any person 'from peaceably entering upon or establishing a settlement or residence on any tract of public land', the President directed that every unlawful enclosure be immediately removed, whether maintained by an individual, association, or corporation.[12] The *New York Herald* published simultaneously a list of illegal enclosures known to the General Land Office. In the most flagrant cases of violation, legal suits were contemplated.[13]

The State of Texas followed the national lead in tightening up the enforcement of its land legislation. *The Galveston News* recalled that Texas had passed a Land Enclosure Act in 1884 insisting that the 'free-grassers' from the Cherokee Strip, who had stretched their wires across the Panhandle of Texas, take down the fences. The State Land Board, under pressure from ranchers, agreed that the remaining school, university, and asylum lands could be leased for six cents an acre annually, but there was no great demand for them at that price. Instead, the cattle syndicates occupied them illegally. Moreover, 'the Scotch Land Grabbers' had indignantly held a protest meeting in Edinburgh against the lease fee. The newly-appointed Grass Commissioners who were now to go upon the lands and enforce the Land Enclosure Act were urged by the newspaper to look into the question of alien defiance of the law. The editor suggested 'If the Grass Commissioners should unearth the true inwardness of the history of land matters in Texas for the past three years, in connection with their duty of bringing the free grassers to terms, and the press dared give publicity to their investigations, some fair reputations might be fractured, and the reign of certain cattle barons would end.'[14]

When the full impact of Cleveland's action was realized, *The Economist* remarked 'it bears out the warning which we gave to the British cattle companies in the days of their youthful enthusiasm to look well to their land titles'. Most of them had paid little heed to the caution and were now to pay the penalty for their rash behaviour.

> On the advice of the unscrupulous Americans who decoyed them into this kind of investment, they believed in their innocence that the 'cattle interest' of the West was strong enough to defy the laws of the country. They took possession of millions of acres of land to which they had no more right than to the City Hall in Broadway. They laid out thousands of pounds in fencing and improvements which will have now to be cleared away. They attempted to get control of the whole grazing area by 'dummying' the river frontages–in other words, making fraudulent entries on them as free selectors. Only children could ever have imagined that the *bona fide* settlers who are crowding into these grazing States would submit to such appropriation of the public estate.

The whole question of land holding in the United States and the validity of titles was a subject worthy of searching investigation by the British investor, in the opinion of the editor. British capitalists had coals of fire heaped upon them over the situation.

> Our land speculators in the Far West cannot be surprised at bringing down a storm of unpopularity on their heads when they fly in the teeth of laws intended to protect settlers, or, worse still, endeavour to undermine them. They have not dealt honestly with the American land system or the American people, and hence the prejudice they have raised against themselves all over the States....[15]

Scottish cattle companies complied with the government regulations. For example, the Prairie Company's fences had been taken down in Colorado in accordance with Presidential demands. Some resentment was expressed in the director's communication to shareholders: 'We are not aware that the removal of the fences will be enforced by the U S Government except upon alien property holders of territory. We fear, however, that this is so, and that this may not be the only illustration affecting this Company of the jealousy with which the Americans regard foreigners in the matter of territorial possessions.' The company had also abandoned vast tracts of land in southeastern Colorado rather than go to the expense of testing the right to approximately 200,000 acres before the United States land office officials. Title to 9,600 acres in the Cimarron Division of New Mexico had proved faulty, and the Scots became involved in a prolonged court battle that was finally settled unfavourably. The Texas Land Board had forced the company to lease 22,000 acres of the Littlefield range within the Canadian Division, acreage that had previously been occupied without cost because it had been surrounded by the leases of other cattle companies and thereby protected. Soon Texas officials announced that the company must rent approximately 67,000 additional acres, that were found not to be owned or leased, at four cents an acre annually.[16] The Swan Land and Cattle Company, in contrast, assured its shareholders that the directors had been careful to abide by the land laws of the United States and that land officials in Wyoming looked with favour upon their transactions. The directors were still concerned, however, over legislation pending in Congress to place stringent restriction on alien corporations owning any land in the United States. They were reassured that no matter what type of law was enacted the United States Constitution would not permit its terms to be retroactive. Under these circumstances, directors proposed to pay for the Union Pacific lands and take immediate possession rather than spread the payment over the next eight years. To raise the £60,000 necessary to secure the title, the directors asked permission to create preferred shares of £10 bearing six per cent interest.[17] In their eagerness to obtain control of vast grazing acreages, many British cattle companies had not exercised sufficient caution to see that the letter and spirit of the United States land laws were obeyed and thus jeopardized the interests of all foreign companies hoping to obtain agricultural, mining, and timber lands in the future.

Debate over the disposition of the western domain and the violation of land laws now passed to a more important phase: the right of aliens, particularly absentee corporations, to own land. After the election, but prior to the inauguration, of President Cleveland, the House of Representatives had received a favourable report from its Committee on Public Lands on the so-called Oates Bill to prevent aliens from holding any land in the United States. The committee announced that the continued acquisition of lands by foreign noblemen would lead to 'a system of landlordism incompatible with the best interests and free institutions of the United States'. In western America immigrants were being brought in each year to become tenants and herdsmen on the vast possessions of these 'foreign lords'. Moreover, it was 'the avarice and enterprise of European capitalists' that had caused them to invest many millions in 100,000,000 acres of United States soil in defiance of the 'rights of honest and humble settlers'. The committee declared that its bill was 'a declaration against absentee landlordism', and maintained that 'American soil should be owned exclusively by American citizens'. The committee recognized that objections would be raised to the bill on the grounds that it would drive foreign capital from the country, but the members were not certain that any permanent harm would result to anyone in the United States.[18] The bill did not pass. The *New York Times* protested the ignorance and narrow-mindedness of the committee's assertion that the exclusion of foreign capital would not hurt anyone in the country. Although the newspaper favoured keeping the Dakota wheat fields and the Colorado ranch lands out of the hands of the British aristocracy, it thought foreigners should be allowed to own homes in the United States. Unquestionably, action was needed to keep the land and cattle companies from holding undeveloped acreage in quantity for speculative purposes and to keep foreign bondholders from gaining possession of huge railroad land grants in cases of bankruptcy and foreclosure.[19] For the rest of the decade, the British press expressed grave concern over the attitude of Representative William C. Oates of Alabama.

The Economist agreed that 'the axiom which used to be so familiar to British investors, that nothing is safer than land, is far from being universally true in the states':

> ... In some of the older States, notably New York, aliens are absolutely disqualified from holding real estate. There are hundreds–we might say thousands–of Englishmen who have spent their lives in New York City, yet cannot own so much as the homes they live in, unless indirectly by getting a friend to hold them in trust. They may have lived for half-a-century under the Stars and Stripes, and be to all intents and purposes American citizens, but failing naturalisation, the law excludes them from the most fundamental right of citizenship....

Even in cases where there were no alien disabilities placed on the statute books of a state, British corporations investing in the United States had been advised by their American lawyers to fortify themselves against possible risks by operating through a native company formed for that purpose. This procedure was not customary among the mortgage companies, but the need was likely to arise.[20]

Petitions against alien landowners flooded the first Congress of the Cleveland administration. Once again numerous bills were introduced. In April 1886 the Judiciary Committee of the House of Representatives reported adversely a bill to prohibit aliens from acquiring title to or owning property within the United States. The majority of the committee feared such legislation was unconstitutional. Representative Oates presented the views of the minority.[21] Three months later another House Committee, that on Public Lands, reported favourably on a similar bill providing that no foreigner, resident or non-resident alien, or any corporation or association in which ten per cent of the stock was held by aliens or foreigners, could acquire or hold real estate in the United States. The committee claimed that the legislation 'has as its basis the proposition that American soil shall be owned by Americans as far as Congress can control it', and insisted once again that a national policy was needed to keep the land in small tracts for actual settlers.[22] Over the objections of the chairman of the Judiciary Committee, who insisted 'this bill will not bear scrutiny', it was passed with an overwhelming majority.[23]

Earlier the Senate had adopted a more comprehensive alien land-holding bill, assuring its legality by specifying that the terms were not retroactive, by protecting inheritance, by exempting any claims guaranteed by treaty, and finally by restricting its application to the District of Columbia and the territories where Congress' power was undisputed. Since 1884 Senator Preston B. Plumb of Kansas, chairman of the Committee on Public Lands, had favoured an absolute prohibition upon any land holdings by corporations, either American or foreign, not absolutely necessary to their declared purposes.[24] In August 1886, when the House measure came before the Senate, Plumb moved to strike out everything following the enacting clause and to substitute the more carefully drafted Senate bill. He was certain the charges against foreigners were exaggerated, but

> If no acre of American soil was owned by a foreigner I should still be in favor of enacting a positive prohibition against such ownership for the future. I think myself that we offer inducements enough to people to come to this country....[25]

The House of Representatives refused to accept the substitution until the second session, so the bill did not pass until February 1887.[26] It was signed by President Cleveland on 3 March.

As finally passed, the law prohibited for the future all aliens or foreign corporations from holding real estate *in the territories* except by inheritance or in the collection of debts. A similar prohibition was placed upon any corporation or association in which more than twenty per cent of the stock was held by non-citizens. No corporation other than those organized for the construction of railways, canals, or turnpikes could acquire or hold more than 5,000 acres of land in the territories.[27] Its terms in no way limited the acreage already held by foreign corporations.

All the Scottish mortgage companies made adjustments to the new law. In the autumn of 1886, the inspector and two directors of the Scottish-American Mortgage Company had visited the Pacific Northwest. They were favourably impressed with Washington and Idaho territories as lending fields, but the Alien Law precluded plans for extending operations in that direction. Business was likewise discontinued in the Dakotas.[28] J. Duncan Smith, the chairman, told shareholders that Britain had wiped such a law from the statute books and added: 'I need scarcely point out to you that so far from coveting the soil of the United States, real estate is the very last thing which a mortgage company wants to have; and therefore, so far as we are concerned, our American friends need be under no apprehension.'[29] The Edinburgh American Land Mortgage also stopped lending in Dakota Territory.[30] Directors of the Oregon Mortgage Company reported that only a small percentage of their funds was invested in Washington Territory. Although they did not propose to prohibit further loans in Washington and Idaho, local agents would be instructed to exercise extreme caution relative to the nature of the security and the character of borrowers. Oregon provided a sufficient outlet for capital. In placing new loans in the territories the company agent would record them in his name, and in case of foreclosure he would hold the land.[31]

Although public opinion in the United States seemed to favour the land legislation of 1887, some critics insisted it was too mild to prevent evasion. But the chief objection came from the territories that wished to attract additional foreign capital for mining. The Governor of Idaho claimed that several important transactions were on the verge of consummation between local mining interests and foreign capitalists when the bill passed, and the negotiations had to be suspended. The Governors of Montana and Utah agreed with him that the law should apply to all types of land ownership except mining claims. The Governor of Dakota, on the other hand, preferred an amendment permitting foreign loans upon land, with adequate protection for mortgage foreclosure.[32]

The *New York Times* emphasized the disappointment among the 'swarm of American sharpers' who had sold mines, ranches, and estates abroad. They would be driven home because the law had frightened most Britishers out of buying anything American. Specific attention was directed to the case of ex-Senator Stephen W. Dorsey of Arkansas, who was engaged in cattle raising and mining in Colorado and New Mexico and who had several million acres to sell when the law was passed. The *Times* suggested that too much land in the Far West was already held by English peers and if they had not resorted to fraud in some cases the law probably would never have been passed. The government had resolved at last to keep the lands for small farmers and keep the syndicates and speculators out.

> Foreign investors should understand the American people do not desire to shut out European capital, but propose that it shall be invested, if invested at all, honestly and in accordance with the spirit of our institutions. They are not willing that it shall be used to support those who steal the public land or for the establishment of vast estates upon which American citizens can live only as tenants of a foreign owner.[33]

The other New York newspapers had earlier taken their stand. After interviewing William A. J. Sparks, the *New York Herald* announced 'The Commissioner seems inspired with the praiseworthy desire to protect real settlers, and his efforts in that direction are worthy of the highest commendation.'[34] In its columns, the land grabs of the cattle barons and the timber frauds received ample publicity. The *New York Tribune* was far more tolerant of the so-called 'land grabbers' who had enjoyed privileges under the administration of Secretary Teller. Even so, as Sparks continued unearthing old frauds perpetrated during the 'halcyon Republican era' and preventing the organization of new ones, 'the sharks' became terrified for fear of 'losing the booty they have acquired'.[35]

As soon as state legislatures realized that the federal law against alien land ownership was to apply only to the territories, several of them enacted laws. Nebraska prohibited non-resident aliens and foreign corporations from holding land, but agreed that any resident alien might convey his holdings to heirs. Lands of non-resident aliens, upon death, should escheat to the state of Nebraska and the heirs would be paid in full.[36] Illinois also decided that non-resident aliens and corporations registered under the laws of any foreign country could no longer acquire lands in that state. Mortgage companies were permitted to take a valid title to real estate and enforce a lien for any debt or liability provided they got rid of all lands so acquired within three years after receiving the title. Personal estates of individual aliens were not affected by the law and each had the right to make disposal during his lifetime.[37] In Minnesota the terms of the federal law were made applicable to the state. The provisions of the act were not, however, to apply to any alien in Minnesota who desired to take up a 160-acre tract of land prior to 1889, nor was it to apply to any land acquired in good faith by due process of law in the foreclosure of mortgages.[38] The Scottish-American Mortgage Company noted the favoured position given their type of company in Minnesota and Illinois, but announced withdrawal from Nebraska. The chairman revealed that the law would be tested before the Supreme Court; meanwhile if Nebraska farmers wanted to pay nine per cent for money when the Scottish company was prepared to loan it at eight per cent, there were many other fields available and eager for Scottish sterling.[39] The Texas legislature passed a law in 1891 prohibiting any alien from acquiring a title or interest in any land within the state, and any deed or other document purporting to convey title to an alien firm was illegal. An exception was granted to the mortgage companies by authorizing any alien to buy, hold, foreclose or sell any land in which he had an interest by virtue of having made a loan upon it. However, such lands had to be disposed of within a six-year period.[40] Because of time limitation, the Scottish-American Mortgage Company ceased lending in the state.[41]

All of these state alien land laws were subsequently amended. The Nebraska statute was declared unconstitutional, and in 1889 a new law, attempting to meet the judges' objections, permitted a non-resident alien who owned land to dispose of it during his lifetime, and if the land descended to his heirs they had ten years to liquidate. The new law also made it possible for alien mortgage corporations to foreclose on property provided it was not held for longer than ten years.[42] The Minnesota law was also subsequently liberalized to protect the title to lands that citizens had purchased from aliens, to exempt small city lots from the provisions of the earlier law, and to provide that the state must take action against an alien corporation within three years after it acquired land.[43] The Texas law was declared unconstitutional and a special session of the legislature in 1892 repealed the legislation and passed a new Alien Law. Non-citizens were still prohibited from acquiring land, but the law did not apply to land currently held in the state as long as it remained in the hands of the present owners. This specification was inserted to please the courts. The new law again favoured the mortgage companies by exempting them from the restrictions of alien ownership and by repealing the section relative to the disposal of foreclosed property within six years.[44] Thus fully protected, the Scottish mortgage companies resumed business in Texas.

The Oregon Mortgage Company was concerned over bills being discussed in the Oregon legislature that would compel foreign corporations to confine their litigation to state courts and would impose an annual licence fee of $750 upon them. Other measures proposed a ceiling upon interest rates and state supervision over foreclosure proceedings.[45] In 1888 the Edinburgh American Land Mortgage Company agreed to co-operate with the Scottish-

13. *Swan Outfit. Western Range Cattle Industry*

14. Skinning a beef on Swan property. Western Range Cattle Industry

American Mortgage Company in securing an amendment to the federal alien land law which would permit foreign mortgage companies three to five years to dispose of lands taken by foreclosure.[46] The directors contributed funds to maintain a lobbyist in Washington, DC. In 1890 Representative Oates introduced another bill prohibiting aliens from acquiring lands anywhere in the United States. Since his new proposal exempted the mortgage companies, the chairman of the Scottish-American Mortgage Company raised no objection. He told his stockholders that English syndicates, speculating beyond all reason, were largely the source of trouble. The Chicago breweries and grain elevators were for the most part English-owned, and the Union stockyards in that city were sold to a London company in 1890 for nineteen million dollars. The proposed Oates bill would give them ten years to liquidate.[47]

The effects of the anti-alien legislation were undoubtedly exaggerated in Scotland, but the land laws of the United States were carefully examined by both promoters and capitalists after 1890. Managers of Scottish property in the United States regularly reported on the effect of legislation to the home offices. All agreed that the prosperity in the territories had suffered severely from the reduction of foreign investment in the 1890s, caused in part by the federal anti-alien law. Powerful interests, particularly in the field of mining, were able to obtain exceptions to the law at the state level and this indicates that many officials were not in sympathy with an embargo on alien capital. Certainly British capitalists were more cautious in investing money in the United States after 1890, and by 1900 the question of alien investments in land in the trans-Mississippi West had ceased to be a serious issue.[48]

Chapter Five

The Scottish Cattle Companies: Crisis, Depression, and Adjustment

Scottish investors fully realized by the end of 1884 that their rush in organizing cattle companies had been ill-advised. Not only had American vendors taken advantage of their enthusiasm by securing profit-sharing contracts that interfered with management, but a few had also misrepresented the nature of the estate and herd they were selling, with the result that some investors had been swindled. Then there had developed unexpected quarantines against cattle exposed to disease, which curtailed the long drives across state boundaries and the international trade in livestock. Most distressing of all was the decision of the United States government to stop the time-honoured practices of the cattlemen using the unoccupied public domain in conjunction with their freehold and leased acreage. So-called 'range rights' no longer existed except in Texas where the land could be rented on an annual basis; the Indian reservations were unavailable for lease.

All of these developments led to major adjustments in the range cattle industry. Yet without any of these unforeseen problems the business, as it was described to the Scots in 1880, was doomed by the basic economic principles of supply and demand. In 1880, according to the United States census, there were only 800,000 range cattle in all Texas and 250,000 in Wyoming. By 1883 Texas could count over 5,000,000 head and Wyoming apparently had approximately 1,000,000. 'What of the fundamental problem of over production at this rate?' asked the *Courant*. 'If there were room in the West for another five years' growth at the same rate as that of the past five years, the States and Territories west of the Mississippi would possess ten head of cattle for every man, woman, and child of the population.' According to the journalist's calculations, by 1889 the American range could produce as many cattle as Great Britain, France, Germany, and Russia possessed *in toto* in 1885. Statistics released by the United States Department of Agriculture indicated the Scottish editor was on the right track. In 1884 the aggregate number of cattle in western America had increased to 20,209,350, in comparison with 19,416,139 in 1883.[1]

In reviewing 'The Crisis in Cattle-Ranching', *The Statist* also insisted that the *basic* difficulty was overproduction. Because the United States could not consume all the beef it produced, exports had increased from 20,000 head in 1871 to 183,000 in 1880. By 1884 Britain alone received 169,257 cattle. Moreover, meat exports from the United States had increased in value within a decade from $2,500,000 to $31,000,000. This increasing volume of trade did not produce profits for individual exporters, and in 1884–5 it was unusually unremunerative. 'But profit and loss can no longer control it. The cattle are there; they are increasing by thousands daily; the pasture they have taken possession of is no longer able to carry them all, and for self-preservation the overgrown herds must be depleted.' Even if it proved desirable, enterprising ranchers could not create more land or produce more grass.[2]

With the future of the range cattle industry so uncertain in 1885 Scottish cattle companies were repeatedly advised to consider carefully the prospects of a reasonable return on capital invested in ranching. That big profits had been earned in the past was beyond question, but equally indisputable was the fact that the gains were due to exceptionally favourable circumstances, including free grass and high prices. The 'boom' had now run its course and the inevitable reaction was becoming manifest.

Companies were urged to study their cost calculations more minutely. For example, *The Statist* took vigorous exception to the circulation in Scotland of a 'comparative statement' of the cattle companies' balance sheets in 1883 and 1884 suggesting that the cost for raising steers for the market ranged from 2s. 6d. to 6s. 1d. per head per annum.[3] The editor pointed out that such 'incredible results' were attained by the simple and fatal mistake of dividing the cost of raising the beasts sold over the whole number of the herd. Had no one stopped to consider that a large portion of the cattle never left the ranch? He suggested that not more than one-fourth of the herd reached the form of mature beef which could be converted into dividends. One should infer that costs were therefore four times the figure recorded. Cost calculations of earlier years he considered 'absurd' and chided the directors for boasting of being able to raise and deliver a steer to the market for less than 10s. a head.[4]

The year 1885 was also memorable for bad prices. The market for young stock was greatly disorganized. According to southern plainsmen, the difficulty all began with Cleveland's order to clear the herds out of portions of the Indian country within forty days. Too many cattle, unable to find a range, had to be sacrificed. Prices were so low that some ranchers preferred to drive their

TABLE 4. American cattle companies in 1885

		Sales *net average realized per head for steers* *1885*			*1884*	
	numbers	*1 year* $	*2 years* $	*3 years and upwards* $	*3 years and upwards* $	*valuation per head incl. bulls* $
Prairie	22,068	17.51	23.53	24.57	33.75	16.66
Swan	9,600			36.62	45.27	25.97
Texas	10,781			24.51	29.97	14.87
Matador	17,508	12.72	19.74	28.50	24.00	17.88
Hansford	3,331			24.40	30.23	24.74
Arkansas	5,145			26.75	29.15	27.34
Pastoral	5,455			27.72	33.09	25.00
Powder River	4,569			31.01	35.01	28.37
Western Land	5,619		25.93	30.88	35.15	26.46
Cattle Ranche	1,806			28.33	32.22	24.99
Western Ranches	3,313			37.81	32.13	27.39

herds back home rather than sell them. Table 4,[5] above, indicates the declining price for three-year-old steers in 1885 in comparison with that realized in 1884; it also reveals the exceptionally low prices obtained for young cattle by three Scottish ranches.

The range cattleman had still another adverse experience to face in 1885. The winter of 1884–5 was unprecedentedly severe, particularly on the southern plains. There was a thoroughgoing blizzard followed by months of extreme cold. Snow drifted into the draws and canyons where the only grass was found. Whole herds began to wander, and encountering a barbed-wire barrier were unable to go farther and hundreds died there. Numerous cows, weakened by hunger and by fighting the storm, slipped their calves; others did not live long enough to raise their young. Financial journals were fretful because the sanguine 'Cattle Kings of the West' were unwilling to face reality and admit the tremendous damage caused by the weather. Rather than dwelling on the misfortune, much less proclaiming it to the public, many ranchers chose to interpret the bad luck as a blessing in disguise. One journal concluded that shareholders in cattle companies would never be told the whole truth of the disaster of the 1884–5 winter, not because the directors wanted to mislead them, but because of the difficulty in arriving at the truth. A full inquiry would be needed to assess the median losses in the Indian Territory, the Texas Panhandle, and Colorado.[6]

The first clue was to be found in the calf brands. Each annual report that appeared expressed disappointment. Even on the best managed ranches, like the Matador, the calf crop was 7,000 to 8,000 short. There was the additional mortality among other cattle, and the directors of the Matador had written down the herd two and one-half per cent to take care of the loss.[7] Western Ranches had wintered a herd in the Indian Territory, and when spring came 2,515 had been lost.[8] The Texas Land and Cattle Company reported calf brands in the state generally one-third to one-half below expectations[9] (see Table 5, below[10]). The total number of new animals branded by the above companies in 1885 was 116,319 as against 126,500 in 1884, a decrease of 10,181 calves.

In March 1886 *The Economist* published a summary of factual information on the eleven leading Scottish and English cattle companies revealing the changes during 1885. These enterprises, only one-third of thirty-odd promoted since 1879, represented a capital of £3,947,000, some 3,319,000 acres of land and 672,000 head of cattle. The financial results of 1885 were admittedly unsatisfactory. Detailed figures are shown in Table 6, pp. 118–19.[11]

Interested observers noted that only the Matador had increased its dividend, paying seven per cent in 1884 instead of six per cent. The Prairie again announced its ten per cent; Western Land and Cattle also paid ten per cent, representing a five per cent drop from 1884. Elsewhere there was a decline in profits, and in some cases, like the Cattle Ranche and Land Company and the Arkansas Valley Company where the dividend had been passed for two consecutive years, disaster was feared.

Dismal as they appeared, *The Economist's* figures did not tell the full extent of the financial weakness in the cattle companies.

TABLE 5. American cattle companies in 1885

	calf crop	
	1884	*1885*
Prairie	26,481	27,714
Swan	21,428	20,236
Texas	14,986	17,949
Matador	24 136	19,501
Hansford	7,000	4,300
Arkansas	3,234	2,386
Pastoral	7,339	5,800
Powder River	9,187	7,475
Western Land	7,262	7,084
Cattle Ranche	4,223	2,224
Western Ranches	1,224	1,650

TABLE 6. American cattle companies in 1885

	land			*capital*	
	owned acres	*leased acres*	*total herd*	*debentures, loans and preferred stock* £	*ordinary share capital* £
Prairie	156,862	32,278	124,212	291,767	294,055
Swan	578,853	nil	123,460	288,340	461,660
Texas	388,174	520,966	106,322	240,000	240,000
Matador	424,296	256,367	94,441	200,000	300,000
Hansford	76,640	124,000	37,734	17,594	209,740
Arkansas	16,023	6,080	24,315	124,994	125,000
Pastoral [American]	300,692	208,891	45,885	164,289	172,050
Powder River	nil		48,625	100,000	200,000
Western Land	75,343	nil	35,469	100,000	100,000
Cattle Ranche	nil	153,607	13,500	5,600	100,000
Western Ranches			18,050	100,000	112,000

Among the earlier Scottish companies, California Pastoral was no longer able to meet the dividend on its preference shares paid in 1883 and 1884[12]; the Missouri Land and Live Stock Company passed its dividend; and the Wyoming Cattle Ranche, paying six per cent to its shareholders, found its herds so short that the wind-up of the company was imminent.[13] Of the newer companies, only the Cresswell paid a dividend–six per cent.

The major companies weathered the storm reasonably well, but their annual reports reflected the general trends in the industry. The Prairie ranches had branded over twelve hundred more calves than in 1884. This was three thousand under expectations, but nothing comparable to the drop experienced elsewhere on the range. Moreover, a herd of 8,000 head being transferred by the Prairie Company to comply with the new federal government land regulations strayed during the winter storm and only 2,086 were rounded up. Cattle sales reflected the downward trend in prices resulting in a drop of £25,000 in the annual income of the company.[14] The Swan Land and Cattle Company reported that Wyoming had escaped the extreme cold found on the southern range, but spring storms were severe in 1885 and the calf brand was down to 20,236, or forty per cent of the breeding females recorded on the books. Of greater concern was the declining market. Steers that sold for an average of $54·17 in 1884 brought only

capital		*dividends*		
shares		*per annum*		
amount £	*paid* £	*1885* %	*1884* %	*1883* %
10	5	10	10	20½
10	6	6	10	9
10	5	5	6	12½
10	6	7	6	8
5	5	nil	7	6
10	5	nil	nil	10
10	5	5	8	
5	5	nil	4	6
100	stock	10	15	15
5	5	nil	nil	5
5	5	4	7	

$46·58 in 1885. Income was correspondingly less for other classifications. The Chicago market had been glutted chiefly because southern ranchers had sent immature stock, usually driven north but no longer welcome there, directly to the slaughterer. In addition, a crisis had developed in American banking in 1884 and many western bankers called in their loans and restricted advances to cattlemen who were forced to raise necessary cash by sending excessive numbers of cattle to the market.[15]

In this year of crisis, western cattlemen gave serious consideration to their problems and to the future of the range cattle industry. Everyone agreed that the Earl of Airlie had understood the crux of the business when he pointed out in 1881 that the larger the ranch operation the cheaper it was to raise cattle. Extensive ranges were essential to the large corporate companies because their costs mounted as the ranges shrank. In early days they favoured the open range and fought all fencing because it was the grass they wanted and not the land. Competition with the smaller rancher and granger for grass and water had steadily increased and both resorted to fencing. In the case of settlers, their action was perfectly legal for they had filed claims under the Homestead and Pre-emption laws, and the ranchers were helpless. When, on the other hand, homesteaders were blocked by illegal wires stretched by large cattlemen, they called for and received help from the sheriff or the federal marshal. Under these conditions, the great majority of cattlemen recognized that the larger outfits would have to be broken up. It seemed inevitable that the time had now come for smaller herds and fenced breeding pastures only on freehold land.[16]

The stockman was also grievously concerned over his relations with the railroads and the stockyards. The large meatpacking corporations of the Midwest not only controlled the major meat markets of the nation but also had working agreements with the stockyards in Chicago, Kansas City, and Omaha to control the supply of cattle. The rancher was certain to be exploited by such arrangements if the cattle associations did not come to his aid. In Wyoming, a constructive working relationship finally evolved between the railroads and the cattlemen as the two most powerful economic interests in the territory.[17]

Ranchers also knew there was a change in the market demand for beef. Quality rather than quantity was wanted, so the day of Texas cattle was coming to an end. Cattlemen realized that the range business was on the way out, but the cattle industry, they insisted, was there to stay. With fenced enclosures, selective breeding, and winter feeding, ranching could continue. They also knew that their battle with the homesteader was a losing one, as it had been throughout the history of the nation. They were aware that the overstocked and overgrazed ranges were vulnerable to the retribution of nature. They were also cognizant of the steps necessary to be taken to relieve their plight, but how many would have the initiative to act in time to avoid catastrophe?

THE DEPRESSION OF 1886–8

The adverse trend in the cattle business continued in 1886. *The Statist* published a table of results of British-American companies' operations. The detailed financial report was as shown in Tables 7 and 8 on p. 121.[18]

An analysis of the herd, calf crop, and sales for 1885 and 1886 was also presented. With the exception of Western Land and Cattle Company of London and Western Ranches of Edinburgh, which paid five per cent and four per cent dividends respectively, all the major British companies carried debit balances forward. The value of all shares had taken a major tumble. The most striking features of annual operations had been the falling-off in total sales and the low prices obtained. For example, the Prairie Company in 1885 had evaluated its herd at $16·87 a head and had realized an average price of $20·75; in 1886 the reverse situation existed, an evaluation of $22·46 a head with sales averaging only $17·90.[19]

TABLE 7. Comparative statement of American cattle company dividends and stock values, 1884–7

	share		*price 21st Feb.*		*dividends*		
	amount £	*paid* £	*1887*	*1886*	*1886* %	*1885* %	*1884* %
Prairie	10	5	26/0	80/0	nil	10	10
Texas	10	5	32/6	87/6	nil	5	6
Matador	10	6	72/6	105/0	nil	7	6
Hansford	5	5	30/0	85/0	nil	nil	7
Arkansas	10	5	15/0	43/9	nil	nil	nil
Pastoral	10	5	37/6	95/0	nil	5	8
Western [Land]	stock		77½	117½	5	10	15
Cattle Ranche	5	5	240	25/0	nil	nil	nil
Western Ranches	5	5	61/0	70/0	4	4	7
Swan	10	6	45/0	105/0	nil	6	10

TABLE 8. Comparative statement of size of herds, sales, and prices, 1885–6

	net average realized for steers		*valuation per head*		*herd*		*sales*	
	1886 $	*1885* $	*1886* $	*1885* $	*1886*	*1885*	*1886*	*1885*
Prairie	17.90	20.75	22.46	16.87	92,439	124,000	13,867	22,608
Texas	20.74	24.51	12.89	14.87	89,250	98,364	7,616	10,781
Matador	21.14	28.50	18.49	17.88	95,066	94,441	12,947	17,508
Hansford	23.67	24.40	19.60	24.40	27,000	37,734	1,643	3,331
Arkansas	24.47	26.78	26.26	27.34	25,266	24,315	3,142	5,145
Pastoral	26.37	27.72	25.00	25.00	45,483	45,885	2,956	5,455
Western [Land]	27.25	30.88	26.57	26.46	32,558	35,469	3,028	5,619
Cattle Ranche	25.58	28.33	26.69	28.55	13,638	13,500	1,365	1,806
Western Ranches	27.25	37.81	27.05	27.39	17,887	18,050	3,170	3,313

The smaller Scottish cattle companies, almost without exception, passed their dividends in 1886. The Wyoming Cattle Ranche Company was finished, with more than £100,000 lost in the enterprise.[20] The same desperate situation was noted in London. Cattle companies failed to pay a dividend and carried forward a deficit. In August 1886 the Powder River Cattle Company went into voluntary liquidation and was struggling to reorganize as the

International Cattle Company, Limited. This company represented a £200,000 loss. Dakota Stock and Grazing Company also wound-up business after losing approximately £70,000.[21]

The annual report of the Matador Land and Cattle Company frankly admitted what every interested party knew: the outstanding feature of the range cattle industry was the low level of prices that had been discouraging to both breeders and feeders, so much so that many men, forced to realize their assets, had been ruined.[22] The Swan report concentrated on the themes of bad weather, falling prices, outbreak of disease, and the increasingly small yield of calves. The directors were convinced that the continuing deficiency in marketable steers and the calf crop indicated that the vendors had overestimated the size of the herds at the time of sale and legal action was contemplated. This situation undermined public confidence in the company for the first time and the preference shares issued to raise funds to pay for the Union Pacific lands, bought originally on time, were not taken up by the Scottish investing public.[23] Then suddenly, in May 1887, the Swan Brothers announced bankruptcy. Scottish capitalists, already concerned over the shortages in their herd, refused to come to the aid of Alexander Swan.[24] He was relieved of his managerial duties and legal action was taken against him and his associates as the original vendors. The directors expressed unfeigned regret at this turn of events.[25]

The severe climate on the open range in the winter of 1886–7 was the greatest calamity of all for the range cattle industry in these depression years. The previous summer had been dry and unusually hot, and extensive prairie fires occurred. As a result, there was a shortage of feed, cattle were thin, there was no market for the younger animals, and only an extremely mild winter could have prevented suffering of cattle on the open range. Unfortunately, as early as the first of November snow began to fall, and by the end of January the northern range was experiencing one of the most severe blizzards in its history. Cheyenne newspapers reported that a forty-mile-an-hour wind accompanied by blinding snow was forcing ranchers indoors and cattle to wander aimlessly. 'As things turned out it was simple murder.... The owners were mostly absent and even those who remained could not move about or size up the situation.'[26] The chinook for which the stockmen prayed never materialized, and when the losses, through death and mutilation, were counted in the spring, ranchers knew that the policy of using the open range for cattle without providing winter food and shelter was too great a gamble to be continued. Some ranchers claimed to have lost sixty to seventy per cent of their herds. Their widely publicized distress led to exaggerated

TABLE 9. Comparative statement of cattle companies' balance–sheets for year 1888

	herd		*calf crop*		*sales*	
	1888	*1887*	*1888*	*1887*	*1888*	*1887*
Prairie	83,970	90,541	13,229	19,062	10,335	8,863
Texas	90,455	95,850	15,584	18,234	16,080	9,622
Matador	96,353	96,545	16,198	22,456	13,429	14,605
Hansford	28,300	28,160	4,662	4,740	3,777	2,099
Arkansas	19,542	22,000	1,561	2,524	2,905	2,211
Pastoral	50,511	51,427	5,755	7,345	5,881	5,091
Western [Land]	25,266	30,209	2,939	4,633	2,012	1,874
Cattle Ranche	16,763	16,050	2,764	2,820	1,408	1,248
Swan	50,000	56,856	10,891	8,943	5,087	5,676
Western Ranches	13,474	12,298	1,049	644	2,980	1,013

estimates of the total destruction and created panic in the range country.[27] 'The cowmen of the West and Northwest were flat broke. Many of them never recovered.'[28] Many firms also began to liquidate holdings.

Careful studies have now estimated the loss from frozen cattle on the northern range at slightly more than fifteen per cent, but the animals which did survive were so emaciated that tax assessors reduced the evaluation of cattle holdings in Wyoming Territory by thirty per cent.[29] Some companies that had overestimated the size of their herds for years took advantage of the opportunity to reduce them to a realistic figure and blame everything on the weather. The cold winter seems to have given the final push to an industry already on the road downward. It did not doom the range business at the height of its glory, as suggested by some. The factors were already present that necessitated the complete revamping of the cattle business.

Annual reports of the British-American cattle companies provided additional evidence that the depths of the depression had already been reached (See Table 9, above[30]).

The calf crop had fallen off drastically everywhere except on the lands of the Swan Company and Western Ranches. Their improvement of 1888 was partially explained by the fact that these two companies had reported tremendous losses twelve months before when their herds were recounted. In general, the herd statistics indicated that the big outfits, like the Prairie and the Texas, were greatly depleted. In contrast some of the smaller herds, like those of Western Ranches, Cattle Ranche and Land Company, and Hansford Company, were beginning to grow again.

TABLE 10.

	net averaged realized for 3-year-old steers		*valuation of herds per head*	
	1888 $	*1887* $	*1888* $	*1887* $
Prairie	19.89	18.64	19.20	22.94
Texas	15.80	17.32	12.94	12.92
Matador	19.04	16.41	17.00	17.00
Hansford	22.10	19.87	18.70	18.79
Arkansas	25.44	21.32	22.50	22.50
Pastoral	26.72	25.81	25.00	25.00
Western [Land]	20.00	18.00	27.07	25.99
Cattle Ranche	26.94	19.74	25.71	25.65
Swan	35.24	29.43	25.00	25.00
Western Ranches	47.38	28.90	22.64	25.18

Annual sales of stock in 1888 were definitely above those of 1887 with the exception of the Matador that appeared to be restricting sales in hopes of increasing the size of the herds on its ranches.

Increased sales may have been explained by the fact that for the first time in several years cattle prices were slowly rising. As Table 10 above indicates, only the Texas Land and Cattle Company received less for its steers in 1888 than in 1887. Spectacular rises were reported by the Swan Company and Western Ranches.

Capital accounts did not reflect any marked improvement. All the companies had passed their dividends in 1887. The Matador was able to distribute two shillings a share in 1888, Western Ranches paid five shillings, and the Hansford Company declared a three per cent dividend. Most of the companies had written off their losses of 1886–7 by reducing the capital account. Some had called on shareholders for additional payments to speed a programme of rehabilitation. By March 1889 most of the cattle shares had begun to rise on the market. Table 11 on pp. 126-7 supplies additional detail.

In 1888 *The Economist* bluntly summarized, in an exaggerated way, the reasons why the English and Scottish cattle companies had been so unremunerative. In the first place, purchase prices for land and herds had been, in most cases, about four times actual value. This basic factor, along with the continuously falling market for the last seven or eight years, was enough to ruin any company. In addition, many organizations had purchased herds by book count, as was the standard range custom, and paid for two or three times as many cattle as were delivered. Third, the majority of these ranchers were on the public domain of the United States to get the feed without cost, and when the pressure of settlement forced them off the lands suddenly, they had to sell cattle that should have been kept. Many ranches were also located on the prairies of the Dakotas, Wyoming and Montana, a land of blizzard, too far north for the successful raising of cattle on the open range. While grass was excellent and cattle might flourish during the winter for several years, there would soon come along one season when the temperature would drop, the wind would blow to hurricane velocity, the cattle would be swept away by thousands, and all the profits of previous seasons would go with them. And finally, there was management: using shareholders' money to build 'castles on the prairies' and dress all the servants in red livery was not sound business and should be discontinued. The editor thought it unfortunate that the British people invested in American ranches at the time they did because of the fashionable craze.[31]

In spite of warnings about pitfalls in the paths of investors in the cattle business and its tirades against the practices of the British companies between 1880–3, the editor of *The Economist* urged reinvestment of British capital in the industry. Now was the very time to buy American cattle ranches, when no one was interested in them. With prudence, investments in cattle ranching in 1888 would probably prove the most profitable ever made in the United States.[32] Later in the year *The Statist* called attention to the rising price of beef in Chicago. With the growing improvement in the cattle trade, shares in some companies, particularly the Prairie and Swan, were considered a good investment at the current market price.[33]

Those who were now advised to invest in western American cattle companies were entering a different business from that of their predecessors eight years earlier. The open range cattle industry was largely a thing of the past. The British-American companies were entering a period of transition and adjustment by no means easy, and most of them would experience a struggle for survival during the next decade.

THE CHANGING INDUSTRY AFTER 1888

Revival in the affairs of the Prairie Cattle Company did not come so quickly as *The Statist* had predicted. The company's capital assets were reduced by the loss of real estate with questionable titles; expenses were increased by the necessity of renting land that had once been used without charge. Sheepherders of northern New Mexico overran the Cimarron Division. Breeding on the

TABLE 11.

	capital			dividends		
	ordinary share capital £	*amount* £	*paid* £	*1886*	*1887*	*1888*
Prairie	352,866	10	6	nil	nil	nil
Texas	312,000	10	6 10/	nil	nil	nil
Matador	300,000	10	6	nil	nil	2/ p. sh.
Hansford	125,844	3	3	nil	nil	3%
Arkansas	148,240	10	6	nil	nil	nil
Pastoral	173,225	10	5	nil	nil	nil
Western [Land]	100,000	stock		5%	nil	nil
Cattle Ranche	100,000	5	5	nil	nil	nil
Swan	537,357	10	7 2/	nil	nil	nil
Western Ranches	78,400	3 10/	3 10/	4%	nil	5/ p. sh.

open range there had produced a minimal crop of calves, and in 1892 the company abandoned the area and moved the herds north to the Arkansas Division in Colorado. All breeding operations were thenceforth conducted on the Canadian Division in the Texas Panhandle. Far more damaging was the disastrously low price for cattle. Losses between 1885 and 1888 amounted to £81,657. The directors found it necessary to call upon shareholders to make an additional payment of £1 on their £10 shares in each year from 1888 through 1890. Thus, £480,000, or £8 a share, was called on the £600,000 authorized capital. Once this was done, the company petitioned the Scottish courts to write off £5 from each share to take care of the shrinkage in assets. The capital wiped out represented ninety-five per cent of the total amount distributed in dividends and bonuses on the paid-up capital between 1880 and 1885. No dividends could be paid because the company maintained a 'suspense account' on its books. In March 1895 a special resolution was passed by the shareholders reducing capital to £165,000, divided into 60,000 shares of £2 15s. each, with £1 15s. paid-up. The Scots thus accepted an additional loss of £105,000. This pioneer Scottish-American company set the pattern for the remainder in its capital reorganization.[34]

The Missouri Land and Livestock Company inaugurated a vig-

prices of shares	
1889 March 16th	*1888 March 16th*
20/6 £7 paid	12/ £6 paid
27/ £7 paid	10/ £5 15/ paid
48/9	50/
30/ £3 paid	21/ £5 paid
nil £6 10/ paid	nil £5 7/6 paid
nil	nil
45/	55/
21/	20/
£7 10/ dis	5/
60/3 £3 10/ paid	45/ £5 paid

orous campaign to sell its lands in 1888 and for the next three years dividends of three to five per cent were available for distribution. In 1891 discoveries of lead and zinc in southwestern Missouri prompted the payment of a bonus of 4s. A reverse trend set in during 1892. Financial panic the following year made collections difficult, the dividend had to be skipped and it was not renewed during the next three years.[35] The California Pastoral and Agricultural Company had resolved to liquidate and in 1889 made an agreement to sell three-fourths of its land providing for an initial payment and three instalments. Income from the first payment, plus that from the disposal of portions of the herd, was used to pay the preference dividend up to date. When the second payment on the land fell due in August 1891 it was not forthcoming and the contract had to be cancelled. After 1892 all payments to the preferred shareholders ceased.[36]

Following the failure of Alexander H. Swan, the Swan Land and Cattle Company was gravely demoralized. John Clay assumed the responsibility for managing the company during the crisis and struggled against the vagaries of weather on the northern plains, the low price for cattle, the problems of land management, and the hostility of the shareholders. In March 1892 £8 had to be written off every £10 ordinary share; earnings justified the payment of a single year's dividend on the preference shares, but by 1895 the payments were still five years in arrears. In 1896 Clay left the organization and went to work for Western Ranches.[37]

No company could match the success of Western Ranches during the 1890s. The cold winter of 1886–7 had destroyed so many cattle that the calf crop was reduced by sixty-one and two-thirds per cent, but neighbouring ranchers reported an eighty per cent drop. The problem of an overcrowded range was thus dramatically eliminated. The directors wrote off the loss by reducing each share by £1 10s., and began to restock the depleted range by buying southern cattle. The managers of this property had apparently found the key to successful ranching–the large importations of southern cattle, the placing of selected Wyoming cattle on the range for fattening purposes, the systematic use of scattered pastures for feeding, and the marketing of only those classes of animals for which there was a demand. Between 1889 and 1895, the company paid annual dividends between fourteen and twenty per cent. By 1896 the original shareholders had received dividends equal to their total investment in spite of the capital reorganization of 1888.[38]

The Dundee cattle companies were in the same predicament as those of Edinburgh. By the time a continuous improvement in the western cattle trade was discernible, shareholders of the Texas Company who had received more than £65,000 in dividends had lost capital assets worth £150,000. The Matador operations were more costly. Capital reorganizations wiping out £200,000 overshadowed the £60,000 paid in early dividends. The smaller Hansford Company had distributed thirteen per cent in dividends prior to a forty per cent reduction in its capital account. But none of the companies had to liquidate, and by the mid-nineties the tide had begun to turn.

The pattern of developments on the Texas and Matador ranches in the 1890s is worthy of comment. The Texas Company concentrated on breeding cattle on the Laureles property in south-Texas and using the Horseshoe range in the Panhandle for fattening cattle for market. During 1890 the directors decided to lease the Horseshoe range to the Cattle Ranche and Land Company. Drought hit south Texas the next year and continued into 1892, the cattle had to be moved, and the company found it necessary to lease lands in the Indian Territory to replace the Horseshoe range. In spite of valiant efforts, many cattle died in south Texas and the calf crop was drastically reduced. Drought had proved as deadly as the cold of winter farther north. During these years the company also was engaged in land promotions which included building railroads across its domain and making Corpus Christi

15. Hands sitting at chuckwagon. Matador Land and Cattle Company

16. Murdo Mackenzie viewing fat steers in stockyard, 1900 (see p.129)

on the Gulf of Mexico a seaside health resort and cattle shipping centre. The deferred interest in the Texas Company, held by Underwood, Clark and Company, still troubled the Scottish directors. In 1893 the deferred shares were replaced with preference shares, the capital account was rearranged by writing off £3 a share, and for the next two years the company was able to pay small dividends on both the preference and ordinary shares, the first since 1885. In 1895 prices were the highest ever paid for southern cattle–$24 a head–and a turning point had been reached.[39]

Murdo Mackenzie, formerly employed by the Prairie Company, became manager of the Matador in 1890, and immediately set about verifying the size of the herd. The actual count of the round-up was between 17,000 and 18,000 short of what the company had claimed, so £2 was cancelled off every share, or £100,000, representing a third of the paid-up capital. The directors made a capital call to restore the loss. The range in Texas was considered ample for the breeding herd, but Mackenzie was anxious to separate the two-year-old steers by sending them north to a pasture for fattening. In 1892 the company started sending these animals to the ranges of Western Ranches in South Dakota. The new manager was also having all company lands resurveyed. The land titles had originally been taken in the names of trustees. Lawyers now advised that they be transferred to the company name because the Texas legislature had restricted future purchases of lands by aliens, and in case of the death of a trustee the company might have difficulty in re-registering the land in its own name. For the first time settlers were encroaching upon the leased lands of the Matador Company, and collectively they used their prior rights between 1888 and 1891 to lease 100,000 acres that had been used for ranching. Governor James S. Hogg of Texas had come to power as a reform governor, and a part of his programme was to check the growth of British and other foreign corporations. The Texas legislature of 1892 passed laws prohibiting acquisition of Texas lands by any alien and demanding that those who held real estate either become citizens or dispose of the land within ten years. The same terms were applied to corporations on the assumption that the public lands would be made more readily available for the 'common people'. Such confiscatory legislation was immediately tested in the federal courts, and the British cattle companies knew that within a short time these laws would be declared unconstitutional. Meanwhile, they were not strictly enforced. Like all the Texas companies, the Matador suffered from the extreme drought of 1892, but the situation was in part alleviated by having available northern ranges to which a part of the herd could be driven. All these difficulties were forgotten when the market began to improve. In 1895 the average price for cattle was higher than any year since 1883. The rate received for cows was double that of 1892. The company seized this opportune time to reduce the capital account by another £100,000 so that small dividend payments could be resumed on the remainder.[40]

In surveying the situation of the larger Scottish cattle companies between 1888 and 1895, it appears obvious that all, with the exception of Western Ranches, had existed on the brink of disaster and liquidation. Six of the major companies, still operating, had written off approximately £1,320,000, or $6,600,000, from their capital accounts. Only the Missouri Land and Live Stock and the California Pastoral had avoided capital reorganizations. These same eight companies had paid out dividends totalling £680,000, or $3,400,000, in the halcyon years, so the capital loss above dividends distributed was about $3,200,000.

A far more important fact was that none of these enterprises had been forced to liquidate. A few small Scottish companies such as the Montana Sheep and Cattle Company, the Chalk Buttes Ranche and Cattle Company, and the Deervale Ranche Company, that did not enter the business until 1884 or 1885, had folded, but only one Scottish organization of note, the Cresswell Ranche and Cattle Company, ceased ranching operations in the 1890s. Losses in the few Scottish companies that had collapsed amounted to £220,000, or $1,100,000, bringing the total investment capital lost between 1887 and 1895 to £1,540,000, or $7,700,000. This amount was sizeable when compared with the total dividend distributions of $3,400,000, but the Scots still possessed some very valuable properties.

In contrast with the Scottish-American cattle companies, the majority of the London companies did not survive the depression of the 1890s. Shareholders of the English companies launched in 1882-3 were only too willing to take their losses and get out of the business. For example, Cattle Ranche and Land Company, Western Land and Cattle Company, the Arkansas Valley Land and Cattle Company, and the Nevada Land and Cattle Company had no assets worthy of note at the time of their dissolution. Liquidation of these four English companies cost shareholders a minimum of £570,000, or $2,850,000. Some of the companies had paid only one dividend in their entire history, and the total distribution of all four companies was less than £100,000, or $500,000. The English had lost $2,500,000 that could never be regained.

The London companies launched after 1883 apparently profited from the experience of those begun earlier, for, when the depression years came and they too elected to terminate operations, some assets remained to be liquidated. For example, the American

Pastoral Company, the Espuela Land and Cattle Company, and the Cedar Valley Land and Cattle Company still had Texas estates that they hoped would produce some revenue. However, these three English companies had never paid more than one or two dividends to their stockholders, a total of only £30,000, or $150,000, through the years. They had written off $400,000 from the capital accounts, little of which was likely to be regained, so the total loss in the English companies in the 1890s was at least £970,000 or $4,850,000. With the addition of £470,000 lost by shareholders in ventures like the Dakota Stock and Grazing Company and the Powder River Cattle Company, which gave up before 1890, the companies registered in London had squandered a minimum of $7,200,000 in the American Cattle Kingdom through their major and most active companies. Total losses were undoubtedly much higher, for many smaller enterprises had been wiped out and some of the latest promotions, like the United States Cattle Ranche Company and the Wyoming Hereford Cattle and Land Association, had not revealed their position. An estimate of $10,000,000 loss through the English companies probably would not be far from correct.[41]

TWENTIETH-CENTURY DEVELOPMENTS

Many of the cattle companies that had survived the years of crisis, depression, and adjustment, 1885–95, moved toward liquidation before the outbreak of the World War in 1914. The three English companies still possessing acreage made the most of the increased demand for land at the beginning of the twentieth century. The Cedar Valley Company was able to return about one-third of the capital invested by its shareholders by using the income from land sales. The Espuela Land and Cattle Company sold its Spur Ranch in 1908 and after paying off outstanding mortgages and liens was able to pay a cumulative preference dividend that had been outstanding for twenty years. American Pastoral, the last of the English companies, disposed of its LX ranch in 1914 and used the income to repay shareholders the face value of their shares as reduced in the reorganization of 1888.[42] One Britisher was moved to remark 'In this game the Englishman does not shine.'[43]

Liquidation of the Scottish companies presents a contrast to that of the companies sponsored in London. Scottish care in the original selection of land, the wisdom of managers of their companies, and the patience and persistence of the shareholders combined to make reasonably successful enterprises out of potential failures. The Missouri Land and Live Stock Company profited from the wave of migration into southwestern Missouri from the states north of the Ohio River that sent land prices soaring between 1896 and 1900. The company concentrated on the disposal of its lands with the view of terminating business. Sizeable dividends and bonuses were paid every year until the wind-up in 1909. Shareholders in this enterprise not only had their initial investments returned, but both the founders and the latecomers made worthwhile profits either in dividends prior to 1886 or in capital bonuses during the last five years of the company's existence. Success had come, of course, from profitable land sales, not from the ranching aspects of the business.[44]

The California Pastoral and Agricultural Company, unable to meet its preference dividend in 1901, was forced into a capital reorganization whereby £100,000, or forty per cent of its paid-up capital, was written off. The ranch in the San Joaquin Valley was sold in 1911 and as payments were made during the next four years the twentieth-century shareholders received better than a threefold return on their investment. This income more than compensated for the capital lost at the time of the 1901 reorganization.[45]

After 1895 the Texas Land and Cattle Company started making small profits, and in the next decade investors were paid, by means of annual dividends, a return of thirty-two per cent on their £5 shares. However, the primary interest of the company was in selling unwanted acreage to neighbouring Texas ranchers. In 1901 Mrs Richard King purchased 111,243 acres of the Laureles Ranch at $3 an acre. As income was received from land sales, the debentures were paid and the preference shares redeemed at par. In 1906 Mrs King through her manager, Robert J. Kleberg, offered to purchase the main block of the Laureles Ranch, 190,000 acres, for $825,000. This land purchase represented approximately one-third of the acreage which in 1956 comprised the King Ranch, the largest privately-owned ranch in the United States. Since 1895, shareholders had received approximately £197,000 in dividends and capital repayments. The land sale of 1906 and the disposition of the herd made available an additional £244,650 to be distributed among investors whose shares were valued at £144,000.[46]

As early as 1893 the Dundee managers of the Hansford Land and Cattle Company had become dissatisfied with the location of their Adobe Wells Ranch along the Canadian River, and had purchased another property in the Pecos Valley of New Mexico. Between 1899 and 1904 there was a cycle of dry years in the Pecos Valley, and the Hansford herds, like the rest, were gradually depleted. Starting in 1906, the company sold its freehold lands, and leased range rights whenever a purchaser could be found. When final liquidation was agreed upon in 1912, company assets were sufficient to repay the outstanding capital, but none of the individual shareholders reaped any great rewards.[47]

After 1895 the Prairie Cattle Company adopted a general policy of reducing its New Mexico holdings along the Cimarron and consolidating the range rights along the Arkansas in Colorado and the Canadian in Texas. The herd on the Canadian range was hard hit by drought in 1901 and the company raised additional capital to buy a new spread, known as the Romero Ranch, for breeding purposes. As opportunities permitted in the next three years the company disposed of the Canadian Division. The years 1909 to 1913, in contrast to those from 1886 to 1908, were tremendously profitable ones for shareholders in this pioneer Scottish endeavour. Dividends began at seven and one-half per cent for 1909 and by 1912 exceeded eighteen per cent. The key to this prosperity was found in the price of cattle, the average income from steers increasing in value from $36·46 in 1909 to $45·59 in 1910, and to more than $50 after that season. An opportunity came in 1914 to sell the Romero Ranch to the Matador Company for £163,000–acreage that had cost only £94,000 twelve years earlier. This good fortune caused the larger shareholders to organize a pressure group to sell the JJ Range in Colorado during the period of high cattle prices. The directors counselled patience but the outbreak of World War I terminated the debate. British capitalists were urged to realize on their dollar investments to support the war effort and the Prairie Company voted to liquidate. The time had now come to check the profit and loss account. The company earnings distributed between 1895 and 1913 were sufficient to repay the total losses, above dividends, from the inception of the company through the depression of 1886–94, more than two and one-half times. Although this first Scottish venture in the range cattle industry of the American West had had its ups and downs, the shareholders who had remained to the end made ample profits.[48]
Nowhere among Scottish-American cattle companies, with the exception of the long-lived Matador, was as much return made on an investment as in the case of Western Ranches. After distributing dividends equal to one hundred per cent return on the face value of its shares, the company modified the Memorandum of Association in 1896 to permit the directors to engage in land mortgage business. Within the next five years shareholders received another one hundred per cent return. After experiencing two cold winters on the northern Plains, that of 1903–4 and 1909–10, the shareholders decided to liquidate the ranching business and form a new company, Western Ranches and Investment Company, Limited, concentrating on mortgages. In November 1919 Clay informed his associates that he doubted whether the business could be continued with benefit to the shareholders. There was no prospect of borrowing cheaply in the United States; it was

equally impossible in Scotland. No corresponding increase in interest rates on mortgages could be obtained. The old cattle company had paid dividends averaging eight per cent per annum on the original capital. The directors expected to give shareholders in the investment company £9 for every £5 share in addition to their dividends.[49] According to the final calculation of profits at the wind-up in 1921, the original shareholders, who had retained their investment from 1883 to 1919, received more than double their original capital after having averaged better than a nine per cent annual dividend for thirty-seven years.[50]

The Swan Land and Cattle Company learned that the change in its management by the removal of John Clay did not alleviate its problems. Prices for cattle remained low and the cold winters of 1902–3 and 1903–4 resulted in tremendous losses in the herd. Marketing was upset in 1904 by a strike among the packinghouse employees in Chicago. Thoroughly discouraged with the vagaries of the weather, the directors voted to introduce sheep raising on the range in 1905. The sheep business had an inauspicious beginning. Profits, if any, were made on wool sales, not on the sale of sheep. Earnings never justified more than two and one-half per cent dividends. By 1911 the sheep and wool business was in a major depression, and the real estate market was stagnant; the winter of 1912–13 was more disastrous than any previous one, killing many of the animals. The Scottish courts were notified in 1917 that the company had been unable to meet the dividend on its preference shares for the six previous years. The courts agreed the preference shareholders could be paid off fifty per cent in cash and the balance owed them paid in debenture stock bearing six per cent interest.

With the entry of the United States into the World War, the demand for wool for military uniforms sent the price soaring, and the next year the United States government purchased the entire clip at a price five and one-half times as high as the average price in 1911. The bottom fell out of the wool market again in 1920. A programme of gradual liquidation was begun in 1924. The next year the business of the Swan Land and Cattle Company was transferred to an American Board, to be wholly independent of Scottish management. The Scots maintained a financial interest through a Board in the United Kingdom. Everyone recognized by the 1920s that the Swan Company had not been a financial success either in the cattle or sheep business, and that the land assets were likely to be far short of the capital invested through the years. In 1956 efforts were still being made to sell the remaining real estate on the best possible terms.[51]

The Matador Land and Cattle Company launched a programme

of expansion in the twentieth century with the purchase of the Alamositas Ranch of 210,000 acres in the Texas Panhandle, approximately one hundred and seventy-five miles north of the main ranch. New northern pastures were obtained by leasing 530,000 acres in the Cheyenne River Indian Reservation of the South Dakota Sioux from the United States government, and 50,000 acres from the Canadian government in Saskatchewan. Immediately following this expansion cattle prices took a sudden plunge downward. Collapse was blamed on the conspiracy and manipulations of the Beef Trust in Chicago, the strike of the packinghouse employees in retaliation, and the exploitation by the railroads whose charges and services were fixed to the advantage of the stockyards and the distributors of meat. Between 1903 and 1908 profits justified small dividends ranging from two and one-half to three and three-fourths per cent. Murdo Mackenzie concentrated on improving the Matador herds. By 1908 Matador steers were winning prizes at the International Livestock Show in Chicago. Finally, in 1911 the Grand Champion Award was won and Mackenzie had earned the reputation he was seeking for the herds.

In 1910 the Matador Company began a decade of prosperity. High prices prevailed, and Matador stock commanded the highest. Company dividends rose steadily to 1914, and for the next six years the annual payment to shareholders was fixed at twenty per cent. Additional profits went into a reserve fund. All this was possible because prices boomed as never before during the war years. During this period of prosperity the Scottish directors worked on schemes to improve the value of their real estate. Agreements were made with the Quanah, Acme and Pacific Railway Company to build a line across the main ranch, to sponsor a town site, and to sell acreage along the railroad to prospective cotton farmers. In 1914 the United States announced that the Matador lease in the Cheyenne River Indian Reservation would be cancelled to enable the Indians to use the land for their own herds. To take care of their stock, the Matador management secured a five-year lease to 10,000 acres in the Fort Belknap Indian Reservation in Montana. This was not sufficient, so a short-term lease was made to 110,000 acres adjoining the Alamositas Ranch, and the 120,000-acre Romero Ranch, belonging to the Prairie Cattle Company, was purchased. Income from land sales at the main ranch was continuous, and great interest was displayed in oil leases there.

After 1918 cattle prices started a downward trend, and in 1921 they dropped fifty per cent because of the uncertain financial picture. The Matador Company dividend was cut in half, to ten per cent, and the next year it was cut in half again. Only by dipping into the reserve fund could these reduced payments be made. When the United States and Canadian governments both levied heavy protective duties on cattle crossing the international boundary, the Matador Company gave up its Canadian leases and replaced them with a two-year lease of 350,000 acres in the Pine Ridge Indian Reservation in South Dakota. Boom times returned to the cattle business in 1927, when steers brought eighty per cent more than the previous year, and these high prices continued through 1929. The directors were able to place an additional £50,000 in the reserve fund, bringing the total to £200,000, equal to the entire paid-up capital of the company.

Accompanying the disaster on the New York Stock Exchange in 1929 and the resulting depression in the United States, there was another tremendous drop in cattle prices. Animals shipped from the Matador in 1929 had brought an average of \$66·41. In 1930 they brought \$39·83. Continuous low prices and drought combined to produce an annual deficit in 1931 and for the first time since 1887 the Matador Company had to pass its annual dividend. By 1932 prices were the lowest in thirty-seven years. Nature continued to conspire against the ranchers. After a dry spring in the Panhandle of Texas, dust storms raged through the summer of 1934. In Montana, the springs of 1933 and 1934 were very wet and cold and the summers brought visitations of grasshoppers that ruined the feeding pastures. Not until 1937 did the Matador Company begin paying dividends again, distributing three per cent.[52]

The prosperity of the Matador Company appeared unbounded during the 1940s. By 1948, Chairman William D. MacDougall announced that the directors had secured a voluntary agreement among the shareholders to limit annual dividends to thirty per cent. Even greater profits were in store because the British government, on 8 September 1949, devalued the pound sterling from \$4·035 to \$2·80, a reduction of approximately thirty per cent. This was the equivalent of a bonus on all dollars called home from the United States by the Scottish company.[53] While the shareholders had subscribed only £200,000 to the enterprise, plus any premiums above par value of shares paid by individual purchasers, their combined equity had now reached £1,274,000.

In December 1949 a major oil strike was made about ninety miles from the Matador Ranch. A year later Lazard Brothers and Company of London proposed to purchase the Matador Land and Cattle Company. Nineteen million dollars was involved in the transaction. During the eight months of negotiation of sale, shares in the Matador rose from \$7 to \$28 on the New York and London exchanges. Chairman MacDougall requested a halt in the trading of shares until final arrangements for the transfer were made in August 1951. Matador shareholders in the United Kingdom received £9 6s. 6d. a share, while those in the United States accepted $23·70. Lazard Brothers agreed that if oil or other valuable minerals should be discovered in the future on the Matador's ranges, they would share the royalties equally with the vendors.[54] As early as 1942 an agreement had been made by shareholders of the Matador Company to divide each £6 share into six £1 shares.[55] Later, three-fourths of the capital was returned so that the shares represented only 5s. in 1951. Thus, Matador shares were sold for over thirty times the capital represented by each share, after having averaged approximately fifteen per cent annual dividends or bonuses for thirty years. Scottish capitalists who so optimistically invested their funds in the range cattle industry of western America, even in their moments of wildest fantasy, could not have dreamed of such a 'bonanza'. Individual profits, of course, depended upon the market price at the time of the purchase of shares. Heirs of the original promoters, if they held their Matador stock, were well repaid for their forbearance with the ups and downs of the industry. Astute investors who purchased shares in the depression of 1930–5 shared in the profits without long suffering.

A BALANCE SHEET

At the close of the nineteenth century, British investors in the range cattle industry apparently had suffered a major financial loss. Few, if any, of the heavily-capitalized companies could claim to have made legitimate profits from their ranching operations since 1882–4. In the aggregate, the English companies had lost approximately $10,000,000 and the Scots somewhere between $7,000,000 and $8,000,000. In the twentieth century, however, many cattle enterprises were able to recoup their losses through increment on land, and profits from the continuous, though erratic, rise in the price of cattle. We have noted that three English companies, the American Pastoral, Cedar Valley, and Espuela, after selling their estates, succeeded in returning the capital invested by their shareholders. The six Scottish cattle companies liquidated between 1906 and 1921 paid their shareholders a total of approximately £1,925,000, or $9,625,000 above their combined capital accounts. Some companies, as the Prairie and Hansford, had made a portion of their income from the ranching business. Others profited greatly by the sale of herds in a period of high prices, but most profitable of all was the increment from land. Although the Scottish companies had written approximately $7,700,000 from their capital accounts as lost, in the dismal years,

1887–95, earlier dividend distributions reduced this deficit to approximately $4,300,000. The conclusion seems inescapable that the Edinburgh and Dundee companies, as a group, in the end regained all their investment capital and had about $5,000,000 more accumulated. When scattered among all the Scottish companies, this profit was negligible for all the efforts expended over three decades. It is also true that individuals who elected to sell their cattle company shares, or who were forced to do so, in a period of crisis or depression had taken great personal losses. Yet for every investor in the Scottish-American cattle companies who lost money in this way, there was another who obtained the securities in a depreciated market and sooner or later reaped the profits. The $5,000,000 favourable balance in the composite capital accounts, moreover, could not offset the $10,000,000 lost by promotions in London. However, the British 'losses' of capital in the range cattle industry, 1885–95, were not losses, in many cases, but only temporary depreciation. Even this temporary depreciation, like the figures on the destruction of herds in the 'great die-up' of the 1886–7 winter, has been grossly exaggerated.

We have already noted the exceptional income received from real estate by cattle companies liquidating after the close of World War I. Care must be exercised, however, not to overemphasize what may appear to be dramatic profits. When calculating the total capital return, the comparatively weak position of the pound sterling on the international monetary exchange and the general inflation of prices through the years become vital factors. A pound taken home in 1920, and certainly one obtained in 1950, was not nearly so valuable as one invested in 1880. Even so, it seems obvious that the Scottish people, as a nation, profited on investments in the American cattle business on a long term basis.

Chapter Six

Adventures in the Mining Kingdom

When news reached Britain of the discovery of gold in California, London financiers eagerly organized joint stock enterprises to explore the slopes of the Sierra Nevada for new deposits or to purchase quartz-lode claims already found by men lacking the necessary capital to exploit them. In 1849 at least eight companies were registered to work California mines, and additional ventures were launched each year until 1855 when the excitement abated.[1] At the peak year of interest, 1853, twenty Anglo-California gold-quartz mining companies were active on the London market, representing an estimated investment of $10,000,000.[2] Many companies did not progress beyond the process of registration. The typical company remained in business for two, certainly not more than three, seasons. Quartz mining necessitated capital outlays for the introduction of crushing and milling machinery. Technical problems immediately arose because the nature and hardness of quartz in California differed from that elsewhere in the world and the British, like others, were unprepared or unwilling to engage in costly experimentation. Information about general mining conditions in California was also fragmentary, mining companies had difficulty in obtaining a land title, and on occasions the English were defrauded. Most of the undertakings proved disastrous for the participants, and, after suffering heavy losses throughout the 1850s, 'the English turned their backs upon California as a field for profitable investment'.[3]

The Scots appear to have been far less interested than the English in these earliest mining activities. No evidence has been found that any Scottish company was organized for purposes of gold mining in the two decades following the California discoveries. This does not prove, or even indicate, that Scots had no financial stake in mining during the 1850s because many wealthy men of northern Britain placed their investments through London financial houses.

Although the Civil War in the United States caused an abrupt termination of mining investments by the British, the situation had greatly altered by 1870. California mining was established on a firm basis, federal law granted a private title to property, and labour costs had been materially reduced. The Mining Kingdom of western America had also spread eastward from the Pacific slope. Along the eastern slopes of the Sierra Nevada gold and silver had been discovered, resulting in the establishment of the Washoe mines of western Nevada. Simultaneously gold had been found in the heart of the Colorado Rockies. Major rushes to these two areas developed in 1859. Some miners, disappointed in these new fields, wandered northward into the Snake River Valley in search of new placers that could be worked by a man without capital. They drifted from north to south along this stream working every tributary flowing in a westerly direction. In 1860 they made discoveries on the Clearwater Fork, in 1861 on the Salmon, and in 1862 on the Boise. Some crossed the mountains to the Montana region, and starting in 1862 each of the next three seasons produced a rush and another boom town. A few years later promising silver-bearing quartz had also been found in Utah. In each case the initial mineral discovery led to the establishment of many mining camps as prospectors fanned out all over the vicinity. Thus, in the decade of the 1860s mining discoveries had led to the establishment of territorial government for Nevada, Colorado, Idaho, and Montana. Nevada had even achieved statehood. In addition, the transcontinental railway had been completed in 1869, and this improvement facilitated the examination of mining claims by prospective buyers. The new telegraph enabled superintendents to communicate quickly with headquarters whether in New York or London.[4] In these same years British legislation concerning the joint stock company with limited liability was being clarified and codified.

The great boom in British export of capital, 1870–3, was accompanied by a frenzied speculation in the shares of overseas mining enterprises in London. One scholar has estimated that the nominal capitalization of companies floated in England to operate overseas mines reached an annual volume of approximately £40 million during 1872 and 1873.[5] In this four-year period, later described as the 'first mining mania', sixty-seven mining companies, capitalized at about £14 million, were registered to operate in the western United States outside California. In addition, twenty-seven companies, representing over £4 million, were active in California.[6]

Although Nevada became the favourite field for the location of English mining companies, California was next in line, and major enterprises were also started in Colorado and Utah. Their success varied widely. The Sierra Buttes Mining Company, Limited, reputedly worked the most profitable mining properties in California for the remainder of the century. The Richmond Consolidated Mining Company, Limited, owning several mining properties in Nevada and operating a smelting and refining works in Eureka, was destined to pay dividends totalling a 324 per cent return on its capital from 1872 to 1895. In contrast, the Ruby Consolidated Mining Company, Limited, operating in the same territory, experienced an unhappy history, including several reorganizations prior to its demise in 1895. Two mining organizations located in Utah Territory, the Flagstaff Silver Mining Company, Limited, and the Emma Silver Mining Company, Limited, were to have a similar history and end.[7] These companies gained such notoriety through the English financial press that they were known to the investing public by the abbreviated titles of 'Emma', 'Ruby', and 'Flagstaff'.

Scottish interest in these western American mining companies with London headquarters may best be illustrated by the history of the Emma Silver Mining Company. Approximately half the shares of this company, capitalized at £1,000,000, were held in Scotland. Within two years after the enterprise was launched there was ample evidence of overcapitalization, misrepresentation of the Utah property, and secret payments, in shares or cash, to vendors and to American and British promoters, all of which combined to indicate that a scandal was in the making. Embittered Scots demanded the appointment of an investigating commission that could hire an engineer to make an independent inspection and report on the mine. They also insisted on the election of two Scots to the Board of Directors to replace the chief vendor and his legal adviser from the United States. It was further suggested that the company's office be transferred from London to Glasgow. Soon the Scots were convinced that fraud had been perpetrated, and led by Alexander Macdougall they voted out the Board of Directors in 1875 and placed their own countrymen in control of a new Board. The new company policy was to file suits in the New York and London courts against everyone involved in this promotion. Although the Scottish investors failed to prove fraud on the part of the American vendors in the United States courts, they were successful in obtaining a court decision against the chief British promoter and secured a financial reimbursement from him. The experience with this and similar companies no doubt prompted the Scots to keep their mining investments in the United States to a minimum during the 1870s. When they expressed a renewed interest in the 1880s they insisted, when possible, that the home office be located in Scotland rather than in England.[8]

Just how much capital flowed into western America for mining operations during the London 'mania' of 1872–3 cannot be exactly determined. Only the better-known companies seeking funds from the public were listed in the Stock Exchange Year-Books. Joint stock companies utilizing limited liability were required by law to file a statement of their capital and shares with governmental authority, but little is known about private companies unless the press called attention to their unusual financial success or difficulty. True, the nominal capital of public limited companies can easily be totalled, but the amount actually invested can only be estimated. Although all recognized that the investment had been heavy, a decade later *The Economist* recalled 'Looking back over the mining mania of 1871, it has been ascertained that out of more than a hundred ventures then brought forward only ten are now in existence, and but half that number ever earned dividends.'[9] It was bitterly suggested 'there is a pretty general belief that the profits were never honestly made; that, as a matter of fact, the ore bodies which yielded the dividends were planted by human hands and not by nature'.[10]

The disastrous results of British mining investments made between 1870 and 1873 were largely the result of manipulations by vendors and company promoters, at the time of issuing prospectuses, to obtain title to the American property, and to raise initial capital. The abuses, as explained in the paragraphs that follow, occurred in all types of company promotion in Britain. However, they were more pronounced in the floating of mining companies than, for example, cattle or land mortgage enterprises. This was explained, in part, by the speculative nature of mining operations throughout the world.

By 1870 professional company promoters were present in London who devoted their time to a systematic search for enterprises that were available for purchase by a public company. They often represented a small group of investors, usually the seven necessary to form a limited liability company, that was described as a 'syndicate'. Vendors of western American mines, or their agents, were also plentiful, congregating in hotel lobbies and public places where they might establish contact with the representatives of investors. Having found a prospective vendor, the promoter would negotiate to see if he could obtain the mining property on advantageous terms for the proposed public company. The price that was paid for a mine was usually three or four times higher than that which the property could command locally or in the eastern cities of the United States. The promoter negotiated a 'bonding contract' whereby he agreed to buy the mine at a stipulated price on behalf of the contemplated company. If the company was floated within a specified time, the property was acquired on the basis of the terms in this contract. Should the promoter and his 'syndicate' fail to float the shares of the company, they had no obligation to the owner of the mine. No risk whatsoever was borne by the British promoter and his associates. Moreover, he usually was able to prevail upon the vendor to take a portion of the purchase price agreed upon in shares of the proposed company rather than in cash. The companies floated were always capitalized at figures somewhat in excess of the cost of the mining property in order that the expenses of organization, salaries, and working capital for development and the installation of improved equipment could be met for a year or two until a systematic mining operation was established.[11]

The people of Britain were invited to subscribe for shares in the proposed company through the issuance of a prospectus. The statutes dealing with company promotion during the 1870s contained no provision concerning these prospectuses. Copies did not have to be filed with the Companies Registration Offices. Under the circumstances, the prospectus became a promotional document that circulated widely, combining colourful presentation of fact, usually some exaggeration, and occasionally outright misrepresentation. Invariably the prospectus quoted reports of mining engineers and appended their endorsements and predictions of outstanding financial success. Without shame, the promoters deleted any conditional phrases or qualifying statements from the official reports of mining engineers prior to using them in the prospectus. Abridged versions of the prospectus were printed in mining journals and newspapers, sometimes on several different pages of the same issue. On occasions, an application blank was provided for the reader, adjoining the prospectus, where he could enter his name, address, and the number of shares desired, to be clipped and mailed to the company office.

As the statutory law was silent on the prospectus, any person relying on statements made in the document that later proved to be false could only bring action for deceit at common law. Even this recourse was available only to initial subscribers, not to shareholders who had later bought shares on the market. The shareholder had little hope of winning a case because all the promoter had to do was to establish the fact that he honestly believed his statements were true when they were made and the case of fraud was dismissed. The promoter could be accused of stupidity, credulousness, and negligence, but not convicted of dishonesty. If the shareholder persisted in his legal action against the company he would seek a recision of his contract to pay the subscription price of his shares. In such a suit it was necessary to prove misrepresentation in the prospectus. It was irrelevant whether the misrepresentation was innocent or fraudulent. However, the companies convinced the courts that they were bound by the formal prospectus and not by the advertised abridged version published in newspapers and periodicals. It was the latter, of course, rather than the official document that contained the misrepresentation. If the subscriber had as much as glanced at the formal prospectus at the time of his application for shares, the promoters were not bound by any advertised version. It was the practice to print the formal prospectus on a different page in the same issue of a journal where the advertisement of the prospectus appeared. The latter was more dramatically presented, more readable in form and generally more appealing. Invariably this advertisement referred to the formal prospectus as the basis of the contract. Shareholders were hard put, under these circumstances, to assert that they had not seen the formal prospectus. Thus affairs were arranged to make possible collaboration between the company promoter and the mining engineers. In a period when the standard of business ethics was low, mining engineers were plentifully available who, for an appropriate fee, would write optimistic reports on speculative mining properties that could be edited to suit the ends of the promoters and the vendors.[12]

In addition to the abuses associated with the prospectus, company promoters did not hesitate to manipulate the market price of shares in the initial offering to the public. As soon as the prospectus appeared, the company released a block of a few hundred shares for trading purposes. Purchases and sales were processed through the Stock Exchange with all transactions at or above the par value of the shares. Brokers often bought and sold shares simultaneously for the same client. The public noticed Stock Exchange reports that shares were being traded at or above par, gained confidence in the enterprise, and often invested. Company promoters rationalized that this was an essential and ethical procedure because no share could initially be sold under par and no payment could be made as underwriter's fees or commissions, for such expenses would result in the shares being worth less than par.

The public was also deceived concerning share values by the practice of declaring an initial dividend shortly after a company had initiated mining operations. This dividend was usually paid out of capital, but the outlay was not sizeable because a limited number of shares had been subscribed for. On the strength of the dividend declaration, shares rose above par and trading was brisk. Another means of making a company more attractive to investors was to obtain the services of a man of title or of great business distinction as chairman of the Board of Directors. Newspapers and mining journals often printed general accusations that promoters offered handsome fees, blocks of shares, and other inducements to get these acceptances, but specific companies or individuals were not named for fear of libel. When the subject was brought up, such arrangements were always vigorously denied by all those who were indirectly charged.

By 1870 an operating arrangement had been worked out whereby the paid-up shares that promoters received for their services were concealed. Any company being floated was responsible for the purchase price, or consideration, paid for a mining property and this amount had to appear, according to law, both in the prospectus and in the memorandum of association. As mentioned, the usual practice was to pay the vendor partially with paid-up shares. Secret agreements, ancillary to the contracts of sale, were often concluded with the vendors awarding a specified amount of the purchase money or shares to the promoters. Thus, both vendor and promoter were vitally concerned with all methods used to rig the market and increase the value of shares.

The total effect of such operations was that practically all mining properties had to be sold at greatly enhanced prices to the English investor. If the secret contract between vendor and promoter was not used, an alternative method was for the vendor to sell to an individual or an 'exploring syndicate' that would shortly thereafter re-sell at an exorbitant mark-up to the promoters of a public company. This second price was the figure that appeared in the prospectus and the memorandum of association, and the amount paid the original vendor for the property was a closely guarded secret. Profits of such negotiations were usually shared with the promoter and less frequently with the vendor. The latter usually had nothing to complain about since he had received as much or more for his mine than he could have hoped to obtain at home.

Final arrangements had to be made in these security transactions to convert shares of doubtful value into cash. Both vendors and promoters and their friends awaited the day when the rigging of the market had placed share values high enough to make the maximum profit. The amount of the vendor's shares was public knowledge. The promoter, however, had usually designated friends who subscribed for a large number of shares to be registered in their names but actually held for him. Certainly any shares received as promotional fees by means of secret agreement were held in the names of others. As soon as optimistic reports appeared noting that shares were selling above par on the market, the reserved shares were sold. Meanwhile, the promoter, in all probability an officer or a director of the company at this point, made public statements boasting of his resolve to hold the shares originally allotted to him for purchase and officially registered in his name. Promoters often explained these practices to American vendors, if they were naïve enough to need an explanation, and they followed the same procedures. As we have noted, the Companies Act of 1862 required that every public company file an annual register of stockholders showing the names, addresses, and occupations of investors, the number of shares that they held at filing time and the number of shares traded during the year. This document could be inspected at the Companies Registration Office, but few investors took such pains. In time, insiders to a company promotion sold their shares without resorting to intermediaries because so few investors went to the trouble to inspect and analyse these company documents.[13]

Although the Companies Act of 1867 provided that 'every prospectus of a company and every notice inviting persons to subscribe for shares in any joint-stock company shall specify the dates, and the name of the parties to any contract entered into by the company, or promoters, directors, or trustees thereof, before the issuance of such prospectus',[14] the courts ruled that only those contracts had to be revealed that were intended to bind the company. As long as the company organizers stated in the prospectus the price which the company had to pay for the property acquired, they were immune to prosecution.[15] The London *Mining Journal* suggested that if the courts interpreted the Companies Act literally concerning the remuneration of financiers and promoters out of the purchase money, the directors of nine companies out of ten would be open to attack.[16] The courts apparently shunned their responsibility in outlawing a practice that had gained universal acceptance. The alternative method of using a middleman or an 'exploring syndicate' to purchase a mining property for a vendor then 'marking up' the price when re-selling to the company actually expecting to work the mine was dealt a death blow by the courts in 1877 when the 'mark-up' device was outlawed. The courts also suggested that promoters of companies acted as trustees for shareholders and were not to derive personal profit out of the transactions of companies they were organizing.[17] This decision, of course, came too late to check the boom of 1870–3.

The press on both sides of the Atlantic had much to say about the 'mining mania' of 1870–3. At the beginning of 1870, the leading mining journal on the Pacific Coast noted, 'Our mines are attracting the attention of European capitalists, and already several have passed into the hands of English companies. This is but the beginning; we have plenty of developed workings, which, if properly managed, would surely yield profits large enough to attract foreign capital.'[18] In contrast to the attitude of some British observers, the same publication expressed admiration for the caution which the English capitalists were exercising in the examination of mines, and thought their conduct was well-calculated to stop the sale of worthless properties. Thorough investigations by competent mining engineers were lauded as safeguards both to the investors and the mining owners of good mines. The opportunity for profits was not to be overlooked.

> There are many good mines west of the Rocky Mountains, which, by enlarging their works and developing further, might be made to pay handsomely, but which, for the scarcity of capital and the high rates of interest here, are unable to make the requisite improvements, but which in European cities, where there is often a plethora of money, and a less rate of interest prevails, would be the best investment that could be presented to the notice of capitalists.[19]

Observing the rising tide of enthusiasm for mining securities in 1871, the London *Times* began a campaign to show the dangers involved in haphazard investment. As a result of the bold editorial policy of Marmaduke Sampson, city editor, in exposing the perpetrators of various business frauds, this city newspaper was described by other periodicals as 'the thunderer'. However, there was no evidence that The *Times* editor was aware at this time of the system whereby the promotion fees of mining company organizers were concealed. Instead he harped on the theme that American vendors were trying to take advantage of English speculators. American vendors were described as western adventurers with minimum capital and character who could not find a Wall Street banker to co-operate with them.[20] Mining journals in both countries thought *The Times* was unjustly outspoken in its criticism of the mining industry. The London *Mining Journal*, an influential weekly trade journal describing the activities of mining companies throughout the world, did casually admonish speculators to be aware of the deceitful practices of American vendors of mines, their agents, and engineers. The question 'Will American mining pay?' was thoroughly discussed, pro and con, in the columns of English periodicals, such as the *Mining Journal* and the *Mining World*.[21] Not until the speculative orgy was over in 1874 was the role of the syndicate as a 'middleman' between vendor and public recognized, nor was the role of the promoter in overcapitalizing the company as a means of getting his reward made known. Lack of knowledge of these operations during 1870–3 may have been a factor indirectly fostering the extensive speculation, but once the practices were public knowledge there is no evidence that promoters modified their operations.

As a single aspect of the sharp contraction in British overseas investments beginning in 1874 and lasting until the end of the decade, there was a marked decline in the number of overseas mining companies registered in Britain and the total nominal capitalization of this type of enterprise. The aggregate nominal capitalization of overseas mining companies floated in London fell from an annual average of £40 million in 1872 and 1873 to £1·6 million in 1876 and reached a low point of £1·4 in 1879. The pattern in western America was the same as that elsewhere. The number of active companies registered to work on the mining frontier east of the Sierra Nevada, steadily declined from the peak year of 1871, when there were twenty, to not more than two or three a year for 1874–9. Beginning in 1873 almost as much capital was involved in company reorganizations as in new enterprise, and in the crisis year of 1874, £8 out of every £10 of nominal capital was designated for reorganization purposes.[22] In California only five new companies were launched in the entire period, 1874–9, in comparison to twenty-seven in the boom years, 1870–3.[23]

While their English cousins organized dozens of mining and smelting operations in western America during the early 1870s and lost heavily in the depression of the close of the decade, experienced Scottish financiers refused to sponsor this type of investment. Leading Scottish businessmen and financiers in Edinburgh and Dundee were preoccupied with organizing investment trusts and taking advantage of the limited liability legislation to register mortgage and security investment companies. Periodic reports on the progress of London-promoted mining companies in the Scottish journals indicate a wide reader interest. Many Scots held stock in the Emma, the Flagstaff and the Richmond Consolidated. No doubt London provided ample opportunity for the investor wishing to risk funds in mining. They did not wait for Scottish-sponsored mining ventures to be launched.[24]

The records of only three limited companies promoted and registered in Scotland for the purpose of mining in the western United States during this decade have been located, one each in Utah, California, and Colorado (see Table 13, pp. 188-9). These enterprises represented a small outlay of capital and existed for only a few years. There is no evidence that financial success came to their sponsors. The only company launched during the 'boom' was the Utah Cotton Wood Mining and Smelting Company, Limited, 1872. This was a private company, registered by the legally-required seven individuals, who were the only shareholders, engaged in examining several silver-lead mining locations near Honeycomb Gulch, adjoining the Big Cottonwood Canyon south of Salt Lake City. The promoter was John E. Watson, a Glasgow accountant, who prevailed upon four merchants, a solicitor, and a lithographer none of whom had any mining experience, to join him in signing the memorandum of association. The enterprise was wound up in nine months; no actual mining was carried on, and the losses were confined to the promoters.[25]

Another Glasgow promotion, the Kirkland Gold and Silver Mining Company of California, Limited, purchased a gold mining claim on the Hathaway Quartz Ledge, on the outskirts of the town of Ophir in Placer County, California. The company was capitalized at £4,000. In this case the sponsors were manufacturers, mercantile clerks, bleachers, and a coalmaster. Following the usual pattern, the vendors received fully-paid shares in partial payment for their property, the majority of the remaining shares were retained in the hands of three Scottish promoters. However, the public was invited to subscribe for shares and the company did attempt to work the property. Disappointing reports were received from California and it became necessary to sever relations with the vendors. The stockholders voted to wind-up the business in 1883 after a vain search for additional capital.[26]

Several Dundee merchants registered the Atchison Mining Company, Limited, in 1875 to purchase the Atchison Mine in the Gold Hill District, near the town of Salina, eight miles from Boulder, Colorado. Two Colorado miners, who managed the mine and mill, retained an interest in the enterprise through paid-up shares received when the property title was transferred to the Scots. The company was authorized to raise £6,000 and this amount proved inadequate to work the mine and operate a ten-stamp mill. Within two years the Scots were earnestly seeking additional capital but with little success, owing to the failure of the property to produce dividends. By 1879 the shareholders petitioned for a dissolution because the company's liabilities were overwhelming. At this time various issues of shares had pushed the authorized capital to £27,000 and the working assets were over £10,000. Including borrowed funds, this venture may have cost the Scots from £12,000 to £15,000.[27] At best these Scottish efforts in western mining can be classified as the speculations of inexperienced men. Evidence is too fragmentary to establish any pattern or principle of investment.

Accompanying the acceleration of all types of British overseas investment in 1880, following the doldrums of the later 1870s, there was a modest revival in the formation of overseas mining companies. The aggregate nominal capitalization of enterprises of this type registered in Great Britain steadily increased until a peak year was reached in 1888. In this year the total was just short of

£47 million, exceeding for the first time the peak years of 1872 and 1873 when the total had been £40 million.

In spite of the disclosure of the exploitive features of company promotion beginning in 1877, excitement of new mining discoveries throughout the world initiated a general upsurge in mining investments. For example, a major factor ending the dullness of the market was the discovery of gold in southern India in 1880, followed by the diamond excitement in South Africa and the development of new gold mining districts in South America. Another significant development affecting this upsurge of investment was the exceptional success reported by a few mining companies in 1884–5. During 1886 there was a sharp increase in the number of new mining companies registered and for the next three years a speculative mania produced a 'boom' not unlike that of 1870–3. Reports of unexpected and phenomenal profits in mining had a tendency to fire the imagination of British investors, and periodically, as in the years 1886–8, the spirit of gambling in the world-wide mining lottery seemed to pervade the investing populace. Although they knew the odds of success were slight, many small investors of moderate means seemed eager to take the risk. The spirit of speculation became rampant and the aggregate of countless small investments in mining shares swelled the national total to amounts significant in the world-wide investment pattern.[28]

In North America, British mining investments increased significantly and steadily between 1881 and 1885. However, most of the flow of capital was for the purpose of reorganizing older companies in need of increased funds for development work rather than for launching new ventures. The comparatively few new companies registered were concentrated in Colorado. By this time the mining industry of Colorado was more interested in the extraction of silver than gold. In addition to their transfer from gold to silver mining, Coloradans vigorously experimented with new techniques for handling all refractory ores. The Caribou mine, producing quantities of silver, had been discovered in 1869. There was active silver mining in San Juan county, in the southwestern corner of the territory, in 1871–2. Shortly thereafter the great silver deposit, known as the Little Pittsburg, was unearthed near Leadville. The organization of the La Plata Mining and Smelting Company, Limited, to operate a public smelter there precipitated a rush of London capital to the Rocky Mountains. At first the English concentrated their operations near Leadville in Lake County and at Lake City in Hinsdale County in the southwestern part of the state. By the time statehood was obtained in 1876, English investors considered all of Colorado their province. Emphasis on Colorado investment became even more pronounced in 1886 with the opening of the new gold mining area at Cripple Creek, and that state shared with California the largest percentage of London capital in western mining endeavours.[29]

The British financial press inaugurated a vigorous campaign to squelch the renewal of excitement in the stock exchange. In June 1881 *The Economist* declared that mining was 'the most risky of all investments':

> In January last there was recorded in these pages the introduction of ten mining companies. February, though a shorter month, brought us twelve such ventures; and the list in March was swelled to fourteen. April, however, brought seventeen new mining concerns before the public; and this number was again capped in May, when twenty such companies made their appearance.... These few figures tell us most clearly that there is an increasing rage for these most venturesome so-called securities....

As a warning to the public, the editor described in detailed and exaggerated language all the abuses that had been resorted to in the past in floating mining companies:

> ... As a rule, mining shares are in the first case applied for, not by investors, but by speculators. A company is formed, two or three mining captains' reports are readily obtained, some picked lumps of ore are assayed, (by means of which assays possibly the name of the Bank of England actually makes its appearance on the face of the prospectus,) and an allotment is made to a small sprinkling of gulled investors, a large number of gamblers who anticipate premiums, and often a considerable balance to parties interested, whose intention it is also to sell on the first opportunity. Then comes the real question of floating the shares into other hands, by the combined circulation of coloured reports, stories of 'important discoveries,' and puffing generally....[30]

The *Scottish Banking and Insurance Magazine* concurred with *The Economist* on developments, reporting that a day never passed in the first months of 1881 without the advertisement in Scotland of a new British mining venture, and on some days there were as many as six. Few of these joint stock enterprises were so modest as to promise ten per cent return, more often it was two, three or even five hundred per cent. *The Scotsman*, an Edinburgh newspaper, was upbraided for printing such advertisements without a word of warning. The magazine editor remarked 'Scotland has considerable credit with the speculating world for a thrifty and wealthy population, while its newspaper press is under the selfish and easy influence of highly paid advertisement.' Getting down to cases, the journal reminded the public of a Rocky Mountain mining company offering an eighty-per-cent dividend when its prospectus first appeared and then with the publication of a letter from an unknown person in the mountains, the promise went up to one hundred per cent.

> If one-half or even one-fourth of this promise were true, Denver would be deserted in no time and leave no one there to keep bar or fill the pulpit–all would be off to the mines. ...There are thousands in Denver who would feel themselves wronged and with their pre-eminence as marksmen with six shooters, it would not be a particularly healthy locality for vendors to reside in, after disposing of so valuable a property so far away from home.[31]

Although the enthusiasm of the 1870s for mining investments in western America, and elsewhere, had failed to excite experienced capitalists or the rank and file of investors in Scotland, the new furore of 1880–1 affected all sorts and conditions of men and even 'the hard-headed folk in the North' succumbed to its influence. The reason for this dramatic shift in interest was the decision of the highly successful directors of the Scottish-American Investment Company of Edinburgh to sponsor a mining enterprise.

Just as these capitalists had made their initial investment in cattle ranches through Faulkner, Bell and Company of San Francisco they also turned to this company for advice in matters of mining. At the beginning of 1881 Charles Sutherland came to Edinburgh from California for the purpose of floating a company to purchase a mining property in Sierra County, including four mines known as 'The Bonanza', 'General Garfield', 'The Hunter', and 'The Justice'. He was accompanied by James Davidson Walker of Faulkner, Bell and Company. In consultation, Walker and Sir George Warrender, Chairman of the Board of the Scottish-American Investment Company, agreed to purchase Sutherland's claims for $400,000.[32] The Scottish Pacific Coast Mining Company, Limited, was registered in March 1881, with a capital of £100,000 in £10 shares. Faulkner, Bell and Company subscribed, £10,000. The reputation of the Edinburgh directors was so well established that £85,000 was immediately paid-up.[33]

An initial dividend of two and one half per cent was paid in July 1881, but the revenue account of that year showed a deficit. No dividend was paid during 1882–3, and finally, in June 1884, the shareholders sent an investigating committee to California.[34] Their report was disheartening. Sutherland had come to Scotland with an option to purchase the property for £66,000. The additional £14,000 secured from the Scots through the intercession of Walker had been divided between the two men as a sales commission. Thus, the wily and experienced Edinburgh capitalists had been victimized by the *modus operandi* that had prevailed in London during the early 1870s but had since been thoroughly exposed. To say the least, they were guilty of mistaken confidence in their San Francisco agent. To make matters worse, miners at the Scottish property, while digging in their tunnel during the first year of operations, had come upon the old workings of another company operating across the mountain ridge. The pay-channel of ore had been cleared away. In short, the Scots had been swindled and operations had to be suspended. The real value of the mine, if any, was on another's claim, and Sutherland, under questioning, could only suggest that a new purchaser might be willing to assume the £8,000 indebtedness of the company and pay the stockholders one-third of any future earnings.[35]

In February 1885 the Scottish Pacific Coast Mining Company agreed to voluntary liquidation under the supervision of the courts. The liquidator tried to force Walker, a company director, to make a refund on the ground that he had circulated a fraudulent prospectus by not revealing his secret contractual understanding with Sutherland. The facts of the case were similar to those in London described earlier and the Scots could get no legal redress. Investigation revealed that the vendor and those associated with Faulkner, Bell and Company had sold their shares as early as 1882. A compromise financial arrangement was finally made in 1898. Once partial restitution had been made, the shareholders received 4s. 6d. per share from all assets other than the mining rights in Sierra County, California. When the claims were sold, another 2s. 4d. a share was paid. At a general meeting in 1899 the legal life of the company came to a close.[36] At least $225,000 had been squandered. Perhaps more important, the canny Scottish financiers were somewhat abashed to receive such a major set-back in western America.

This experience with the Scottish Pacific Coast Mining Company shaped the pattern of Scottish investment in western American mining in at least three important ways: Edinburgh was never again to become the headquarters for a significant mining venture in the nineteenth century; future Scottish overseas mining companies were to be sponsored by men of lesser capital and reputation, usually with headquarters in Glasgow; and when the great 'boom' of 1886–8 developed in London the problems with this company were so well-known that the excitement for the most part passed Scotland by.

The Scottish-American Mortgage Company, of Edinburgh, the friendly competitor of the Scottish-American Investment Company for profits in the United States, likewise made an initial investment in western American mining in the 1880s. Sheriff J.

Guthrie Smith, company chairman, visited New Mexico in 1881 on business for the mortgage company and the Prairie Land and Cattle Company. Frank L. Underwood showed him reports from engineers attesting to the unusual value of copper ores in the Copper Mountain District near Clifton in southeastern Arizona Territory.[37] He also noted the annual report of the acting governor of Arizona Territory in 1881 that remarked 'Besides its silver and gold, Arizona can show some of the largest copper deposits on the continent. Among them should be mentioned the famous Clifton mines.... This is a perfect mountain of copper ore. Its vast extent is not yet known. As far as workmen have penetrated, they have encountered rich ore.'[38] The upshot of these conversations was the organization of the Arizona Copper Company, Limited, in 1882, Scotland's most heavily capitalized mining venture of the nineteenth century. Although the early history of this company was a discouraging one, the property was to prove, in time, to be exceptionally valuable. Success was so long in coming, however, that the record of this company did not counterbalance the negative outlook toward mining venture in Scotland created by the history of the Scottish Pacific Coast Mining Company.[39]

While Scotland's leading capitalists still wrestled with the problems growing out of their major mining investments of 1881–2, *The Economist* announced the changing climate of opinion in London during 1885: 'The market for mining shares has undergone a wonderful transformation during the past few weeks, a great rush of speculative business having completely broken up a state of extreme stagnation which had lasted for several years.'[40] *The Statist* had also noted the trend and reported sadly 'The weary waiting and bitter disappointment which followed the mining mania of 1880–1 are now matters of history – perhaps almost forgotten by those who did not lose money. The majority of the concerns so gaily floated have disappeared into the limbo of liquidation.'[41] A word of warning was once again issued about foreign mines, particularly those in the United States:

> ... When novices meddle with foreign or Colonial mines, they play to lose. That is almost certain.... Taking the best case, that of a fairly honest mine, which might be worked at a profit under prudent management, it will be so loaded up with debentures, ordinary shares, preferred shares, and what not, that only an El Dorado could stand the brunt of it. The Americans themselves have very few mines of that class. They are got up exclusively for export....
>
> The getting-up of mines for the British market is an industry which has been cultivated by the financial genius of all nations. Our American cousins, of course, take the lead

in it; but they have competitors of every race, and we might truly say of every colour.[42]

The Scots, who had so recently tried their hand at gold mining in California and copper mining in Arizona, had already turned to Colorado in 1884. For obvious reasons Edinburgh investors shied away from all proposals for new mining ventures. Dundee residents concerned with overseas investments were occupied with the problems of the Arizona Copper Company. American proprietors of mining operations therefore came to Glasgow to seek the funds necessary to keep their declining enterprises going. Several merchants along the Clyde, who had no mining experience, registered a private company known as The Scottish Colorado Mining and Smelting Company, Limited, with an authorized capital of £250,000 in £1 shares. American shareholders in the Century Consolidated Mining and Smelting Company that owned mines and ore supplies in Boulder County, Colorado, exchanged their shares for 147,000 new ones in this company, and the Scots provided £5,000 cash in exchange for preferential shares entitled to a cumulative dividend of ten per cent per annum. If the business became profitable, plans called for a campaign to interest the public in the remaining stock. This was not the case: experiments with new smelting practices failed; the property had to be sold because mortgagors threatened to foreclose and the tax collector would not wait for back taxes. The whole assets of the company were swept away.[43] An American agent also prevailed upon Glaswegians to register the Richardson Gold and Silver Mining Company, Limited, to underwrite mining operations on three lode claims, all located in Russell Gulch, three miles from Central City. Capital of £50,000 was immediately subscribed, with £37,000 represented by ordinary shares going to the American owner and £13,000 by preferential shares awarded to Scots, who were guaranteed a one hundred per cent return on their cash before giving up their privileged position. Although the owner-manager had optimistically guaranteed a dividend of twenty per cent a year for the first two years, his plans must have gone awry for the company lasted a single year.[44] The third and largest investment proposed during the year was in the Colorado Silver Mines, Limited, that anticipated the purchase of several blocks of silver mines in Cunningham Gulch about seven miles from Silverton in San Juan County for $250,000 in cash and $250,000 in shares of the company, nominally capitalized at £200,000. The Chicago vendor and Glasgow promoters issued an elaborate prospectus quoting the *La Plata Miner* to the effect that the 'Pride of the West', principal mine of the seven to be transferred, was thirty feet wide and produced ore worth $65 a ton, including silver, lead, and some gold.

Scottish money was to be used to erect an elaborate concentration plant. The press reported potential dividends estimated at from fifteen to twenty-two per cent a year. This project, highly publicized both in the United States and Scotland, was not mentioned anywhere in the press after a few short months and all evidence suggests that the public did not subscribe for the shares.[45] In this single year American mining agents had learned that inexperienced Scots could be gulled into providing cash for mining concerns in the doldrums and with an uncertain future. The exchange that they demanded for cash was preferential shares. More often than not the company, as initially set up, was privately organized by men of moderate means, experience, and ability. If the decision was made to seek funds from the public, the company sponsors were not adverse to the circulation of a glowing prospectus of doubtful validity. Fortunately the investing public demonstrated caution, financial losses were comparatively small, and only the Scottish promoters suffered the penalty for their folly.

During the London boom of 1886–8 only one mining company was sponsored in Scotland, the Feather-Fork Gravel Company, Limited, to operate in Plumas and Sierra counties, California. A brief summary of the history of various mining techniques is essential to understanding the nature of this venture. In the first upsurge of English interest in California mines, 1870–3, the dominant type of investment had been hydraulic operations along the Feather, Yuba, Bear, and North Fork of the American rivers, all tributaries of the Sacramento River flowing out of the Sierra Nevada. As a result of the initial success of the Sweetland Creek Gold Mines, Limited, along the Yuba River, five additional hydraulic mining companies were launched within that three-year period. The British had scarcely started work when the farmers of the Sacramento River Valley complained about the damage being done to their farms and orchards by the debris washed down the mountain tributaries. The protest was organized on a twofold front, judicial and legislative. In the ensuing struggle between the agricultural and mining interests for political dominance, the British mining companies contributed money and time as well as such behind-the-scenes leadership as aliens could judiciously expend in a domestic political crisis. By 1880 it was clear that the farmers had won. Although the debris controversy ended in disaster for all hydraulic mining companies in California, most English-owned enterprises were doomed to failure before the legal battle came to an end.[46]

One type of hydraulic mining operations, known as 'deep placer mining' whereby shafts and tunnels were sunk to locate and exploit buried deposits that had been laid down by rivers in earlier geological ages and subsequently covered by debris, regained lost popularity in the 1880s because the gravel selected was largely free of dirt and debris and could be washed thoroughly without polluting the river systems.[47] Through San Francisco bankers, several Glaswegians had loaned £12,000 at ten per cent to help finance this type of hydraulic operation by California companies. Convinced that large-scale gravel operations would be profitable, they negotiated with an Oakland promoter to purchase every available claim along the headwaters of the forks of the Feather River. A company was formed, capitalized at £300,000 with 150,000 £1 shares transferred to the various vendors of approximately sixty-five mining claims. As usual, these shares were classified as deferred and their holders were to receive no dividends or have any control over the business until a sum equal to the amount called up on preferred shares, purchased with Scottish cash, had been paid. Moreover, the sums already loaned to several California companies whose claims had been taken over, were recorded as partial payments on preferred shares. By 1890 £1 had been called on each of 75,000 preferred shares and several Glasgow businessmen held as many as six to seven thousand shares. Publishers Walter and Robert Blackie and Leonard Low, millionaire shipbuilder of Glasgow, were among the heaviest investors.

In 1892 the Scottish company was concentrating its attention on the Thistle Shaft along five miles of the Gibsonville Channel, three miles south of the town of Gibsonville. This shaft had been sunk 535 feet to penetrate volcanic capping over the bed of an ancient river channel. Depth of the underground gravel deposit was one hundred feet in places, but the stratum of pay gravel was only a few feet. Each shaft leading into the deposit contained two cages upon which ore cars were hoisted from the bedrock to the rim; the empty cage went down as the loaded one was drawn up. There was room for only four men to work in these underground shafts at one time, but there were seventy-five employed by the company in other capacities at a $3 wage for an eight-hour day. Ore was transported to Downieville along a pack trail and then by a rough road to Oroville, fifty miles away, where there was a railroad. For years, carloads of gravel, averaging a ton each, were removed from the former river bed. Periodically work was suspended at one shaft and a new station opened up elsewhere along the channel. In 1895 the company erected a large boarding house for its employees, a covered dump house of fifteen thousand tons capacity, and a reservoir holding thirty thousand gallons of water for washing. Such capitalistic outlays necessitated periodic reorganization of the securities held in Glasgow. Profits were significant but they were all ploughed back into the operation and the

Scots never earned any dividend. The directors finally agreed in 1902 that they did not have a paying business and wound up their operations. Meanwhile, they had underwritten a thorough test of this type of mining with the best technological equipment that could be obtained. The difficulty was not inadequate funds or management, but inadequate gold deposits.[48]

The boom in overseas mining company formation in London suddenly collapsed toward the close of 1888, and two years later the export of British capital abroad came to a sudden halt with the Baring crisis of 1890. Decline in mining investment, that was apparent well in advance of the general economic depression, had been caused by numerous reports of fraud and extravagance and the general failure of the vast majority of mining enterprises to earn profits. Since the Scots had never been involved in the boom of promotions, the fluctuating pattern was not felt. Several prospecting companies, like Scottish California Gold Quartz Mining Company, Limited, and Leechman Prospecting Company, Limited, were financed and directed in Glasgow by an investment group composed of a merchant, a shipowner, a stationer, an accountant, and a solicitor, all of whom obviously knew little about mining. They employed San Francisco 'mining engineers and experts' to find suitable properties for purchase, but nothing worthy showed up and they lost only the small cost of their searches.[49] Other Scots provided funds to refinance and expand operations of the Creston Gold Mining Company in Saguache County, Colorado, but their support was not sufficient to save the enterprise.[50] The only Scottish mining endeavour of significance in this period was an attempt on the part of Edinburgh residents to introduce a new technological process for extracting gold from refractory ores in the Grass Valley District in California. The Pollok process included a roasting operation to induce oxidation in ores containing sulphur, iron, and pyrites prior to chlorination. The method had been used successfully in the Transvaal of South Africa, in Queensland, Australia, and in Chile, so patent rights were purchased to make an experiment in western America. An experimental claim, 'The Tracy' in Grass Valley, was purchased from an Omaha vendor. The Scots moved cautiously, shipping over a limited amount of experimental equipment from Glasgow. They installed a hermetically sealed chlorinating cylinder to further refine the refractory ores roasted by the Pollok process. Along with a few thousand pounds of ore and the customary chlorine-producing reagents, water was forced into the cylinder until a one hundred pound pressure was attained. The entire cylinder was then rotated. After the strong chloride liquor had dissolved out the gold in an hour or two, the contents were discharged on a filter bed lined with lead. The precipitated gold was collected from this bed every week or ten days and carefully washed until it gave no reaction when tested for gold chloride.[51] The company had crushing machinery to handle three times the amount of ore being used in the experiment, and contingent orders had been placed with a Glasgow firm to manufacture six of the chlorinating cylinders if the experiment proved successful and popular. However, results did not justify expansion so the Grass Valley, California, Gold Extracting (Pollok Patents), Limited, gave up after four years of work, 1890–4. The Scots had expended a modest £11,000 on a justifiable experiment that might well have paid them handsome dividends.[52] Two directors of the Second Scottish Investment Trust Company of Edinburgh, Holmes Ivory and J. Dick Peddie, were active in the management of this experiment and the trust company had invested funds directly. The majority of the shareholders were military and professional men.

Although the early 1890s were years of greatly reduced overseas investment, the Scots plodded along at their usual registration rate of about one new company a year in western America. Their interest was concentrated on Colorado exclusively between 1890 and 1893. The search was still for silver rather than for gold. One group of Glaswegians organized the Mining Development Syndicate (of Colorado) to find a promising claim. Unable to employ a satisfactory agent after two years, the Scots granted paid-up shares in their £20,000 company to several Colorado mining men in Denver, Silverton, Leadville, Boulder, and Caribou, hoping that a financial stake would spur their efforts to locate a worthwhile property. When this scheme failed, the Scottish directors allied with a London mining engineer who promised to help. After eight years of disappointment, the search was abandoned. Perhaps what was classified as bad luck was in reality a blessing in disguise because of the continuous fall in the price of silver.[53]

Another Scottish syndicate headed by Leonard Low, purchased H. A. W. Tabor's famous Poorman mine in the town of Caribou, the Grand Island District, twenty miles west of Boulder. As early as 1859–60 prospectors from the Central City area had roamed over the hills near Caribou but did not recognize the silver ore there. A decade later an old prospector saw a shipment of Nevada silver ore, observed the similarity with what he had seen at Caribou, and went back to locate the Poorman mine in 1869.[54] Peak production was reached between 1883 and 1888 when the mine had been sold to the Tabor Investment Company. In spite of Tabor's optimistic predictions about the property, little work was done in the next three years and he appeared to be holding it for speculative purposes.[55] The financial structure of the Poorman

Silver Mines (of Colorado), Limited, and its contract with Tabor included several innovations. The £130,000 capitalization was divided into 103,000 ordinary shares and 27,000 deferred shares. Holders of ordinary shares, that were in reality preferred shares, had a prior right to a fifteen per cent annual dividend. Once this was paid, yearly profits were to be divided with one-third to the ordinary shares and two-thirds to the deferred. Tabor took the bulk of his payment in 90,000 ordinary shares, but he also received 5,000 deferred shares, and £10,000 in cash. Glaswegians who subscribed for the remaining shares obligated themselves for £35,000 and periodic calls on these shares within the next eight years totalled £23,000. Several Scottish merchants and industrialists had subscribed for a thousand shares each.[56] As soon as the Scots took over the property, the mine was pumped out, new machinery was installed, and the *Boulder Herald* reported the mine was producing more silver than any other in the country.[57] The price of silver fell faster than the mine could increase production so operations were shut down.[58] Finally, the secretary reported the details of the company's demise to the Registration Office:

> ...The property has not been worked in many years and it was some years ago taken possession of by parties in America who had advanced monies on account of the property. The Directors would have put the company in liquidation a considerable time ago, but they had hoped that the price of silver would improve, and that probably some arrangement would be possible with the parties now in possession of the property for its being restarted, or that it might be sold on terms which would admit of some reversion to the shareholders. The recent fall in the price of silver and the difficulties in which the property now is, make any realisation in the directors' view, impossible, and there being no assets on this, I was instructed to take the company into liquidation.[59]

The chief problem was getting a quorum to attend a meeting that might authorize a legal end to the company. All evidence suggests that Tabor had unloaded the Poorman mine as the ore supply was approaching exhaustion and when the market for silver was on the downgrade, at the same time reserving a share in any profits that might develop as a result of the shrewd use of development capital provided by the Scots.

Through the Tabor Investment Company, the Scots managed to experiment with a new process for extracting the residue of gold and silver from the tailings accumulated at mines worked in earlier decades. A Glasgow company, known as the Cassell Gold Extracting Company, Limited, controlled a new patented process

17. *Clifton 1898, Arizona Copper Company's Colorado incline* (see p.165)

18. (overleaf) (a) *Morenci between 1905 and 1913;* (b) *Supply train brought up from Clifton to Morenci for Arizona Copper Company*

18 (a) *and* (b)

that it wished to try out in Colorado. However, a Denver company with rights to the MacArthur-Forrest process objected because their procedures were similar. Through the Tabor enterprise a consolidation of patents was arranged in the Gold and Silver Extraction Company of America, Limited, with an authorized capital of £110,000. This company was managed by a brewer, a shipowner, a doctor, and a director of the former Cassell Gold Extracting Company. During 1895–6, Scottish shareholders raised £38,600 for this unprofitable experiment, and Tabor and his friends began selling their shares. The company management insisted that the business was enduring and in 1902 cajoled shareholders into authorizing sale of £25,000 in debentures to raise capital. Two years later the directors elected to shift their operations to Jefferson County, Montana, where it was hoped the tailings would be more successfully and profitably worked than those in Colorado. When the time came to buy up additional mining dumps, the shareholders balked at a fantastic proposal to issue preference shares to new subscribers and grant them a bonus in ordinary shares. Instead they elected to accept their losses and close the business.[60]

Looking back over thirteen years of investment in the American mining kingdom since 1880, the Scots could not be proud of their ventures. Experienced Edinburgh capitalists, so successful in other types of investment in the United States, ran into serious difficulty in mining. Nevertheless, Glasgow solicitors and accountants encountered little difficulty in locating ironmakers, wine merchants, and ship builders who were willing to risk a few thousand pounds in the search for gold and silver, to introduce a new technical process, or even to underwrite or refinance a declining mine. They concentrated their investments in California and Colorado between 1880 and 1893, losing at least £150,000 in the Sierra Nevada and £75,000 in the Rockies through limited companies registered in Scotland. Most companies invested little and lost minimal amounts. The bulk of the California losses resulted from the swindle of the Pacific Coast Mining Company and the failure of the Feather-Fork Gravel Company. At the same time, much of the money had been spent on reasonable experiments in deep gravel operations and new processes for reclaiming gold and silver. The status of experiments in refining copper ore in Arizona had not yet been reported. Although the overall results had been disappointing, the record of mining companies registered and directed in Scotland had not been either as extensive or as miserable as that of the English. The wily Scots deliberately refrained from following the London investment pattern after their initial participation in the mania of 1881–2. They were unaffected by the cycle of 'boom and bust' as reported in London, nor were they concerned over the sudden popularity or decline of various mining districts in western America that seemed to control the flow and ebb of English capital. In the total British picture, the Scottish-registered companies risked little capital. Their total nominal capitalization for the entire period 1880–93 totalled £1,350,000, of which only a fraction was actually expended. By comparison, during a nine-month period of 1886, fifteen Anglo-American companies were registered in London with a capitalization of £2,560,000.[61] The fifty-six Anglo-American mining companies whose shares were dealt with on the London market in 1887 represented a nominal capital of £11,000,000, but, according to one authoritative journal, the actual amount subscribed to United States mines by English investors since 1870 was nearly £20,000,000. Only seven of these companies had paid consistent dividends. The editor of *The Statist* bitterly concluded 'So disappointing, indeed, have been the results of American mining to English investors that the feeling is largely entertained that it is only the rubbish that has found its way to this market, the few successful ventures having falsified the expectations of the vendors.'[62]

Many factors play a part in the poor record of Scottish mining ventures in western America. Perhaps foremost among these was lack of knowledge about mineral properties and inexperience in the science of their operation. Speculators, for the most part accountants, clerks, tradesmen, and lawyers, were in the forefront of many promotions and they worked with small capital in hopes that they would strike it rich in a wild gamble. Much of their illogical activity was based upon the unethical promotions of unscrupulous Americans. Even some of the more legitimate, continuous and systematic explorations in the mining of western America came to nothing because of the inability to find a reliable agent. Communication was far from perfect. Most skilled Scottish capitalists found sufficient and more reliable investments in land mortgages and railway securities, and their decision to concentrate on these worked for their personal profits and for the best interest of the homeland.

Chapter Seven

The Arizona Copper Company: Scotland's Greatest Mining Venture

Under sponsorship of the directors of the Scottish-American Mortgage Company, the Arizona Copper Company, registered in 1882, had a heavy capitalization of £875,000 divided into 160,000 preferred shares of £5 and 75,000 deferred shares of £1. Preferred shares, held by those subscribing investment capital, were to receive a cumulative preference dividend of ten per cent per annum. Any additional profits were to be split, with one half going to the preferred shareholders, to be divided among them as a group, and the other half to the deferred shareholders. These last shares were largely held by capitalists in Edinburgh who sponsored the mining company and by the American promoters who had received deferred shares for their services. The investing public, eager to participate in a company launched under such promising auspices, applied for the shares many times over the number available and these securities were being exchanged freely after allotment at a forty per cent premium. The financial risk was great and the company history was turbulent.[1]

As early as 1868 a prospector and Army scout, Robert Metcalf, had displayed a sackful of rich copper ore in Silver City, New Mexico, which had been taken from a mountain peak alongside Chase creek, a tributary of the San Francisco River, about one hundred miles to the west. A storekeeper who was present obtained and forwarded the ore to his financial backer Henry Lesinsky [Leszynsky] in Las Cruces. Lesinsky had worked in the gold mines of Australia and the silver mines of Nevada before joining his uncle, Julius Freudenthal, and his brother, Charles Lesinsky, in the mercantile business. The sight of rich ore fired Henry's imagination and soon he was off to the mines with Metcalf, the Silver City merchant, and four armed men. Their trail led into unknown and dangerous country. After four days of riding, they discovered fresh moccasin tracks left by Apaches and decided it was best to travel by night. At last they encamped at the foot of a mountain designated the 'Longfellow' by Metcalf, who had first found copper there. After dismounting, unpacking and tying their horses, the men found a cave in which to cache their food and blankets, and climbed the hill to see the blue and green croppings of copper ore. On their return, excitement turned to dismay when they found the horses and supplies gone. The prospectors realized that these had been stolen by a small band of Apaches who had followed them unnoticed for several days. Exercising caution, the fortune seekers returned on foot to the nearest ranching outpost. Metcalf and Lesinsky both feigned a lack of anxiety, or even concern, about the discovery. Metcalf's patience was exhausted first, and in 1870 he asked Lesinsky to take an interest in the mine and become his partner. After much haggling, Lesinsky secured a controlling interest for $10,000, with the understanding he would furnish supplies from his stores in Las Cruces and Silver City, with Metcalf paying his proportionate part. Lesinsky returned to Las Cruces, and with his uncle and brother organized the Longfellow Mining Company. In 1873 Metcalf sold his remaining interest to Lesinsky for $20,000, and the entire Longfellow property passed into the hands of the three partners.[2] Metcalf was willing to sell the Longfellow because the previous season he had ascended the Chase creek canyon for about seven miles to Shannon Mountain and there located another group of copper claims, the most promising of which he named for himself.[3]

Another group of miners from Pinos Altos, a gold camp near Silver City, had prospected in the area during the summer of 1870. Although disappointed in finding no paying gold deposits, these men had observed copper outcroppings. Their enthusiasm for copper mining was so meagre that they did not register claims until 1872 when the ownership of the 'Arizona', 'Central', 'Yankie', and 'Moctezuma' were recorded. These four claims were purchased by E.D. Ward, a wealthy Detroit steamboat owner, who paid the discoverers $2,000 for each location and all expenses of preliminary development and patent. Ward incorporated the Detroit Copper Company and sent out an old steamboat captain, inexperienced in mining, to operate the mines. Miners interested in these various claims had organized the Copper Mountain Mining District.[4]

Throughout the seventies, owners of the Longfellow struggled to develop their property, brought in Mexican metal workers, experimented with primitive smelters, and worried about getting men and supplies through Apache country. In 1873 they erected the first adobe smelter with a capacity of about a ton of ore a day. The fuel used was charcoal supplied from rude kilns in the Burro Mountains, eighty miles distant. Burro trains carrying out the partly-refined copper, moulded into pigs of 150 pounds, stopped on the return to process and load charcoal in the mountains. There was no doubt about the richness of the ore. The outcropping on the surface of the Longfellow was only about 250 feet, but as the miners sought the vein they penetrated ore everywhere they dug. The place was turned into an open quarry. An early shipment of seventy-five tons of ore was carried by pack train to Silver City and from there to La Junta, Colorado, a railroad terminus, eight hundred miles distant from the mines. Transported by rail to a Baltimore refinery, this ore yielded thirty-five per cent copper. From the beginning, the greatest drawback to development of the rich deposits was the inadequacy of transportation.[5] The Texas Pacific Railroad was being built across Texas towards New Mexico and the Lesinsky Brothers watched its construction eagerly, announcing that once the railroad was completed they would employ a thousand men at the Longfellow and that the entire Clifton district could support ten thousand.[6] To connect the mine and furnace, the Lesinskys built a 'baby-gauge' railroad twenty inches wide. In the early years, mules provided the motive power, but nevertheless this railroad was the first constructed in Arizona. In time the line was extended from Chase creek up a dizzy incline into Morenci, the site of the Detroit Copper Company's furnaces, by way of 'Yankie', 'Humboldt', and other copper mines. Lesinsky and his associates also acquired the Coronado group of mines, and then extended the narrow-gauge line up the canyon to these claims and those of Metcalf.[7] During the time the copper deposits were worked by the Lesinsky Brothers, an estimated 20,000,000 pounds of copper bullion was produced in their furnaces.[8] The ore smelted was rich carbonate, that averaged about twenty per cent metal, but much of the copper was lost because of the crude methods of treatment. The slag dump became a treasure at a later day when its contents were reworked by improved furnaces and refineries.[9]

By 1880 mining journals in San Francisco and New York were printing accounts from the Arizona newspapers about the fabulous wealth of the region. According to these articles, usually written by mining engineers, a force of approximately one hundred and ten men, Mexicans and Chinese, worked at the Longfellow, at least five hundred more were employed elsewhere in the Clifton area, an additional one thousand were used as woodburners and freighters, and, in all, 25,000 were supported by the copper operations. An estimated 50,000 tons of twenty to twenty-five per cent copper ore was in sight at the Longfellow. At the price of twenty-three cents a pound in 1880, the total income from this mine alone would run between five and six million dollars. Mining engineers insisted profits 'almost beyond arithmetical computation' awaited capitalists with funds sufficient to build an adequate smelter and provide a transportation outlet.[10]

Value of these properties was immeasurably increased when the Southern Pacific Railroad, which had replaced the Texas Pacific in constructing the line along the thirty-second parallel through Arizona and New Mexico, finally reached Lordsburg. Only seventy miles from the mines, this new connection would soon simplify transit to the Gulf of Mexico ports, and from there the copper ore could be shipped to refineries along the Atlantic coast or to Swansea, Wales. Realizing this, the Scots seized the opportune moment to purchase all the available properties at the confluence of Chase creek and the San Francisco River and to organize the Arizona Copper Company. The leading groups of mines obtained were the Longfellow, Coronado, Metcalf, and Queen. Lesinsky and his partners received $1,200,000 for their holdings and Metcalf was given $300,000. Try as they would, the Scots could not prevail upon Ward to sell his Detroit Copper Company.[11]

In addition to the mining claims, the Scots purchased the reduction works in Clifton consisting of three furnaces for smelting ore and a company store. With a predominantly Mexican population of 10,000, this mining camp was the metropolis of Graham County. It boasted of 'a newspaper, the *Clarion*, a school, 2 hotels, 8 stores, and saloons more than sufficient for its needs'.[12] The surrounding country was devoted to cattle ranches where men divided their time between raising steers and fighting Indians. In the year that the Scots took over the copper operations, the Apache Indians attacked miners on the outskirts of the district. They remained in the hills around Clifton until 1885.[13]

In characteristic fashion, the Edinburgh syndicate spent capital lavishly in making improvements in the mining and processing of copper ore. When the Scots took over operations, coke obtained at the rail terminus in Lordsburg was replacing charcoal, but the intense heat produced by coke forced a modification in refining operations with the substitution of copper water jackets in the furnaces. In addition to remodelling the old furnaces, construction was begun on a new and larger one. The Southern Pacific Railroad was approached about a co-operative project to construct a branch railroad from Lordsburg, New Mexico, to Clifton. Realizing that construction of the line was imperative, the Scots, without waiting for a reply, authorized a road survey.[14]

J. Duncan Smith, managing director, spent the winter of 1882–3 in the United States on an inspection trip for the various Scottish companies under his direction. Upon his return, shareholders were called together in extraordinary session to hear a discouraging report. In spite of the potential wealth of the mines, profits had been negligible for several reasons. The crude and inconvenient arrangement of the old smelter, where coke had to be carried up to the furnace floors on the backs of men, had raised labour costs excessively. Cost of freight to New York where the bullion was further refined pushed production figures higher. At the same time copper prices had steadily declined, dropping from seventeen to fifteen cents a pound within the short period since the Scots took over. Finally, a cave-in at the Longfellow mine had cut off access to the richest deposits of ore.[15]

In addition to the problems in Arizona, shareholders were in disagreement concerning the financial structure of the company. A scheme had evolved for the commutation of deferred shares. The plan was to purchase these shares held by Underwood, his American associates, and the original directors at a premium and then to convert them into a second issue of preferred shares at the rate of £2 for each old £1 deferred share. Some of the original preferred shareholders expressed reservations on the grounds that they were losing their preferential position and demanded equal representation on the Board for holders of preferred stock. The Americans also objected for quite different reasons. They apparently still anticipated annual profits far in excess of ten per cent and wanted to hold on to their claim of one-half the annual profits above that figure. The directors, caught in the cross-fire, suggested that Scottish capitalists who had been invited to join the Board had refused because they disliked the existence of two classes of shares. Fearful that litigation might develop, the directors consulted lawyers, who concluded that the proposal might lead to legal difficulties because it would involve 'a purchase by the company of its own shares, not authorized by the memorandum of association'. Many shareholders were unhappy over the impasse that had developed.[16] Moreover, although an initial quarterly dividend had been declared in November 1882, on the basis of six per cent a year, continuing outlay of capital on railroad and smelter construction coupled with a reduction in the margin of profits made the declaration of dividends impossible. In this time of difficulty, the Board strengthened the prestige of the company by securing the services of Sir George Warrender as a director. Leading shareholders suggested that this appointment was only a beginning in the right direction and insisted that a mining engineer of known competence be added to the directorate.[17]

The investing public in Scotland followed developments with inordinate interest, and newspapers and magazines published all available news, printed letters from correspondents, and volunteered editorial comment. The editor of the *Scottish Banking and Insurance Magazine* critically appraised the first annual company report, noted that the figures of potential production were much less than those in the prospectus and that statements were more carefully guarded than in 1882. In his opinion, the directors had demonstrated little managerial skill. Immediate profits for investors were now clearly impossible.[18] When the narrow-gauge Arizona and New Mexico Railway connecting Clifton and Lordsburg was completed in July 1883, one correspondent of *The Edinburgh Courant* immediately suggested that this further increased the risk of shareholders: 'In addition to the working of a mine subject to 'Caves in', falls in the price of copper, and visits from hostile Indians, they have now to operate nearly ninety miles [actually seventy] of railway, and pay interest on its cost of construction.'[19] In this man's opinion, there was no hope for profits.

The discouraging reports and adverse public opinion caused 'Arizonas' to drop 6s. each week in July. This brought forth many letters from stockholders. Some suggested the increased exchange of shares at depreciated prices was caused by rumours of litigation with the American vendors that would embarrass the company. Others stated that some shareholders were ready to call for an inquiry into company management. The more sanguine insisted that investors should hold their shares until the end of the next financial year of the company, to disregard the rush to sell stock fostered by 'bears' who were gambling on the fluctuations on the Stock Exchange. The £5 preferred shares were selling for 56s.[20] The correspondence became so acrimonious that the *Courant* finally issued a statement that 'as far as this journal is concerned we...would be glad neither to see nor hear anything further about Arizona until it suits the directors to make public some authentic official information as to what is being done at the mines'.[21] Future letters were acknowledged, but the contents not printed.

The situation was so confused that various interested parties made arrangements to send inspectors to Arizona to procure reliable information. Colin Mackenzie, a Scottish director, returned and reported that four smelters were operating in Clifton, a new deposit of rich red oxides had been found on a hitherto unworked claim, the Longfellow was reopened, the ore from the Coronado was proving to be of exceptionally high quality, and a tramway there had been completed.[22] Meanwhile, a group of stockholders, dissatisfied with reports from official representatives of the Board, employed H. R. Lewis and Company of London to make an 'unbiased appraisal'. This agency sent a University of Pennsylvania engineer into the Southwest to find the answer to these questions: Is the company a legitimate enterprise? How valuable are the properties? Will the railroad pay? What is the whole investment likely to earn in a year? His final report estimated the value of the mining holdings at $3,000,000, with an earning power of fifteen per cent per annum. When this news was released, the editor of the *Scottish Banking and Insurance Magazine* inquired as to the purpose and validity of unofficial inspectors' reports.

Who were the people who secured the aid of Lewis and Company? Was it the disgruntled, or an unofficial action of the Board? Was this a scheme to raise public estimation of the company? Lewis and Company announced permission had been given to make the report public, yet who had granted the permission? Arizona shares had risen slightly following the report, but soon tumbled to a new low of 43s. At this stage of developments, the editor elected to take steps to end the anxiety by sending an agent of his journal to Arizona to see how the mines were managed, to check on the value of the property and the possibility of profits. This was deemed justifiable because the public had been 'open-mouthed' looking for news since the heavy investment following issuance of the prospectus. According to the editor, the directors were apparently trying, by inspectors' reports and occasional vague statements, to push up the price of shares. The managing director of the Arizona Copper Company was notified of the magazine's intent and asked to postpone the annual September meeting until an investigator could return. Meanwhile, the magazine published a list of shareholders with their respective holdings. Attention was called to the fact that J. Guthrie Smith and J. Duncan Smith had invested trust money. The name of Frank L. Underwood of Kansas City was conspicuously absent. When inquiry was made at the Arizona Company offices, it was explained as a clerical omission. Had he really pulled out? Bankers in Trinidad, Colorado, and Cimarron, New Mexico, had reduced their holdings. Were the Americans preparing to leave the enterprise entirely? The editor promised to write about the 'notorious company' in every issue to come. The emotional anxiety was increased because many investors in Arizona copper had also purchased shares in the Scottish Pacific Coast Mining Company seeking California gold. Mounting evidence suggested that the highly successful Edinburgh investment syndicates were about to experience their first financial reverses.[23]

The Clifton *Clarion*, speaking for Arizona residents, continued its praises of the improvements made by the energetic Scots. In August digging was being concentrated at new mines in the Metcalf group, particularly at the 'Little Annie'. Tons of copper ore were being piled up. At the 'Little Giant', 'small lumps of copper are found, about the size of hen eggs, which are nearly pure copper'. A new blacksmith shop was constructed near the company store.[24] The Copper Mountain District was so valuable that New Mexico residents started a movement to have the Arizona-New Mexico territorial boundary line resurveyed. The Governor of New Mexico was convinced the property was in his Territory and promised the creation of a new county carved from Grant and Socorro counties in New Mexico, with Clifton as the county seat, if his opinion was confirmed by the survey.[25]

The long-awaited director's report was released to an extraordinary meeting on 20 October 1883. The original capital account had been expended: £583,000 had been spent for the mines, £100,000 had gone into new furnaces, £100,000 in the construction of the railway to Lordsburg, and preliminary expenses had consumed the balance. Additional mining development and tramway construction had been financed on credit and these obligations totalled £268,652. Attempts had been made to procure long-term loans in the United States, with Underwood's endorsement, but these had not been forthcoming. To take care of the current difficulties, the directors proposed to issue £300,000 in redeemable debentures secured by special assignment of the railroad to trustees. These were offered at ten per cent annual interest for a ten-year period, but the company was empowered to redeem them any time after five years by paying an additional ten per cent. To make matters worse, a legal flaw had been found in the company's land titles. When the company was being formed, Duncan Smith had sought legal counsel in Trinidad, Colorado on the land tenure question. He had been advised that the United States statutes did not prohibit the acquisition of mining property by aliens once the title had passed from the government. After complying with statutory requirements, such as registration, an alien corporation could purchase real estate from a private individual or company and hold such property in the territories of the United States. Underwood and Company had elected to organize an American corporation under the laws of Arizona Territory, known as Arizona Copper Company of Clifton, that purchased the mining properties. The Edinburgh company then became the trustee for the land holdings. London legal opinion now suggested this was not in line with the memorandum of association that spoke only of buying and working mines and failed to mention holding land titles, or for that matter operating railroads. The company was in a position to be challenged for violating British law.[26]

When these developments were made public, a barrage of comment reached the newspapers. The editors of the *Dundee Advertiser* and *The Edinburgh Courant*, stunned into silence, printed them without comment. At this point William Lowson of Dundee retired from the Board of Directors because of 'unpleasant insinuations' against him and his co-directors. Sheriff Guthrie Smith relinquished the chairmanship and George Auldjo Jamieson, a lesser shareholder but a man with mining experience, agreed to pilot the company out of its insolvent condition. Upon retiring, members of the old Board admitted the company had not met expectations, but insisted that it possessed the richest mining land in the United States and future developments would prove the wisdom of the heavy investment. The ever-critical editor of the *Scottish Banking and Insurance Magazine* concluded 'No one seems to believe in the concern but the directors themselves.'[27]

The newly-organized Board acted swiftly in an attempt to restore public confidence. The members proposed to cancel the anticipated debenture sale and to solve both questions of financial embarrassment and land title by organizing a new company with broader powers, the Arizona Trust and Mortgage Company, Limited. This new company had a capital of £360,000 divided into 120,000 shares. A call of £1 a share was to be made and invitations issued for debentures at seven-per-cent interest up to the limit of the uncalled capital, £240,000. Once the funds were raised, £350,000 was to be lent to the Arizona Copper Company on security of the entire property in Arizona. The Copper Company was to pay ten per cent on the loan. Thus, the total liability of the company was increased to £1,225,000.[28] Sir George Warrender and the men associated with him in the Scottish Pacific Coast Mining Company, still had confidence in western mining investments and they constituted a majority of the Board of the Arizona Trust and Mortgage Company. William J. Menzies became president and James Cowan, James L. Lawrie, and Thomas Nelson assumed obligations as trustees. Thus, the two Edinburgh investment syndicates interested in western America since 1873–4 merged their resources to see this mining venture through the crisis.[29] The memorandum of association was drawn so that the trust company had ample power to hold title to the lands in possession either of the Clifton corporation or by the trustees of the Edinburgh copper company. Procedures were also established for the future amalgamation of all the various companies associated with the production and sale of Arizona copper.[30]

Still sympathetic to the copper venture, the *Courant* urged the public and old shareholders to subscribe to the new company.[31] The more cautious *Scottish Banking and Insurance Magazine* insisted that everything depended on the basic value of the mining property. Those going into the new trust company were part owners of the mines. As long as the £35,000 annual interest payments were forthcoming, investors would get a good return on their money, but the editor obviously thought this would not be long.[32] Nevertheless, applications for both shares and debentures were rapidly received and the trust and mortgage company proceeded through the final stages of registration. Even the copper undertaking's greatest critics admitted that the mortgage company was secure, in part from the value of the narrow-gauge Arizona and New Mexico Railroad, and foreclosure would always protect the trust investors.[33]

This company reorganization by no means solved the problems of the Scottish investors. The new Board had employed a San Francisco mining expert to report on the current situation in Arizona. Meanwhile, deficits continued to pile up and during the financial crisis all work not immediately productive had been shut down. The railroad was opened to public use for passengers and freight in an attempt to bring in revenue. During March 1884 Arizona shares dropped to an all-time low of 8s., representing only eight per cent of the original investment. The next month the report from the independent mining engineer arrived concluding that the price originally paid for the mines was far beyond their actual value. Managerial incompetence had caused additional losses to the company. Furthermore, the erection of new smelting works had been on too large and elaborate a scale for the promise of the mines. Only the Longfellow had yielded a profit; the Queen and Coronado had been operated at a great loss and work there should be suspended; the Metcalf, if properly managed, might show a slight profit.[34] Immediately following release of this report to the press, three of the directors, Sheriff Guthrie Smith, Duncan Smith, and Thomas J. Gordon, resigned from the directorate. The only directors left were Sir George Warrender, Jamieson, and Colin Mackenzie. Duncan Smith agreed to remain on as managing director but without a seat on the Board. The prevalent opinion was that the original directors, although men of ability, finally recognized the fact that they did not know anything about copper and were now acting on the principle of self-preservation.[35]

In an editorial exposé, *The Edinburgh Courant* accused all the 'inner circle' of the company, with the exception of Duncan Smith, of speculating in shares, buying when prices were low and selling when high. Evidence was present to show that Lowson, Gordon, Guthrie Smith, Underwood, and an associate Willard R. Green, had made profits of £13,080. The directors had withheld official information from the shareholders while they took advantage of the intelligence to buy or sell shares advantageously. The editor placed most of the blame on Underwood, who was already demanding exorbitant prices for his deferred interest in the Prairie Cattle Company from Scots desiring to terminate all business connections with his Kansas City firm. The newspaper suggested that the American banker believed 'that men who have money live for the benefit of men who have brains.... He has been the lion they feared, and they [the Scots] have been the jackals that assiduously purveyed for him.... When he was not selling shares at a big premium he was dictating a new secret agreement to give him some fresh advantage over the unsuspecting shareholders.' The *Courant* editor, who had exercised more patience with the Board of the copper company than most Scottish journalists, bristled in indignation at the realization that he, too, had been duped and concluded 'Never has a Board... presumed... to put its shareholders so completely on one side. Never a Board so coolly and systematically strained its authority; never one so liberally helped itself out of the common fund, and did so little for its extravagant fees.'[36]

Company affairs had indeed reached a crisis. No clear title was yet in the hands of the directors, and when it was ascertained that Underwood contemplated the speedy removal of his large capital resources from Scotland, the new directors of the copper company were forced to take legal action to preserve recourse to these funds, in hopes of protecting the shareholders against any additional loss. By their manipulation of the company shares, the original directors, many of whom were men of distinguished reputation, had made themselves liable for charges before the court. Jamieson called a meeting of shareholders and asked for a vote of confidence in handling the delicate negotiations. The chairman explained at great length the circumstances that had brought the company to its lamentable condition. The time had come, he thought, for the American vendors to know that the company was prepared, if driven to extremities, to force fulfilment of all its claims. On the other hand, the Board had no intention of being the instruments of vindictiveness against the first Board of Directors. If the shareholders wanted to push affairs to the bitter end, they should elect another group of directors. Neither would the new Board follow an imbecile policy of not demanding a financial settlement from all concerned. Their chief aim was to avoid litigation and to adjust the conflict of interests on a rational, equitable basis. The remaining directors had agreed to continue to occupy their places on the Board only with the distinct understanding that their decisions would not be questioned by the shareholders. They resigned in a body and were re-elected with the stockholders fully aware of the situation. The new Board hoped to avert the ruin of the company and, if that were impossible, to take steps to mitigate the destruction. Should the matter of land titles ultimately be overcome, and the company relieved of financial pressure, there was still hope that some moderate degree of prosperity might be attained. No promises were made and the chairman noted 'it certainly need surprise no one if the termination of the company should be found only in liquidation'.[37] On situations like this, *The Statist* of London commented:

> One of the most curious, and for the cynical person the most entertaining, studies in psychology is to be found at a meeting of shareholders of a Mining Company that has come to grief. ... It will be an exceptional indignation meeting if there are not a few clergymen present, and a shrewd lawyer or two; possibly two or three authorities on 'sound investments,' and a small crowd of hard-fisted fellows who are generally credited with being well able to take care of their money. The retired trader or the superannuated civilian, who has fancied all his life that his light was being hid under a bushel, often takes to Mining Shares in his old age, just to show his friends what he might have done had his opportunities been equal to his ability and his pluck. Sooner or later he lands in the inevitable mess.... [The mine] generally takes the shortest cut it can find into bankruptcy, and its life is a fitful succession of liquidations and reconstruction, as in the case of the much-lamented Emma Mine, or the rocket-like Arizona. And yet what swarms of long-headed men were drawn into both these 'wild-cat' speculations![38]

In July 1884, the directors called an extraordinary meeting of stockholders to dissolve the Arizona Copper Company, and to found another company with the same name. In the process, several legal manipulations secured the land title and absorbed the deficit into the capital account. All assets and liabilities of the old company, including the debt to the Arizona Trust and Mortgage Company, were transferred to the new Arizona Copper Company registered in August 1884.[39]

By the end of 1884, the Arizona Copper Company had established an efficient mining and railroad business. A thorough inspection of the mines revealed that the earliest reports about a 'mountain of copper' existing near Clifton were correct and that the adverse reports from the San Francisco expert a few months earlier had been misleading. The Longfellow remained the principal mine owned by the company. Located about five miles from the smelter, this claim near the summit of a rugged mountain rising 1,500 feet above Chase creek had been opened by a tunnel 200 feet below the apex of the mountain. A second tunnel was being dug 200 feet below. Over five miles of underground passages had been excavated to reach the large ore chambers. The Metcalf group, three miles up the creek, were also along the slopes of another 1,200-foot mountain peak. One of these mines, the 'Little Annie', had been pierced by two tunnels to extract the rich red oxide ore. The 'Oriental', adjoining the 'Little Annie', showed traces of old Indian workings where the red men had extracted chrome iron and bromide for their paint. This mine, the 'Little Giant', and the 'King', all in the Metcalf group, had extensive deposits, but their exact size was not yet determined. The Coronado group, five miles further upstream, was approached by an incline leading from the narrow-gauge railroad that ran up the canyon. A tunnel was driven through this mountain for 1,200 feet following the ore vein. Ore obtained here contained silica and had to be mixed with other ores to smelt easily. In all, the Arizona Copper Company owned some forty claims. The smelting and refining works were located at Clifton near the confluence of Chase creek and the San Francisco River, a tributary of the Gila River. Here the face of a towering cliff of 500 feet had been blasted down for over 100 feet and four terraces formed on which the buildings and machinery of the company had been erected. On the upper terrace, fifty feet above the furnace floors, ore bins had been built. These were compartmentalized and the narrow-gauge railroad ran along the dividing partitions so that the cars could deposit ore from the mines in the proper bin. When needed the ores and fluxes from this storehouse on the highest terrace were drawn off by opening gates to tramways conveying the materials to the crushing house on the second terrace. Once prepared for the furnaces, the ore was delivered to storage rooms on the third terrace. Coke bins were also located here, along with special containers for fine ore that needed no crushing. The narrow-gauge railroad network connected all these structures on the third level with the mines, smelter, and the rail line to Lordsburg. Thus, a minimum amount of labour was needed to deliver ore to the smelters. All the bins were filled daily so that the smelters could run throughout the night. Five furnaces were kept in operation constantly. Three of these, built by Messrs Fraser and Chalmers of Chicago, had a sixty-ton daily capacity; two others, constructed by Messrs Rankin, Brayton, and Company of San Francisco, were capable of handling thirty tons each. The San Francisco River had been dammed and a flume constructed, utilizing the flow of water to generate power for turbine wheels and blowers. Should this source of power become unavailable, engines had been installed to meet the emergency. No enterprise in the American West for the production of copper bullion had been so well organized and equipped.[40] The plant had a capacity to produce 30,000 pounds of copper a day, and, in the month of November 1884, 640,000 pounds of bullion was actually produced, ninety-seven and one-half per cent fine. As only one refining process was necessary, these mines were considered to be in shape to compete effectively with those in the Lake Superior region.[41]

Unfortunately, just as the problems of refining and transportation had been solved, another development seriously disturbed the management and the shareholders: the overproduction of copper. Reductions in the cost of production could not keep up with declining price. When the company was projected, the price of copper was nineteen cents a pound; in January 1885 it was slightly more than eleven.[42] During the last three months of 1884, cost of producing copper at Clifton was in excess of the price that could be realized. Reductions in wages and the selection of the better ores for smelting brought a small margin of profit in the first quarter of 1885, but not enough to counterbalance the losses at the close of 1884. The company managed to pay the interest on all borrowed money out of profits from the railroad and the store. The Board solemnly announced 'There can be no profit directly from the manufacture of copper, until the market price rises.'[43] The financial situation remained unchanged for the next two years. The mines continued to produce quantities of copper bullion but at a loss. Profits from rents, store sales, and the railroad were used to pay the interest owed the Arizona Trust and Mortgage Company. Chairman Jamieson laboured valiantly, hoping to earn enough to make a payment on the principal.[44]

At the annual meeting of both companies in 1886, shareholders agreed to a programme of amalgamation and each appointed a committee of shareholders to confer with the respective Boards in working out an understanding.[45] The Arizona Copper Company had travelled a devious and rocky road, but now the enterprise was to have a unified organization and, for the first time, harmony and respect existed between directors and shareholders. As the editor of *The Statist* later observed 'Starting with a maximum of confidence and unbounded expectation on the one hand, and a minimum of experience and practical knowledge on the other, it really was little wonder that the earlier direction of this company's affairs should so quickly furnish a new illustration of the old adage "Pride goeth before a fall".'[46] When the fall came, it was severe, but the company picked itself up, reorganized and looked to a profitable future.

During 1887 attempts had been made to organize several European syndicates to gain control of the world supply of both copper and tin. A predominantly French syndicate, with Paris headquarters, was finally successful, and early in 1888 the directors of the Arizona Copper Company were requested to join the organization in a desperate effort to drive up the price.[47] There were misgivings about the ability of any association to maintain

19. (a) *Ore car employees of Arizona Copper Company, Clifton, about 1893;* (b) *Morenci, Arizona*

20. Sir George Warrender, Director, Scottish-American Investment Company, Limited, Edinburgh

the price of copper in face of the increasing supply. British investors had holdings in the copper mines in Spain, the Cape of Good Hope, and Chile, as well as in the United States. Although large-scale copper mining in the United States was of recent growth, the Lake Superior, Montana, and Arizona mines had quickly become sizeable producers. Their output was so large that any syndicate, attempting to control production, had to enter into contracts for their ore.[48]

The copper association gave the Arizona Copper Company a three-year contract for its entire output. Directors of the company planned to submit the agreement negotiated in Paris to the shareholders, but other members of the syndicate raised objection, so the officers 'accepted, with reluctance but with no hesitation, the responsibility for closing the transaction'. They did announce that if the minimum price the syndicate expected to demand was obtained and only the minimum of past production was reached, the average revenue would be approximately £80,000 annually under the agreement, enough to pay a dividend. They summarized their viewpoint as follows:

> It would be impossible, and it would, if possible, be inexpedient to lay before the shareholders all the reasons which have induced the Board to go into this arrangement. The Directors are themselves unanimously and strongly of the opinion that the transaction is prudent and advantageous, and they have the satisfaction of knowing that this is the view entertained by the trustees of the Mortgage Company.[49]

This agreement marked a turning point in the company history.

Plans of the syndicate meanwhile received harsh criticism. W. B. Lawson, city editor of the *Financial News* of London issued a pamphlet, 'The Crisis in Copper', in which he applied the disparaging title of *ring* to the group attempting to control the supply and price of copper and thereby enhance the value of company shares on the world's stock exchanges. He denied the possibility of success for the scheme in view of rapidly increasing production coupled with steadily reducing consumption. Lawson's negative outlook toward the copper industry was already well known, for he had written an article, 'The Deluge of Copper', in the London *Times* during 1885 that undoubtedly had aggravated the already distressed copper market throughout the world. *The Engineering and Mining Journal* of New York challenged Lawson's view:

> We think it too soon yet to predict the actual effects of the current price of copper.... We cannot believe that the return of 16½ cents, which, until recently, was a low price, and one under which the consumption of copper rapidly increased is now fatal to its use.

> While a cheaper metal may replace it for some purposes, the demand for entirely new applications is growing. For instance, no substitute for copper for electrical transmissions of power has been or is likely to be proposed. Here we have an entirely new field for copper, which promises to be to the copper trade what steel rails are to the iron trade.
>
> The cost of mining, smelting, and manufacturing copper is really the element which will determine its price, and the experience of the past few years proves that the price to which the metal dropped was too low to secure the supply for the world's wants.[50]

At the end of 1888, Jamieson announced that annual earning of the company, due to sales to the syndicate, was £130,000, six times the annual average for the last five years and sixty per cent more than had been anticipated at the time the agreement in Paris had been reached. The initial success of the syndicate forced the price of copper up to seventeen cents a pound and copper shares began to exchange hands on the market at an ever-increasing figure. Writing an editorial on Arizona Copper, the editor of *The Statist* remarked 'The present price of the shares have certainly ample room for participating in the advance which has already taken place in shares of the leading companies.' This comment caused an active business in Arizona shares, and within the third week of September 1888 the price had risen from 23s. to over 33s. This price was still deemed low in view of the current earning capacity of the company.[51]

The prosperity of 1888 made it possible for the Arizona Copper Company to start shedding the last legacy of the initial mismanagement. The directors of the copper company and the trust and mortgage company agreed upon a programme of gradual amalgamation and a reorganization of capital. As an initial step, £1 was written off the preferred £5 shares in the copper company to take care of an operational deficit built up prior to 1888. Total indebtedness to the trust and mortgage company amounted to £438,751. Directors of the copper company agreed to issue £266,000 ten per cent debentures to partially meet this obligation. These funds were converted into first mortgage sterling bonds of the copper company, and were delivered to the trust directors with an additional £90,000 cash. On the basis of this partial payment of the indebtedness, shareholders in the copper enterprise were permitted to participate with the trust certificate holders in any distribution of profits that might accrue from copper operations. No longer did the annual fixed interest charges of £35,000 stand in the way of a declaration of dividends.[52]

Shareholders received no benefit from this amalgamation, however, for the copper syndicate was never again as successful as in 1888. It struggled to maintain the price of copper above fourteen cents a pound for three years, but in 1891 copper values began to slide back to the levels of 1885–6, until an all-time low was reached in 1894.[53] At the annual meeting of 1893 the shareholders of the Arizona Copper Company were told of the impact on their enterprise. Although cost of production had been steadily reduced each year since 1888, the fall in copper prices had left a deficit.[54] Among other discouraging developments, a spring flood of 1891 had cost the company $100,000. High water had destroyed the homes of Mexican labourers, the approaches and bridge of the Arizona and New Mexico Railway across the San Francisco River were washed away as well as an iron bridge across the Gila River at Guthrie.[55] In spite of all these setbacks, the Scots doggedly persevered with their enterprise. Large quantities of copper bullion were produced each month. When sulphide ores were found, a concentrating plant was erected to produce sulphuric acid from the residue in processing the copper. Like dozens of other innovations introduced by the Scots, this experiment proved a financial success.[56]

Two developments in 1895 indicated that a new chapter in the long company history had begun: a capital reorganization made possible the final absorption of the trust and mortgage company, and the appointment of a new general superintendent James Colquhoun. Holders of certificates in the mortgage company received a bonus of £1 6s. 6d. on each share. Funds for this purpose were raised by an issue of six and one-half per cent 'A debenture stock' (£135,000). Debentures of the old mortgage and trust company bearing ten per cent interest were bought up and a new issue of terminable debentures issued by the copper company (£100,000). The third ranking debenture series were those of the copper company now classified as 'B debenture stock' (£181,239). The more important capital account of the company was complicated and consisted of the following issues in the order of the claims upon the resources of the company:

£633,060 representing the original fully-paid preference shares, now £4, entitled to a cumulative preference dividend.

£40,000 representing 160,000 newly-created 'ordinary preferred' shares of 5s., largely held by the trustees, with nothing called, but entitled to a ten per cent cumulative preference dividend and half the surplus profits above the payments of ten per cent on all classes of shares.

£5,050 representing fully-paid 'ordinary deferred' shares, long-standing at £1, entitled to ten per cent following

> payment on the preference shares and half the surplus above the payments of ten per cent on all classes of shares.[57]

Colquhoun introduced four processing improvements during his first three years on the job: a leaching plant; a sulphide concentrating plant; a power plant run by a gas engine; and a Bessemer plant. He justified his decision as follows:

> The first, combined with concentration, solved the problem of the treatment of low-grade oxidized ores; the second proved that the lowest grade sulphide ore could be treated at a profit; the third showed the way to cheap power; and the fourth enabled us to obtain the full value of our product. Our mining has kept pace with the general forward movement of our metallurgical work, and as a result we are now extracting ore from timbered slopes for a price which in former years would have been deemed impossible. While doing this work, the development of the mines has been so little neglected that the company has more ore in sight than its present plant can do justice to.[58]

In addition to these processing improvements that greatly increased the volume of copper ore produced at an all-time minimum cost, the company benefited from the rising price of copper. Starting in 1895 the average price per pound on the world market rose steadily until it reached seventeen cents a pound in 1899 and held on at better than sixteen cents for the next two years. Between 1900 and 1910, only once did copper prices drop below thirteen cents, and in 1906–7 they were at nineteen and one-half and twenty cents a pound, a higher figure than was obtainable when the Arizona Copper Company had been launched twenty-five years earlier. The high price of copper, beginning in the 1890s, was the result of increased uses for copper, particularly for wire used in electrical communication. Science and technology had provided improvements in the mining and metallurgical industry and coupled with increasing consumer demands had produced a revolution in copper production and marketing.

This happy combination of circumstances made possible the payment of a dividend of 2s. 6d. on each of the old preferred shares for 1894–5, after the interest payments were made on all debentures. For the first time in history, since the initial dividend of 1882, investors had received a payment. They had waited twelve long years. The dividend was increased to 4s. for 1895–6, and to 6s. for 1896–7. By 1898 there was a reserve fund of £141,388.[59] Twenty-five per cent of all earnings beyond the payment on preference shares was being set aside to redeem debentures. The London *Mining Journal* observed:

> Considering the exceedingly promising outlook for copper

> the reports of all copper mining companies should be attentively studied by investors, for, as we have frequently said of late in these columns, copper companies at the present moment are more attractive than gold mining companies. To the ordinary investor the Arizona Copper Company is not so well known...but now that its prospects appear to be greatly improving, it lays serious claim to the studious attention of the investor.[60]

In 1899 the Arizona Copper Company produced 9,467,401 pounds of copper, and annual profits reached £158,000.[61] Once again the mining press in London commented:

> For some weeks past, and at the present moment, Arizona shares are one of the most popular amongst copper specialties. Recently the price has literally been going up by leaps and bounds, probably because they are cheaper than many others, and are, therefore, more within the range of the small investor. They will continue to be popular for some time to come, there can be no doubt, for the outlook for copper is as promising as it could be.[62]

George Auldjo Jamieson, the chairman of the Board who had pulled the company through the trying years, died in 1900, but not before he knew the venture was a success.[63]

During the first two decades of the twentieth century, Arizona Copper Company's business was tremendously profitable. The directors were able to liquidate all the outstanding debentures, consistently pay ten per cent annual dividends on all three classes of securities, and then distribute large dividends to the ordinary shareholders. Table 12 on p. 182 reveals the profits distributed for 1901 to 1911.

The largest percentage of these dividends went to stockholders who had underwritten the company in crisis years. The preferred shares of the founders received only ten per cent annually. By 1904 each of the 5s. 'ordinary preferred' shares created at the time of the 1895 merger had drawn dividends of £2 1s. 6d., or better than an eightfold return. The 'deferred ordinary' had received an equal amount, or more than twice the face value of the stock.[65] In this year the ordinary stocks were standardized in capital value at 5s.[66] From 1904–7, 15s. 1d. was paid in dividends, representing better than another three-fold return on capital. Each subsequent year, up to the outbreak of World War 1 in 1914, a thirty-five per cent dividend was declared on ordinary stock.[67]

While the profits flowed home to Scotland in flood proportions, the management in Arizona had to deal with the ravages of actual floods along Chase creek and the San Francisco River. On 9 June 1903, at the time of a great new mining strike, heavy rains in the

TABLE 12.

year to Sept. 30	*free profits* £	*amount carried to reserve* £	*dividends* £
1901	320,329	30,000	323,162
1902	246,469	40,000	205,019
1903	301,518	50,000	252,515
1904	287,939	40,000	252,515
1905	361,099	50,000	309,512
1906	303,138	80,000	423,504
1907	434,461	108,000	309,512
1908	288,138	90,000	214,518
1909	320,435	80,000	214,518
1910	227,646	20,000	214,518
1911	262,340	45,000	214,518
total	£3,353,512	£633,000	£2,933,811[64]

mountains caused the waters of Chase creek to rise, retaining dams for concentrates burst, and a sea of mud 'as thick as molasses' swept down the canyon, destroying scores of modest dwellings built by the Mexican workers. An estimated fifty Mexicans were drowned, but only thirteen bodies were recovered, the rest being carried away in the flood waters. Damage was estimated at $100,000 and the mining companies of Clifton came to the relief of the needy. Then, in January 1905, flood damage was concentrated in the town of Clifton where the floor of the Arizona Copper Company's smelter was covered with water six feet deep. Damage on this occasion was estimated at $300,000. A third flood struck Clifton in December 1906, and another score of Mexican workers lost their lives. Entire adobe houses, one of which stayed intact, floated down the creek.[68] These vagaries of nature were not only costly but the tragic loss of life was also very damaging to morale.

In 1909 the farmers in the Gila Valley complained that the tailings from the great concentrating mills at Clifton were polluting the irrigation waters taken from the river between Solomonville and Fort Thomas. They also claimed that debris and barren silt was being deposited on the agricultural lands during periods of overflow so that crops would no longer grow on the damaged land. The farmers finally took the matter to the courts for redress and the mining companies were forced to construct large dams for impounding the tailings.[69]

During the World War, beginning in October 1915, the most serious labour trouble ever known in the Southwest developed. Five thousand mine workers, mostly Mexicans, in the camps at

Clifton, Metcalf, and Morenci struck for union recognition and higher wages. Managers and professional workers at all the copper mines in the district, fearing bodily violence, left the Clifton area as soon as the first outbreak occurred. A temporary camp was established at Duncan. A decision was made in December to send 500 non-union men into the district, protected by a force of United States deputy marshals under orders from the federal court in Tucson, on the pretext of doing assessment work on unpatented claims. The situation was so critical that the Arizona Copper Company suspended its operations from October 1915 until February 1916, and again during the summer and autumn of 1917. The company benefited from the tremendous demand for copper during the war and the resulting high prices. Certainly the income was sufficient that the labourers might well have received a sizeable wage increase. Annual dividend distribution in each of these four war years, after the payment of income taxes, totalled from sixty to eighty per cent of the total capitalization of £678,110. For 1917–18 the value of copper production was £2,085,112. The reserve fund stood at £1,005,175.[70]

The Scots purchased the holdings of the Shannon Copper Company, in nearby Metcalf, during 1919, and soon thereafter a sudden slump in the copper market found the Arizona Copper Company overexpanded. Decline in the value of copper continued into 1920–1, so that the bullion produced for the year was worth only $2,350,000. As a result, only dividends on the preference shares were paid and the reserve fund had to be dipped into. The directors elected to stop work in Arizona in May 1921.[71]

The Scottish company had a major asset in a very large low-grade deposit, known locally as the 'Clay Orebody', that joined its claims and extended into the nearby Phelps Dodge holdings. In 1917 engineers had blocked out forty-seven million tons of ore in this deposit, but more capital was needed for development than the depleted treasury of the Scots could supply. The directors thought it a good time to sell, and Phelps Dodge was eager to buy. In October 1921 resolutions were passed sanctioning an agreement to sell the entire company holdings including the Arizona and New Mexico Railway, to the Phelps Dodge Corporation of New York. The price the Scots demanded in exchange for their deferred ordinary shares was 50,000 fully-paid shares of $1,000 in the New York corporation, representing ten per cent of its stock. The Americans were also to pay the dividends on the preferred shares and the preferred-ordinary stock for a five year period and then retire these securities, worth about £675,000, at par value. The Arizona Copper Company had a right to nominate a director of Phelps Dodge as long as the company held ninety-five per cent of the 50,000 shares. The Arizona Company continued in existence only as an investment company to hold these Phelps Dodge shares. Owners were requested to deposit their shares with the company but reserved the right to dispose of them at will.[72]

The Scots had not parted with their copper mine in Arizona without some vigorous opposition from a minority of stockholders. James Colquhoun, who was primarily responsible for the financial success of the company in the twentieth century, recorded his version of events when the decision to sell had been announced.

> ...During the prolonged negotiations which followed, many rumours were set afoot resulting in a great advance in the price of shares and so, when the final terms were announced to the hopeful shareholders, there was consternation on every hand. The blow fell like the news of a second Flodden. The shareholders who had held on for the big price and the speculators who had bought to make a profit were as one in their exasperation and indignation, and it was in this frame of mind that the clans gathered for a great meeting at which the fate of the Company was to be decided....The assembly was stormy, and devoid of all the charms which adorn the meetings of Y.M.C.A.'s....The [deferred] shareholders had counted upon at least 4 pounds per share and the directors met them with an offer of 18 shillings....
>
> A thousand shareholders were present and when the Board filed into the room a few shareholders gave expression to their feelings in a manner not unusual at a boilermaker's meeting....The only portion of the Chairman's able speech which attracted appreciation was the announcement that 15 minutes would be allowed for refreshments. The crowd at once proceeded to the nearest bars, and when fortified with the wine of the country, they again drew up in line to meet the shock of battle....[73]

Final amalgamation with Phelps Dodge was temporarily delayed because of taxation troubles. The Arizona Copper Company had made a claim for repayment of British excess profits duty. The Government recognized this requested refund to the extent of £300,000, but simultaneously made claims for the failure of the company to pay certain income taxes.[74] Since 1895 the Scots interested in the Arizona Copper Company had received, as a group, more than a tenfold return on their investment. Holders of the deferred shares of 5s. appear to have received a great deal more personally, and they still retained an indirect interest in the copper business through their shares in Phelps Dodge Corporation.[75]

Many factors were responsible for the success of the twentieth century: technological advances; high prices for copper; and most important, a skilful and forward-looking management willing to make innovations in refining, marketing, and promotion. Scotland's greatest venture in the Mining Kingdom had paid off handsomely for those who had exercised patience and others who had retained confidence in the company during its darkest days. Moreover, the enterprise at Clifton was among the largest and most important in the history of the mining industry in Arizona and in the American West.

Chapter Eight

Widening Horizons in the Mining Industry

Although the export of British capital overseas had slowly increased annually after 1886, reaching a peak in 1890 that for the first time exceeded the previous high point of 1872, the next year witnessed such a rapid decline that the annual export returned to a level below that prevailing when the general upswing started. The period, 1891–5, was characterized by continuing decline in overseas investment. In 1894 the flow of capital was estimated at £20·1 million, less than a quarter of the amount of 1890. Some recovery was noted in 1896, but the flow of capital overseas the next year diminished to the normal level for the decade. An all-time low was reached in 1898, but the last two years of the century were again at the normal level for the decade. During the 1890s Britain continued to loan in the United States but on a much smaller scale than before, so that the percentage of United States investment in the world total was less than in the period 1870–80.[1]

Investment in mining enterprises had a tendency to reflect this overall pattern during the decade, but there were notable exceptions. A precipitous drop in the nominal capitalization of overseas mining companies occurred in 1891 and reached a low point of £12 million in 1893. Although the general flow of capital overseas continued low in 1894, mining investment began to increase. British foreign and colonial mining enterprise in 1895 eclipsed any preceeding year of the century and an unprecedented number of companies, 881 in all, were registered, chiefly to operate in the gold fields of South Africa and West Australia. Total capitalization approached £100 million. There was a slight tapering-off of activity in 1896 but mining investment continued abnormally high for the rest of the decade, the nominal company capitalization averaging annually between £55 million and £72 million. Where the United States was concerned, the boom of 1895 was not felt in the western mining states. A striking change was recorded the next year when the amount of new British capital invested was £6,000,000, a remarkable advance on the early years of the decade. Of this amount, £1,000,000 was invested by ten English companies in the Cripple Creek District, Colorado. This American boom helped to keep the total mining investment figures high and to cushion a more dramatic reduction in African and West Australian investments. A slight decline came in 1897; there was only a fair amount of activity in 1898. Then in 1899 new investments matched the peak year of 1896, followed by a precipitous drop in 1900 to about one-third, or a total of £1,825,000.[2]

In 1890, the year in which the Baring crisis precipitated an abrupt end of economic expansion, a Directors Liability Act was passed forcing greater responsibility upon the company promoters, and this may well have been an additional retarding factor on new enterprises, particularly in the field of mining. Up to this time British common law had assumed that the author of a prospectus was honest. The courts had taken the position that promoters had to know that certain statements were untrue at the time of their publication to be liable for damages, and the burden of proof was upon those who doubted their integrity. As earlier noted, the result had been flagrant misrepresentation in promotional literature for two decades. The writer of a prospectus could be as careless as he wished without fear of retribution. This new act made company promoters and directors who authorized the issuance of a prospectus liable to pay compensation for losses incurred by persons who relied on untrue statements in the prospectus or other notices, reports, or memoranda that included an invitation to subscribe for shares or bonds. The burden of proof was now shifted to those who issued the prospectus to show that they had reasonable grounds to assume the statements in question were true. The law specifically required promoters and directors to restate or quote an engineering expert fairly and to be prepared to show that they had reasonable grounds to believe that the authority quoted was competent to express an opinion. This last provision was particularly aimed at those who so often misquoted or omitted qualifying statements from the reports of mining engineers.[3]

Just as the Scots had not lessened their interest in western American mining during the period of decline, 1891–3, the investing public appears to have been unaffected for the rest of the decade by the declining cycle of overseas investments so apparent in London. Both 1894 and 1895 witnessed an increase in the number of companies registered over the previous year, and 1896 was a boom year in which six new enterprises were launched, more than twice the number in any previous twelve-month period (see Table 13, pp. 188-9). As in the past, Glasgow was the home office for most of the limited companies that sought to exploit American mineral wealth. Silver properties failed to interest the Glaswegian,

TABLE 13. Western American mining enterprises registered in Scotland

		registration date	*nominal capital £*	*Scottish headquarters*	*winding up*	*active*	*location*
1	Utah Cotton Wood Mining and Smelting Company, Ltd.	1872	6,000	Glasgow	1872	no	Big Cottonwood Canyon, Utah
2.	Kirkland Gold and Silver Mining Company, Ltd.	1875	4,000	Glasgow	1884	yes	Placer County, California
3.	Atchison Mining Company, Ltd.	1875	6,000	Dundee	1880	yes	Boulder County, Colorado
4	Scottish Pacific Coast Mining Company, Ltd.	1881	100,000	Edinburgh	1899	yes	Sierra County, California
5	Arizona Copper Company, Ltd.	1882	875,000	Edinburgh	1921	yes	Graham County, Arizona
6.	Scottish Colorado Mining and Smelting Company, Ltd.	1884	250,000	Glasgow	1894	yes	Boulder County, Colorado
7.	Richardson Gold and Silver Mining Company, Ltd.	1884	50,000	Glasgow	1885	yes	Gilpin County, Colorado
8.	Colorado Silver Mines, Ltd.	1884	200,000	Glasgow		no	San Juan County, Colorado
9.	Feather-Fork Gold Gravel Company, Ltd.	1886	300,000	Glasgow	1902	yes	Plumas and Sierra Counties, California
10.	Creston Gold Mining Company, Ltd.	1889	160,000	Edinburgh	1891	yes	Saguache County, Colorado
11.	Grass Valley, California, Gold Extracting Company (Pollok Patents), Ltd.	1890	30,000	Edinburgh	1894	yes	Nevada County, California
12.	Poorman Silver Mines (of Colorado), Ltd.	1891	130,000	Glasgow	1899	yes	Boulder County, Colorado
13.	Mining Development Syndicate (of Colorado) Ltd.	1892	20,000	Glasgow	1900	no	Colorado
14.	Gold and Silver Extraction Company of America	1893	110,000	Glasgow	1904	yes	Colorado
15.	Bear Creek Alluvial Gold Mining Company, Ltd.	1894	65,000	Glasgow	1898	yes	Rocky Bar, Idaho

16.	California Gold Production Syndicate, Ltd.	1894	55,000	Glasgow	1899	yes	Sierra County, California
17.	Prescott Development Syndicate, Ltd.	1895	100,000	Glasgow	1902	no	Arizona
18.	Alaska (Glasgow) Gold Mine, Ltd.	1895	44,000	Glasgow	1901	yes	Nevada County, California
19.	Redhill, Ltd.	1895	75,000	Glasgow	1899	yes	Nevada County, California
20.	Diamond Hill Gold Mines, Ltd.	1896	455,000	Glasgow	1908	yes	Broadwater County, Montana
21.	Gold Basin Mining Company, Ltd.	1896	150,000	Glasgow	1896	no	Mohave County, Arizona
22.	Glasgow and Western Exploration Company, Ltd.	1896	30,000	Glasgow	1921	yes	Utah, Nevada and Colorado
23.	Jumper Gold Syndicate, California, Ltd.	1896	45,000	Glasgow	1914	yes	Tuolumne County, California
24.	California Consols, Ltd.	1896	60,000	Glasgow	1912	yes	Tuolumne and Shasta Counties, California
25.	Atlas Mines Syndicate, Ltd.	1896		Glasgow	1902	yes	Tuolumne County, California
26.	Highland Chief Mining Company, Ltd.	1897	30,000	Glasgow	1897	no	Deadwood, South Dakota
27.	Bull Creek Mineral Estates, Ltd.	1897	42,000	Glasgow	1897	no	Christian County, Missouri
28.	Longfellow Gold Syndicate Ltd.	1898		Glasgow	1902	yes	Tuolumne County, California
	Nonpareil Gold Syndicate, Ltd.	1906	6,000-10,000	Glasgow	1910		Tuolumne County, California
29.	Scottish California Mining Syndicate	1898		Glasgow		no	Tuolumne County, California
30.	Crystalline Gold Mines, Ltd.	1898	65,000	Glasgow	1902	yes	Tuolumne County, California
	Crystalline Mining Company, Ltd.	1902		Glasgow			
31.	Arizona Copper Syndicate, Ltd.	1899	100,000		1900	no	Graham County, Arizona
32.	Mineral Hill Copper Syndicate, Ltd.	1900	5,000		1905	no	Yavapai County, Arizona
33.	St. Patrick Gold Mine, Ltd.	1900	80,000	Glasgow	1908	yes	Cripple Creek, Colorado
34.	Herman Mining Company, Ltd.	1903	30,000	Glasgow	1907	yes	Placer County, California
35.	California Copper Syndicate, Ltd.	1901	30,000	Glasgow	1902	yes	Fresno County, California
	Fresno Copper Company, Ltd.	1902	175,000-400,000	Glasgow	1907	yes	
	Fresno Copper Company, Ltd.	1907	100,000	Glasgow	1914	yes	
36.	Scottish Tonopah Gold Mining Company, Ltd.	1904	3,000	Glasgow	1908	yes	Esmeralda County, Nevada
37.	British Arizona Copper Company, Ltd.	1913	25,000	Dundee	1924	yes	Arizona

perhaps due to disappointments in Colorado and the continuing decline in the price of that metal in the nineties. Emphasis was placed upon gold. The quest was no longer confined to California and Colorado, but extended to every mining state in the West.

In 1894 a miner of Rocky Bar, Idaho, arrived in Glasgow and prevailed upon a group of Scots to register a private company, the Bear Creek Alluvial Gold Mining Company, Limited, to work his Idaho mine. All the shares in this company, capitalized at £65,000, were registered in the name of the vendor with the exception of seven, one for each director as required by law. The directorate was composed of a wine merchant, a book agent, a manufacturer, an oil merchant, a shipbuilder, a barrister, and an accountant. Apparently the purpose of registration was to establish a vehicle whereby the public could be asked to loan £16,000 debentures as working capital. One American journal expressed the opinion of many in suggesting that this was 'rather a novel proposal', but the scheme worked, for residents of Glasgow, the nearby villages of Dunoon and Lenzie, and even Manchester, provided these essential funds.[4] Two years later the company was reorganized with a larger capitalization and the holders of £10 debentures were granted fifteen £1 shares in the new company. There was no other alternative than the loss of their loan.[5] The inevitable collapse came within a few months. This Idaho speculation provided a prime example of the irresponsibility of both the vendor and the directors as well as the incredible gullibility of some investors.

In 1896 Scots became interested in the Diamond Hill mines, located near Hassell, eight miles southwest of Townsend, Montana. A syndicate formed by a Broadway financier agreed to send two Glasgow coal merchants, James Nimmo and George A. Mitchell, and several mining experts to Montana to study the claims and decide whether a company should be formed to work them. The quartz was known to produce quantities of low grade ore and capital was eagerly sought to conduct a large scale experiment to see if profits could be made from its processing.[6] The Scots agreed to take the risk and the Diamond Hill Gold Mines, Limited, was registered with the huge nominal capital of £455,000, divided into 305,000 preferred shares and 150,000 ordinary shares. The American vendors were willing to sell their property for 150,000 preference shares, and members of the syndicate subscribed for 75,000 preference shares and 50,000 ordinary. The rest were to be made available to the public. Both the American vendors and the members of the original syndicate were to be reimbursed £5,000 for the expenses of promotion and investigation.[7]

Montana state officials were convinced that this Diamond Hill project was of great importance to the mining industry of the Northwest because it would prove whether modern mechanical appliances for handling large quantities of low-grade ore at a minimum cost could yield a reasonable return on capital. Every Montanan interested in mining watched the progress at Diamond Hill hoping for success. The Scots constructed a dam and power plant on the nearby Crow River to provide electricity to operate a mill of one hundred and twenty stamps. When completed, the power was found insufficient. It was not possible to use steam power to augment the supply because the cost of fuel would exceed the margin of profit from the low-grade ore. As an alternative, the directors hoped to purchase and transmit electricity from a Missouri River plant at Canyon Ferry.[8] Development work proved expensive and the original working capital of £50,000 that the American vendors had claimed would be sufficient to build the power plant, provide machinery, and pay expenses was exhausted the first year. Directors found it necessary to advance personal funds to finish payments on the crushing and milling machinery and to provide the wages of workmen. At this juncture, the debenture holders petitioned the Scottish courts to stop all work, but the directors pled for time. If the property were abandoned and the wages of workmen left unpaid, they would have the right to work the property for what was due them. A complicated scheme of financial reorganization was achieved in 1898, and for ten years the Scots worked doggedly before agreeing to terminate the effort. They never had a paying business. This experiment, which would have proved a boon to Montana mining, if successful, cost the Scots at least £60,000.[9]

Simultaneous with these undertakings in the Northwest, other Scots sought opportunities in the Southwest. A group of Glasgow clerks organized the Prescott Development Syndicate, Limited, and employed Theobald B. Comstock, engineer and mining expert of Prescott, Arizona, to seek promising properties, with the understanding that he would receive one-sixth of the profits coming from any properties he recommended for purchase. Between 1895 and 1902, the Scots squandered almost £40,000 in fruitless explorations.[10] Another exploring syndicate acquired an option on the Gold Basin mines near Hackberry, Arizona, at the northern end of the Hualpai Valley, in Mohave County. A Chicago lawyer travelled to Scotland to promote a company to take over the mines from the syndicate. With the aid of a report from a Los Angeles 'mining expert' he found Glasgow accountants, cashiers, and clerks who were willing to register a company with nominal capitalization of £150,000. Plans called for purchase of the mine at £120,000, payable in £30,000 cash and £90,000 deferred shares.

The remaining £30,000 the promoters hoped to secure from the public. Final arrangements hinged upon a new inspection of the mines. Reports were decidedly unfavourable and fortunately the company was quickly dissolved.[11] Thus the Arizona ventures came to naught.

South Dakota was the scene of another Scottish mining venture. John E. Watson, a Glasgow chartered accountant, whose offices were the centre for promotional activity, interested several iron merchants in purchasing the Highland Chief Mining Company near Deadwood. In this case a company, known by the vague title of the Smelting and Development Company, Limited, capitalized at £30,000, was registered without a prior adequate inspection and shareholders were asked to pay up 10s. on each £1 share. The property proved valueless, the Scots had an unsaleable mining company on their hands, and had lost £13,000 in the endeavour.[12] Another Glasgow chartered accountant promoted the Bull Creek Mineral Estates, Limited, to purchase a tract of mineralized land in Christian County, Missouri, from a London company, known as the Missouri Mining and Land Company, Limited. Payment to the Englishmen was in preferred shares and the Scots were promised the return of their entire capital plus a six per cent annual dividend before the investors in the old London company were to receive payment. Within a year a liquidator had been appointed and the Scots were doomed to disappointment again.[13]

The widespread and somewhat frantic search for paying western mining enterprises is perhaps best illustrated by the history of the Glasgow and Western Exploration Company, Limited. In 1896 the Coats family of Paisley, thread manufacturers, sponsored this organization to 'explore, finance, and develop' mining properties in western America. Initial capitalization was £6,000 in £1 shares of which the Coats clan held 4,700.[14] In 1898 a block of mines near Milford, Beaver County, Utah, was purchased from the Montreal Mining and Smelting Company and plans made to erect a smelter. Later in the year another subsidiary, the Adelaide Star Mines, Limited, purchased several well-known mines at Cherry Creek, in White Pine County, Nevada. Funds were expended in digging new shafts, erecting hoisting machinery, building an air compressor plant at the mines and a concentrating and smelting plant at Golconda, Nevada. Mines and plant were connected by railroad.[15] A third Coats enterprise was the Meldrum Tunnel and Mining Syndicate, Limited, which owned a short tunnel and railroad near Ouray, Colorado. The company failed and had to be dissolved in 1900. At least £30,000 was lost, more than two-thirds of which belonged to the Coats.[16] Each enterprise begun by the Glasgow and Western had individuality as a limited company, but the parent company controlled all the offspring, chiefly through the dominant interest of the Paisley threadmaking family. When the exploration activities expanded in 1898 the parent company had increased capitalization to £30,000, with two-thirds of the stock reserved by the Coats. Their western American investments as a whole did not prove profitable, and in 1913 liabilities forced the termination of the Glasgow and Western. Business continued until 1921 when all the properties had at last been sold or liquidated.[17]

Thus the Scots had searched in vain. Not a single paying mining property had been found. Even the Glasgow bankers and solicitors handling the extensive funds of the Coats family had been unable to find an enterprise languishing for funds that would reward investors. Scottish capital, totalling approximately £230,000, had been used unsuccessfully for experimentation, primarily in Montana, Nevada, and Colorado. Most of the money had come from an unsuspecting public, usually misguided by a Scottish promoter who hoped to share profits with an American vendor in exchange for his service in promoting the company.

Nowhere in the West were the Scots as active in mining endeavour as in California. In 1895 the British consul in San Francisco called the attention of his countrymen to the revival of interest in gold mining in California during the previous two years. Decline in the price of silver had caused miners to turn their attention once again to gold. Recent improvements in methods of treating gold ores meant that the same mine that had previously failed to produce sufficient gold to pay for extraction costs could now be worked at a profit. For this reason capitalists were chiefly interested in partly-developed properties that could be worked with new methods, rather than in mere prospects.[18] The California State Mining Bureau confirmed the consul's observation that a mining revival was underway in the state. Mines that had been abandoned as unprofitable by old methods were being drained, retimbered, and opened up; placers, considered exhausted, were being worked again; and hydraulic mining, under legal regulations was resumed. The greatest boom of all was expected in quartz operations. The change was reflected in the labour market, for in 1896 there were two miners at work for every one employed the previous year.[19]

Well-established British investors began quietly investigating California mines with a view to purchase. Cecil Rhodes and his friends, so prominent in South Africa, were among those expressing interest. This diversion of experienced and well-advised investors from South Africa to the western United States stimulated a revival of interest in California on the London stock market.[20]

In contrast to the London activity, San Francisco mining stock brokers observed that speculation in mining shares was never so quiet, while mining was never more active. All over the state new mines were being worked, new mills built, and old mines reopened, but the public was persistently staying away from the exchanges.[21]

In spite of their years of experience in the field of mining investment, Britishers' methods of mine selection remained under attack from consular officials, London financial journals, and California newspapers. *The Economist* reprinted an indictment written by the British consul in San Francisco:

> When a proposition for the investment of money is brought to the attention of English capitalists, instead of sending out a man who is thoroughly well informed upon the subject at issue, whether it be mining or water development...in nine cases out of ten they select some person who, while usually very much of a gentleman, and quite a pleasant fellow, understands no more about the business than the Ameer of Afghanistan. He is often a retired army officer, and generally a distant or rather impecunious relative of one of the leading investors. The first thing that he generally does is to erect a very handsome and commodious residence for himself as superintendent. In one case in the Northern part of the State [of California] $100,000 was expended on the house and grounds of the superintendent of an English mining company and $200,000 on the mill before it was discovered that they had no ore.[22]

Western editors insisted that the large share of profit derived from the promotion of companies was still going to middlemen in England or Scotland, and that in nine cases out of ten the Britishers were themselves to blame for their losses.

The California Gold Production Syndicate, Limited, is a case in point. Organized in Glasgow, this company had an authorized capital of £55,000 in £1 shares to purchase and work the property of the Saint Charles Hill Gold Mining Company, a quartz and drift mining operation located 'between Goodyear's Bar on the east and Fiddle creek on the west, at 2,000 ft. elevation above the Yuba River'. The vendor, Robert Stevenson, mining engineer of San Francisco, received 25,000 fully-paid shares in the new company. His Glasgow agent, John M. Murray, a chartered accountant who specialized in promoting mine companies, received 20,000 shares fully paid. The few remaining shares were set aside for sale, and members of the Coats family, with their penchant for mining investments, provided most of the cash. The available capital was spent in development work, but the ore recovered proved of little value so the company terminated its existence within five years.[23]

Between 1895 and 1898 dozens of exploring syndicates were organized in Glasgow in hopes of finding a promising California mine. These were usually private ventures, in the initial stages, with capital limited to a few hundred pounds to finance the search. If a property was found, capitalization was increased and the vendor received his compensation in shares along with the Glasgow promoter or contact man. Average life of these companies was two years, although occasionally the financial structure was so confused liquidators worked for a decade under court supervision to straighten out affairs. If the activities of the syndicates never got beyond the searching stage losses incurred averaged £2,000 although a few of these undertakings cost the sponsors as much as £5,000. Among Scottish exploring companies in California in this period were the Plumas Placer Syndicate, Limited; Diadem Mines Development Syndicate, Limited; Crownpoint Gold Syndicate, California, Limited; California Mines Financiers, Limited; and the Seine River Syndicate, Limited.[24] Several Glasgow citizens like Thomas Lawson, a jeweller, James Ferguson, a butcher, George Mitchell, James and Adam Nimmo, coalmasters, were associated with most of the companies. Among the exploring companies that went so far as to take over and work a mining property were the Alaska (Glasgow) Gold Mine, Limited, and Redhill, Limited, with holdings in Nevada County. Shareholder lists reveal that those who invested were ill-prepared for mining ventures. Retired Army and Navy officers were the largest shareholders in the former company. Investors in the latter included the well-known confectioner Andrew Buchanan, an ironmonger, a warehouseman, a teacher, a printer, a stationer, and even a student who subscribed for two shares.[25] The end of one of these enterprises, described as follows, was typical: 'The company is not carrying on business now nor is it in operation. It was discontinued some years ago and its mines abandoned. The only other asset is some shares in a limited company which are worthless. The shareholders lost all interest in the concern and all attempts to get a quorum at a meeting were unsuccessful as there are no funds.'[26]

Although the search generally proved unrewarding, the Jumper Gold Syndicate, California, Limited, that had secured several quartz claims in the heart of the Mother Lode country in Tuolumne County in 1896, chanced upon phenomenal success. The syndicate began like all the rest with a small capital, in this case £9,900. It was sponsored by the determined jeweller Lawson, the coalmaster Mitchell and the butcher Ferguson. The Scots eventually raised £45,000 to purchase the 'Jumper', the 'New Era', and the 'Gold Rule' mines, all located on a ridge four miles south of Jamestown near the village of Stent. All had been worked periodically since the 1860s, but their potential was untested and unknown. For example, one official reported that the owners of the Gold Rule stated their mine had not been worked in 1871; other accounts suggest that $48,500 worth of gold was produced in 1870 and 1871.[27] The Jumper was the principal mine of the group obtained by the Scots. In the early days an effort had been made to work it by selecting only the better ore, but when the new manager assumed direction for the Scots he thought the geological conditions were such that this method did not produce the best results. The practice of selection was abandoned for stoping everything between the walls. Although this at first appeared an extravagant and unnecessary action, the results proved eminently satisfactory.[28] From time to time rich strikes were made. On one occasion a single blast knocked down $3,000 worth of 'high grade'; for some days thereafter very rich ore was found, said to be worth $10 a pound.[29]

When news of this development reached Glasgow, shares in the company sky-rocketed in value. There was a wild scramble to secure some of the unissued shares, followed by feverish buying and selling of those in individual hands. In 1898 company capital was increased to £100,000, with the new issue being prorated among old subscribers.[30] Development work at the Gold Rule increased production there for the next three years, but the Jumper continued to be the bonanza. The labour force was increased from fifty to one hundred and twenty-five. Additional stamps were installed to increase milling facilities from twenty to fifty and finally to sixty stamps. Average ore value was $5·25 a ton; at times it ran as high as $7·85 a ton. California officials reported 'The Jumper is one of the best worked and best managed mines in the state. It is heavily and properly timbered. The walls are hard–that is there is no trouble from swelling ground. The main shaft is down 1285 feet, and is equipped with air and electricity. There are nine levels at the mine.' Although production records after 1896, when the Scots took over, are not complete, gross output of the Jumper mine has been estimated at $3,000,000.[31]

Between 1900 and 1904 shares in the Jumper Gold Syndicate remained at a premium and could not be purchased, but the property was worked out by 1906. Recognizing the situation, the directors reconstructed the company, reducing the capital by half, £50,000 in 10s. shares. Each old subscriber was credited with 8s. paid up on the shares held and 2s. was provided for further work.[32] During 1914 the Scottish company turned the property over to lessees; eventually they sold out to a French company, which had so little success the mill was shut down in 1919.[33]

The success of the Jumper Gold Syndicate naturally caused the Scots to concentrate their California mining activities in Tuolumne County. Lawson and Ferguson organized the Longfellow Gold Syndicate in 1898 to acquire the Longfellow and Tough Nut mines in the Big Oak Flat District, and dividend income from the Jumper was reinvested in hopes of duplicating the success. The choice of mining property was logical because the Longfellow was also known as a 'pocket mine' that had rewarded its successive owners in the 1850s and 1860s. The Scots went to work in earnest, draining the mine, sinking a shaft four hundred and fifty feet, building a stamp-mill, concentrating works, and a cyanide plant.[34] By 1902 they gave up and transferred operations to an adjoining property through the Nonpareil Gold Syndicate, Limited.[35] Undoubtedly a significant percentage of the profits from the Jumper were left behind in Tuolumne County rather than going home to Glasgow.

Others tried to emulate the success of the Jumper syndicate. California Consols, Limited, with directors from Leith, Edinburgh, and London as well as Glasgow, purchased the Louisiana Gold Mine, eight miles east of Sonora, and two quartz claims near Cherokee. When these properties did not pay off, they purchased others in Shasta County. More money was lost by this syndicate than most.[36] Other Tuolumne County operations included the Atlas Mines Syndicate, Limited, which took over a claim on Jackass Hill, one mile north of Tuttletown, and a mill site near Robinson's Ferry on the Stanislaus River.[37] On the slopes of Whiskey Hill near Jamestown Scots acquired five quartz claims and a fifteen-stamp mill by paying vendors $170,000 and assigning to them one-eighth of the stock in the Crystalline Gold Mines, Limited, organized to develop the property. The public subscribed for 19,000 £1 shares. When the claims proved of little value, the California vendors agreed to accept the final instalment of $20,000 in paid-up shares.[38]

In spite of the failure of every effort to find a mine whose potential was equal to that of the Jumper, losses of these various exploring syndicates were not as great as in the past, for the Scots had learned to pay the vendors of American mines in shares exclusively, to provide a limited capital for development, and either cease work or shift the centre of operations quickly if the returns were not favourable. The only sizeable loss in Tuolumne County was through the Crystalline Gold Mines; to a lesser extent by California Consols. The combined capital squandered by the half-dozen syndicates working there was only twenty-five to thirty per cent of the profits made from the Jumper mine.

Having abandoned all hope in Tuolumne County, the Scots

once again, in 1903, expressed an interest in northern California gold mines through the purchase of the Herman mine, north of Deadwood, Placer County. The mine had produced annual profits since 1895, so the Scots agreed to pay £30,000 for the property, £20,000 of which was in shares and £10,000 in cash. The Glasgow promoters were shrewd enough to make an initial payment of £2,000 and await developments. The remaining ore in the mine was of such low-grade that profits from production did not equal the funds expended on development work so the venture was terminated in 1907.[39] Thenceforth, the Scots abandoned their search for profitable gold mines in the Sierra.

From the overall viewpoint, the outstanding characteristic of Scottish mining investments in western America during the 1890s was the dominance of inexperienced and unscientific men. In contrast, the English worked systematically, employing the services of the best-equipped experts in the world to conduct painstaking investigations. Among those at work were the Exploration Company of London, backed by the Rothchilds and headed by Hamilton Smith. The Anglo-Continental Syndicate of London had one of its directors, Edmund Davis, in the field. John Hays Hammond made inspections in the United States as well as elsewhere in the world.[40] If a property was deemed worthy, the English were never frightened away by high prices.[41] In comparison to the English, the Scottish activity was minimal.

Viewed from the world perspective, British mining investment capital was pouring primarily into South Africa and West Australia. As noted, the funds sent to the United States during the decade were concentrated in Colorado, chiefly in Cripple Creek, so that the world-wide boom was not fully felt in California even though it appeared substantial from the local viewpoint. Scottish activity in California and elsewhere between 1895 and 1897 was a vital part of a larger movement. For example, there were fifty new British mining companies in North America in 1895 with five times the nominal capital of those of 1894; in 1896 the number increased to one hundred and three with double the amount of capitalization of the previous year. In California alone, eight English mining companies filed registration papers in 1895; seven the following year.[42] Peak year of registrations for the decade was 1897 when fourteen London companies were begun to work in California.[43] After that the level of activity returned to that of 1895 for the rest of the decade.

Although the opening year of the twentieth century witnessed a continuing flow of British capital overseas, the years 1901 and 1902 marked another low in foreign investment with the annual totals less than half that of 1900. The figure for 1902 was £9·8 million, but in 1903 the average pattern of £21·1 million was recorded. Beginning in 1904 there was steady increase in overseas investment by the British until the outbreak of war in 1914. A glance at the figures for the decade shows a decided upswing for 1905–7, a temporary set-back in 1908–9, and an enthusiastic revival, 1910–13. The annual figure of overseas capital export was £198·2 million in 1913 or nine times the annual average for the 1890s. When foreign investment activity had been accelerated after 1904, capital flowed both to the Americas and the Empire. In 1911 investments in America, North and South, came to fifty per cent of the total as compared with forty per cent in 1885.[44] However, British capital coming into the United States represented a smaller percentage of the total channelled to the Americas in the years after 1890 because the nation had built up its own capital reserves.

The pattern of overseas mining investment did not coincide with the general flow of funds abroad. The decline of 1901–2 was certainly observed, but the fluctuations of the next ten years did not affect the investment in mining. A total of approximately £37 million was the nominal capitalization of British companies registered to invest in foreign and colonial mines in 1903 and with the exception of a slight upswing in 1906, the amount invested each year for the next four gradually declined until a low of approximately £15 million was reached in 1908. Each year witnessed the launching of from seven to twelve companies to operate in the United States. Between 1902 and 1904 the annual nominal capitalization of these enterprises ran from £1·5 million to £2 million, but beginning in 1905 United States mines met with little favour. By 1908 the North American section of the mining market was recognized as being on the downgrade. Year after year fresh capital for new enterprises became less and less. Edward Ashmead, who for thirty-three consecutive years had prepared a table of new mining companies registered in London as a special annual feature of the London *Mining Journal*, commented in his final summary 'The United States used to absorb a lot, but the mines taken up by people over here failed to attract. The English capital spent by us in the States on its mines somehow brought us no profit. For years past a really good mine–and there are abundance of them in the States–never fell into the hands of the English capitalist. The United States can always find money to work its own mines when they are worth working.'[45] From this time forward to the outbreak of the World War in 1914, the American market was described as being in a state of apathy.

During the first decade of the twentieth century, Parliament made another valiant attempt to end the abusive practices of company promoters that had become commonplace in the nineteenth century. A Directors' Liability Act was passed in 1900 enumerating regulations that must be met before the Registrar of Joint Stock Companies could issue a certificate of incorporation. The company prospectus, dated and signed by all the organizers and proposed directors, had to be filed with the Registrar and so stated on the face of the prospectus. Company prospectuses had been publicized far and wide in the past, but never before had the document been filed with governmental authority. The law also provided a long list of items that these prospectuses must contain. The memorandum of association, including the names and addresses of signers and the number of shares subscribed for by each of them, was to be included. There was nothing new in this provision, but in addition, if any of the signers had been issued shares either partly or fully-paid, this fact had to be stated. Promoters were required to specify the number of shares that had to be subscribed before the company would be officially floated and the shares allotted. Names and addresses of the vendors of the property to be acquired by the company and the amount paid to them in cash, shares, or bonds was to be revealed as well as the number and value of all shares issued as 'fully-paid' and the consideration for which they were given, the amount of commissions paid for the procuring of subscriptions to shares, and funds paid to any promoter. Directors and promoters also were required to reveal the full nature and extent of any interest they had in the property to be acquired by the company.[46] Legislators had acted on the assumption that publicity concerning the activities and manipulations of company promoters would force them to adopt higher standards of conduct. The weakness of the law was that it made no attempt to prohibit specific abuses and to provide penalties. Moreover, by limiting the applicability of the new rules relative to prospectuses to companies inviting the public to subscribe for shares, the way was still open to abuses.

Some organizers complied with the regulations and made information public that they would have preferred to keep secret, as in the past, but they were in the minority. As always, the majority found ways and means of avoiding the release of information. Taking advantage of the fact that the reform legislation applied only to those companies inviting the public to subscribe for shares, promoters declared there would be 'no initial public issue'. Capital stock of a new company was allotted privately to promoters, vendors, and directors. Only then were the shares listed for trading on the stock exchange. A propaganda campaign, including highly favourable reports of interviews with company officials, was launched to induce the public to buy shares on the open market. Stockbrokers were offered commissions for securing subscriptions.[47]

Parliament found it necessary to extend its policy of compelling the disclosure of information by the enactment of the Companies Act of 1907 whereby private companies were required to reveal the same type of information demanded from the public ones in 1900. Such companies were to file this data in a 'statement in lieu of a prospectus' that would be available for public inspection in the Companies Registration Office. Moreover, promoters had to establish a time and place for inspection of all material contracts. No longer was it possible for any corporation to avoid disclosure of facts that might repel prospective investors. At last secret agreements had been eliminated.[48]

In the twentieth century the Scottish quest for gold turned to new fields. The first, and perhaps the greatest, was at Cripple Creek, Colorado, only thirty-five miles from Pike's Peak. Gold seekers had thoroughly inspected this region during the rush of 1859 but found no paying placers. The district acquired a bad reputation in the 1870s, when unscrupulous men salted mines in hopes of producing a boom, and miners had a tendency to stay away thereafter. Delay in the discovery of wealth at Cripple Creek also can be attributed to geology, for the ores were unfamiliar tellurides and the veins did not crop out on the surface. These veins, once unearthed, contained gold in combination with other elements, chiefly tellurium, a nonmetallic element that had a tin-white lustre. The great discovery was made in 1891 and capital came from all parts of the world hoping to share the wealth of this new field. From 1893 through 1897, 3,057 new mining corporations were organized to work the district, with an average capitalization of a million dollars. The wealth of Cripple Creek helped absorb the blow dealt the silver industry of Colorado by the demonetization of the metal and the resulting rapid fall in price. Moreover, the total mining production of Colorado gradually increased until 1902, when the output of precious metals exceeded three million dollars a month.[49]

Significant English investment in the Cripple Creek region appears to have developed in 1895 when half a dozen companies, modestly capitalized at under £100,000, were registered. The next year found the interest of English investors at a high point when a dozen or more companies, each capitalized at a figure between £50,000 and £250,000, were active in the region. Combined nominal capital of the enterprises was in excess of £1,000,000. As late as 1897, the English, who had accepted the early, exaggerated reports of the phenomenal wealth of the strike, were still disappointed. Interest was greatly stimulated when Winfield S. Stratton sold his Independence mine to the Venture Corporation of London, in 1899, for $10,000,000. Stratton's Independence, Limited, one of the largest English firms ever to operate a western American mine, was continuously in the public eye for the next ten years, both in the United States and Great Britain, and the events connected with it largely shaped English attitude toward the Colorado gold field.[50] The mine had been purchased on the basis of information and estimates contained in the inspection report of the Colorado State Geologist, Thomas A. Rickard, an Englishman by birth. In 1900 John Hays Hammond made a thorough examination of the property and reported that ore reserves had been greatly overestimated, and Rickard was forced to admit that his report was based on information furnished by the mine foreman rather than from personal inspection. Rickard was replaced by Hammond as consulting engineer and was paid £10,000 for a single year's engagement, probably the highest salary ever paid by any Anglo-American mining company. The British sought redress for their losses in the courts claiming that Stratton had represented the ore in sight as worth $7,000,000 at the time of sale when he knew it was only worth $2,000,000. The company asked for $6,000,000 from Stratton's estate, as the estimated amount of deliberate overevaluation, but the courts refused on the grounds that Stratton had not taken his payment in cash but in shares of the company. The fact that he had immediately marketed them through the Venture Corporation had no bearing on the case. Moreover, the English had taken $10,000,000 worth of ore out of the mine by August 1907.[51]

Unlike the English, the Scots were more cautious in their participation in the Cripple Creek gold rush, but they could not resist at least one venture. A syndicate, dominated by the Coats family and primarily sponsored by Henry Coats of Perth, acquired the St Patrick Lode claim from the Gold Belt Mines Investment Company of Colorado. In addition, a processing plant owned by the Mount Rosa Mining, Milling, and Land Company, inspected and approved by a London engineer, was bought. The Scots paid $150,000 in cash and in addition 40,000 £1 shares, representing half of the company capital, went to the vendors in Colorado Springs. The remaining shares were placed on the market to raise capital to develop the St Patrick claim, and 28,000 were purchased by Archibald Coats of Paisley. The mine proved a disappointment. The American shareholders, who participated as original investors in the Gold Belt Company, began selling their shares in 1901. The Scots raised another £20,000 by increasing stock.[52] A reorganization became necessary in 1904 when capital was reduced from £100,000 to £30,000. Old shares were given preferential status in the new St Patrick Gold Mine, Limited, and though they were nominally worth 5s. the holders were credited with only 4s. paid-up. Over seventy-five per cent of the capital had been wiped out, and by 1908 the enterprise was abandoned.[53]

Renewed activity and widespread interest in the mining possibilities of Nevada resulted from the discovery of gold at Tonopah in May 1900. Before the twentieth century south-western Nevada was virtually unknown to map compilers. It was a land of scattered, rugged mountains between long stretches of sandy wilderness, sparsely clothed with sagebrush. Some cattlemen and sheepmen knew the area only vaguely, and a very few prospectors had ever penetrated the country.[54] Like most gold discoveries, the find at Tonopah was mere chance. James L. Butler and his wife, driving a pack-train through the wasteland, picked up stones to hurl at their recalcitrant burros and recognized the rock as mineralized quartz. On a return trip through the region they gathered some ore samples and turned them over to the district attorney of Nye County, offering him half-interest in the claim for the assay fee. The lawyer, equally impoverished, offered half of his half to an Austin engineer who learned that a ton of the ore would produce $80 in gold and $600 in silver. The partners later returned to the richest outcrop at Mizpah Hill and staked off every foot of ground. They filled two wagons with ore and started back to Austin. The rush to Tonopah was on.[55]

Within five years more than thirty mines were being developed in the district. By 1905 the total output at Tonopah had been $9,000,000 of which $7,000,000 worth of ore had been hauled across sixty miles of desert for smelting. There was another $40,000,000 worth of ore blocked out in the mines, and ultimately Tonopah was to add $125,000,000 to the world's supply of precious metal. A thriving town of stone and frame buildings had risen in a sandy wash between two mountains to become the county seat of Nye County and for a time the financial centre of Nevada. Five thousand residents boasted of being served by electric lights and a house-to-house water and sewage system at this outpost in the wilderness.[56]

The discovery at Tonopah was but the first between 1900 and 1904. Next, there was Lone Mountain, fifteen miles west, later Goldfield, twenty-three miles south where the ore was even richer, and finally Bullfrog, seventy-eight miles south of Goldfield. Hundreds of mines were discovered, companies formed, and stock sold from a few cents to a few dollars a share. The boom was characterized by overprospecting, overcapitalization, and overpopulation.

Glasgow's John M. Murray, the chartered accountant who had by now achieved modest fame as a mine promoter, registered a private prospecting company, known as the Scottish Tonopah Gold Mining Company, Limited, in May 1904, with a capital of £3,000 to seek a worthwhile property in southwestern Nevada. Among his associates was Andrew Bonar Law, member of Parliament. In 1905 the company obtained the IXL and Golden Star mining claims near Tonopah. Company capital was increased at this time to 10,000 £1 shares, with a large block of the securities going to the vendors. The property was not a paying proposition and the company was terminated in 1908 with modest losses.[57]

Professor Russel Elliott has pointed out that the isolation of these new mining camps forced development of the entire southern part of Nevada, established north-south routes of travel, and gave the economy of the state a unity that had been previously lacking. Small operations, like that of the Scots, could not solve the problems of inadequate transportation, water, fuel, food, and building material. Tremendous capital was needed to extract and process the ores of the district. In each mining camp only one or two companies emerged, capable of exploiting the properties thoroughly and scientifically.[58]

The major innovation in the pattern of Scottish mining investments in western America during the twentieth century was the development of an enthusiastic interest in copper properties. In this respect, the Scottish viewpoint coincided with that of their English cousins who had waited to the century's end to invest in the red metal. Observing the struggles of the Scots in Arizona, the English had demonstrated very little interest in copper mining between 1870 and 1890. Only two ventures were made in the entire twenty-year period. In California, a London firm of Dorset and Perkins had purchased the 'Leviathan' mine in Alpine County in 1869, upon the report of W. T. Rickard that it was 'one of the richest copper mines in the world'. A smelting works was erected, a German metallurgist placed in charge, and the copper ore produced forwarded to England by way of San Francisco for further reduction. Profits were not forthcoming so the mine and furnace were shut down in 1872.[59] In 1889 the Union Copper Mine at Copperopolis attracted the attention of English capitalists who were negotiating for the property, when the eastern owners decided their deposit was larger than they had realized and refused to sell.

Then, in 1894, another group of Englishmen negotiated the purchase of the 'Lost Confidence' Mine and Iron Mountain Mine in Shasta County, for $300,000, from a San Francisco Company. They organized Mountain Mines, Limited, with a capital of

£100,000 and erected a small smelter. Their properties had previously been worked for iron and silver. They found that the ore was not free milling and had too much base metal so the project was on the verge of abandonment. At this point a mining inspector suggested that the ore was far more valuable for copper than for silver or iron. A new company, Mountain Copper Company, Limited, with a capital of £1,250,000 was registered at the end of 1896, paid Mountain Mines £1,120,000 for the Iron Mountain Mine and immediately began erecting a new smelting works at Keswick, Shasta County, near Redding. Discovery of a large copper deposit coincided with an increase in the world price of copper that began in 1895. The company quickly became an important producer. Between 1895 and 1898 California's annual copper production increased from 226,000 to 21,500,000 pounds, largely as a result of this British enterprise.[60]

The success of this company caused a flurry of excitement in London about the prospects of copper investments. Moreover, all evidence pointed to the fact that the Arizona Copper Company was at last engaged in a profitable business. However, the investing public was reminded of the long, troublesome history of this Scottish enterprise, the financial and technical problems, and was advised to abjure the purchase and management of copper enterprises. To satisfy an interest in copper, Englishmen were urged to invest in an American-controlled company.

In 1895 the Anaconda, Montana's huge copper undertaking capitalized at thirty million dollars, turned to European investors for subscriptions to one-fourth of the company stock through the Rothchild and Exploration group.[61] A correspondent of *The Economist* was soon suggesting that the English stockholders in the Anaconda sell back their shares to America. Copper and copper shares were thought to be 'dangerous things to touch. The supply, the demand, the metal market, the inside manipulations, are all unknown factors. I would say this to English investors: "Leave the Americans in undisputed possession of their own copper mines. They know more about them than we do." '[62]

In spite of all warnings, the high prices prevailing for copper between 1899 and 1902 naturally stimulated a world-wide interest in the industry.[63] London investors sought out copper mines that might be purchased in western America and Scottish investors, with less resources, followed their lead. They focused attention on the only two areas where the British had previous experience with copper enterprises, Arizona and California. A New Arizona Copper Syndicate, Limited, purchased eight claims in the Clifton district, adjoining the properties of the Arizona and the Detroit copper companies. Starting with a nominal capital of

£100,000, the company placed a block of 20,000 £1 shares on the market at half price.[64] Capitalizing on the name 'Arizona copper', which worked wonders among investors, the concern was extravagantly advertised in the eastern United States markets. The Prescott *Daily Citizen* suggested the prospectus and circulars issued proved the enterprise was not legitimate, but a scheme 'gotten up to bleed the tenderfoot who never saw a mine'. Investigation proved that the company's claims were essentially undeveloped; it was not even certain the bottoms of its shafts were mineralized. The newspaper summarized its findings:

> A group of undeveloped prospects which mining men deem worthless; a proximity to the Arizona Copper Company's properties, which fact they use in their prospectuses to the fullest extent, and an unalterable nerve, are the stock in trade of this fake company which is selling stock in the East, by utterly false representation, at prices which place a valuation of several million dollars on the property.[65]

The editor was concerned about the effect on the Arizona mining industry:

> Arizona seems to be suffering from several 'enterprises' of this class at present, and she owes it to herself to publish them to the world. The territory is full of legitimate mining propositions, and men who have money to invest can do so safely and profitably by coming here and investigating for themselves or sending able men to do so for them. Buying stock of unknown companies with undeveloped properties, at big figures, is nothing short of foolhardiness.[66]

The Scots appear to have participated in several copper enterprises of the type to which the editor referred. In 1900 a group of Glaswegians registered the Mineral Hill Copper Syndicate, with a capital of £5,000, to buy the 'Mineral Hill' and 'Examiner' claims, of unproven worth, in Yavapai County. Scottish officials were notified in 1905 that the company had not carried on business for three years. The property, upon examination, turned out to be worthless.[67] The only legitimate Arizona copper enterprise sponsored by Scots in the twentieth century was the British Arizona Copper Company, Limited, sponsored in Dundee during 1913. The promoters raised £25,000 in a private company to acquire the holdings of the Cleopatra Copper Company. Well-known Scots, Alexander Mackay, James M. Balfour, and Henry David Lawrie, were among the partners, each of whom held at least a thousand shares. The property was worked systematically for three or four years but by 1920 the directors admitted that no additional development work had been conducted the previous year. Extending the depth of the mine, the only way in which any significant ore might be found, was very costly and, with the discouraging outlook of the copper market, was not sufficiently promising to justify the expenditure that might be required. The directors decided that company capital was in excess of its needs so 12s. 6d. out of each £1 share was returned. This was indeed an innovation, for joint stock companies, almost without exception, continued to bombard subscribers for additional funds through the years, always with the promise that with a little more time and expenditure dividends would certainly be forthcoming. This company continued work in a modest way for the next few years with its £10,000 and finally in 1924 abandoned the effort.[68]

California copper provided a more legitimate outlet for Scottish investment capital in the twentieth century. The new discoveries in Shasta County by the Mountain Copper Company, combined with the high price of copper, ushered in the modern period of the industry in the state. Of lesser note was the 'foothill copper belt' that stretched from the crest of the Sierra Nevada for nearly one hundred and fifty miles down the Sierra slope in Madera, Fresno, and Tulare counties, on across the San Joaquin Valley, and up the eastern slope of the Coast Range to its summit.[69] The two largest mines in Fresno County were developed by British capital: the Copper King by the English and the Fresno Copper Mines by the Scots.

The Copper King came into British hands in 1899 amidst complaints from both the London *Mining Journal* and the New York *Engineering and Mining Journal* that there had not been adequate inspection to determine the size of reserves or the suitability of the ore for smelting. The English immediately built an expensive smelter on the site rather than send the ore to Vallejo for processing. Within a few months the shares rose to fantastic heights on the market and rumours suggested that a new copper syndicate was trying to get control. Within a year the bubble had burst, shares were below par on the market and could not legally be sold at the figure they would bring. Large shareholders had to underwrite the enterprise. Mismanagement was painfully apparent. The smelter's construction had been delayed, no exploratory work was conducted to prove the value of reserves, and prolonged and costly litigation had been necessary to secure a valid title to the company's land.[70]

In spite of the apparent problems of this company, Glasgow's John M. Murray sponsored the California Copper Syndicate, Limited, in 1901, to buy three claims in Fresno County adjoining those held by the Copper King. Nominal company capital was £30,000, £24,000 of which went to the vendors in paid-up shares. This private syndicate organized the Fresno Copper Company, Limited, the next year with a nominal capital of £175,000 and invited the public to subscribe for the £1 shares. In accordance with the new law of 1900, the company filed its prospectus. It had the characteristics of a promotion tract. The company's eighty-acre property sixteen miles northeast of Fresno, was connected to a branch of the Southern Pacific Railroad, three miles away, by a good wagon road. Fresno, a town of 15,000, was on both the Southern Pacific and Santa Fe lines, so transportation facilities were ideal. Electric power needed for hoists and drills was available from the San Joaquin Valley Electric Company and timber could be procured at a large mill six miles distant from the mine. So all the essentials were easily available. The Scots had been reassured by a number of experts about the value of this property and the information was shared with prospective investors through the prospectus. An Oakland 'mining expert' had 'no hesitation in affirming that the Fresno is from several points of view the best located and most desirable copper property in California today'. A San Francisco copper authority insisted 'The work done on this property has exposed a remarkable body of ore, and in my opinion, has proved the existence of a very valuable mine'. From Los Angeles a mining engineer also reported 'From a careful examination of the surface indications, and of the large bodies of copper ore exposed by the shafts and drifts, I am convinced this property can be made one of the largest producers on the Pacific Coast.'[71] Such glittering generalizations were apparently sufficient to satisfy many prospective investors, but no one had ventured to estimate the value of ore on the property.

The American vendors received £105,000 for their property in paid-up shares. On the basis of the glowing prospectus, 23,000 additional shares were immediately sold and 10s. called up on each. This £11,500 scarcely took care of the preliminary expenses, so promoter Murray launched a comprehensive programme of alternately raising and spending capital. In June 1903 nominal company capital was increased to £225,000. One half of the new issue, 25,000 shares, were to be placed on the market at a 10s. premium with the initial shareholders offered a preferential position in the subscription lists on a pro-rata basis. According to reports from California, large quantities of ore were being brought to the surface of the mine daily. Foundations were being laid for a new smelter and other buildings. The only discouraging note was that contractors were three months behind with construction schedules, due to labour troubles, and the management was afraid the machinery that had already been ordered would arrive before adequate preparations were made for its installation. The company also continued to purchase lands, including a gold quartz claim, within easy access of the copper mine and smelters. To raise development funds in 1904, a portion of the real estate was sold to a similar copper promotion known as the Glasgow Copper Syndicate, Limited, for $100,000.[72] The Scots planned on an elaborate scale: extensive improvements were made on the ground, including a hoist and pump for the main shaft, an air compressor, electric light plant, sawmill, machine shop, assay office, buildings for offices and residences, and a copper smelter. The smelting plant consisted of two furnaces of two hundred tons capacity, a converter shed, and a power house. A railroad had been surveyed to replace the wagon road connecting with the Southern Pacific branch, and before the roadbed was finished a locomotive and several ore cars had been ordered and delivered to the mine. These operations were very expensive and at the close of 1906, the Fresno Copper Company was capitalized at £400,000 and had raised at least £100,000 in cash for its operations.[73]

Once the smelter was completed, the trial run brought a most serious problem to light. The ore was expected to produce an average of at least seven per cent copper and $2 in gold to the ton, but when it was sampled *after* the smelter had been completed it assayed only two per cent copper and practically no gold. There were thousands of tons of ore on the dump, and exposed in the mine, which were too low in grade for profitable treatment.[74] The Glasgow promoters had no alternative but to liquidate the old company and register a new enterprise under the same name in 1907. The £400,000 capital was reduced to £100,000. The Scottish investors had only £10,000 remaining out of the £100,000 they had provided. In desperation, the remaining funds were used to explore the mine to greater depths hoping to find better ore. The company sold 100,000 tons of low grade ore on the dumps to be delivered over the spur railroad line on which $40,000 had been expended. But after 1908 the Fresno Copper mine was idle.[75] For the next few years an engineer, watchman, accountant, and a few workmen were employed to keep the mine free from water and the machinery in good working order to facilitate inspection by any interested purchaser. The property was mortgaged in 1911 and thereafter, each year, shareholders were faced with the decision of whether to wind-up the company or contribute a small assessment to finance the mortgage. The inevitable end came in 1914 and ten years later the company sold its real estate, 2,500 acres, for a nominal sum.[76]

As is the case with mining investments, ninety per cent of the Scottish efforts brought no return. The historian finds difficulty in explaining why well-informed people with an urban, commercial and industrial background were repeatedly duped into impossible ventures. The excitement of a plunge into gold and silver mining has always appealed to men and will continue to do so, no matter how risky the project, how dim and sketchy the plans for its development, and how grandiose the prospectus. Something approaching £1,000,000 was squandered by the Scots in the search for wealth between 1900 and 1915, but the one rich strike in the California gold fields–the Jumper of Tuolumne County–returned more than half that amount of capital to Scotland. In addition, Arizona Copper's estimated £6,000,000 in dividends between 1901 and 1921 completely overshadowed nineteenth-century Scottish losses in mining speculation. Perhaps the discovery of one good mine counterbalanced the score of failures in the eyes of the venturesome.

Chapter Nine

Single Purpose Ventures: Transitory, Exciting, and Unprofitable

In addition to their basic interest in the expanding railway network, the land mortgage business, the range cattle industry, and the mining kingdom of the western United States, Scottish investors sponsored projects to reclaim land for agricultural use and to introduce settlers interested in this acreage in California, Missouri, Iowa, Minnesota, Texas, New Mexico, and elsewhere. They also secured large timber tracts in northern California, and vineyards, orchards, and orange ranches elsewhere in the state. In the Pacific Northwest, the Scots built a railway and financed a flour and sugar mill. Although these single-purpose ventures were widely diversified, transitory and far less significant, both in the history of Scottish overseas investment and in the economic development of the western United States, their short histories were exciting, and provoked an inordinate amount of discussion and debate both among western Americans in the vicinity of their operations and among the investors back in Scotland. The history of each endeavour is a tale worthy of telling.

LAND, RECLAMATION, AND COLONIZATION SCHEMES

Scottish capitalists organizing companies to make land purchases worked on the assumption that large blocks of strategically located land could be secured for cash, held until the surrounding country developed adequately, and then sold in smaller parcels at a rewarding profit. The railroads holding extensive land grants were eager to part with acreage, particularly in return for gold or sterling. British investors, through their American agents, sought out in particular those lands covered with marketable timber or of potential agricultural value. To hasten the harvest of profit, some companies organized colonization movements to populate their lands with farmers.

Among the pioneers was the Glasgow Californian Land Company, Limited, registered in April 1877 to purchase 30,000 acres of land on Roberts' Island in the delta of the San Joaquin Valley.

The Scots paid £75,000 for the tract and guaranteed to raise an equal sum for development work. The American seller contracted to build the necessary levees, dams, and sluice gates for the reclamation and protection of the land, which was subject to overflow, and to superintend their maintenance for a period of five years. He also agreed to plough and harrow not less than twenty-five thousand acres of land for the first planting of seed. The estimated cost of this reclamation was £54,000 to be forwarded from Scotland in instalments as the work progressed. The price for preparing the ground for cultivation was to be 16s. an acre, payable on the planting of each successive one thousand acres. This enterprise was sponsored by a half-dozen leading merchants and ironfounders of Glasgow, who immediately provided £30,000 to start work in California. It was understood that the vendor was not to obtain his securities for the real estate until the Scottish investors received an initial dividend of six per cent on their capital.[1]

This endeavour of the Glasgow capitalists had an interesting historical background. To the west of Stockton, California, there were several hundred thousand acres of swamp and overflow land. For twenty years this land was thought to be of no value except as a home for fowl and wild hogs. At the time of California's admission into the United States in 1850, Congress granted this acreage to the state, the customary procedure in disposing of overflow land. State authorities immediately sought to utilize the gift by granting small farming plots at $1·25 an acre to individuals who hoped to reclaim the land with ditches and levees. Interest in the property continued to mount during the 1860s, and soon several heavily-capitalized companies organized projects to reclaim large blocks of the land.[2]

In May 1870 Captain William C. Walker, superintendent of the Tide Land Reclamation Company, inaugurated the work of reclaiming Roberts' Island, eighteen miles eastward from Antioch. There were to be ninety miles of levee constructed, including the damming of about thirty sloughs. It was estimated that the land could be reclaimed for $2·50 an acre. New ditching machines were to be given a thorough test and if they were not able to do the work 'at a less cost than muscle, then the latter will be brought into requisition'. By employing one to two thousand workmen it was proposed to complete the reclamation work in a single season.[3]

This first major attempt to reclaim Roberts' Island was not successful, but by 1876 Morton C. Fisher had succeeded in drying out the upper portion of the island, consisting of twenty-two thousand acres, at a cost of $140,000. Fisher owned fifteen thousand acres and the rest was broken into small plots, several of which were farmed by Chinese. Fisher wanted to reclaim the lower part of the island, which he also owned, and he sought the necessary capital in Scotland. The Glasgow company was organized, with the understanding that he would be the managing director in California.[4]

With Scottish capital, a massive and expensive levee was built around the entire island and another one across it to divide Fisher's land from that belonging to the company. Some thirty-six thousand acres on the lower division of the island were reclaimed by this work at a total expense of $350,000, or about $10 an acre. Because the project was far more costly than the reclamation of the upper half of the island, the Scots called up the entire authorized capital of £75,000, in addition to the vendor's interest, £75,000.[5] Another cross levee was later built on the Scottish property, so that Fisher's personal estate was known as the upper division while the Scots controlled a middle and lower section. Once the land was dry, the tules had to be burned off, the sod turned over with ploughs, and the roots cut off squarely. After a few weeks of exposure to the sun, the roots could be burned out of the clods of earth. The expense of preparing the soil by extirpating the tule roots was about equal to that of reclamation, so when the lands were fitted for the cultivation of the first crop, the Scots had invested $26 an acre.[6] The *Stockton Daily Independent* reported developments:

> ...A more complete and thorough change cannot be imagined than has been effected upon the tract of land which so lately was wholly unproductive. The bog has been apparently thoroughly reclaimed. Roads have been made to connect the farm buildings,...and a person traveling over the country can hardly realize that only five years ago it was a tule swamp. While much more remains to be done before all this immense body of land will be thoroughly reclaimed, enough has been done to prove that reclamation is possible, and that the capital here expended will prove a profitable investment.[7]

Although some Japanese, Hindus, and Mexicans had worked on the construction of the levees, Chinese coolies were so prominent as labourers that local residents referred to the works as 'China Levees'. The agitation against the Chinese was at its height in California in 1879 and Stockton papers came to their defence:

> ...the three thousand Chinamen who for three Summers found employment in the mud and water upon Roberts' Island building those substantial levees which have converted a vast swamp into tillable land, and the unsightly and worthless tule wastes into vast fields of luxuriantly

> growing grain, have done more for the advancement of civilization, more to better the condition of white laborers of this State than has been or ever will be accomplished by the three thousand sandlotters, who have, during the last three years, been accustomed to gather each Sunday in San Francisco to listen to speeches against land monopolists, Chinese, and to complain of the Government which has granted them protection and given them greater liberty than they know how to appreciate or enjoy.[8]

The Scots continued to invest in the agricultural operations on Roberts' Island. The capital of the Glasgow Californian Land Company was increased in 1880 by the issuance of £30,000 in preference shares entitled to six per cent annual dividends. Another £30,000 in preference shares, drawing ten per cent annually, was authorized in 1881, and soon the company capital stood at £355,000. The directors began the release of Fisher's shares that had been held in security.[9]

Agricultural cultivation was expanded each season between 1880 and 1884, but before the Scots could receive a systematic return on their investment, disaster struck. The evening of 17 March 1884, the cross levee separating the upper and middle sections of Roberts' Island gave way. The first telegraphic dispatches reaching Sacramento announced that 21,000 acres planted in wheat had been inundated.[10] Men bringing the tidings to Stockton reported that the first break was about twenty feet wide. Apparently the foundation of the levee was defective and the pressure of water so great that a strong stream was forced underneath and boiled up like a real spring in the wheatfields inside.[11] Fear was expressed that the other cross levee on the Scot's lands, between the middle and lower sections of the island, might wash out. If this levee broke, the whole island would be inundated.

By morning the break was one hundred and fifty feet wide and water was pouring over the levee into the middle division, making a waterfall four feet high. The broken levee was one of the largest on the island, ninety to one hundred and twenty feet wide at the base, thirty to forty feet at the top, and nine to ten feet high in places. When the alarm had first been given, one hundred and fifty repairmen were rushed to the scene, but after the superintendent saw the nature and extent of the break, he realized manual labour was useless and ordered all work stopped. Water swept over the island knocking down the tall grain as it went and travelling about as fast as a man could walk. When it became known that there was no hope of mending the levee, the farmers packed their household furniture in wagons and started for more habitable country. Initial reports had not exaggerated, for some 21,000 acres of land, covered with a knee-high stand of grain, was laid open to the ravages of the water. Loss was estimated at 650,000 bushels of grain, worth at least $500,000.

By 20 March the break in the levee was closed. Using a heavy sledge hammer, workmen had driven two rows of piles into the ground fifteen feet deep across the opening. The space between the lines of piles was filled with brush and sacks of earth. Although the water was falling rapidly, most of the farmers' crops were ruined. A few contracted with pumping companies to remove the troublesome water from their tracts as a final effort to save their plantings.[12] Early in April the repairs were described as secure and permanent. There was only a trifling loss on the lowest division, chiefly from seepage over forty or fifty acres, but with this exception the Glasgow company's property there was unimpaired. The great damage had been in the centre of the island.[13]

San Francisco papers reported that ploughing and planting activities were being renewed in December 1884. Farmers who were interviewed reported that the black adobe soil in the delta was ideal for ploughing. 'The prospects are flattering and the farmers are cheerful', the reporter revealed, and some renters on the Scottish company's lands were confident of excellent crops.[14] After such a calamity, the newspaper man looked upon the situation with sanguine eyes.

However, by 1890 an estimated 350,000 acres of fresh-water tidelands had been reclaimed in the Sacramento-San Joaquin Delta. Thousands of acres of wheat and barley grew in what had once been impenetrable bogs of tule and flag. Expert agriculturalists pronounced the land as some of the richest in the world, equal if not superior to the diked land of Holland. Profits could be made by both the capitalist and the renter when the weather was right.

> It is doubtful whether there are better inducements offered in any locality for the investment of capital, than can be shown to exist in the prospective profits to be derived from the purchase and thorough reclamation of this character of lands adjacent to the San Joaquin River....Some of the shrewdest capitalists of California have already invested largely, and although it requires time to make the reclamation perfect...the success attending efforts already made is incontrovertible.[15]

Reclaiming these lands had come about only as a result of costly and patient experiment. Later observers insisted that the Glasgow Californian Land Company had placed its levees too near the river bank and that a breakthrough was inevitable when immense floods of water came down in the spring of the year. After hundreds of thousands of dollars were lost they rebuilt their levees farther back, brought up solid earth from the river bottom, and dug wider ditches to relieve the overflow. These ditches also served as waterways for transportation. The Santa Fe Railroad later laid its tracks across the land improved by the company.[16] Yet the Scottish investors who had made their contribution by trial and error paid heavily. In June 1886 the shareholders of the Glasgow Californian Land Company agreed 'that it has been proved to the satisfaction of This Meeting that the Company cannot by reason of its liabilities continue its business and that it is advisable to wind-up, and accordingly that the company be wound-up voluntarily'.[17] At least a million dollars had been lost.

The Glaswegians were not alone in their real-estate promotion. Syndicates in Dundee and Edinburgh, composed of well-known manufacturers and capitalists, who had first recognized the potentiality of Scottish-American investments, also tried land promotions. The early history of the Dundee Land Investment Company organized in 1878 to purchase acreage in western America through Jesup, Paton & Company, has already been told.[18] Two years later Edinburgh capitalists followed suit. The directors of the Scottish-American Investment Company registered the Scottish American Land Company with a nominal capital of £100,000. The company was empowered to purchase land or acquire it by grants, to cultivate and improve it by machinery or roadbuilding, and to sell or otherwise dispose of it.[19] Sir George Warrender served as president of the company, William J. Menzies was vice-president, and John Clay, Thomas Nelson, and Patrick Sterling served with them on the Board of Directors. By 1881 £7 was called-up on the first five thousand shares issued and £2 on a second issue of five thousand, making the working share capital £45,000. Approximately £34,000 additional was borrowed on debenture. The company paid a ten per cent initial dividend for 1881–2, but for the next two years there was no distribution.[20]

In March 1884 the shareholders were notified that the lands held by the company in the United States had been materially reduced. In view of the prevailing sentiment against alien land ownership, it was necessary either to enlarge the basis of company operation or instruct the management to inaugurate a programme of liquidation. The shareholders elected to sell the company real estate to Alexander Peddie, a Scot residing in Iowa, for £54,000, payable in instalments over five years.[21] The mortgages on other Iowa lands were retained, and, in November 1885, these were estimated to be of greater value than the outstanding debentures. As a result of the sale to Peddie, the directors hoped to repay all

21. *William J. Menzies, Director, Scottish-American Investment Company, Limited, Edinburgh*

22. Oregonian Railway Engine no. 5, Yamhill County

23. Widening the Oregonian Railway to standard gauge

the shareholders their entire capital with six per cent interest, after allowing for company expenses both in Scotland and Iowa. For 1884–5, a small dividend of three per cent was paid, but for the next five years there was no distribution. The directors announced, however, in 1892 that the redemption of debentures was completed, and in the following year the company went into voluntary liquidation in order that the capital might be repaid to the shareholders as funds permitted. Although it appears doubtful, the investors may have succeeded in getting their money out of this enterprise. Certainly no significant profits were made.[22]

Scottish interest in southwestern Missouri lands purchased from the St Louis and San Francisco Railway has been noted in the account of the Missouri Land and Livestock Company. Leverett B. Sidway, a land and farm loan agent of Chicago, who promoted and managed this combined land and cattle venture, had earlier apprised Edinburgh capitalists of the availability of these railroad lands. Upon his recommendation, the Missouri Land Company of Scotland, Limited, was established at the close of 1880 to take over 142,000 acres of land in Barry County, Missouri, at $1·25 an acre, or approximately £35,000.[23] In contrast to the early success of the Missouri Land and Livestock Company, similarly organized under the same American auspices, land sales of this company appear to have been few and it experienced difficulty in making any profits for the first seven years. In 1887–8 a dividend of five per cent was paid, and for the next five years the directors were able to distribute from three to six per cent.[24]

In 1902 the Scots admitted they had made an unfortunate investment and a resolution was passed to reduce company capital to £47,500 by returning 5s. on each share to investors. The Board of Directors was now composed of only three men: a gentleman landowner, a chartered accountant, and the Professor of History in the University of Edinburgh. In 1908 the company had 71,098 acres of land in its possession, evaluated at only £16,777, while the capital account stood at £37,500. Four years later the Scots began selling their lands at every opportunity, returning the capital to the shareholders. Slightly less than 40,000 acres remained in the company's hands in 1919 to pay off the final shares, valued at £12,500. Shareholders voted to wind-up the next year, but formal action was not taken until 1933. The liquidator reported in 1937, and again in 1939, that his job was not finished, and he died in 1943 with the task still incomplete. Scottish officials struck the company from the register in 1948.[25] Certainly the investors had earned a pittance for their pains and were fortunate in getting their investment returned from these lands.

A fifth land promotion, the American Land and Colonization

Company of Scotland, was incorporated in March 1881 during a particularly distressing time for the Lowland farmers. This company proposed 'to help emigrants in their selection of a new home, to arrange for their transit by sea and by land, to offer them farms of an extent and description suitable to their means and tastes, to aid in the erection of their homesteads, and to permit payments in yearly instalments'. The Glasgow company had a nominal capital of £500,000 in £10 shares. An initial £60,000 was raised during 1881 and the directors secured a tract of 84,000 acres of land in Pipestone and Murray counties in southern Minnesota. The company also purchased half interest in the town of Woodstock, the terminus of the St Paul and Sioux City Railroad in Pipestone County. In conjunction with the railroad, a 'commodious' hotel and land offices were constructed; a small land boom was promoted and some transactions brought as high as forty per cent profit. During 1882–3, Jesup, Paton and Company were the American representatives.[26] In June 1883 the directors announced that 42,964 acres had been sold or leased, declared an annual dividend of eight per cent, and established a reserve fund.[27] During the next two years declining profits were added to a small reserve fund.[28] When the directors saw little prospect of improvement, they proposed that six of the largest shareholders be appointed liquidators. Each shareholder in the company was paid a bonus of 5s. a share, and the liquidators expected to return all the paid-up capital with the additional possibility of a substantial bonus.[29]

In March 1883 Sir George Warrender, William J. Menzies, and Colin J. Mackenzie of Edinburgh, who were associated in the Scottish-American Investment Company, organized another land venture, the Texas and New Mexico Land Syndicate, Limited. They were contacted by the New York vendor of the Reuben Ross Land Grant who arranged for the transfer of this Spanish grant located in west Texas. The company was prepared to invest £20,000 in improving and cultivating this land in anticipation of future sales. Nothing was to be paid the American owners until validity of the Spanish title could be ascertained. On the advice of lawyers in America, the Scots abandoned the idea and wound-up their company in 1885, having lost nothing but their time and the legal and promotional fees.[30]

Most Scottish land companies of the early 1880s experienced only fleeting financial success. When the first dividend of ten per cent was announced by the Scottish American Land Company, eager investors pushed the value of the first issue of shares, with £7 called, up to £8 12s. 6d. The second issue was selling at £3, exactly fifty per cent higher than the paid-up capital. Within the year these dropped to £6 17s. 6d. and £2 respectively, amounting to a capital depreciation of £13,750. Shares of the Missouri Land Company of Scotland, with £4 paid-up, had dropped from £3 18s. 6d. to £3 13s. 6d. during 1882–3, a reduction in stock values of £2,270.[31] By 1884 the Scots had put four and a half millions sterling into land companies in the United States, Canada, and Australia, and had accepted the liability for a million and a half more uncalled capital. Four of the companies, including Canada North-West Land Company and the Scottish American Land Company, had to pass dividends. Only the Missouri Land and Livestock Company was able to maintain the expected ten per cent per annum. Depreciation in the stock of the land companies was estimated to be nearly three times as large as the gross profit they yielded to the proprietors.[32] Much of this temporary depreciation became permanent loss when many of the companies folded in 1884. In this year Scottish capitalists largely abandoned their search for wealth through the direct purchase and sale of land.

The same promoters who demonstrated such patience in handling mortgage and cattle company investments, seemed unwilling to wait for the increment in land values to bring them profits. The inability to maintain consistent dividends, that placed them in a weak competitive position in securing loans from fellow Scots through debentures, coupled with concern over alien land legislation, may offer a partial explanation. At any rate, the few new companies registered after 1884 were private ventures not inviting financial support from the general public. An example may be found in the Park Red River Valley Land Company, Limited, of 1885. Several Scottish farmers and seed merchants who owned small farms in Cass County, Dakota Territory, agreed to pool their lands and resources to plant, cultivate, and market wheat. Each man subscribed for one share of stock for each acre of land he brought into the combine. The co-operative venture was not successful and the dozen promoters who had paid £3 a share in 1885 had to contribute another £1 in 1890. The income from the wheat crop of 1892 was so small the company elected to cease business. Between £25,000 and £30,000 had been lost.[33]

A final speculation in real estate was conducted in Nevada. The South Nevada Land and Development Company filed articles of incorporation in Edinburgh in March 1913, so that it might, as an American corporation, solicit funds in Scotland. The promoters, led by Peter Buol, Las Vegas' first mayor, were buying up acreage, improving it by irrigation, and then subdividing and selling lots near the growing town of Las Vegas, Clark County, Nevada.[34] Scots were invited to subscribe to $100 shares in the enterprise, and $85,500 was soon raised. For years there was no financial return and when the company manager in Nevada died in 1932, affairs of the company were depressed by litigation over water resources, unpaid taxes, and the absence of a market for land during the economic depression. A Los Angeles shareholder took over the company lands as trustee and paid the back taxes in 1936. The Scots assured him there would be no more funds forthcoming and urged that the less valuable lands be sacrificed to protect the more promising. When this procedure did not suffice to meet indebtedness, default was the only solution. Upon the death of the trustee in 1943, large acreages surrounding Las Vegas were a part of his estate. The heirs agreed to divide the income with the Scottish shareholders in the land company on an equal basis. By 1948, $36,000 had been sent to the Edinburgh headquarters. The Scots thus received back about forty-five per cent of their investment and nothing in dividends.[35] Investors of the twentieth century learned again what the Scottish capitalists of the 1880s had experienced: land promotions in western America were too risky, not likely to bring financial rewards, and should be left to local residents.

TIMBER AND AGRICULTURAL PROMOTIONS

As soon as Scottish investors realized in the late 1870s that forest lands could be purchased in large blocks and that there were potential profits in cutting and processing the timber, limited stock companies were rapidly formed for this purpose. As in other lines of endeavour, William J. Menzies of the Scottish-American Investment Company was the leading promoter. In the summer of 1880 Menzies, Alexander Mitchell, a Glasgow timber merchant, and other Scots formed a partnership with Cook and Brothers of Montreal and Toronto to organize the British Canadian Lumbering and Timber Company, Limited. The syndicate secured control of over 800,000 acres of land, including pine timber 'limits', or cutting-rights, in Quebec and Ontario and approximately 5,800 acres in Michigan and 1,200 in Wisconsin, all held in fee simple.[36]

The success of this company during the initial year prompted the organization of the American Lumber Company, Limited. Herman H. Cook, the Toronto lumber merchant, came to Edinburgh to interest the Scots in the purchase of additional limits in Ontario and the northern Michigan peninsula. Menzies brought together several of his capitalist friends, including timber merchants of Edinburgh and Glasgow, to draw up another Memorandum of Association to acquire pine lands in the United States and Canada and to engage in the business of lumberers and timber merchants. The nominal capital of this company, registered in April 1882, was £412,000.[37]

The first subscription amounted to £212,000, of which £130,000 in deferred shares went to the vendors of the timber lands.[38] After several directors made a brief tour of inspection, the Ontario limits, with the exception of those on the Serpent River on the north shore of Lake Huron, were handed back to the Canadian vendors at the price originally paid for them. As a part of the financial adjustment at this time, the vendor's deferred shares were cancelled and replaced by a smaller cash payment for the Michigan lands. Shareholders were informed that lumbermen, working as independent appraisers, had affirmed the value of the white pine remaining in Michigan. When the lumber was placed on the market, however, it was found 'not of the quality in demand' and the price received did not cover the annual expenses. The directors found solace in the fact that all the lumber companies were in difficult straits as a result of the decline in annual consumption of timber during 1883. Of greater import was the knowledge that new flaws had developed in the company's titles to its timber rights in Michigan. In some cases the Scots had purchased a temporary permit to cut the standing timber, but did not have any permanent right to the land.[39] The Michigan lands were finally taken back by the vendor at $2 for every estimated hundred feet of timber in place of the $3 originally paid.[40]

In January 1884 an extraordinary meeting of the American Lumber Company was called to consider winding-up procedures.[41] The *Scottish Banking and Insurance Magazine* thought the absence of public excitement about the failure of this company remarkable, since the American vendors had earlier learned that the company could not carry on the business for which it was started, foresaw disaster, and had got out on the best possible terms.[42]

A published list of shareholders revealed sixty-two investors from Edinburgh with Nelson, Menzies, and Warrender, of the Scottish-American Investment Company, the largest holders. In Glasgow there were thirty-seven stockholders, and in Dundee, thirty. Among the heaviest investors in the latter community were the Dundee Investment Company and William Mackenzie. There were six stockholders in Aberdeen and the remaining shares were scattered among the lesser Scottish communities. The largest single investor was Archibald Coats, manufacturer of Paisley, who held a thousand shares.[43]

In November 1884 the liquidator revealed that there were nine judicial actions against the company in the federal court at Marquette, Michigan, for sums amounting to $15,000 and two actions in the Canadian courts amounting to $14,000. All parties claimed the Scottish company had illegally cut timber on their lands. Nothing was left of the company but the chattel assets, and the liquidators were unable to realize on them because of the depression in the timber business. The Scots could not escape legal liability, and practically all the capital placed in the venture was lost.[44]

Scots were repeatedly warned to avoid the timber industry. At the annual meeting of the Lumber Manufacturers' Association of the Northwest in Chicago, during October 1885, the president reported a fifteen per cent decline in timber prices since 1883 and a ten per cent reduction below the amounts sold in 1884. To maintain prices, a further twenty per cent reduction in sales was urged for 1886. *The North-West Lumberman* reported 'The lumber trade of the country at large, and especially of the North-West, has this season made a mistake in supposing that there could be an advance in prices preceding a rise in volume of demand. . . . An attempt has been made, . . . to create an artificial demand by shaking higher prices (on paper) in buyers' faces. But the effect has been a dismal failure. . . .'[45]

Capitalists directing the Scottish-American Investment Company invested heavily in another timber and lumber enterprise in California. Joseph Russ and Company of San Francisco, timber merchants, owned several mills and logging railroads in northern California and apparently had access to unlimited forest. During 1882 partners of this company approached Faulkner, Bell and Company of San Francisco concerning a scheme to secure additional redwood groves in Humboldt County and enlarge the transportation and manufacturing facilities there. Plans were laid to form a syndicate strong enough to dominate the logging business in northern California, and James D. Walker, a partner in Faulkner, Bell and Company, who was already well known in Edinburgh as a purveyor of mines and cattle ranches, hurried to Scotland to secure the capital essential for the new company.

The upshot of his trip was the registration of the California Redwood Company, Limited, in July 1883, to acquire 72,000 acres of redwood forest in Humboldt County. Authorized company capital was £900,000. Half of this amount, approximately $2,250,000, was immediately called and paid-up. The Scots agreed to pay £732,000, in cash and shares, to this California syndicate for land and timber in Humboldt County, and for the mills, wharves and tugs belonging to Joseph Russ and Company. After the redwood had been cut, plans called for the disposal of the lands for grazing and agricultural purposes.[46]

Walker, Russ, and his partner, David Evans, all maintained a personal financial interest in the California Redwood Company through their shares and debentures. The Board of Directors included the Scots, Sir George Warrender (chairman), Blyth, Menzies, and Nelson, along with the three Californians. To avoid legal complications over foreign ownership of land, all titles were to be left in Walker's name and actual operations managed from San Francisco.[47]

In Eureka, California, *The Humboldt Standard* reported the news about this 'biggest transaction in California in recent years'. When the launching of such a company had first been reported on the village streets, stories had been discounted because the mills had been working on reduced schedules and lands had been selling at trifling figures as a result of the depressed timber market. Nevertheless, the wealthy Scots had purchased two mills in the Eureka district, one of these located on an island in the bay opposite the town, and a third in nearby Trinidad. These mills could process 170,000 feet of lumber daily, and a fourth, under construction, would have an additional capacity of 90,000 feet. The Freshwater and Humboldt Logging Road, about nine miles long, and the shorter Trinidad Logging Road had been acquired with all the rolling stock.

The flow of Scottish capital made possible immediate expansion. A new railroad was being built up the Elk River Valley. Orders had been placed for four new locomotives, 20,000 tons of railroad iron, and the metal parts to construct one hundred new flatcars. The Scottish company announced its intention to find a market for redwood in northern Europe. The first two shipments, 1,500,000 feet of timber, had been sent to Glasgow. In time, the trade was expected to include markets in Mexico, South America, and Hawaii. By the end of 1883 the company was shipping two million feet of lumber per week, making it the leading manufacturing company in Humboldt County and one of the largest in California.[48]

In October 1883 the California Redwood Company advertised a £300,000 debenture issue in the Scottish journals, with certificates of £200 and £100 running for five years at an annual interest of seven per cent. The property of the company and the £450,000 uncalled capital were listed as security. The directors estimated the annual profit from their undertaking at £100,000, over four times the interest on these debentures. Surveyors had evaluated the company's redwood timber at $10,500,000. As a further protection for the debenture holders, a sinking fund of $1 for every one thousand feet of timber cut had been established.[49] The accounts for 1883 showed a profit of £12,681, but no dividend was declared. Expenses had been much larger than anticipated because of the continuous purchases of timber lands and the expansion of processing equipment. Plans had been made to acquire a lumber yard in San Francisco for the storing and seasoning of timber.[50]

By 1884 rumour was spreading that the California Redwood Company was involved in a gigantic scheme to acquire title to the public lands of the United States by means of fraudulent entries under the Timber Land Act of 1878. This law permitted the purchase of 160-acre tracts of timber land in the states of California, Oregon, and Nevada, and in Washington Territory for $2·50 an acre. Only citizens of the United States, or those declaring intention of citizenship, were entitled to register a claim. Moreover, the purchaser had to declare that he did not apply for the land as a speculation but for his own exclusive use, and that he had not either directly or indirectly made an agreement or contract whereby the title acquired from the United States might be used for the benefit of other persons. The applicant had to take an oath to this effect before the registrar and receiver of the land office in the district where the land was situated. Those swearing falsely were guilty of perjury and would lose both the money paid for the land and the title, and any grant of conveyance they might have made would be declared null and void.[51] Newspapers suggested that timber barons, in defiance of the law, had resolved to gain possession of the redwood forests of northern California and had hired agents 'to scour the country for such impecunious and other vagabonds as could be found, who, either from ignorance or recklessness, were willing, for a consideration of from twenty-five to fifty dollars, to commit the perjury necessary to obtain'[52] 160-acre timber tracts which cost $400 each, with $10 additional for fees. All payments were made by the agent, who appeared to have an unlimited amount of cash, and with the aid of a pliant official as registrar and receiver in the Humboldt district, the certificates were speedily issued. These were immediately transferred to a partner of Joseph Russ and Company and eventually conveyed to Walker at Faulkner, Bell and Company. Land applications had been presented at the local land office in batches of twenty-five at a time. The San Francisco companies had dispatched a lawyer East to speed up the issuance of the final patents in the General Land office in Washington.[53]

The rumour that reached the general public in 1884 was not unfounded. At the very beginning, soon after the first group of certificates reached the capital, government officials grew suspicious and, fearing universal fraud, suspended issuance of final patents and sent a special agent to California to investigate. He was bought off by the timber scouts, but later in 1883 a second investigator, Wilson T. Smith, went West and obtained conclusive evidence that some ninety entries of timber lands, embracing about 14,000 acres, had been fraudulently made, transferred upon certificates of entry, and retransferred before patent to Faulkner, Bell and Company.[54]

On the basis of this evidence, the grand jury of the United States district court at San Francisco issued an indictment against eight men involved in the transactions. In each case bail was placed at $5,000.[55] *The Bulletin* of San Francisco connected the California Redwood Company with the trial and invoked a reply from the company lawyers who finally felt compelled 'in justice to state' that the lands held by the company were issued years ago and that the Scottish venture was in no way connected with the frauds.[56] Somewhat abashed, *The Humboldt Standard* announced:

> . . . it is to be regretted that sufficient testimony could be adduced upon which to base an indictment. It is nevertheless true, that the law is no respecter of persons, and in its vindication alone are the rights of citizens safe. . . . Faithful and conscientious officials in high and humble stations is [*sic*] the only guarantee for the protection of the rights of the people. If flagrant violations of the law have taken place, it is not the fault of the law but the blame rests with those who are entrusted with its execution.[57]

The whole sordid affair was summarized in a San Francisco magazine, and a bitter complaint recorded against foreign land grabbers:

> On every hand we hear the cry ad nauseam, of land-grabs, fraudulent grants, land-thieves, etc. These charges are principally made against our own citizens, and to some extent they are, doubtless, well founded. But of late a new element seems to have entered the field in the shape of syndicates from abroad, wielding immense capital, and who have already commenced, in defiance of our laws, to grab public lands of enormous value, and practically rob our citizens and despoil us of our most valuable forests.[58]

The story was reprinted by the *Financial and Mining News* and soon the Scottish public learned of the alarming developments. Already apprised of the situation, the directors of the California Redwood Company had dispatched Menzies and Blyth to the Pacific Coast to inspect the property and examine the land titles.[59] The Scottish directors cabled from San Francisco: 'No occasion for anxiety about Redwood title; rigid independent inquiry is showing entirely favourable result.' Another Scot, John Robertson, wired his Edinburgh firm: 'Spent six days in Redwood; my investigations entirely confirm prospectus. I have seen lawyer who examined title. I am satisfied all is in perfect order.'[60] Meanwhile the United States Senate passed a resolution requesting the Secretary of the Interior to report about entries on the public lands by foreign corporations.[61]

According to the estimates of a special agent of the General Land Office, possibly 100,000 acres of land had been fraudulently registered. When he discovered the scheme of fraud in all its details, he was offered a bribe of $5,000 to suppress the facts and abandon the investigation. As we have seen, he produced sufficient evidence to justify the grand jury indictments. For his pains the agent was subsequently suspended from duty and afterwards dismissed from the service at the instance 'of great influence brought against him from the Pacific coast and in Washington'. In the fall of 1884 patents were issued in one hundred and fifty-seven cases reported by the agent as fraudulent. The officer in the General Land Office responsible for the case had suppressed the evidence and misled the Commissioner to secure the transfer of 22,000 acres of land, valued at $440,000, to the perpetrators of the fraud. All these facts came to light after the appointment of William A. J. Sparks as Commissioner of the General Land Office in the Cleveland administration. The Democratic commissioner cited the case to illustrate 'that the ramifications of fraud extended into the General Land Office at Washington', and to present 'some of the difficulties of special agents when their discoveries implicate wealthy and influential persons'.[62]

Another special investigator, appointed by Sparks, arrived in northern California in January 1885. Representatives of the redwood syndicate soon discovered his presence and attempted to defeat the renewed investigation.

> Some of the witnesses were spirited out of the country; others were threatened and intimidated; spies were employed to watch and follow the agent and report the names of all persons who conversed with or called upon him; and on one occasion two persons who were about to enter the agent's room at his hotel for the purpose of conferring with him in reference to the entries were knocked down and dragged away.[63]

Conclusive evidence was again produced that David Evans and Charles H. King, partners of Joseph Russ and Company, along with Walker, were the prime manipulators of the timber-land grab. They had enlisted the services of Charles E. Beach, 'an old experienced land sharp', a brother-in-law of Evans, and a brother of the registrar in the local land office. From the backroom of a saloon, three blocks from the land office, various persons were hired to go about Eureka and the surrounding area to find individuals who would sign applications for land and transfer their interests to the company.[64] Fifty dollars was paid for each 160-acre tract thus secured, and the company's 'agents' received an additional $5 for each applicant enlisted. No attempt was made to keep the solicitation secret:

> Sailors were caught while in port and hurried into a saloon or to a certain notary public's office and induced to sign applications and convey the lands to a member of the firm. Farmers were stopped on their way to their homes, and merchants were called from their counters and persuaded to allow their names to be used to obtain title to the lands.[65]

Operations were conducted on a large scale. A local lawyer testified to drawing up four hundred and fifty deeds, a Eureka notary public admitted preparing eighty-one certificates in a single day, and the recorder for Humboldt County stated that three hundred and forty-nine deeds, in favour of David Evans, were drawn up in his office on one occasion. Thus the Scottish syndicate, according to various estimates, had fraudulently obtained from 57,000 to 64,000 acres of the most valuable timber land in the United States, appraised by various persons from $6,400,000 to $11,000,000. Commissioner Sparks had thoroughly aired the affairs of the California Redwood Company.[66]

In May 1886 the Californians who had been indicted were freed when a federal jury in San Francisco quashed the charges. The *New York Times*, recalling the indictments, complained that the men would 'resume business at the old stand'. It inquired if the Department of Justice was unable to hold someone responsible for such a shameful failure to enforce the laws.[67] In November 1886 Cleveland's Secretary of the Interior requested the Attorney General to institute new suits to secure the cancellation of patents on one hundred and fifty-one entries granted during the presidency of Chester A. Arthur.[68] At the trial, held before the registrar and receiver at Eureka, California, over one hundred entrymen came forward to testify that they had been persuaded by agents of the land syndicate to make illegal entries. Commissioner Sparks reported that in disclosing such facts they sacrificed their own interests and were subjected to bitter persecution and personal indignities.

> . . . Many of these witnesses were employees of the defendants and their associates and they knew that they would forfeit their situations and deprive themselves of an opportunity of making a living for their families in the vicinity, while, on the other hand, if they failed to testify, they would be liberally rewarded. One of the entrymen while on the witness stand was attacked by the attorney for the defen-

> dants and cruelly beaten, for no other reason than that he had dared to testify to a conversation between himself and the attorney, wherein the latter had attempted to bribe him not to appear as a witness in the case.[69]

In Edinburgh the shareholders had agreed to wind-up the California Redwood Company in April 1885, after reporting an indebtedness of £146,768. The news was bitterly received, and one Scottish journal observed:

> Scarcely has the wreck of that unfortunate venture, 'The Scottish Pacific Coast Gold Mining Company, Limited,' with its precious freight of £95,000 of hard-earned Scotch money, disappeared beneath the waters of liquidation, than another galleon, 'The California Redwood Company, Limited,' hailing from the same port,—No. 123 George Street, Edinburgh,—launched under the same auspices, with a still more costly freight,—also of Scotch money,—has met with a like disaster.

No reference was made to the embarrassing land fraud. The reported causes of failure involved problems of a Board in Edinburgh trying to manage a manufacturing and trading business six thousand miles away. Agents in California who had been granted too much control over the management, were deemed incompetent, and they had spent money recklessly. Moreover, debentures had been issued at too high a rate of interest. Much blame was placed upon the directors of the Scottish-American Investment Company. One editor noted 'no other venture of theirs has succeeded', and suggested that their original success was 'more by luck than good guiding'.[70]

Liquidators notified the debenture holders that the estimated value of company properties and the uncalled capital amounted to £414,543. The entire indebtedness to debenture holders was £369,000. They were warned, however, that all shareholders, particularly the Californians, would not be able to pay the capital call, and only £239,000 could be raised in Scotland.[71] The editor of *The Edinburgh Courant* raised the question as to whether liquidation should be made on a voluntary or judicial basis. Representatives of the Scots who had investigated the status of the company's property in California had submitted a report 'highly unflattering to the vendors and certain other persons in California responsible for the conduct of the Company's business'. Fortunately, the vendors had taken 30,000 deferred shares in partial payment for their timber lands, carrying with them a liability of £5 a share. The Californians were confronted with a £150,000 debt in place of what they thought would be a valuable reversionary interest. The Edinburgh Board now called upon them for £2 a share. The vendors immediately began to negotiate to relieve themselves of this liability, but the Board was unreceptive. The Scots insisted the mess was all the making of the vendors and managers in America and that 'it would be rather too much in keeping with what has gone before if they were allowed to escape from responsibility'. The Californians pressed for a judicial liquidation. Whether the liquidation was judicial or voluntary, the *Courant* thought the whole of the unpaid capital must be paid-up.[72]

As the Interior Department investigation continued, San Francisco attorneys, who had examined the entrymen's deeds to Evans and the transfers from Evans to Walker to eliminate all legal flaws, testified that Walker knew what had been done to get the land and that he had agreed to the project with King before the lands were registered. When this report was published, the Scottish company organized the Humboldt Redwood Company, Limited, in August 1885, for the primary purpose of getting the lands transferred from Walker to new trustees.[73] Walker then stated that the Scotch capitalists also knew that the land they agreed to purchase was still public domain and that the matter had been fully discussed with them in Edinburgh. The General Land Office concluded that the testimony proved a conspiracy had been entered into by Walker, King, and the Scottish capitalists to acquire the timber lands before any of the entries had been made and when they knew that the lands had not been entered. The Scots were going to have difficulty in maintaining the defence of innocent purchasers.[74] Several well-known Scottish capitalists had extensive funds tied up in the Humboldt Redwood Company. Sir George Warrender had £12,000 in the business; Nelson, £15,000; Archibald Coats, £7,000; Blyth, £5,000; and a dozen more had between £4,000 and £6,000 invested.

In December 1885 liquidators of the California Redwood Company made an agreement of restitution with Russ and Evans. The mills in Eureka and Trinidad, along with 17,000 acres of redwood lands, reverted to the Californians. In turn, Russ and Evans agreed to return all the preference, ordinary, and deferred shares they owned in the Scottish company, worth approximately £500,000, and to hand back £40,000 in cash and £72,000 in debentures, part of the price paid for the northern California property. A portion of this money was to be used to compensate the Scots for the stores they had left behind, the cut timber and logs, and for a shingle mill they had built. However, this business deal involved only a portion of the California properties of the company. Nothing in the agreement with the two partners of Joseph Russ and Company was to be construed as a release of claims the California Redwood Company had against their other partner, Charles H. King, or Faulkner, Bell and Company.[75]

With permission of the court, the original timber company was reconstructed as the Edinburgh and San Francisco Redwood Company, Limited, with a reduced capital of £120,000. Debenture holders in Scotland agreed to take 12s. cash return on each pound lent and to leave 8s. with the new venture. Thus £100,000 of unpaid share capital, held as security for the debentures, could be released to pay the California creditors of the company in full. All interest in arrears on the debentures was also paid, and since the remaining property was sufficient to pay the new loans, this group was satisfied. The shareholders, on the other hand, had lost heavily—possibly as much as £250,000.[76] The new company did not propose to engage in cutting, sawing, and carrying timber, because it was deemed too expensive and involved a business to be carried on so far away from Edinburgh. The directors planned to get other lumbermen to take up their lands and carry on operations either on a rental or royalty basis. Nelson represented the original promoters on the new Board, but the remainder were debenture holders. The management was divorced from the Scottish-American Investment Company.[77] The questionable land titles remained the responsibility of the Humboldt Redwood Company.

The Edinburgh and San Francisco Redwood Company from the outset found lumbering business on the Pacific Coast in the doldrums. Until 1885 the lumbermen of California had successfully formed a pooling arrangement to regulate prices by limiting the supply. They estimated that California would use 150,000,000 feet of redwood lumber annually, and each manufacturer had a quota to ship to San Francisco. In the fall of 1884 these combined quotas were twenty per cent more than sales, so orders for reductions were sent out. Mendocino lumbermen refused to agree, sold their lumber under the current price, and broke the market. Prices tumbled rapidly and redwood was being sold for less than the cost of manufacturing and shipping.[78] Under these circumstances, the Scots were unable to promote much local interest in their forests. Although a few sales and leases were made, income was only sufficient to meet the interest on debentures. No dividend was paid, and by the close of 1890 only £15,512 in cash assets was in hand. Three years later this was reduced to £9,698.[79]

The Scots elected to ask the United States courts to restore to the company various 160-acre tracts of land registered on the basis of timber and pre-emption claims in 1883 but later cancelled by the Commissioner of the General Land Office. As a new settler took up the land on which a patent had been denied, the Humboldt Redwood Company, holder of the questionable titles, brought suit to prove that the settler held the quarter section of land in trust for the company rather than possessing it outright. The Scots did not deny the fraudulent nature of the original entries, but introduced evidence to prove the company knew nothing of the fraudulent character of each entry at the time the acreage was purchased. In April 1897 the United States district court in San Francisco declared that the holder of a certificate of purchase to public land, based upon a pre-emption or forestland entry, acquires only an equitable title to the land, and a purchaser of such a certificate could not acquire any greater right than the entryman possessed. The purchaser could not be protected even though he was unaware of fraud in making the entry. Moreover, the court disallowed the Scots' claim that the action of the Commissioner in cancelling the entry of public land without notifying the holder of the certificate was void. Moreover, the fact that the Commissioner's action had not been approved by the Secretary of the Interior in no way altered the position of the holder of the cancelled certificate. If the Land Office made an error, then the company should have exhausted every effort to have it corrected there. Failing in this, the company could not set up its claim in another court against a registrant of a patent approved by the Land Office.[80]

The California press rejoiced that the timber land was still the property of the government and kept open to entry. The decision of 1897 settled fourteen suits involving the title to two thousand one hundred acres in Humboldt County and was applicable to 30,000 to 40,000 additional acres owned by various and sundry purchasers.[81] Litigation continued to the United States Supreme Court, where the district court's decision was upheld in 1900.[82]

Early in 1901 the Edinburgh and San Francisco Redwood Company sold all its lands with a clear title in the Trinidad district for £195,000. Half of the sale price was received in cash, and by borrowing £32,000 the directors were able to pay off the outstanding debentures, £114,000, in May 1901. The company retained small acreages in the Elk River Valley until 1904 when the company was wound-up.[83] The debenture holders had succeeded in regaining their loans to this timber promotion with interest, but the shareholders of the old California Redwood Company, who had hoped to recoup some of their losses by the reconstitution of the company, were sorely disappointed. Extravagant management, guilty of overexpansion at a time when timber prices were declining, and the legal complications over the fraudulent registration of claims to timber lands had combined to produce the disaster.

A group of Glaswegians organized the Scottish Carolina Timber and Land Company, Limited, in 1884. In comparison with the Edinburgh promotions, the beginning was modest with an authorized capital of £40,000. The Scots used the bulk of this capital to purchase approximately 40,000 acres of land in Madison and Haywood counties, North Carolina, northwest of the city of Asheville. This acreage, located in the Appalachians along the North Carolina-Tennessee border, was covered with pine forest. The plan was to cut the timber, improve the land for farming and cattle raising, and ultimately promote immigration to the site and establish a Scottish colony there.[84] From the first season's timber cutting the shareholders received a dividend of eighteen and one-half per cent, twelve and one-half per cent in new shares and six per cent in cash. Authorized capital was raised to £80,000 in 1885 and to £200,000 the next year. Lumbering operations mushroomed. Unfortunately for the investors, the efforts for 1886 produced a profit of only £474. The company's sawmill was in full operation throughout 1887, but the debit at the year's close had risen to £5,467. Lumber prices were too low to justify continuation of the enterprise and by 1899 it was wound-up.[85]

Between 1893 and 1895 Glaswegians also operated the Woodruff Land and Timber Company, Limited, which had purchased 5,000 acres of land in Woodruff and Cross counties, Arkansas. The vendor received £14,000 for his acreage, originally obtained from a St Louis railroad, chiefly in the form of ordinary shares in the company. For promotional work the Scots subscribed to an additional £12,500 in preference shares entitled to a ten per cent dividend. The venture did not prove successful and after a Scottish inspector reported the timber to be inferior, the company was liquidated.[86] The Scots had tried land and timber promotions along the Atlantic and Pacific coasts, in the Great Lakes area and in the Mississippi Valley, but nowhere did they experience financial success.

While some sought to enhance their fortune through the purchase of redwood forests in northern California, other Scots proposed to grow grapes and oranges in the southern part of the state. With the sponsorship of two Edinburgh wine merchants, a Glasgow engineer, and several businessmen of Leith, the Scottish Californian Orange and Vineyard Company, Limited, was registered in September 1884. The authorized capital was £50,000 in £2 shares. The declared objects of the company were exceptionally broad, emphasizing real-estate promotions, the buying and breeding of cattle, sheep, goats, and hogs as well as operating orchards and vineyards.[87] Of the first issue of 10,000 shares, only 4,515 were sold, with £1 called on each. With this money the directors purchased an eighty-nine acre ranch with fifty acres planted in fruit trees and grape vines. From their various operations, the promoters hopefully expected to make an annual profit of fifteen per cent. Ernest Watson, son of a Glasgow engineer and director, was sent to Duarte, California, as general manager.[88] But young Watson was not successful, and the Scottish shareholders, with the exception of Watson and his Glasgow friends, began to dispose of their shares. By 1888 there were only eleven shareholders left. When a second pound was called on each share at the close of 1895, all investors but the company officers withdrew. Upon Sir William Renny Watson's death in 1901, his estate included 4,380 shares in the company. Five years later the enterprise came to an official close with a loss of at least £6,000.[89] The Scots' imagination had been excited by the land boom in southern California during the 1880s, and at one time they had planned to transport Scottish citizens to work on their estates. But their plans had ended in disappointment and with them a dream of providing a young son with an economic start in the United States was destroyed.

Another attempt to raise fruits and cereals in southern California was made between 1893 and 1896 by a company known as the St Mungo Fruit Growing Company of California, Limited. The chief promoter was Lord Hamilton, a resident of Motherwell, who secured financial support from a tea merchant, a confectioner, a clergyman, and a hotel keeper in nearby Glasgow. These men subscribed £5,466 of an authorized capital of £15,000 to purchase land on the outskirts of Fresno. The sale of produce and animals raised on their lands did not produce a profit and in 1896 the directors voted to wind-up. The property purchased by the Scots was exceedingly dry, and there was difficulty in disposing of it. No evidence of sale has been found, and apparently everything invested was lost.[90]

In 1900 a Glasgow wine importer prevailed upon his legal counsel and two other importers to join him in promoting two private companies, each with a capital of £1,000, to transport California wines to Scotland. These companies were known as the California Vineyards Association, Limited, and the California and Australian Vineyards Union, Limited. The Memoranda of Association suggested that great plans were afoot 'to carry on the business of wine and spirit brokers, distillers, brewers, maltsters, yeast makers, wholesale and retail wine, spirit and beer merchants, bonded storekeepers, coopers, dealers and blenders of British and foreign spirits, wines and other liquors . . .'. Evidence suggests that the companies did not transact much business of any kind, and by 1904 winding-up proceedings were under way.[91]

The last and largest of the Scottish efforts to make a southern California vineyard a paying proposition was launched in 1901 when the Barton Estate, extending over nine hundred and sixty acres, with buildings, plant machinery, and livestock, was purchased in Fresno County. Company capital was £56,000 in £1 shares. Twenty thousand of these that had a preferred status were held by the California proprietors, and the remaining 36,000 deferred shares were to be sold in Scotland. This was an unusual arrangement, for the Scots usually demanded the preferred shares when financially underwriting a new or expanding business, and left the deferred securities in the hands of American borrowers. The promoters intended to 'carry on the business of growing and purchasing and selling grapes and other fruits, and of manufacturing wines, brandies, and other spirits, including the barrels, casks, jars, bottles, and other vessels'. The Scots secured a going concern, for the company inventory at the time of transfer included four hogsheads of brandy and thirty-one hogsheads of port in bond at Cardiff.[92] Profits were not forthcoming and in 1907 a financial reconstruction took place. Each of the 36,000 deferred shares was reduced in value to 15s., and provision was made to increase the number of preferred shares to 35,000, thereby increasing capitalization to £62,000. At this time a special resolution provided that the company would be 'private', with the shareholders limited to twenty and no funds solicited from the public. The grape-growing and wine-making endeavour continued until 1920 when the company sold out its interests to a Fresno resident. The agreement for liquidation provided each shareholder would receive 1s. 4d. for each preferred and each deferred share, irrespective of any right given the preferred shareholders in the Articles of Association. The Scots thereby obtained a return of approximately £4,300 on a £60,000 investment.[93]

Another twentieth-century agricultural project was begun in 1911 when Charles R. Wingate of Alameda County, California, interested several Glaswegians—an accountant, a marine insurance broker, and a chemical manufacturer—in organizing the Aqua Fria Land Company, Limited. With a £20,000 capitalization the company proposed to purchase lands in Butte County. The Scots, through the management of Wingate, cultivated a peach and almond orchard and experimented in growing alfalfa and raising livestock in conjunction with it. The ranching-farming project, later known as the Los Almendros Land Company, Limited, continued successfully until the death of Wingate in 1923 when the land passed from Scottish hands.[94]

In their land promotions the Scots had everywhere experienced failure. The flow of capital into forest lands, vineyards, orchards, and orange ranches reached high tide in the 1880s. After that, the experienced financiers withdrew; but even into the twentieth century less opulent Scots insisted on trying these single-purpose ventures in land development, and in each case lost virtually all their investment.

TRANSPORTATION AND MANUFACTURING ENTERPRISES

In spite of ambitious plans to expand their mortgage operations throughout western America in the 1880s, Dundee investors retained a primary interest in the Pacific Northwest at the beginning of the decade. Advances on Oregon and Washington real estate, particularly farm lands, had been lucrative enough in the 1870s to build sound financial foundations for the companies guided by William Mackenzie. Such success encouraged the capitalists of Dundee to sponsor the construction of a railroad and other Scots to promote flour and sugar manufacturies in the Greater Northwest.

In their railway promotion, the Scots were to challenge the position and interest of another European entrepreneur in western America, Henry Villard. Villard had started his career as a railroad promoter and financier in 1873 when the association of German bondholders in the Oregon and California Railroad Company chose him as their representative in the Pacific Northwest. Having arrived in the United States in 1853 as a German immigrant boy, he became an itinerant journalist, learned of the West's potentialities, and immediately following the Civil War studied public and corporate finance as secretary of the American Social Science Association. Upon his arrival in Oregon, after a brief visit to Germany in 1873, he quickly acquired the interests of Ben Holladay in the Oregon and California Railroad Company. Once in control of this corporation, he set up the Oregon Railway and Navigation Company to purchase and take over the operations of the powerful Oregon Steam Navigation Company, which owned a fleet of steamers running between Portland and San Francisco. This newly organized firm planned to construct a main railroad along the southern bank of the Columbia River to connect with the Oregon and California Railroad at Portland, thereby gaining a southern outlet to California, and to build feeder lines into eastern Oregon and Washington Territory. A monopoly of Northwestern transportation was envisioned.[95]

Meanwhile, William Reid, spokesman for the Scots, conceived the plan of purchasing small, independent rail lines in the Willamette Valley and combining them into a transportation system, ostensibly for competition with the Oregon and California Railroad, which had stopped construction south of Portland at Roseburg in 1872. If construction proved unprofitable, the fear of competition might stimulate Villard and his German investors to buy out the proposed line. Reid found his Dundee associates interested in this railroad investment, but none of their Scottish-American enterprises, either in Dundee or Portland, was authorized to engage in such a business.

On 4 May 1880 the Oregonian Railway Company, Limited, was registered in Scotland for 'constructing, reconstructing, diverting, equipping, owning, operating, leasing, or selling, transferring or disposing' of railroads in Oregon and Washington Territory or from any point there to the rest of North America. The company declared a special interest in a line running from Astoria or Portland southward through that part of Oregon west of the Cascade Mountains. A grandiose scheme was outlined to build across the mountains near the middle fork of the Willamette River and to make connections in eastern Oregon with lines leading into the territories of Washington and Idaho or the states of Nevada and California. Ample provision was made for the acquisition and operation of wharves, steamboats, canals, bridges, express and stage lines, telegraphs, turnpikes, clay or plank roads. In short, legal powers were obtained to build a transportation empire in the Northwest if fate and finances proved favourable. The Earl of Airlie's name headed the list of those signing the Memorandum of Association. He was joined by his business associates, Thomas H. Cox, William Lowson, Thomas Leng, William Mackenzie, and Peter M. Cochrane, all of Dundee. The authorized capital of the enterprise was £160,000.[96]

As a start, the company planned to purchase and complete, and possibly extend the Dayton, Sheridan, and Grand Ronde Railway, a narrow-gauge line three feet wide, running through the lower Willamette Valley. The directors of the company, under the chairmanship of Cox, borrowed £95,000 for which they issued first mortgage bonds, bearing six per cent annual interest, due in fifteen years. As security, the bondholders received a mortgage on the railroad and a claim on the unpaid capital of the shareholders. After purchasing several short lines on each side of the Willamette River, the company resolved to unite the two major sections of their railroad by erecting a bridge across the Willamette River and extending the road into the city of Portland. In December 1880, the shareholders voted to increase the company's authorized capital to £400,000, and an immediate issue of 16,000 shares raised the subscribed capital to £320,000. To procure additional funds for this expansion, the company also borrowed £119,700, for which they sold a second series of bonds, or deeds of security, to run for twenty years. Although these securities were less desirable than those backed by a first mortgage, the reputation and wealth of the company's directors made them easily marketable.[97]

The threat of expanding competition was of sufficient concern to Villard to justify the lease of all the lines and properties of the Oregonian Railway Company by his Oregon Railway and Navigation Company on 1 August 1881. The lease was for ninety-six years at an annual rental of £28,000. By this negotiation the Villard interests not only liquidated a potential competitor with a terminus on the Columbia River but also secured additional time before resuming construction on the Oregon and California Railroad. Two months later, the Oregonian Railway Company announced that the lease had been executed and delivered and the first instalment on the rent received.[98] Relations between the two companies were cordial for the next two years. In November 1882 shareholders in the Scottish concern received a dividend of 4s. a share.[99] Payments were regularly made by the lessee up to the following November.

In 1883 the Oregon and California Railroad resumed construction southward to form a junction with the Central Pacific at the Oregon-California state boundary. By the end of the year, one hundred and forty miles of track was laid as far as Ashland, but an additional year was needed to complete the last thirty-eight miles, including tunnelling through the Siskiyou Mountains. Much of the capital invested had come from the sale of surplus lands in Portland.[100]

This extensive construction proved expensive and strained the credit of all the Villard transportation enterprises in the Northwest. His railway promotions, including the Northern Pacific, brought him to insolvency. Early in 1884 the Oregon Railway and Navigation Company, without warning, repudiated its lease made with the Scottish company, and, on Whitsunday 1884, refused to pay the rent that had come due. Panic developed among the shareholders in Dundee, and within a few days Oregonian Railway shares dropped 65s. While the directors remained discreetly silent, the bondholders became alarmed over the security of their loans.[101] The *Dundee Advertiser* suggested that in the absence of fuller information bondholders should press severely on the company for a settlement.[102]

The bondholders, in special session, debated whether to liquidate, in which case the shareholders would lose everything, or to postpone liquidation but ask shareholders to call-up at once the outstanding capital and transfer the money to the bondholders. No final decision was reached, but a committee was appointed to represent the bondholders before the company's directors, and immediately a circular was sent to the shareholders requesting a private meeting.

The editor of *The Edinburgh Courant* expressed an understanding for the bondholders' viewpoint: 'Naturally they turn their eyes to the nearest realisable assets, and as it happens to be the £4 per share of uncalled capital, they demand that it should be at once called up and paid over to them.' Unwilling to admit defeat, the journalist was certain the railroad could be worked profitably:

> It is a very cheap line of its kind, having cost altogether about £2600 a mile. It is fairly well located in a rising agricultural State. Against these advantages have to be set the want of an efficient terminus and the fact that it is paralleled through its whole length by a competing line – the Oregon and California. The former drawback might be remedied at comparatively small cost, for the present northern terminus is only twelve miles from Portland, the principal port of Oregon, and once connected with Portland it should get its share of such traffic as is going.

Why not delay action long enough to send a Scottish agent to Oregon to take the railroad from the hands of the lessees and run it? The editor concluded:

> . . . Dundee will have no more American leases—or anything else American—for a while; but it would be a scandal, as well as a folly, if repudiation so flagrant and shameless as there has been in this case should go unpunished, as it certainly will if the Company is prematurely forced into liquidation.

Agitated Dundee shareholders, fearful of financial ruin, wrote to the American minister in London to inquire if an injunction could be obtained to keep the company legally alive until the United States courts could review the validity of the lease.[103]

In May 1884 shareholders of the Oregonian Railway Company voted to issue 20,000 preference shares of £1 each to raise the £12,000 interest due on the company bonds and to provide sufficient money to commence legal proceedings against the lessee company. It was also agreed to call an extraordinary meeting the following month to consider the voluntary winding-up of business and the appointment of a liquidator. When the shareholders subscribed to only fifty per cent of the preference stock, two of the directors, Cox and Leng, pledged £5,000 each to test the validity of the lease made with the Oregon Railway and Navigation Company, provided other shareholders took up the additional £2,000 in the issue. Four of the largest shareholders issued a second circular urging co-operation and support for the generous offer.[104]

At this stage of the negotiations, the shareholders had paid-up £6 on each share, a sum of £192,000, all of which had been spent on construction. They still had a liability of £128,000, but the outstanding bonds totalled £214,700. If the entire company capital was paid-up and the venture liquidated, the shareholders would lose everything and the bondholders would still be £86,000 short. Each of the directors had subscribed for one thousand to fifteen hundred shares, and others in Dundee had purchased in the aggregate close to three thousand shares. In July the Scottish courts agreed that the small number of bondholders who had petitioned for the winding-up of the company were within their legal right. However, as the company had paid the interest on the petitioners' bonds within the twenty-one-day time limit for legal payment of debts, and as the petitioners represented but a small percentage of the total bondholders, the court refused to order termination of the company against the wishes of the shareholders and directors. The Oregonian Railway Company was now prepared to sue the Oregon Railway and Navigation Company in the federal courts for violation of a contract.[105]

While the legal proceedings were pending, Reid urged the Scottish investors to put up more capital for the railway enterprise. According to his reports, the company had in its possession one hundred and sixty-three miles of railroad constructed at a cost of $12,150 a mile. In addition, it possessed a wharf on the Columbia River at Portland, the surrounding property, and the right-of-way through the city. These assets, along with the rolling stock, were valued at $2,248,420. Reid suggested that with an additional $521,000 the company could complete the line into Portland, restore the bridges destroyed by the neglect of the Oregon Railway and Navigation Company, purchase a new locomotive, and recondition the remaining rolling stock. Such an expenditure would push the cost up to $14,500 a mile. The Portland promoter pointed out the contrast between that figure and the $70,000 a mile expended on its competitor, the Oregon and California Railroad: 'The total cost per mile of your line,' he remarked, 'would only be about one-half of their mortgages and debts per mile.' He was certain that the lighter, narrow-gauge road could be completed successfully, and even be extended to the western coastal towns. The Scottish investors paid little attention to his scheme which proposed that five additional shillings be raised for every pound already invested.[106]

The judicial hearing was postponed while the two corporations filed charges and replies with the United States Circuit Court in the District of Oregon. Villard's company based its case largely on the fact that nothing in its Articles of Association permitted the company to make a lease. In December 1884 Judge Matthew P. Deady reviewed the legal papers and declared 'the denial of indebtedness is clearly frivolous'. The court was not prepared, however, to dismiss all the legal arguments presented by the Oregon Railway and Navigation Company and granted a further delay while both parties presented final evidence.[107] On 18 March 1885 Judge Deady announced his decision in favour of the Scottish company. According to Oregon law, three or more persons were authorized to form a corporation to engage in any lawful enterprise or business and this, in the judge's opinion, included the power to buy and sell or lease a railway. In October 1878 the state legislature had passed a law placing a foreign corporation on the same footing with a domestic corporation, upon its compliance with the laws governing registration and regulation. Furthermore, the Oregonian Railway Company was recognized by the Oregon legislature as an existing corporation, lawfully engaged in the construction of a railroad in October 1880, when it was granted wharfage privileges and a right-of-way through the city of Portland. After establishing the legal existence of both corporations, the judge declared that 'a contract of a corporation, though invalid for want of power in the corporation to make it, may, if not illegal, be enforced against such a corporation, where it has had the benefit of consideration therefore'. The lease was thus declared a legal contract and the Oregonian Railway awarded the first half-year's unpaid rent, amounting to £400, plus interest and court costs.[108] The defendants were given forty days to appeal to the Supreme Court, but before the appeal could be taken, the entire penalty had to be consigned to the court.[109] Immediately the Scottish company brought action for the second unpaid instalment of rent due in November 1884, amounting to $68,131. Another suit in equity was also introduced against the Oregon Railway and Navigation Company to make good the extensive dilapidations on the narrow-gauge, estimated at $150,000 to $200,000. The outcome of all these cases depended upon the validity of the lease which had been established by the first decision of the court.[110]

With renewed optimism the shareholders agreed to meet the semi-annual interest on the company's bonds by paying up 5s. on each share. As the litigation continued for many months, these periodic payments were gradually using up the uncalled capital, and bondholders were in danger of being left with nothing but the rapidly depreciating railroad. Fearful that three or four years would pass before the Supreme Court disposed of the case, the editor of the *Scottish Banking and Insurance Magazine* urged a compromise. He suggested: 'The Oregonian Railway itself—a narrow gauge one, "starting from, and leading to, nowhere"—with several bridges down and otherwise only partially worked, will daily become of less value, and by the end of the struggle won't be worth anything.'[111]

When the original contract had been made, the Scottish company had agreed to finish thirty-one miles of track then in construction, but two months later the Villard interests elected to take over construction and agreed to operate and keep in good repair the entire lines. In April 1885 the Oregon federal court considered the Oregonian Railway Company's request for an injunction requiring the Oregon Railway and Navigation Company to fulfil its legal obligation to maintain the railroad property. The Oregonian Railway insisted the construction was never completed and through negligence two bridges over the North and South Santiam rivers had been allowed to wash away. Judge Deady concluded:

> As a general rule a contract to build or repair will not be specifically enforced in a court of equity. It is said that if one wont [*sic*] build another will; and if there is any loss sustained the remedy is at law, for damages. And this is specifically so as to contracts like the covenant in the present lease, to repair during a period of many years.

Although the injunction was denied, the Court agreed to appoint a receiver with authority to operate the railroad and use the proceeds for current expenses and repairs. Moreover, the court authorized the receiver to borrow money on the security of the road, sufficient to put it in repair, and suggested that the Oregonian Railway Company later bring action at law to recover the amount expended.[112] In July 1885 the ten per cent annual dividend on the preference shares was declared, 'but to be payable only as and when their rents have been received and are available for dividend'.[113]

As the legal battle continued, the Oregon Railway and Navigation Company denied that the lease had ever been legally executed. Four additional cases were taken up on 16 April 1886, and all the various arguments against paying the rent were reviewed. Once more the Oregon federal judge declared that a covenant to pay rent in semi-annual instalments over a period of years was in the nature of a series of undertakings or obligations assumed at the same time. His earlier decision making possible the recovery of any one of these instalments had already determined the validity of the lease and the liability of the Oregon Railway and Navigation Company for each of the unpaid instalments.[114] These totalled $234,000 by October 1886. One Scottish journal remarked: 'Apart from the gain to the Company thus impudently attempted to be defrauded, it is matter for congratulation that the US Law Courts have all through the successive stages of this tedious litigation upheld the inviolability of contract which must be of first principle in all mercantile transactions.'[115]

In March 1889 the United States Supreme Court, to the surprise of everyone, reversed the decisions of the circuit court in Oregon and released the Oregon Railway and Navigation Company from all its financial obligations to the Scots. Justice Samuel F. Miller read the decision declaring that when a statute made a grant of power or franchises to a private corporation, construction of the grant in doubtful points should be against the grantee and in favour of the government. This general rule applied with greater force to Articles of Association organizing a corporation under general laws, as in the case of Oregon corporations. The power to lease a railroad was not, in the court's opinion, to be presumed from the usual grant of powers in a railroad charter. Unless authorized by legislative action, one company could not transfer a railroad, its appurtenances and franchises, to another company by lease, nor could the second company receive and operate them under such a lease. The constitution and general laws of Oregon did not authorize a railroad corporation to obtain a railroad by lease. Moreover, the Oregon law did not confer upon a foreign corporation the right to lease a railroad in the state, but only the right to construct or acquire and operate one there. Justice Stephen J. Field dissented in a terse statement:

> . . . I cannot perceive what public policy of the State is sustained by denying to a foreign corporation, which has by her permission constructed a railway therein, the right to lease its road to a domestic corporation. It would rather seem, if any considerations of public policy are to control, that such a policy would favor a transfer of the road from foreigners to her own citizens. When the transfer is made the State can exercise over the road, its management, and the charges for its use, the same authority which she could have previously exercised.[116]

The only alternative for the Dundee company was liquidation. Several directors, including Cox, Leng, Lowson, and Cochrane, informed the Scottish courts that the company could not pay its debts. The whole assets of the company included the railways in Oregon, on which there was a lien for \$318,000 spent by the receiver, and £2 2s. 6d. uncalled capital on each share. Debts included £214,700 in two bond issues and £49,000 borrowed from the British Linen Company's Bank in Dundee. Through the purchase of ordinary and preferred shares, first and second mortgage bonds, and the granting of loans, Forfarshire residents had invested nearly \$3,000,000 in the Oregonian Railway Company, and \$2,250,000 appeared to be lost.[117]

24. *Section gang at the Oregonian Railway Depot at Sheridan, Yamhill County, about 1888*

25. (overleaf) (a) *The Salem (Oregon) Capitol Flour Mills Company, Ltd.* (see p.243); (b) *Barn and threshing scene on a farm near Woodstock, Minnesota, sponsored by the American Land and Colonization Company of Scotland in the early 1880s*

25 (a) *and* (b)

Meanwhile Villard's insolvency had also hastened the bankruptcy of the old competitor, the Oregon and California Railroad. It was purchased by the Southern Pacific Railway Company in 1887 to complete the last segment of its line between Ashland and the Oregon-California boundary. Reid seized the opportunity to sell what remained of the Oregonian Railway Company to the Southern Pacific, thereby assisting the bondholders to recoup a small percentage of their investment.[118] In the end, Dundee investors still lost $1,250,000.

Reid's unpopularity in Dundee knew no bounds. The resentment was general and bitter as a result of the 'abundant and chastening crop of litigation and vexation' for which he was primarily responsible. Mackenzie later gave his impressions of 'Dundee Reid' to the public:

> In American parlance he had a champion reputation as a first-class Ananias! In departure from the truth he had a practised facility. Senator Nesmith, the humourist mentioned in Sir John Leng's book, is reported to have said that there were three liars in the State of Oregon, and that William Reid was two of them. This is the man who brought to our unfortunate town that sad misadventure the Oregonian Railway, which cost our citizens something like a quarter of a million sterling and years of weary suspense and fierce and futile battle.[119]

Scots participated in another aspect of the economic development of Oregon, the flour milling business. The Capitol Mills of Oregon, capable of manufacturing seven hundred barrels of flour per day, had been erected by the City of Salem Company, an American corporation. Most of its shares, however, were held in Scotland. When additional capital was needed to increase operations in 1883, the Scots elected to register a limited company at home and thereby control management policies. The Salem (Oregon) Capitol Flour Mills Company, Limited, had an authorized capital of £100,000. The first call for funds was limited to £60,000 in £5 shares with approximately sixty per cent of the shares reserved for company directors. Investors, who were invited to contribute £1 for each share upon application, were told that the company had hopes of early twenty-five per cent annual dividends.[120]

But the second annual meeting, in December 1886, dispelled these expectations: 'Early in this year the Directors resolved in consequence of the condition of the trade, and the losses already apparent, to suspend operations and to confine the work to the realisation of the wheat and flour on hand. The mills were closed in June and no new business has been gone into.' With the exception of one shipment of flour to Liverpool, all consignments to Britain had lost money for the firm. Local trade in Oregon had been quite unprofitable. Not only was the entire paid-up capital of approximately £15,000 lost, but the mills themselves were seized by Oregon creditors as security for their loans. Although the shareholders recognized that all their investment was lost, several Scots who had lent the company £2,150 insisted that a liquidator, appointed at their request by the Scottish courts, secure the repayment of this money. As late as 1902 the liquidator notified the court of his failure in this mission because American citizens had obtained a prior legal claim to the company's property.[121]

The Scots also tried their hand at raising sugar beets and operating a sugar refinery in eastern Washington during the 1890s. The manager of John Walker and Company, sugar refiners at Greenock organized a syndicate investing £7,000 in the Washington State Sugar Company, Limited, to acquire leases to three thousand acres of land in Spokane County and a sugar factory in the village of Waverly. Washington residents also raised £30,000 for the enterprise. By 1898 the company needed additional capital to remodel the Waverly plant and purchase additional factories, so Glaswegians organized a new joint stock endeavour known as the Scoto-American Sugar Syndicate, Limited, to raise £3,000. The company spent most of its resources fighting restrictions on alien business activities in the State of Washington.[122]

Evidence suggests that the Scots were no more successful in manufacturing sugar than in processing wheat. Fortunately for the investing public, these manufacturing concerns were private companies with a limited number of stockholders, and their failure did not constitute an economic tragedy as in the case of the Oregonian Railway Company. In each enterprise legal restrictions on the business activities of foreigners or adverse court decisions had been a major factor in their financial failure.

Chapter Ten

Patterns and Problems of Scottish-American Investment in the Late Nineteenth Century

By the mid-1880s numerous mortgage companies, both foreign and domestic, were operating throughout the trans-Mississippi West. They had played a significant role in financing the attempt to subdue the Plains to the plough, in underwriting cotton cultivation in the South, and in opening the Pacific Northwest. Between 1888 and 1894 most domestic mortgage companies concentrating on loans in the Plains States failed. There were many interrelated causes, primarily from the vagaries of the weather. Beginning in 1887 the Plains country experienced a series of dry years. Drought and the resulting short crops usually resulted in an increase of prices, thus alleviating the disastrous plight of the farmer; but in these years the prices for agricultural products were greatly depressed. Many settlers were unable to meet the payments on their mortgages. Companies were forced to foreclose and their real-estate holdings grew to unmanageable size. Moreover, their capital had been converted into land at a time when real-estate was a drug on the market.[1]

Various mortgage companies had vigorously competed for the privilege of financing the farmer in the American West. The Scottish companies not only had to meet the competition of domestic concerns, but also to vie with one another as a result of their simultaneous action in entering new geographic areas and initiating loaning operations. Certainly, by the close of the 1880s the Scottish mortgage companies were encountering stiff competition everywhere. *The Economist* reported that 'In "Wall Street" parlance, some of the distant States in the West are literally "plastered" over with these mortgages, and the number of foreclosures, already very heavy, is increasing at a threatening rate'. The whole of central and western Kansas was covered with mortgages, and at least 5,000 farms had been abandoned in 1889 owing to the inability of mortgagees to meet their obligations. Foreclosures were occurring with undesirable frequency in Iowa, Missouri, Minnesota, Nebraska, and Dakota. Because interest rates ranged from eight to fourteen per cent in the West, rivalry for business suddenly became keen at the decade's close. Many companies were advancing from fifty to seventy per cent of the appraised value of farms and hoping to forestall an inevitable drop in interest rates. The financial journal suggested:

> At first the Western farmer borrowed money, mainly for the purpose of improvement, to which extent borrowing may have been perfectly legitimate. The last few years, however, his borrowing has too often been of a very different character—in fact to tide him over crop failures and unprofitable seasons. The wonderful productiveness of a virgin soil had made him oversanguine and careless of the future, and he trusted in Nature to pay his debts.[2]

When criticized for this exposé, *The Economist's* correspondent professed a desire 'to inspire caution about a business which has been pushed to unwholesome excess, and which is based upon unsound conditions'.[3]

The Scottish-American Mortgage Company admitted that 1888 had been only a 'fairly prosperous' year in the United States. The demand for money had been maintained notwithstanding the increased competition, but in some sections there was a noticeable tendency to lower the rates of interest. Although southern crops were expected to be good, the harvest on the northern Plains was uncertain because of inadequate rainfall. The company now operated in thirteen states. The directors elected at this time to increase the capital by issuing 25,000 new shares at a premium of £1 per share.[4] As previously noted, the other four Scottish mortgage companies also increased their capital at the decade's close, unmindful of any possible collapse in their operations.

The Edinburgh Courant had already recognized the pattern of activity among the Scottish mortgage companies:

> The companies operating in America have from the first year of their lives been steadily progressing westward. As each new State got settled up, and the rate of interest fell, they had to look out for fresh fields and pastures new. The earliest of them started in Chicago after the great fire. . . . As Chicago mortgages ran out the money was transferred to Iowa, Missouri, and the great corn states of the Upper Mississippi. With wonderful rapidity they, too, were flooded with foreign capital, chiefly Scotch, and they naturally lowered their price for it. Then came a new move westward into Texas, New Mexico, and even as far as Southern California. . . . but it is only a question of time when the irrepressible Yankee became rich enough to be independent of his Scotch uncle. . . .[5]

Competition had forced the numerous mortgage companies with United States headquarters to grant more and more freedom of judgment to their local agents. Individuals working on a commission basis had a tendency to be overgenerous in approving loans. In some cases, careless business practices had been engaged in, and even fraud was common.[6] In contrast, the Scottish companies insisted that their agents adhere to the basic guiding principles established in the 'home office' when making loans. Those who stepped out of line were quickly held accountable. Nor could the established mortgage companies of Edinburgh and Dundee be criticized for casual or unsystematic business practices. However, they were not immune to fraud. Agents of the Scottish-American Mortgage Company in Dallas, Texas, and Yankton, South Dakota were guilty of defalcation. The defaulting agent in Yankton died insolvent in 1892 and the directors wrote off £12,500 for the loss.[7] His name was studiously withheld from the public because he was a Scotsman and a neighbour of the managing director, J. Duncan Smith.[8] The upshot of this situation was a thorough-going reorganization of the lending procedures by local agents. The Edinburgh American Land Mortgage Company also suffered losses through the dishonesty of the same Dallas agent, but Jesup, Paton and Company, its American representatives, succeeded in acquiring enough real estate to cover most of the loss.[9]

THE IMPACT OF DEPRESSION IN THE EARLY NINETIES

Subnormal business conditions developed in Europe at the close of 1889. A four-year wave of rising security prices, speculation on the stock exchange, and overinvestment overseas was checked. The British in particular had been guilty of excessive activity in Latin America, and the upheaval associated with the transfer from empire to republic in Brazil coupled with a financial crisis in the Argentine brought embarrassment to many investment companies. Baring Brothers, for example, were deeply involved in the Plata River region and, when the crisis came, were so imprudently illiquid that the house was forced to cease business in 1890. The firm had large holdings in United States securities, such as the Santa Fe Railroad, which had to be sold immediately. Such forced sales caused the prices for all American railroad and industrial stocks to drop rapidly. The United States market was further depressed because British capital had to be withdrawn from the United States and used temporarily to bolster the unstable security markets at home.[10]

The depressing effect of the Baring crisis upon the American stock market was especially acute because only a few months preceding it there was an outburst of speculative activity in railway securities resulting from the passage of the Sherman Silver Purchase Act of 1890 by the United States Congress. European investors expected this legislation, practically doubling the amount of silver coinage in the United States, to bring about a currency inflation. In anticipation of this trend, American stocks, good, bad, and indifferent, were purchased in quantities not equalled since 1885, and prices rose by leaps and bounds during the first half of the year.[11] These were the months when the new investment trusts were buying heavily. In midsummer the flow of capital to the United States was shut off abruptly because of the British financial crisis. British investments in the United States during the last quarter of 1890 were the lowest of any similar period since 1887.[12] This sudden shifting in the market placed the newer Scottish investment companies in an unfortunate plight. The Edinburgh Investment Trust found it necessary to write down the value of its investments £11,500 for each of three years, 1890–3. The Scottish Investment Trust of Edinburgh, the British Investment Trust, and most other new companies found it necessary to take similar action. Some companies were forced to reduce dividends; others transferred funds from securities to land mortgages.[13]

The financial difficulty had a contrasting effect upon the well-established companies that could take advantage of the declining prices on the stock exchange to buy more securities at depreciated prices. The Scottish-American Investment Company of Edinburgh was able to declare a fifteen per cent annual dividend in 1891, the largest that had been distributed since the recession of 1884. Steps were taken the next year to increase the company's capital from £2,000,000 to £2,500,000.[14] William J. Menzies, the company's managing director, was still convinced that United States securities were an ideal form of investment, and he had earned international recognition as a financial expert thoroughly knowledgeable in American economic affairs, particularly railroad investment.[15] The established Scottish American Trust Companies of Dundee maintained their annual dividends, continued to build up reserves, and congratulated investors on their good fortune in having their money in United States rather than in South American securities.[16]

In spite of the difficulties arising from stiffening competition, the mortgage companies of Scotland did not feel the effects of the financial stringency as quickly as the investment trusts concentrating on securities. The mortgage business was considered so much more advantageous than stock market transactions in 1891 that the wealthiest directors of the established investment trusts of Dundee organized new mortgage companies. Edward L.I.

Blyth and Thomas Nelson, of Edinburgh's Scottish-American Investment Company, were among the directors of the United States Investment Corporation, Limited, registered in January 1891, with an authorized capital of £100,000.[17] The company's authorized capital was increased to £250,000 the next year, and Menzies and John E. Guild, chairman of the Alliance Trust Company and the Scottish American Trusts of Dundee, joined the Board.[18] Guild was also chairman of the Investors' Mortgage Security Company, Limited, launched at this time in Dundee with £1,000,000 of authorized capital.[19]

In these years the Pacific Northwest appears to have been the favourite location for mortgage loans. The agricultural depression in the northern Plains had not yet been felt in the region. Crops were good both in Oregon and Washington, and land values soared because of increased railway facilities. The situation reassured the Oregon Mortgage Company that the Pacific Northwest afforded ample profit on investment; the annual dividend of the company between 1890 and 1893 was ten per cent and additions were made to the reserve fund. New issues of shares were sold to the public at a premium in both 1891 and 1892 until all authorized capital was taken up. Approximately £400,000 had been invested in the Northwest by 1893 and the company had never been so prosperous since its beginning ten years earlier.[20] The success of this company prompted directors of the new United States Investment Corporation, Limited, to initiate plans for concentrating its land loans in the Pacific Northwest, and Portland bankers were invited to sit on an Advisory Board. After a trip to Oregon, Guild was convinced that these Oregonians were primarily interested in real-estate promotions and he urged a policy of caution on the new company. Portland, with a population of 75,000, was reported to have opened up eight extensive residential subdivisions sufficient for a city of 350,000. The real-estate boom had pushed land values higher than those of St Paul and Kansas City. The Scottish capitalist reported that in one area, known as King's Addition, real estate was selling at $80 and $100 a front-foot and he doubted that people living in seven- and eight-room houses could afford such high land values. Because of this inflation and the sudden competition among the many Scottish companies in the area, he urged that not more than one-third of the appraised value of city property be lent. As to farming areas, he recommended that the company postpone agricultural loans in the Northwest. Rural lands along the Willamette, valued at $80 and $100 an acre, he considered far too high when the best cotton lands along the Mississippi delta and the wheat lands in Kansas were declared at $40 an acre. The cost of reclaiming an acre of land from the Oregon forest was at least $75 an acre, far too expensive a process in the eyes of the Scot. However, if such loans were considered, he first recommended the Willamette Valley, then the Umatilla Valley, the Palouse Country, and the Walla Walla Valley in eastern Oregon and Washington.[21]

Under the influence of Guild, the new Investors' Mortgage Security Company, scattered its loans throughout the West and South. Initial loans were placed through the various agents working for the Alliance Trust, such as MacMaster and Birrell in Portland, the Kansas City Investment Company, Caldwell and Judah in Memphis, and Francis Smith and Company in San Antonio.[22] The company appointed an inspector of agencies resident in the United States. Local agents submitted applications for loans to this inspector who, on approval, made recommendations to the Scottish Board, where the final decision was made. On the other hand, local agents were granted the power of attorney to act for the company in foreclosing on loans in default, managing and selling real estate, and seeing that the Scots complied with the national and state laws.[23] Public confidence in the directors of this company was so great that half of its authorized capital, £500,000, was subscribed immediately. Embarrassed by such sudden riches, the company had to invest the bulk of the funds in railroad bonds until such time as mortgages could be carefully placed.

Thus we see that while Scottish investors in securities were plagued by an unstable and generally declining market between 1890 and 1892, those interested in land mortgages encountered only the problems known and expected in the business. Experienced investors began transferring their capital from securities to mortgages. The comparatively strong position of the Scottish mortgage companies interested in the American West had led to the creation of new heavily-capitalized enterprises at a time when similar companies with headquarters in the eastern United States were in the doldrums, particularly those that had a large percentage of their investment in the upper Mississippi Valley.

The European depression and continued speculation on the New York Stock Exchange finally deranged the financial mechanism in the United States. Foreboding indications of trouble appeared during the first half of 1893. With the failure of the Philadelphia and Reading Railway and several large industrial trusts, there followed a general break in stock market prices. Western and southern banks facing collapse withdrew their deposits in New York. During the year 573 banks and loan companies closed. When the Erie Railroad went into bankruptcy in the summer, the stock market virtually collapsed. The overbuilt and overcapitalized railroads of the West were all in distress. In 1894 there were 156 railroads with 39,000 miles of track in receivership, including the Northern Pacific and the Union Pacific. These delinquent lines represented two and one-half billion dollars, or one-fourth of the total railroad capital in the United States. Trade and industry were also disorganized resulting in widespread unemployment. The wages of labour were reduced, and insolvency was general.[24]

The Statist was convinced that the intensity and persistence of the downward movement of stock prices, so painfully evident, could be better measured 'in a wholesale than in a retail manner'. The editors published a list of securities in which the British were primarily interested and noted that their total evaluation in July 1893 was £83,376,000. These same stocks and bonds had been worth £146,916,000 at their highest prices since the Baring crisis. This represented a depreciation of forty-three per cent. Individual securities had dropped in value from fifty to seventy per cent.[25] Surveying the American railroad picture from an investment standpoint in 1894, *The Economist* bitterly concluded 'we doubt if any class of securities, not excluding even mines, has proved so unprofitable'. After reviewing the last decade's dividend history of twenty rail lines, thought to be representative of British holdings in the United States, the editor pointed out that nothing had been received on a nominal capital of $312,867,000, or £62,573,000. Among the twenty railroads falling in this category were the Denver and Rio Grande; the Missouri, Kansas and Texas; the New York, Lake Erie, and Western; the New York, Ontario, and Western; the Philadelphia and Reading; and the Wabash Lines. Twelve of the railroads considered had at one time paid dividends ranging from one to three per cent, but seven of these entered the ranks of the non-dividend paying lines in 1893-4. Only the Baltimore and Ohio, the Illinois Central, and the Pennsylvania had exceeded an average of five per cent.[26]

In these years of desperate depression, 1893-5, the Scottish companies concentrating on American investments met the most severe test since their establishment. The three Scottish American Trust Companies of Dundee were able, because of their conservative borrowing policies of past years, to pay steady dividends during the three crisis years. To do so, the reserves usually carried forward had to be reduced. Robert Fleming had an arduous year in 1894, crossing the Atlantic seven times within the twelve months; most of his time was spent in the United States.[27] The stalwart Scottish-American Investment Company of Edinburgh did not come through the trying period unscathed. The annual dividend was reduced from fifteen per cent to twelve and one-half per cent for 1893, but stabilized at that rate. The company was forced to write down the book value of its securities. Some stocks that had reached a comparatively high price on the market, but which had distributed a minimal dividend, finally had to be sacrificed to maintain steady dividend payments.[28] The British Investment Trust met the situation by reducing its dividend from seven to five per cent. Since the trust was formed in 1889 the world had been subjected to a series of financial crises and the directors were gravely concerned that the total value of the security investments was between six and seven per cent below the value of the capital and debenture stock.[29] The Edinburgh Investment Trust, the Scottish Investment Trust Company, and the Second Scottish Investment Trust Company all followed the pattern of lowering their dividends each year until they were paying only one or two per cent.[30] In spite of the reduced income, none of the Scottish investment companies were forced to liquidate.

The Scottish mortgage companies, that had withstood the Baring crisis and the European depression comparatively well, experienced severe repercussions from the Panic of 1893 in the United States. Agricultural adversity in the southern and western states had been increasing for a number of years prior to the general collapse; in fact, fourteen-cent corn and five-cent cotton had so reduced the rural purchasing power that the earnings of all those handling farm goods or dependent upon farm markets suffered. The corn crop was a disastrous failure in 1894. The falling off of the European demand for wheat caused its price to drop below fifty cents a bushel. The great agricultural staples were reduced to a price level that had not been known since the early forties.[31]

The great Alliance Trust found it necessary to increase the number of foreclosures each year between 1893 and 1895, and the depressed business conditions hindered realization on the real estate obtained. In 1894 the customary annual dividend of twelve and one-half per cent was split, with ten per cent designated as an annual dividend and two and one-half per cent declared a bonus. This action appeared ominous and the directors frankly announced that bonuses should not be anticipated in the future. In 1895 the dividend was cut to eight per cent. The crux of the problem was the continuing ruinous prices for agricultural staples that were bankrupting the American farmer. The price of cotton improved in 1895, but the amount received for cereals was at an all time low.[32] Most of the older Scottish mortgage companies followed the lead of the Alliance company in reducing dividends. The United States Mortgage Company of Scotland was in the unique position of maintaining its dividend of eight per cent annually throughout the depression years.[33]

The plight of those companies loaning in the cotton states adjoining the Mississippi River was aggravated by widespread overflows that flooded the delta lands in the Spring of 1894. The chairman of the Alliance Trust hastened to Memphis, a rapidly growing town of 70,000 and second only to New Orleans as a cotton centre, and spent three weeks with the company's inspector of agencies touring the great delta plantations on both sides of the river. The water had covered young corn and cotton crops and remained too long for a second planting. In the hope of avoiding repetition of the disaster, the United States government, state and local agencies expended large sums of money on public levees. In addition, land owners erected private levees and strengthened old ones in hopes of protecting their property.[34] The Edinburgh American Land Mortgage Company stopped lending in the southern states in 1895 and elected to concentrate its operations in the upper Mississippi Valley where there was more diversified farming.[35]

Agriculturalists in the Pacific Northwest who had enjoyed unprecedented prosperity between 1889 and 1892 now found their income drastically reduced as a result of an exceptionally wet harvest season in 1893, coupled with the price decline for the minimal amount of grain that was produced. The Oregon Mortgage Company was forced to take over large amounts of real estate and to reduce the shareholders' dividends.[36]

The two newcomers to the mortgage business, the United States Investment Corporation and the Investors' Mortgage Security Company, both directed by men affiliated with the Alliance Trust, expanded their loaning business in spite of the general agricultural depression. The United States Investment Corporation extended its operations outside the Pacific Northwest when agents were selected in Minneapolis, Memphis, San Antonio, and Le Mars, Iowa. The Scots associated with these companies attempted unsuccessfully to have one inspector for all the Scottish mortgage companies to supervise local agents in the United States on a nationwide basis.[37]

Events leading to the organization of the Deltic Investment Company, Limited, at the close of 1894, reflected the desperate plight of the mortgage business in the United States. The Ashley Company, Limited, operating a series of plantations in Madison Parish, Louisiana, on which it had foreclosed, was gravely in debt because of the cotton price collapse. Through Caldwell and Judah, Memphis brokers, several Scottish mortgage and investment companies advanced sufficient funds to keep the enterprise solvent. The chief lender, the Alliance Trust Company, had agreed to put up $168,500 on the security of the unmortgaged lands of the company. As indebtedness to Scottish investors mounted, it became increasingly clear that the farming and mercantile operations of the Ashley Company were insolvent, so William Mackenzie proposed that the Edinburgh and Dundee companies take over the business rather than reveal their losses to the Scottish public.[38]

Representatives of the Alliance Trust Company, British Investment Trust, United States Mortgage Company of Scotland, the Canadian and American Mortgage Company, the Scottish Investment Trust Company, and the Second Scottish Investment Trust established a syndicate to undertake agricultural operations in the Louisiana delta. The Scots acquired the mortgages of the Ashley Company for $569,000. Capital was raised for this payment by issuing preferred and ordinary shares in the Deltic Company. The Scots also assumed the outstanding indebtedness of the Ashley Company, representing the money they had advanced in 1893 and 1894, in exchange for shares in the company. After the allocation of the various issues of shares among the participating Scottish companies, the directors employed Caldwell and Judah to manage large cotton plantations at Quebec, Waverley, Shirley, and Ashley in Madison Parish. Not only did the agents become involved with the problems of marketing the annual cotton crop, they also had to determine the extent of cultivation, the crops to be planted, and the type of labour to use. In addition, they had to learn how to manage cotton gins and company stores on an economical basis. Several mass colonization schemes were proposed. The Shakers expressed an interest in establishing a colony on the tract in 1895, and the Scottish directors urged their managers to encourage the move.[39] Only a few families came. This was but the first of many schemes to get satisfactory tenants on the land.

The reduction of dividend income from the Scottish mortgage companies was inconsequential when compared with the capital losses incurred by Scottish investors through similar companies located in the United States. When the Equitable Mortgage Company of New York, the Jarvis-Conklin Mortgage Trust, and the Lombard Investment Company defaulted during 1893, several English companies using them as agents were financially embarrassed. For example, the Colonial and United States Mortgage Company, with its offices in Hull, was forced to make capital calls on shares to remain solvent.[40] The Anglo-American Land Mortgage and Agency Company, associated with the Lombard, was unable to meet the principal on maturing debentures.[41] At least one financial journal thought it noteworthy that the main support for the United States land mortgage companies came from 'the usually shrewd and cautious Scottish people, and the equally shrewd and cautious Yorkshire and Lancashire members of the Society of Friends'.[42] *The Statist* observed that the United States mortgage companies had borrowed more freely than was the custom in Britain. Although the limitations on borrowing money varied, the Scottish practice of restricting loans to the amount of 'uncalled and unpaid capital' was deemed the best. Moreover, the Scottish companies were notable for the extent of reserves built by the accumulations from the past, which supplemented their working capitals. These factors explained their soundness, and many Scots regretted that all their mortgage investments had not been placed through the Edinburgh and Dundee companies rather than directly through those in the United States.[43] Between £7,000,000 and £9,000,000 of British money was tied up by the failure of four of the largest United States mortgage companies and, as noted, a considerable percentage of this had been secured in Scotland.[44]

Professor Allan Bogue has suggested that it was only natural for the American farmer, who failed, to vent his spleen on the mortgage agencies and non-resident lenders. The western settler had been schooled in a subsistence agricultural economy and he found the business methods of commercial farming irksome. In rural areas there was also a feeling of mistrust both for banks and money lenders. When efforts were made by a mortgage company to extract prompt payments in periods of economic adversity, the farmer considered it tyrannical. If the farmer failed, the foreclosure proceedings merely confirmed all his feelings of hostility toward the mortgage broker and the investor.[45]

Mortgage agencies could not be exonerated of all guilt for the debacle of the 1880s and 1890s. The local agents functioned with too little supervision from domestic companies in the United States and they gouged commissions out of the settlers which they did not report to the companies. Moreover, the mortgage companies made no serious effort to teach farmers the business principles of commercial agriculture or to make certain they had a reasonable chance to use their loans successfully. Although Scottish companies made a more serious effort to supervise local agents by issuing detailed instructions on loaning procedures and by appointing general supervisory firms, their efforts were often minimized, or even unavailing, because of the great distance between farm and home office and the time necessary for communications to be transmitted back and forth.

The average Scottish investor, like that of the eastern United States, was largely ignorant of western agricultural life. Success depended upon their confidence in, and the ability of, the directors and managers of the Edinburgh and Dundee companies. The high rate of interest paid on mortgages between 1873 and 1893 had led to excesses in the business, and the Scots had added to the veritable craze to obtain these high rates. However, the Scots did not engage in the reckless practices and financial irresponsibility that characterized many of the domestic mortgage companies. Professor Bogue has fairly summarized the overall situation: '. . . undoubtedly there was much more misunderstanding than malice or avarice, more of ignorance and undue optimism than calculated fraud and, as always on the frontier, much more of suffering than the bountiful resources of the United States might seem to demand'.[46]

PROBLEMS OF SCOTTISH INVESTMENT, 1895-1900

In addition to the alarming problems connected with the depression in the early 1890s, the Scottish capitalists investing in the United States were plagued by difficulties growing out of a British-American diplomatic crisis. In 1895 the Cleveland administration became involved in controversy over the settlement of the boundary line between Venezuela and British Guiana. The United States Secretary of State, Richard Olney, sent a belligerent note to the British Foreign Office demanding arbitration and insisting that failure to comply would be interpreted as a violation of the Monroe Doctrine. The British Prime Minister, Lord Salisbury, who likewise directed foreign affairs, replied that the Monroe Doctrine did not apply to the boundary controversy and was not recognized as international law. At this point, President Cleveland, who had become agitated over the dispute, drafted a ringing message to Congress in December suggesting that the United States draw the boundary line and, if necessary, support its decision by armed force. With enthusiasm and applause, Congress appropriated funds for an independent boundary commission and some Congressmen anticipated war.[47]

American and British financial interests became gravely concerned over the wave of jingoism that swept both countries. Businessmen worked frantically to calm the troubled waters. The directors of the Scottish-American Investment Company of Edinburgh complained that 1896 'commenced under the disastrous effect of President Cleveland's Venezuelan message'.[48] The Scottish American Trust Companies in Dundee were concerned that the post-depression restoration of public confidence in the United States as a field of investment had been so quickly dispelled by the diplomatic crisis.[49] The mortgage companies of Scotland, fearful that diplomatic relations might be severed, knew that their loaning and real-estate operations were in real

26. Chamber of Commerce, Dundee, building in 1855

27. William Mackenzie of the Alliance Trust Company, Ltd., Dundee

jeopardy. When Congressional reaction to Cleveland's message of December 1895 became known in Edinburgh, the directors of the Scottish-American Mortgage Company decided to cease making loans. Each agency in the United States was instructed to await further notification before re-lending Scottish funds. As a result, unemployed cash accumulated for several months and the annual income of the company suffered.[50] The Alliance Trust, on the other hand, was apparently not so frightened and used its influence to get other Scottish-American companies to continue business as usual. The directors were aware that almost one-half of the foreign commerce of the United States was with the British Empire and that this economic tie guaranteed the continuance of 'peaceful and mutually beneficial relations'.[51]

Fortunately for the cause of peace, many Britons agreed with the Scottish capitalists. The ministry adopted a conciliatory tone, co-operated with the American boundary commission, and a geographic compromise was worked out along the line the British had repeatedly offered the Venezuelans.[52] All Scottish-American companies rejoiced at the settlement. Shareholders of the Investors' Mortgage Security Company, for example, were told 'the bonds of brotherhood between the two nations are, by the friendly aid of arbitration, being drawn more closely together'.[53] *The Economist* perhaps expressed the consensus of opinion among British investors in January 1896:

> It is with a sense of no ordinary relief that the country recognizes an improvement in the situation as regards the Venezuelan dispute. It is no exaggeration to say that on this side of the Atlantic there has been the deepest and most intense anxiety to escape from our difficulties with the United States. . . . We feel that war with America would be civil war, and desire to avoid it as much as we would an appeal to arms within the Empire itself. No wonder, then, that the evidence of a better tone at Washington has given universal satisfaction. We have plenty of jingoes and fire-eaters here, but we venture to think that there is not one of them who would regret a peaceful end to the present dispute.[54]

The financial stake of the Scots in the United States at the height of this diplomatic wrangle is clearly revealed in Table 14, p. 258, prepared by William Mackenzie of the Alliance Trust Company.[55] Although this money was not entirely invested in western American mortgages, the great bulk of it was there. Scottish investors were liable for approximately $60,000,000, a sum that could easily have been placed in jeopardy by an outbreak of war. Certainly the concern of investors was justified. The Venezuelan

TABLE 14. Capital of Scottish Mortgage Companies investing in the United States, 1895

company	*capital* £	*debentures* £
The Alliance Trust Co., Ltd., Dundee	1,500,000	2,070,000
American Mort. Co. of Scotland, Ltd., Edinburgh	250,000	238,031
British Canadian Trust, Ltd., Dundee	250,000	248,514
Edinburgh American Land Mort. Co., Ltd., Edinburgh	300,996	379,030
Edinburgh Mortgage Co., Ltd., Edinburgh	18,905	55,000
Investors' Mortgage Security Co., Ltd., Edinburgh	1,000,000	786,726
Oregon Mortgage Co., Ltd., Edinburgh	325,000	325,000
Scottish American Mort. Co., Ltd., Edinburgh	1,274,672	552,947
Scottish Canadian Trust, Ltd., Dundee	50,000	
Scottish Mortgage & Trust Co., Ltd., Edinburgh	142,419	25,667
Scottish Pacific Mort. Co., Ltd., Edinburgh	70,983	70,431
Second Investors' Mort. Security Co., Ltd., Edinburgh	332,744	
United States Invest. Corpn., Ltd., Edinburgh	250,000	223,751
United States Mort. Co. of Scotland, Ltd., Edinburgh	250,000	225,502
Western & Hawaiian Investment Co., Ltd., Dundee	255,000	220,948
Western Ranches & Investment Co., Ltd., Edinburgh	150,000	137,805
	£6,420,719	£5,559,352

crisis had made clear to all, in dramatic fashion, that the Scottish investors' stake in the United States was tremendous, that the risk they ran was at times equally great, and that the economic interests in both countries were justified in bringing pressure on the diplomats to maintain international harmony.

Throughout the decade of the nineties the Scottish investor, as well as the American, was concerned with the vacillating currency policy of the United States government. When the depression came in 1893, most businessmen agreed with President Cleveland that one basic cause had been the attempt to aid the silver interests, thereby undermining confidence in the American dollar. Before the President could assemble Congress to act on his recommendation to repeal the Silver Purchase Act, the chairman of the Scottish American Trust Companies of Dundee was expressing regret to the shareholders that 'there has as yet been nothing done in America regarding the silver question'. Even so, the Scottish investment trusts were, for the most part, not directly concerned with the monetary policy, because they had concentrated on purchasing bonds redeemable in gold.[56] Directors of the Alliance Trust also reported that they had included a gold repayment clause in their mortgage loan contracts.[57]

As the demands of western mining interests and indebted farmers everywhere in the United States for the free and unlimited coinage of silver gained momentum, Scottish investors complained that as long as the currency question remained unsettled the business future of the United States would be uncertain. Although the directors of the Alliance Trust regretted the delay in settling the 'American Monetary Question', their perennial optimism before the investing public continued:

> It [the currency question] occasions in some quarters an alarm and a want of confidence which do not seem to be warranted. The people of the United States are too wealthy and too patriotic to allow their currency to become depreciated, or to occupy a position inferior to that of any other nation. Their ability to pay the cost of whatever course they decide to adopt is undoubted, and even if it be so extreme as to involve the redemption in gold of every silver and every paper dollar now in circulation, their National Debt per head of population would only be about one-third of the amount carried by each of the inhabitants of this country. By what means and how soon a satisfactory settlement will be reached cannot be predicted, but in well informed opinion the present condition of affairs is regarded as temporary, and your Directors see no occasion to expect that investors will ultimately suffer through failure of the United States to maintain its monetary standards and credit.[58]

From its London headquarters, *The Statist* disagreed with the Scots and was convinced by mid-summer of 1895 that

> . . . with the great activity of the Silver Party in the United States, in holding conventions and distributing 'free silver' literature broadcast, with both parties bidding for the silver vote, . . . and with the prospect that no improvement in the currency position will be witnessed until the Presidential election has been held eighteen months hence, it is probable that capitalists will refuse to embark in new enterprises, and that trade in the United States will remain more or less depressed.[59]

When it became clear that the question of future monetary policy was to be settled in the presidential election of 1896, the excitement of the campaign almost paralysed the investment market in the United States. Well-established securities that had hitherto been purchased by investors all over Europe did not attract buyers. A recurring theme through the annual reports of all the Scottish investment and mortgage companies was the unusually severe strain of the presidential election and the resulting shut-down of business that affected all types of investors. With the Republican triumph in November, signalling an adherence to the gold standard, the chairman of the Investors' Mortgage Security Company expressed the feeling of all Scottish investors when he reported to his shareholders early in December 'The great struggle over the Presidential election has terminated happily by the choice of a President [William McKinley] who will not tamper with the currency and who refuses to allow his countrymen to pay their debts in depreciated coin.'[60]

As soon as the political contest of 1896 was settled, American railway securities once again found a market. Before the official opening of the London Stock Exchange on the day following the United States election, an estimated 100,000 shares had changed hands. The financial press reported that 'the "Yankee market" was thronged by a mass of shouting, gesticulating members, vainly endeavouring to make their bids heard amid the babel of incoherent noise'. For several hours confusion was so great that systematic business was out of the question.[61]

In anticipation of such a development, the directors of the three Scottish American Trust Companies of Dundee registered another investment trust known as the North American Trust Company, Limited, with an authorized capital of £500,000. The directors made initial purchases of seventy-one 'first-rate investments' when they were depressed in value during 'the dark era of the Presidential election'. Once the election was over and the monetary policy settled in favour of the gold standard, the value of these securities was expected to make a spectacular rise. The Dundee capitalists obviously were hoping that financial history would repeat itself and that this company would duplicate the success that the parent enterprises had experienced from investing in the depths of the 1873 depression. By the close of 1898, the new company appeared to be well on the road to success. Market value of their securities was almost £100,000 greater than the total share and debenture capital of the company. By the century's end the entire £500,000 share capital had been issued and an equal amount borrowed, making £1,000,000 available for investment. All shares had been sold at a premium, six per cent annual dividends were being paid, and £50,000 had been set aside in a reserve fund.[62]

At least one group of Edinburgh capitalists agreed in 1899 that the time was ripe to enter the investment field in the United States. In September, R. H. Guild and James Ivory organized the American Trust Company, Limited, with an authorized capital of £100,000. The Scots immediately purchased railroad bonds of the Atchison, Topeka and Santa Fe, the Union Pacific, the Northern Pacific, and the Norfolk and Western. A second series of purchases was made in several Edinburgh mortgage and investment companies such as the Investors' Mortgage Security Company and the Scottish-American Investment Company. Then they turned to industrials and manufacturies—American Beet Sugar, American Steel Wire, American Cotton Oil, and Federal Steel. Shares were soon obtained in the Westward Ho! Gold Mines, Limited. In November 1900 the directors bitterly disagreed over the heavy investments in industrial securities, with Ivory leading the opposition to the heavy stake in the steel industry. This disagreement foreshadowed a company reorganization two years later; meanwhile company assets increased thirteen and one-half per cent on the paid-in capital and shareholders were receiving a dividend of five per cent.[63]

Observing the outburst of speculation in the last years of the century, the directors of established Scottish investment companies elected to move with caution. The extravagant hopes of prosperity following the election of President McKinley were not immediately realized. Railway traffic did not improve appreciably.[64] There was a reluctance on the part of businessmen to engage in large-scale transactions until the tariff issue was settled. Once the principle of high protective rates was enacted into law, railroad earnings gradually began to increase.[65] The currency question also remained unsettled for many months. At the beginning of 1898 *The Statist* reported widespread apprehension in the United States over the possibility that the Democratic party might win the congressional elections. Such an eventuality would mean that the silver question would be fought all over again in the Presidential election of 1900. Cautious investors were warned to consider what would happen to securities of the leading railroads of the United States in case of a silverite victory and the adoption of a silver standard. If railroad income in the United States during 1897 had been received in silver instead of gold, according to the editor, the profits available for railroad dividends would have disappeared and the average railroad would have been unable to meet its fixed charges.[66] The security market was uncertain, not only because of tariff and currency policies but also because of the Spanish American War. Investors were convinced that the manpower and resources of the United States would certainly end in victory. The uncertain factor was the amount of time the effort would take. When the victory came quickly, there was an outburst of buying on the market during the first months of 1899.[67] In the ups and downs in the volume of shares traded and the fluctuation in values between 1896 and 1900, two trends were clearly discernible. First, the demand was for the securities of gigantic industrial corporations rather than for the railroad securities that formed the basis of Scottish investments. Second, the general improvement in business taking place in the United States had resulted from the investment of domestic, rather than European, capital. The capital resources of the United States had increased so enormously that the Scots were finding difficulty in locating profitable outlets for their money.

The financial journals in the United States were greatly agitated by the apathy of British investors who watched the revival of speculative activity. Although in 1897 the prices of railway shares reached the highest quotation in five years, the British were indifferent to the boom. A major deterrent to the renewed flow of capital, according to the editor of *The Economist,* was the bitter experience of investors who had been 'fleeced by drastic reorganizations and mulcted in heavy assessments', while powerless to exercise any effective control over management.[68] *The Statist* was accused of 'being animated by a hostility toward the United States', because it did not encourage 'the wild speculation that is now going on so fast and furiously in Wall Street'.[69]

In spite of pessimistic analyses from London, the Scottish-American Investment Company realized that the outcome of the Spanish American War had restored confidence in the United States and that money had been brought out of hiding by its citizens to dispel the idea that prosperity was to be achieved only by the adoption of a silver currency. Not only had the cost of the war been paid by loans raised within the United States, but immense amounts of capital had been placed in investments. Prices had risen rapidly, prosperity had returned, and consequently political discontent was decreasing. The Scots thought the next Presidential election was likely to turn not upon the secondary issue of making silver a legal tender but upon whether or not the United States should launch a programme of imperialism. The securities of the company materially advanced in value on the stock market in 1898; the next year was described as 'one of unbounded prosperity'. The directors agreed the time had come to raise the dividend from ten to eleven and one-fourth per cent after placing £50,000 in the reserve fund.[70]

In surveying the condition of the British investment trusts begun in 1888 and 1889, *The Statist* insisted that the securities purchased at inflated prices during these years had not regained their value by 1897.[71] The British Investment Trust, for example, reported in February 1897 that the evaluation of its securities showed them to be about four per cent less than the amount of debentures and capital stock. This depreciation had virtually disappeared by 1898, and in 1899 the company's securities were worth more than its combined capital and debentures. At this time the directors elected to reveal the diversification of the company's holdings: 72·4 per cent in railroad securities of various types; 13·1 per cent in bonds of water, gas, electric light, and cable companies; 1·5 per cent in state and municipal bonds; 6·4 per cent in bonds of industrials; 6·6 in stock of industrial concerns including land and finance projects. A total of £2,113,241 was invested. No investor could have asked for greater detail than that supplied by the British Investment Trust in 1899. By 1900 the company was able to raise its dividend to six per cent and recommend an increase in capital.[72]

While the Edinburgh Investment Trust, the Scottish Investment Trust Company, and the Second Scottish Investment Trust Company were less successful than the other Edinburgh and Dundee investment trusts between 1897 and 1900, they all managed to increase their dividends by the end of the century.[73] The Scottish companies, as a whole, were in far better financial position than the English. *The Statist* reported that the reserves of six of the investment trusts in England had disappeared by 1897, the reserves of ten companies were lower than in 1892, and only two remained as high.[74]

Scottish companies concentrating on real-estate loans found their mortgage business was not sharing the prosperity of the United States in the late nineties. Annual reports to shareholders all dealt with the same themes: the comparatively slight increase in farm income in the United States, the competition for loans among the various companies that led to a reduction of interest income for all, the increase in the number of mortgage foreclosures, and, most important, the increasing amount of real estate for which there was no market. Most of the mortgage companies found it advisable to reduce their annual dividend during this period. In 1896-7 revenue of the Scottish-American Mortgage Company dropped more than twenty-five per cent below the previous year and the annual dividend that had been reduced to ten per cent a year earlier was further reduced to seven per cent.[75] The United States Mortgage Company of Scotland reduced its dividend from eight to five per cent in 1897.[76] The United States Investment Corporation held out until 1900 before reducing the dividend from six to four per cent.[77] Reserve funds, that remained a source of protection for debenture holders, had to be dipped into on occasions to make annual payments to the shareholders. This was the case of the United States Mortgage Company of Scotland in 1898.[78] The Scottish-American Mortgage Company used its entire contingent fund and an additional £50,000 from its reserve fund to reduce the value of its real estate as it appeared on the company's books in 1900.[79] Directors of the powerful Alliance Trust maintained a note of optimism in their annual reports and continued to pay an eight per cent annual dividend, higher than any of the other mortgage companies. However, the company experienced the same declining fortunes in its mortgage business. Earnings were largely stabilized by the profits from the bond and stock department.[80] By 1900 shareholders were reminded that although the annual report was satisfactory, it was not nearly so good as in the years before the Panic of 1893, when annual dividends from ten to twelve and one-half per cent were paid and large sums allocated to build up a reserve fund of £200,000. Nor were shareholders ever likely to see the high dividends again because of the falling rates of interest in the United States. The chairman admitted that the current demand for mortgages was slack because farmers had become more conservative borrowers since the depression of 1893-5.[81]

Those mortgage companies concentrating in a single geographic area of the United States, had to deal not only with the general nation-wide trends in the mortgage business, but also with regional problems. The United States Mortgage Company of Scotland, which had loaned heavily in the southern cotton states and in the ranch country of Texas, was unusually hard hit in 1897 when several large ranches in Texas fell into company hands. Thereafter, correspondence with agents in the Lone Star state dealt with matters of ranch management, and inquiries and reports relative to rainfall and the conditions of the range.[82] The Oregon Mortgage Company noted that conditions in 1896 were better in the Pacific Northwest than elsewhere because both Spokane and Seattle had benefited from mining developments in British Columbia and Alaska, and the trade with China and Japan was gathering volume. Most important, the price for wheat was comparatively high in the Northwest. Prices continued high during 1898 and 1899. The company experienced its quota of foreclosures, but when the Portland manager reported that the appraised value of the company real estate was realistic the directors elected to increase the dividend from five to six per cent in 1899. Their optimism proved premature. Spring frosts followed by rain during the harvest season reduced the wheat crop in the Northwest and this was accompanied by a decline in price. The number of foreclosures spiralled upward, real estate was a drug on the market, and in July 1900 the directors used the entire reserve fund to write down the value of the real-estate account.[83]

In these dismal years for the Scottish mortgage companies, the West of Scotland American Investment Company, Limited was organized in Glasgow to take over the properties of the American Land and Colonization Company of Scotland, which had been forced into liquidation in 1895. Although the Memorandum of Association empowered the reconstituted company not only to improve and sell this land but also to deal in mortgages and investments, its limited capital was primarily used to promote the disposal of lands in the upper Mississippi Valley, chiefly in Minnesota.[84]

The Statist had sent a correspondent to the United States in 1899 to survey the American business scene. In an article entitled 'The Prosperity of the United States: Will It Continue?' he concluded:

> The American people no longer feel the necessity to economize, and their greater outlays have already caused an immense improvement in the iron trade and a considerable recovery in the cotton, woollen, lumber and other trades. The advances in wages already conceded and the increased employment have affected the spending capacity of large numbers of workmen. Old works are being reconstructed and new ones started to meet the increasing consumption. In brief, all the indications exist of the American nation having entered upon a prolonged period of prosperity.[85]

European investors remained sceptical toward the business revival in the United States and continued to sell securities. This was deemed desirable by most American businessmen, who felt that the depression of the nineties had been partially brought on by the sudden withdrawal of foreign capital and that it would be well to repay all European investments. The typical businessman thought the only circumstance that might check the tremendous business prosperity would be the election of a Democratic President committed to free silver. After the passage of the Gold Standard Act by Congress in 1900, political observers agreed that in times of prosperity a sound-money government was not likely to be replaced by one that might upset finance. As the capital resources of the United States appeared sufficient for all the needs of business and agriculture, the enterprising Scot was destined to encounter increasing difficulties in finding a profitable outlet for his money there in the twentieth century. So he began to seek out more lucrative fields.

Chapter Eleven

Twentieth-Century Trends

When the people of the United States re-elected William McKinley as President in November 1900, retaining the Republican party in power, Scottish capitalists immediately interpreted the result as a verdict favouring a 'sound monetary policy'. Subsequent adoption of the gold standard by the United States Congress was regarded as a definitive settlement of the 'Silver Question'. These political decisions proved a great stimulus to business. Prices for securities went up rapidly and both the British and American public invested at a greatly accelerated rate. Prosperity was the keynote of the years 1900-14.

The established investment companies in Edinburgh and Dundee profited from the rapid rise in stock market prices. The Scottish-American Investment Company reported in 1900 that the total value of its securities was at an all time high, and each year additional advances were recorded.[1] In 1905 the market value of securities held by each of the three Scottish American Trust companies comprising the 'Fleming group' was from £194 to £213 for each £100 invested in the original trust certificates. Prosperity was also reflected in the steadily increasing dividends received by shareholders in most Scottish companies.[2] Earnings of the Scottish-American Investment Company in 1900 justified an increase in the annual dividend from eleven and one-fourth to twelve and one-half per cent, and this level was maintained through 1905. The next year it was increased to thirteen and three-fourths per cent.[3] The British Investment Trust, paying six and one-half per cent in 1900, increased its dividend systematically for the next decade until it was ten per cent in 1910; by 1913 it had reached a maximum of fourteen per cent.[4] Other investment companies were not so prosperous. The Edinburgh Investment Trust, created just in time to experience the succession of crises of the 1890s, did well to maintain a steady seven per cent dividend.[5]

Dividends earned by the stockholders were largely determined by the capital structure and borrowing power of the company.

Those companies established in 1889-90 had issued shares which were in turn divided into preferred stock or shares, with a fixed rate of return, and deferred securities, with an income dependent upon profits. In 1902 the Scottish-American Investment Company received the sanction of Parliament to reorganize its capital to reduce the uncalled liability on shares. The purpose of the directors was to modernize the company structure to increase borrowing power and thereby compete with the earning power of new companies, like the British Investment Trust. At the time of reorganization each shareholder had paid only £2 on each £10 subscribed share in the Scottish-American Investment Company. An additional call of £4 a share was converted into preference stock and the income used to redeem debentures. Simultaneously ordinary shares were reduced to £6. In 1904 the remaining liability of £4 on ordinary shares was extinguished. Both ordinary shares and preferred stock were included in the company's capital account, and since the company retained the right to borrow up to two-thirds of its paid-up capital the borrowed funds could be greatly augmented. In 1906 fresh capital was created so that the authorized amount for the company was £1,800,000, with £600,000 in fully-paid ordinary shares of £2 and £1,200,000 in four per cent preference stock.[6] This pioneer Scottish investment company did not go so far as to permit borrowing to the full amount of its paid-up capital, as the British Investment Trust had done. Even so, the reorganization made possible spectacular increases in dividends on the ordinary shares that reached sixteen per cent for 1910 and two years later had risen to eighteen per cent.

The Scottish American Trust Companies of Dundee had never borrowed any money except for temporary purposes, but in 1895 a new ceiling had limited the directors' borrowing power to fifteen per cent of capital. Then in 1910 the shareholders agreed that the directors could borrow, both for temporary and permanent purposes, a sum equal to the nominal capital. At this time the shares of each of the three companies were selling at twice par value, but the conservative directors took advantage of their new opportunity to borrow an amount equal only to the total par value of shares.[7] The Edinburgh Investment Trust, with a modern capital structure of deferred and preferred shares, decided that nothing could be achieved by a reorganization but, desiring to expand operations, elected to establish a new company rather than increase its own capital. A Second Edinburgh Investment Trust was organized by the amalgamation of two small operations: the St Andrew Company, started in 1893, and the St George Company, begun in 1900.[8]

Although the Scottish-American Investment Company maintained the bulk of its investments in the United States during the first decade of the twentieth century, most of the remaining companies in Edinburgh sought other fields where the financial rewards would be greater. In 1902 the Edinburgh Investment Trust revealed that about two-thirds of its investments were in Great Britain and the Empire, and about one-third in the United States. Since the earnings from British investments were greater than those in the United States, by 1910 the company began to seek more investments at home, hoping to recoup heavy losses resulting from the Boer War in South Africa and its aftermath.[9] In 1913 the British Investment Trust announced that it had £2,500,000 invested in the United States and an additional £1,100,000 in railroads outside the United States, chiefly in Latin America.[10] Directors of the new American Trust Company, while concentrating holdings in the United States, were continuously interested in Latin American securities, such as the bonds of the Buenos Aires and Pacific, and the Mexican Central Railways.[11]

In 1910 shareholders in the Scottish American Trust Companies of Dundee approved an investment clause permitting purchases of 'bonds and stocks of Companies and Corporations in the Western Hemisphere, in our own country and its dependencies, and in the dependencies of the United States of America'. The directors did not immediately take advantage of the wider investment powers. The United States remained the predominant field of interest, with 80·3 per cent of the funds of the First Scottish American Trust Company still invested there in 1912. Two years later this had been reduced to 74·30 per cent.[12]

The falling interest rate in the United States had become a real problem by 1905. *Poor's Manual* reported that the average rate of 4·45 per cent for 1896 had dropped to four per cent. This decline was the primary factor behind the decision of newer Scottish investment companies to withdraw from the United States and seek out areas of the world where money was in greater demand. Companies launched in the 1870s moved slowly, but a policy of reducing the overall percentage of funds invested in the United States was operative in the pre-World War period among all the Scottish companies. The lower percentage of capital invested in the United States by the Scottish American Trust Companies, for example, resulted not so much from capital withdrawn from the United States as it did from placing *new* capital elsewhere. This fact provides evidence for the assertion of economic historians that the most important tendencies in the British economy in the post-World War period had their beginning in the years before the conflict.[13]

Among the holdings of the Scottish investment companies in the United States, railroad securities continued to be of primary importance. More and more emphasis, however, was being placed upon industrials. The American Trust Company had large holdings in the major sugar, steel, rubber, tobacco, typewriter, and electric power and lighting companies.[14] When the Second Edinburgh Investment Trust was registered, the directors not only purchased railway bonds and stocks but also industrials, such as American Car and Foundry and Lackawanna Steel Company; utilities, such as the Helena Gas Light and Coke Company, and the Denver Union Water; and such local promotions as the Edinburgh and San Francisco Redwood Company, and the Prairie Cattle Company.[15] The British Investment Trust reported in 1913 that £1,000,000 out of the £2,500,000 invested in the United States was in industrial securities.[16]

The continuing prosperity of the Scottish investment companies was checked only momentarily by the periodic financial upheavals in the United States during the first decade of the twentieth century. The lag in stock market prices during the recession of 1904 proved but a ripple on the wave of prosperity of the larger Edinburgh companies, such as the Scottish-American Investment Company and the British Investment Trust. The Edinburgh Investment Company directors noted a decline in the value of securities, but not enough to affect the annual dividend.[17] In contrast, to the new American Trust Company the fall in securities appeared to be a 'great financial depression', and the directors immediately inaugurated a policy of exchanging high-priced securities for those subject to less market fluctuation.

Following the business reaction of 1904, there came two and a half years of general prosperity marked by great speculative activity. Optimism was so great that businessmen and investors did not pay proper attention to the strains on the financial system of the country. Trust companies began expanding rapidly and when the Knickerbocker Trust Company of New York failed, in October 1907, a panic was precipitated. Two days later the market plunged downward and for two weeks the runs on banks and trust companies led to many failures in the United States. The financial stringency was acute but short-lived. Unlike the Panic of 1893, this did not lead to a prolonged period of depression. Recovery came so quickly that the events of 1907 were subsequently referred to as 'the rich man's panic'.[18]

The Trust Companies of Dundee reported that the annual revenue of United States railroads dropped $300,000,000 during the crisis of 1907. American business had been running at top speed for too many years, according to the Scots, and there were so many securities on the market that there had to be a halt for want of investment funds. For the first time in its history Dundee's North American Trust Company reported a depreciation in the value of its American holdings, but the total drop was less than one-third the reserve fund.[19] The American Trust Company, hard hit by the recession of 1904 before its portfolio had been properly diversified, was forced to cut its dividend from five to one and one-half per cent.[20] However, these two companies were the exception rather than the rule.

By 1909 fairly prosperous conditions had returned to the United States and the following year wholesale prices reached a peak fifty per cent higher than in 1896. An element of uncertainty still prevailed because of the continuing investigations of the railroads by the Interstate Commerce Commission and the anti-trust suits of the United States against the Standard Oil Company and the American Tobacco Company. Prosperity returned in full force in 1912, but in the following year business was again declining slowly and was slightly depressed when the war came.[21] Periodic complaints by Scottish investors about political interference in the economy of the United States were noteworthy chiefly because they broke the monotony of discussions about increased capital and profits in years of continuing prosperity.

Several new Scottish investment companies were registered during the first decade of the twentieth century to deal in securities both in North and South America. A private company known as the Scottish North American Trust, Limited, capitalized at £100,000, was established in 1905. Investment funds were largely provided by two wealthy families of Edinburgh, John Erskine and James Harrow Guild, and Alfred and Robert F. Shepherd. By 1910 when the Scots sold their interests to Robert B. and Arthur E. Guinness of London and wound-up the company, investments were declared at £197,925.[22]

At the close of 1907 William Mackenzie of Dundee joined Andrew Bonar Law, MP, in organizing the Scottish Western Investment Company, Limited, capitalized at £500,000. This company was to have its headquarters in Glasgow. Robert Fleming agreed to use his experience and connections in investing the company capital for an annual fee plus one-quarter per cent, on all money placed. In 1910 the company capital was increased to £1,000,000 with all new shares being sold at a premium. When Britain entered the war in 1914 this company had £2,000,000 invested in the Americas.[23]

Three additional investment companies with United States interests were registered in 1913-14. The Scottish Colonial Investment Company, Limited, a private company promoted in Glasgow, lasted only two years. One director was bankrupt and the other was on military duty in France.[24] The Scottish American Development Corporation, Limited, of Edinburgh, sponsored by an iron merchant and an oil operator, met a similar fate.[25] Of greater importance was the Glasgow American Trust Company, Limited, capitalized at £250,000 and promoted by the chairman of the West of Scotland Investment Company, which had been in business for very nearly twenty years. The directors hoped to combine the mortgage and investment business.[26] The launching of this new company, sponsored by an established firm in Glasgow, along with the promotion of the Scottish Western Investment Company a few years earlier, meant that capitalists of Glasgow were, for the first time, taking their place beside Edinburgh and Dundee investors interested in United States securities and mortgages. Apparently the heavy industries of the Clyde no longer profitably utilized all of Glasgow's surplus capital. This may well be regarded as one of the most significant developments in Scottish-American economic relations between 1900 and 1914.

One of the greatest changes in the economic picture of the United States in the early twentieth century was in the field of agriculture. The decade from 1890 to 1900 had witnessed the end of the rapid opening up of the fertile lands of western America. The growing domestic market in the United States began to absorb an ever-increasing proportion of staple food products of the farm. Prices for farm products rose more rapidly than railroad rates, enhancing the farmer's margin of profit. Moreover, agricultural prices moved up faster than the general price level, and the average value of farm land advanced at an unprecedented rate. As a result, American agriculture was continuously and unusually prosperous between 1900 and 1920.[27]

The exceptional prosperity of the American farmer was only partially shared by the Scottish mortgage companies that had financed much of his activity in the last three decades of the nineteenth century. This was because the continuing competition from domestic capital forced a rapid decline in the rate of interest. The margin of profit between borrowing in Scotland and lending in western America gradually shrank. On the other hand, agricultural prosperity did make possible, in time, the sale of extensive real-estate holdings which the Scottish-American mortgage companies had acquired in the depression years.

The Scottish-American Mortgage Company maintained a business exclusively in mortgages, with 3,700 loans scattered throughout the United States. The American manager, Henry Sheldon, called upon at the 1901 meeting of shareholders to explain the slow improvement in the land market, concluded his remarks with the following:

> Now that America is beginning to have more capital of its own, I think it is proper that some acknowledgement should be made of the great service rendered to us, in the development of the country, by the use we have enjoyed for so many years of capital sent to America from Great Britain, and especially from Scotland. . . . The money that has come from Scotland to America has been invested in many ways that have been of great service to our people.[28]

At the time of a company reorganization in 1906 to get rid of the liability on shares, to increase borrowing power, and to enlarge the field of operations, a company spokesman noted that the company was thirty-two years old, its dividends had amounted to 328 per cent on the capital invested, or an average of over ten per cent a year, and a £150,000 reserve fund had been accumulated. In spite of its reorganization, the company was unable between 1907 and 1914 to earn profits comparable to those of the earliest investment trusts.[29] Meanwhile, the company pioneers had disappeared from the scene. Duncan Smith died in 1904, and with the retirement of Sheldon from the American managership three years later, the inspection headquarters had been moved from Chicago to Kansas City.[30]

The Edinburgh American Land Mortgage Company also went through a capital reorganization to cut down the liability of shareholders, and noted at the time that throughout its thirty-year history shareholders had received an average dividend of six and one-half per cent.[31] The Investors' Mortgage Security Company built up a reserve fund in anticipation of a capital reorganization in 1906. Scarcely had this been arranged than the company felt the pinch of the Panic of 1907, because it had investments both in mortgages and securities. With the return of prosperity the company expanded its mortgage business into Canada, with Winnipeg headquarters. By 1913 the company was paying ten and one-half per cent dividends, and shares were selling at a premium.[32] The United States Investment Corporation, also engaged in mortgages and securities, was less successful and shareholders had to be content with a smaller annual dividend of between four and six per cent.[33]

The Pacific Northwest enjoyed continuous and exceptional prosperity during these years and those companies with large holdings there, the Alliance Trust Company and the Oregon Mortgage Company, participated to the fullest. At the 1901 meeting of the stockholders of the Alliance Trust, the company agent in Portland,

28 *Princes Street, Edinburgh, about 1903*
29. (overleaf) *Share certificate of the Alliance Trust Company, Ltd., Dundee*

No. 1419

THIS IS TO CERTIFY that William Reoch Ritchie, residing at Anerley Villa, Newport, Fife, as Trustee for himself and the other children of Mrs Amelia Mathers Reoch or Ritchie Anerley Villa aforesaid, is the Proprietor of — Fifty — Ordinary Shares of Ten Pounds each Nos. — 68165 to 68214 — inclusive of

THE ALLIANCE TRUST COMPANY, LIMITED,

subject to the Memorandum and Articles of Association of the said Company and that up to this date there has been paid up in respect of said Shares the sum of Two Pounds per Share.

Given under the Common Seal of the said Company at Dundee this Twenty fourth day of August in the year One Thousand Eight Hundred and Ninety three

James Guthrie. Director

Wm. Mackenzie Secretary

Oregon, addressed the Scots on the subject of the Pacific Northwest:

> It embraces at the present time the two States of Oregon and Washington, which are an Empire within themselves, extending as they do to an area of 180,000 square miles, now only in what may be described as the initial stages of development. Foreign and especially Scotch capital has had much to do with what development has already taken place, and it seems likely to continue, for some time at least, to be an important factor in their growth. In both of these States, public sentiment, with but slight temporary aberrations, has been uniformly sympathetic to foreign capital. . . .
>
> The acquisition of the Philippine and Hawaiian Islands by the United States and the excitement incident to the development of the gold fields in Alaska, have served to direct increasing attention by the American people and others to the Pacific Coast States, with the result that, instead of, as formerly, regarding them as being on the confines of civilization, they are now regarded as the centre of what may truly be called the American Empire.[34]

Real estate acquired by the Oregon Mortgage Company during the depression following 1893 had largely been liquidated by 1904. Four years later, the chairman could report 'The recent financial crisis in the United States has in no way interfered with the prosperity of the Company, having had little effect in the States in which the Company operates, beyond temporary inconvenience.' Upon his return from the Pacific Northwest in 1909, the chairman revealed that irrigation projects near Missoula and Billings, Montana, and Idaho Falls, Idaho, had opened up new agricultural lands and farmers were wanting money for improvements. Farmers in Oregon and Washington were emphasizing market gardening and fruit growing, along with basic wheat cultivation. The company had invested £340,000 in Washington, £100,000 in Oregon, £75,000 in Montana, and £70,000 in Idaho. Between 1902 and 1905 the company had earned eight per cent annual dividends, and in 1906 this was raised to ten per cent. For 1911 an additional bonus of two per cent was paid. In 1912, a new issue of ordinary shares was sold at a premium of fifty per cent and the income placed in a reserve fund.[35]

Although mortgage loan rates continued to fall, there was little change in the percentage of the total investment of the Alliance Trust allotted to the mortgage field between 1905 and 1914. In the latter year, the absolute amount of mortgage business was more than twice that of nine years earlier. In 1915 eighty-three per cent of the total investments of the trust were in the United

States, six per cent in Canada, and eleven per cent in the rest of the world. Mortgage loans represented fifty-six per cent of its investment. Under new Articles of Association adopted in 1906 the holders of ordinary shares were permitted to pay up their uncalled liability and to have that amount converted into four per cent preference stock. By 1914 the company was capitalized at £1,500,000, of which £400,000 was ordinary and £1,100,000 preferred. This capital reorganization was reflected in the size of annual dividends on ordinary shares. Until 1905 it had been eight per cent annually, then systematic increases pushed it to ten per cent in 1906, twelve per cent in 1909, thirteen per cent in 1910, fifteen per cent in 1912, and on up to nineteen per cent in 1915.[36]

The Alliance Trust Company used Scottish capital to develop the natural resources of the United States in many different ways and places. For example, in California the Summit Lake Investment Company was organized to take over 17,481 acres of land along the tributaries of the Kings River in Fresno County, approximately twelve miles west of the town of Laton and thirty miles southwest of Fresno. The company hoped to carry out a programme of reclamation that included the draining of several sloughs along the lower reaches of the Kings River and the construction of levees to hold back the seasonal overflow of the river, the enlargement of Summit Lake so that it could serve as a reservoir, and the improvement of the natural channels of the river and adjoining canals to provide a system of controlled irrigation. A large acreage was to be made available for grain growing, hog raising, and cattle pasturing. An inspector for Balfour, Guthrie and Company, San Francisco, appraised the property at twice the $275,000 the Californians wished to borrow, so Scottish funds were made available for five years at seven per cent annual interest.[37]

The company also continued its efforts to secure control of the Chavez Land Grant in New Mexico. A court of private land claims, sitting in Santa Fe, had reduced the grant to 48,000 acres in 1895, and the Scots accepted the decision rather than risk an appeal to the United States Supreme Court. The approved acreage allotted to the company was carefully selected within the boundaries of the larger grant. The Scots also worked out an agreement, under the supervision of the court, whereby those squatters with the most valid claims were given title, and the court agreed to quiet title of all others. The Alliance Company also purchased the half-interest in this grant held by the Colorado Mortgage Company and became solely responsible for future developments.[38]

The Scots participating in the Deltic Investment Company

agreed in 1900 to abandon the unsatisfactory attempt to cultivate its Louisiana lands by using hired hands, and leased the lands to tenants.[39] This new policy appeared to be no improvement. In 1906 an experiment with Italian labour in the Mississippi Valley was introduced by assigning plots of 200 acres to each of fourteen immigrants. The following year the company agreed to send the editor of an Italian newspaper in Memphis, *Corriere Italiano,* to Italy to seek additional workers. Mackenzie was to join him in Rome. The company wanted to secure fifty Italian families willing to migrate by offering them $150 toward their passage to New Orleans and a cabin in which to live upon arrival at the Ashley Plantation. A few Italian families found new homes, but the fifteen thousand dollars invested in bringing them to America brought no financial return to the Scottish promoters.[40]

The company's acreage was continuously subject to overflow by seasonal flood waters of the Mississippi River and had been inundated four times prior to 1897 when the United States Engineers built a levee. There was no further spring flooding except for a minor break-through in 1903. The company was able to drain its lands, and by 1907 both sales and rentals were increasing. Then the boll weevil struck the cotton crop. The company met this crisis by the establishment of an experimental farm of 500 acres where tenants were taught methods to check the spread of the weevil and the advantages of crop diversification. Soon Louisiana rice production was second only to cotton. In spite of all efforts, the boll weevil destroyed the 1910 cotton crop. The company was unable to collect advances made to tenants in cash, tools, and supplies because many of them were bankrupt. The directors agreed to accept the loss but also voted to make no more loans. Lands lay idle, and in 1913 the company was forced to reverse its policy and to finance farmers on a crop-sharing basis. Farming operation proved unprofitable, and as there was no market for agricultural land the company resolved to exploit the timber resources on the acreage.[41]

Initial offers to purchase timber for $15 to $17 an acre were received in 1911 but the Board deemed the price too low. The next year timber-cutting rights on 19,102 acres were sold to the Singer Manufacturing Company that expected to set up a sawmill in this district where there was sufficient hardwood to make sewing-machine cabinets. The Scots also encouraged construction of a proposed east-west railroad, which would traverse six miles of the company's timberland, by promising the construction company a cash bonus of $25,000 if the line was completed by 1913. Meanwhile, timber experts from Chicago advised the Scots to exercise patience, predicting that the remaining 42, 550, increascluding 27,700 of virgin timber, would produce handsome profits.[42]

The Mississippi River overflowed again in April 1912, and, although there was no serious damage, the flood waters interfered with cultivation, and farmers, buying land on instalments, were sufficiently discouraged to abandon their acreages. New levees protected the property of the Deltic Investment Company in 1913, but there was serious damage elsewhere in the delta and farmers were clamouring for government protection. Congress had appropriated $6,000,000 for the protection of the lower valley in 1912. The Mississippi River Levee Association, presided over by A.S. Caldwell, the Scottish company's agent in Memphis, pressed vigorously for further funds to support a six- or seven-year work programme by the United States Army Engineers to establish protection from Cairo, Illinois, to the Gulf of Mexico. In 1914 Congress appropriated another $3,500,000, but the Levee Association insisted that at least fifty million dollars was needed. Meanwhile, the Scots had accumulated indebtedness on this experiment in Louisiana that amounted to £44,900, and no solution to their difficulties had yet appeared.[43] This chronicle of events in the lower Mississippi Valley is typical of countless efforts of Scots engaged in the land mortgage business in the United States, and illustrates the tenacity which they displayed in handling investments and the way in which their capital was used to sustain or improve an area in need.

As one examines details of the historical evolution of various Scottish-American enterprises during the early years of the twentieth century, certain patterns of development appear clear-cut. The Scots investing in industrials found them more profitable than land mortgages. Yet this advantage was only comparative, for agriculturalists prospered in these years, and the mortgage companies were generally in a sound financial position. There was a tendency for the Scots interested in the stock market to shift from railroads to industrials. Everywhere they encountered competition from domestic investment capital, which meant a lowering of interest rates. Many Scots began to channel the new funds available for investment elsewhere—to South America and to South Africa—in search of greater profits in nations with less highly-developed economies. Although the actual amount of Scottish capital invested in the United States in 1913 was somewhat greater than it had been in 1900, it represented a smaller percentage of the total Scottish capital invested overseas. A new source of Scottish money appeared in these years. The established capitalists of Glasgow, who had found profitable investments in the industries of the Clyde, joined their fellow-citizens in the East of Scotland, chiefly in Edinburgh and Dundee, in entering the mortgage and investment business in the United States in a substantial way. These funds more than replaced the money occasionally withdrawn by some of the older companies for investment elsewhere. In spite of the recessions of 1904 and 1907, the word that best describes these years is 'prosperity'. Just prior to the outbreak of war, however, the business picture, despite good earnings at that time, appeared more uncertain than at any time since the turn of the century.

THE WAR YEARS, AND ADJUSTMENTS IN THE TWENTIES

The chairman of the Investors' Mortgage Security Company caught the spirit of the times when he told shareholders at the annual meeting in 1914:

> Up till now the tale that has been told you at this Meeting has been the story of continued and increased prosperity of the Company. I am not going to suggest that prosperity has ceased, for that is not the case, but you must agree with me when I say that we are living in a severe and strenuous time and this is not the time to say much about prosperity.[44]

The outbreak of the European War in August 1914 immediately checked all programmes of expansion and increased capitalization among the Scottish investment and mortgage companies. Although the value of securities began to decline during the first two years of the war, earnings were maintained well enough to sustain, but not increase, dividends.

By 1916 the Scottish-American companies were rendering great assistance to the British government by making available their credit in the United States. Dollar securities were deposited on loan to His Majesty's Treasury as a part of the American Dollar Securities Mobilization Scheme. The government gave a bonus of one-half per cent on securities deposited. By 1917 the British Investment Trust had deposited United States stocks and bonds worth $7,896,750 with the Treasury.[45] The Scottish-American Investment Company had added securities on deposit that were valued at $8,000,000.[46] Undoubtedly the combined deposits of the Scottish-American companies provided a significant amount of credit that could be used to procure war matériel.

In addition, many companies inaugurated a policy of selling their investments in the United States and bringing home the funds to be lent to the British government. The Scottish-American Investment Company had purchased British government securities to the extent of £1,309,367 by the end of 1916. Sixty-three per cent of their United States investments had either been sold and invested in the war effort or placed on deposit with the Treasury, and the company chairman observed 'It must be no small satisfaction to the shareholders to be able in this way to do a share in helping their country in time of need.'[47] Early in 1917 this company subscribed another £1,000,000 to the new five per cent war loan. The Alliance Trust Company invested an aggregate of £1,076,200 in the national war effort.[48] The three Scottish American Trust Companies and the North American Trust Company of Dundee reported a decrease in the percentage of their investments in the United States during each of the war years.[49] The American Trust Company with a comparatively small capitalization, assumed its responsibility by subscribing £75,000 to the British War Loan, 62,500 francs to the French War Loan, £2,000 to Russian Treasury Bills, and deposited dollar securities in London amounting to $283,500.[50]

Entry of the United States into the war brought many changes. The value of securities shrank rapidly and particular concern was expressed over the effect of the decision of the United States government to take over operation of the nation's railroads. The North American Trust Company reported that the 'bottom had fallen out of the American market' as a result of the transfer from a peacetime to a war economy and the flow of capital to the government through Liberty Loan drives. All annual reports noted the burden of heavy taxation at home and abroad, especially the income tax in the United States, and comparatively small remuneration received on capital loaned or deposited with the British government.[51] In spite of all the gloom, characteristic of businessmen forced to submit to the regulations and taxation accompanying a war, investors' dividends were maintained.

The mortgage companies did not assign so large a percentage of their capital to the British Treasury as the investment companies because their assets could not be so quickly and conveniently converted into cash. Advances made to the American farmer had been called-up from all directions and, through the United States government, he requested the British government to permit mortgage companies in the United Kingdom to extend to him the same consideration granted the Canadian farmer. The British government finally recognized that funds invested in farm mortgages in the United States were employed in support of an industry vital to an Allied victory, and on 3 October 1918 restrictions on the mortgage business were relaxed and the companies permitted to resume reinvesting the principal collections received each year. Both the United States Mortgage Company and the Oregon Mortgage Company then announced that decrease in the total invested in the United States over the last three years had stopped. Relief from governmental pressure had not come, however, until the war was almost over.[52]

Toward the close of the war it was clear to Scottish capitalists that the United States would emerge as a creditor nation. United States citizens had not only bought back stocks and bonds previously owned abroad but had also made extensive purchases of European government securities. The venerable Scottish-American Mortgage Company in 1918 saw no immediate prospect of increasing its business in the United States and the directors utilized the broader investment privileges of the company, acquired in 1903, to place capital at home rather than abroad.[53] The First Scottish American Trust Company of Dundee reported in 1919 that for the first time in history its investments in the United States were below fifty per cent of its total.[54]

Many Scottish companies found that the book value of their assets had suffered depreciation during the war. The British Investment Trust, for example, reported that a valuation of its securities showed a thirteen per cent depreciation.[55] The North American Trust Company admitted in 1917 that its holdings were sixteen per cent below book value.[56] The First Scottish American Trust Company of Dundee was proud of the fact that its position, in this regard, was the same in 1919 as it had been in 1914.

The chairman of the North American Trust Company presented the challenge of the day when he said:

> While war means destruction of life and property, reconstruction in its present day sense means far more than rebuilding of these two elements—it means today the scrapping of old ideas, the destruction of shibboleths of the past, and the remodelling of life and industry on an entirely new foundation. This is the period through which we are now passing. It is fraught with many difficulties, many pitfalls, and in magnitude equals, if it does not actually surpass, the many and varied problems which we have had to face during these days of battle, now, thank God, safely past. . . . I firmly believe we will revive our national and international trade on a sure and lasting foundation.[57]

As a means of adjusting to changing times, consolidations were undertaken by several Scottish-American mortgage companies in the last two years of the war. For example, in April 1918, the oldest Edinburgh company, the Scottish-American Mortgage Company, made plans to purchase the entire share capital of the American Mortgage Company of Scotland for £250,000.[58] The Oregon Mortgage Company acquired the business of the Canadian and American Mortgage and Trust Company.[59]

Another important development was the decision of several companies interested primarily in the United States mortgage field to liquidate this business gradually and assign the funds set free to general security investment both in the United States and elsewhere. The United States Mortgage of Scotland joined the Second Scottish Investment Trust of Edinburgh and commenced a shift of operations into the investment field. In May 1928 the name of the company was changed to United States Trust Company of Scotland.[60] After conducting a business almost exclusively in mortgages for forty years, the Edinburgh American Land Mortgage Company sold its ordinary shares in July 1919 to the British Assets Trust, Limited. Thereafter it was gradually transferred to an investment trust company, changing its name to Second British Assets Trust, Limited, in 1925.[61] The Investors' Mortgage Security Company also decided in 1922 to transfer to investments.[62] The old Scottish-American Mortgage Company revealed in 1925 that it had likewise been engaged in transferring to securities that now represented forty-four per cent of the company's funds. The transfer was continuous; by 1927 securities comprised fifty-eight per cent of the total; in 1929, seventy-five per cent.[63]

The long-established companies interested in United States securities, after due consideration, accepted the fact that the policy of withdrawal and reinvestment at home or within the British Empire was permanent. The pattern had been established just before the outbreak of war for economic reasons and then intensified by the financial demands of the British government during the war. A practice, once thought transitory, now appeared fixed. In spite of the depressed market in the United States, Dundee's Scottish American Trust Companies could realize on securities at their depreciated values, bring the dollars home, and make up the loss through the favourable rate of exchange into sterling. In other words, the advantages of monetary transfer were geographically reversed from what they had been in the years of the companies' beginnings, 1873-75, and they profited again by the exchange.[64] The Scottish-American Investment Company of Edinburgh and the British Investment Trust followed the example of the Dundee companies in liquidating holdings in the United States and reinvesting elsewhere.

This withdrawal from the American field had no adverse effects upon the expansion or operations of the investment companies of Scotland. In 1927 the three Scottish American Trust Companies were reconstructed whereby each increased its capital by £100,000. Three years earlier the North American Trust Company had increased its capital from £1,000,000 to £1,250,000. The newer Glasgow investment companies, excited at the prospects of sizeable profits on the world's stock exchanges, also expanded. The West of Scotland American Investment Company doubled its £100,000 capitalization in 1925. The Scottish Western Investment

Company increased its share capital from £1,000,000 to £1,250,000 in 1929.[65]

Two new investment companies worthy of note were launched in the decade: the Second American Trust Company, Limited, of Edinburgh with a capitalization of £600,000 in 1926, and the Third Scottish Western Investment Trust, Limited, with a capital of £500,000 started in the same year. Shareholders of the first company were told not to assume by the name that an undue proportion of its funds would be invested in the United States. The other company admitted in 1930 that only one-sixth of its investment was in the United States.[66]

A perusal of the annual reports of the Alliance Trust Company for the 1920s serves to highlight the trends within Scottish mortgage and investment companies during the decade because that company was engaged in both. First of all, the directors recognized that the security market was more profitable than mortgages and adopted a policy of reducing its mortgage business. The American farmer was experiencing a depression between 1900 and 1924, not unlike that of 1893-6. He was oppressed by high labour costs, because wages of workers had not dropped from the high wartime level to conform with the falling prices for agricultural products. The Fordney-McCumber Tariff of 1922 resulted in higher prices for his equipment. Prices for staple products were generally low and fluctuated wildly. In 1923 the boll weevil scourge created a short cotton crop and farmers obtained a national average of thirty cents a pound for cotton, almost one-third higher than it had been in 1921. To offset this improvement in farm income, there had been a surplus of wheat in 1922 and a bumper crop in 1923 that led to a drop in price. Storage space at major grain ports was full. The cattle market was also dull in 1923. In April 1924, the chairman of the Alliance Trust Company summarized the situation in American agriculture:

> For the past three years we have not been able to give you a good account of our Mortgage operations in the United States and Canada, and I much regret to inform you that we have experienced another disappointing year. In 1922, the poor crops in America adversely affected our borrowers, but I can not bring forward crop failure as an explanation of the bad results we have encountered for 1923. Speaking generally, and if we ignore certain sections of the cotton belt, the year was comparatively free from crop failure. . . . It has been rather a question of price. With the one exception of cotton —and possibly corn—the prices ruling for American agricultural products during the past season have been very poor, and have left little, if any, margin of profit to our

> borrowers over the cost of production. . . . America is producing food-stuffs in excess of the ability of her consumers to buy.

To the Scots the situation appeared simple: 'It was the old question of supply exceeding the demand.' In 1914 the Alliance Trust Company had £2,345,182 invested in the mortgage business, representing over half of its funds. By 1921, this phase of the company's investment was reduced to forty-seven per cent. At the 1928 annual meeting shareholders were frankly told 'Our Policy is one of withdrawal and realization, but conditions are making its attainment difficult and slow. Conditions were, on the whole, fair during the past year, but the Real Estate market failed to show any improvement.'[67]

By way of contrast, it should be noted that the Oregon Mortgage Company directors observed the same developments in United States agriculture witnessed by the Alliance Trust Company, but they delayed leaving the field of mortgage investment until the end of the 1920s, and therefore met disaster in the 1930s. Prices for sugar beets, potatoes, and alfalfa were sufficiently high between 1920 and 1923 to offset the great losses among the wheat farmers of the Northwest. The directors were forced to admit that 1923 was an unsatisfactory year for the mortgage business and the chairman commented:

> The American farmer is in a difficult position of having to sell his products at the world price, which is at present abnormally low. On the other hand, everything that he buys and all the expenses of production, such as wages and taxation, are still at an artificially high level. The farmer is thus between the upper and nether millstone, and the reaction is all the more severe because of the prosperity enjoyed during the war. This condition of affairs is inevitably reflected in our business, and the outlook at present cannot be said to be any brighter.

Two years later at the annual meeting the chairman remarked again 'to find a parallel for conditions in our Mortgage field it is necessary to go back to the agricultural depression of the '90s . . .'. Yet in defiance of these gloomy observations and with the real-estate account doubling every two years between 1923 and 1927, the directors continued to pay shareholders a ten per cent annual dividend. The customary annual bonus of two per cent was even increased to four per cent for 1923. Finally, in July 1927, the directors made a belated decision to withdraw from the mortgage business in the United States. They rushed into the security market and by 1929 half the company's funds were in this type of investment. At the annual meeting of July 1930, the shareholders were 'greeted with the sad story' of continued foreclosures, rising cost of upkeep for the real estate, and the necessity for reducing the dividend to eight per cent. There was much worse to come.[68]

In addition to transferring its funds from mortgages to securities, the Alliance Trust Company had participated in another trend of the times by introducing a programme of capital expansion in 1921. Shares were placed upon the market periodically until 1926 when the subscribed capital was equal to that authorized, £2,500,000. The securities marketed in 1926 had to be rationed among the stockholders who were permitted to purchase £10 for each £100 already held, but at a price of £25. None complained at the price, because the market quotation for the £10 stock was quoted at £55. Then, in 1927, the authorized capital was raised to £3,000,000, and the amount issued was £2,572,500.[69]

This policy of expansion reflected a general development strikingly manifest in the financial history of Great Britain. At no time had the formation of new investment companies or the expansion of old ones reached such a volume. Between 1923 and 1926 new capital amounting to £15,000,000 had been offered and subscribed in investment trust companies alone. *The Times* had reported in its 'financial review for 1926' that £33,000,000 had been invested in 'financial, land, investment, and trust companies' in the United Kingdom, in comparison with £21,600,000 for 1925 and £17,200,000 for 1924, making a total of £71,800,000. The provincial cities of England were still virtually untouched by the movement, for such cities as Manchester, Liverpool, Birmingham, and Newcastle, broadly speaking, had no investment trusts at all. The activity in Scotland, 'The Home of the Investment Trust', and in London was all the more marked.[70] A half-century of experience had proved the investment trust principle a success. The United States was now a single field in world-wide interest.

Like the rest of the Scottish mortgage companies, the Alliance Trust Company also recognized the advantages of consolidation. In 1918 the company took over the management of the Western and Hawaiian Investment Company, which had 81·8 per cent of its investment in land mortgages. There were rumours of amalgamation, but instead, in 1923, the Western and Hawaiian was renamed the Second Alliance Trust. The policy immediately adopted corresponded with that of the senior company: first, expansion; second, transferring the bulk of funds from land loans in the United States to stock and bond investments; and third, reducing the holdings in the United States to invest on a world-wide basis.[71]

Finally, the Alliance Trust Company had shown the way to make profits. The dividend on ordinary stock steadily increased from nineteen per cent in 1920 to twenty-five per cent in 1927.

In addition to dramatic capital gains, described in detail by the company chairman at the next annual meeting, the reserve fund stood at £2,000,000. This exceptionally large amount had been built up to keep public confidence high and to hold debenture interest rates low, thereby maximizing profits.[72]

In the midst of great success the Alliance Trust Company and its Scottish associates were still left with legacies of the past like the Deltic Investment Company. During 1920 there were heavy rains, both in the planting and picking season, in the Mississippi River delta in addition to the annual visitation of the boll weevil. Both crops and prices were poor in 1921, the most disappointing in the company's entire history. Many white tenants who had defaulted the previous year decided to surrender their holdings. To minimize the idle lands, the company arranged to finance and directly supervise the labour of Negro tenants. The company developed a system of annual rental contracts with an option to purchase, trusting that some renters were men of diligence who would eventually become proprietors. Farming operations became so discouraging that for the next five years the directors elected not to publish annual reports. However, a new source of income materialized in 1925. All timber on the estate was sold on option. The company received $817,932 in cash and in July half of each ordinary share of £1 was repaid.

During the spring of 1927 the Mississippi River went on a rampage. The levee adjoining company lands broke, and 2,100 acres of rented farm land was covered with water, which receded so slowly that there was no time to plant a crop. The directors felt this event had set back the realization on real estate for many years and made flood control a major national question. Congress did appropriate $325 million for control of the Mississippi River. Meanwhile, the season of 1928 passed without agricultural cultivation. In 1929 the deposit of silt left by the flood was removed, but an excessive rainfall brought new floods to the lowlands. The company directors were watching oil and gas developments in the region in the hope that they might provide a substitute income for the depleted timber reserves. By September 1929 a hard-surface road from Shreveport had been completed through the company property and a $7,000,000 bridge across the Mississippi at Vicksburg was about to be opened. Once again the Scots anticipated selling their lands.[73]

In the highly complicated period between 1914 and 1929, certain characteristic patterns of Scottish overseas investments may be discerned. Without question the trends established before 1912 were accentuated by the events of World War I. Competition with domestic capital became increasingly acute because of the growing resources for investment in the United States. The mortgage lending business was in a comparatively unfavourable position because of the widespread agricultural depression, so much so that the Scots largely abandoned this type of economic endeavour, once so profitable. And finally, reduction in profits caused the Scots to accelerate their departure from the United States and seek new frontiers for investment where their capital was more urgently needed and the rewards greater. Withdrawal from the western United States in no way meant a lessening of Scottish interests in overseas investment. On the contrary, most of the established limited companies expanded capital in the 1920s.

THE DEPRESSION AND THE NEW DEAL

When shareholders of the various Scottish-American companies assembled for annual meetings in 1930, Board chairmen scarcely needed to emphasize the crisis before them. The financial press had already reported that between 19 September 1929, when stock values reached their peak on the world-wide exchanges, and 13 November, when they touched bottom, a shrinkage in value of over £8,000,000,000 had occurred in the stock listed on these exchanges. Stock speculations had increased steadily for over six years before the crash. Until 1927 the boom had been kept within reasonable bounds, but in 1928 stocks were being bought not on the basis of earnings but on the estimated return of four or five years hence.

When the economic storm broke over the world in 1930 no area of investment escaped its devastating influence. The chairman of the Alliance Trust Company admitted:

> Trust Companies, in short, must pass through a period more trying than the most cautious pessimist ever anticipated. In the past they have reckoned that by a wide spreading of their investment risk, a stable revenue position could be maintained, as it was not to be expected that all the world would go wrong at the same time. But the unexpected has happened, and every part of the civilized world is in trouble.[74]

The directors found reassurance, however, in the large reserve fund built up in the good years to take care of the bad ones. The chairman of the Second Alliance Trust Company was more optimistic, suggesting that investors who were compelled to sell had done so and that a healthier stock market would soon recover. Moreover, his company was more interested in the strength and permanence of its earning power than in the market price of securities.[75] The annual dividend of the company was raised to twenty-two per cent in September 1930, and remained there for the next three years. By September 1933, he was forced to admit 'the immediate outlook continues to get worse instead of better'. For some time the widespread defaults and reductions in American holdings had been offset by the favourable rate at which the dollar revenue was converted into sterling, but the abandonment of the gold standard in the United States and the devaluation of the dollar ended this possibility. After reviewing the banking crisis in the United States early in 1933, the chairman reported:

> Last, and worst of all, the public at large took to hoarding all the currency and gold it could lay its hands on, and for that disastrous purpose it is stated that the three days ending March 4 last saw $800,000,000 withdrawn from the banks. When the new President took over from his predecessor on the morning of the 5th of March he found the economic life of the United States paralysed by debt and panic. In such circumstances all ordinary measures were useless. He had to adopt whatever devices could be suggested to ease the position immediately, to raise prices, put money in circulation, and restore some kind of confidence. It is said that his measures have not been based on sound principles, but, after all, what are meant by sound principles are rules or principles that have been found useful in the past. Unfortunately, the position in the United States was such that the rules of the past did not apply. The President could do nothing but boldly experiment and subject his experiments to the principles of trial and error. It is not for us to criticize him in this extraordinary situation.[76]

The chairman of the Alliance Trust Company was less charitable when he asserted that the United States government had discovered that an abundance of metallic currency was not the cure for anything. He commented further:

> America, in particular, with the largest stock of gold in the world, finds its production and trade reduced to a catastrophic extent, its army of unemployed greater than that of any other country, and its whole economic system involved in something like paralysis. That is not the fault of the gold standard. It is, as has been well pointed out, the fault of those very causes which have brought about abandonment of the gold standard.[77]

The impact of the world-wide slump on those Scottish companies interested exclusively, or even dominantly, in the security market was reflected in their annual reports that dwelt on themes of security depreciation, decline in annual income, and continuing withdrawal from the United States as a field for investment. For example, the First Scottish American Trust Company reported that the valuation of its investments had fallen sharply during 1930, had continued to decline for the next three years, and then began to rise again very slowly. There was, of course, a time lag between the fall of industrial earnings and the decline in revenue so the company income was not reduced until 1932. Even so, a maximum dividend for the decade was paid on ordinary stock, twenty-seven per cent. After that, dividends had to be cut, and by 1935 they had reached a low of eighteen per cent. As late as 1938 the company's investments were still below book cost. Like the rest of the Scottish investment companies, this Dundee firm had been withdrawing from the United States for some time; in 1933, only a fifth of its funds were invested there and if the depression had not been world-wide the effects of the depression in the United States would have been cushioned.[78]

The American Trust Company noted the same trends. In 1933 an evaluation of its investments revealed that the entire reserve fund of £300,000 was far from adequate to cover the depreciation; after deducting the entire reserve the total decline in security reserves was 19·22 per cent below their purchase price. Recovery came quickly, however, and by 1936 the depreciation was only 12·4 per cent. Between 1930 and 1934 the annual dividend of the company dropped from fourteen to four per cent.[79] The Second American Trust Company somewhat proudly noted that its American securities represented only from eighteen to twenty-two per cent of the total between 1930 and 1936. Their world-wide distribution of investments did not protect them from shrinkage, reported at 20·70 per cent in 1932.[80] Even the venerable Scottish-American Investment Company revealed in 1934 that only forty-six per cent of its investments were in the United States and an equal amount in the British Empire.

Companies investing in farm mortgages felt the disaster of the depression as acutely as the security companies, and the process of recovery appeared more complicated and prolonged. The continuous fall in commodity values after 1922 had been a major factor in producing the general depression in the world's economy. An improvement in prices was further delayed by the imposition of tariffs, quotas, and exchange restrictions. Climatic conditions in the United States brought additional woe to the farmers who were already plagued by ruinous prices for crops. During 1930 drought scorched large areas of the farm belt. Poor crops, coupled with poor prices, meant that interest on mortgages would not be paid, foreclosures would be necessary, and the real-estate market would be exceedingly dull. In 1933 the Alliance Trust Company reported that its mortgage investment business, representing one-eighth of the whole, had gone from a condition of adversity to one of collapse. The loans on which the annual interest was paid represented less than sixteen per cent of the total capital in the mortgage business. Partial interest was paid on less than twenty per cent. Over twenty-two per cent of the funds was represented by loans on which no interest whatsoever was paid, and more than forty-two per cent was represented by real estate paying nothing into the revenue account.[81] The Second Alliance Company rejoiced that only four per cent of its total funds were in mortgages.

Real disaster overcame those companies that had remained exclusively in the mortgage business through the early 1920s. The Oregon Mortgage Company was a case in point. The vast majority of its mortgages in the Pacific Northwest had to be foreclosed and between 1928 and 1931 the nominal value of its real estate increased from £80,000 to £115,000. The company was obliged to drop its dividend from eight to five per cent for 1931. It was thirteen years before the shareholders received an additional distribution. A modest four and one-half per cent was paid for 1944 and by 1948 the annual dividend had reached seven per cent. Many Scottish capitalists felt the directors would have been well advised to have built up a strong reserve fund in the 1920s rather than paying 'fancy bonuses' in addition to ten per cent annual dividends.[82]

The depression years proved the undoing of two recently-established Glasgow companies dealing both in mortgages and securities. Debenture holders of the Glasgow American Trust Company were called together in 1930 and told that the Chicago agents, George Forman and Company, had reported that almost one-third of the $1,752,816 invested with them had been temporarily lost through depreciation. The directors counselled patience, but in 1936, when the debenture loans became due, the holders were told they could not be paid. They agreed to a postponement of the final payment for ten years and each year a small percentage of the borrowed money was refunded until forty-five per cent of the loan had been paid up in 1944. Of course, the stock-holders had been wiped out and in 1946 the company voted to wind-up its affairs.[83]

The West of Scotland American Investment Company found itself in the same plight. George Forman and Company reported that only forty-five per cent of the Scottish investment funds, totalling $2,706,249, could be realized in 1930. Barrow, Wade, Guthrie and Company, accountants of London and Chicago, investigated affairs of the Chicago agents and urged the directors of the Glasgow firm to bring legal action for maladministration of funds. Meanwhile, George Forman and Company transferred some of its assets to the Scots. In this instance, too, debenture holders were asked to delay payment of their loans for ten years. Liquidation of this debt was a slow and painful process, but by 1950 eighty per cent had been repaid and the next year the company was wound-up.[84]

In contrast, the third Glasgow mortgage and investment company launched in the twentieth century, the Scottish Western Investment Company, was comparatively successful during the depression decade. Following the pattern of new investment companies, holdings in the United States had been limited to twenty per cent of the total. Dividend payments were well maintained. The success of this enterprise may be partially attributed to the guiding genius of William Mackenzie and the prestige of the Bonar Laws.[85]

Shareholders of the Alliance Trust Company assembled in 1934 to bewail the failure of the World Economic Conference in London and 'the refusal of the world as at present constituted to function as a business unit'. The leading feature of the year, however, was 'the great American experiment'. Although President Roosevelt was at first admired for having attacked the economic situation with courage and resourcefulness, there were now misgivings about the New Deal. His policy was thought to be 'simply one of revolutionary experiment. It has never been possible to say what course the President would take next, and the final outcome is veiled in complete obscurity.'[86] Five months later, at the annual meeting, the chairman of the Second Alliance Trust Company concurred:

> The position of the United States defies calculation. The New Deal has not brought prosperity and the country is subsisting entirely on hope. No sane man supposes that it can emerge from its present position without further loss and trouble or that the violent operations of the President, even though ultimately beneficial, can be carried out without injury and suffering in many directions.[87]

In 1935 the New Deal looked even less promising. With relief measures pouring millions of dollars into the channels of trade at a rate of expenditure greatly exceeding government income, some Scottish capitalists were convinced that the recovery stimulated thereby could be neither real nor permanent. However, the money supplied from federal government sources had resulted in the repayment of a number of the Alliance Trust Company's mortgages. A reduction in real-estate holdings would have been more welcome, because most mortgages repaid were those paying interest regularly and at a higher rate of interest than could be obtained for money in 1935. Some sales of real estate had been made in the Pacific Northwest where irrigation had improved holdings. The annual dividend on ordinary shares that had been twenty-five per cent since 1929 was lowered to twenty-two per cent.[88]

The Scottish companies welcomed the gradual return of prosperity to the United States in 1936. Everything from cigarettes to automobiles was going up in price and the all-important capital goods indicators, construction contracts and machine tools, were fifty per cent higher than in 1935. Railroad and utility companies were being forced to expand and equip. Although the enormous deficit in the federal government's budget appeared to be a menace, the optimistic insisted that bank controls, easy money and increased taxation might solve the problems of financing.[89]

The Alliance Company not only continued to express concern over the 'wonderland finance' in the United States but also regretted that industrial recovery had not extended to agriculture. The mortgage business, still representing ten per cent of the company's funds, was so depressed that the directors suggested it might eventually become a definite capital loss. In 1937 legislation for the relief of the American farmer had just begun to simplify the task of realizations of mortgage loans, when the Agricultural Adjustment Act was declared unconstitutional by the Supreme Court. The company chairman, however, thought the President was 'a singularly resourceful person' who was conscious of the farmers' political power, and the Scot was convinced the agricultural interests would somehow get the consideration due them.[90]

When the business recession of 1937 occurred, the spectacular declines on the New York stock market provoked a tirade from the presiding officer at the annual meeting of the Second Alliance Trust Company:

> . . . we must remember that that market is the victim of gambling operations to an extent for which we find no parallel on our side, and wild and disorderly movements are the natural result. The economic position gives no apparent justification for what has happened. There is a large demand for goods and services accumulated during the depression still not satisfied, money is easy and likely to remain so, and there is a strong revival of agriculture—the country's greatest industry and the basis of its prosperity and its export trade. On the other hand, we cannot treat such movements as have taken place as if they had no significance at all. They show real lack of confidence somewhere, and without reasonable confidence healthy and sustained recovery cannot take place. The trouble lies in the political sphere. The wild methods of government finance, President Roosevelt's attitude toward big business—particularly the Utility

> Companies—the success which has attended the shock tactics of organized labour and so on, have tended to sap confidence. We can hope, however, that the great resources of the United States and the energy and ability of its business community will enable it to overcome all the difficulties which politicians put in its way.[91]

Any decline in the value of the company's United States securities, now representing twenty per cent of the total, did not preclude the raising of the annual dividend on ordinary stock from eighteen to twenty per cent. The Alliance Trust Company, with seventeen per cent of its interests in the United States, also increased its distribution among shareholders from twenty-two to twenty-three per cent; both companies, therefore, appeared to have survived the crisis unusually well and were now on the road to prosperity. The capitalization of the Alliance Trust Company, with £3,250,000 authorized and issued, remained the same after 1934.[92] It was the most heavily capitalized investment trust company in Europe at the outbreak of the World War of 1939.

In these years of crisis, the Alliance Trust Company was attempting to liquidate its real estate in the United States acquired as a legacy of the mortgage business. As early as 1927, E.D. Fleming, employed by the Dundee office since 1889, was charged with the responsibility of visiting the various agencies for this purpose. The process of realization was complicated because the properties were varied and scattered. One holding in west Texas was the Palo Duro Canyon in Randall County. Once a part of the Goodnight Ranch and the site of its headquarters, this well-known landmark had passed into the hands of the Arnold Brothers. In 1920 the Alliance Trust Company lent B.S. Arnold $67,500 on the security of his 18,550-acre ranch. Interest payments on the loan ceased in 1933, and four years later when Fleming visited the mortgaged property the Scottish company's only income came from tourist fees paid to visit 'The Grand Canyon in Miniature'. Four hundred Civilian Conservation Corps men were making roads and trails, building tourist cabins and hostels, and constructing an artificial lake to make the area a state park. When the project was completed, the Scots expected to sell the site to the State of Texas for a park at a price sufficient to repay its loan with interest as well as most of a second lien of $150,000 that Arnold had borrowed elsewhere on his cattle.[93]

When occasion afforded, revenue-producing real estate in urban areas had been obtained in exchange for farms and orchard sites held by the Scots. In the Pacific Northwest, the Scots owned and operated the Washington Park Manor in Portland, Oregon, a three-storey modern brick apartment house containing twenty-five three- and four-room suites. In 1934 only $100,000 remained outstanding in Oregon, out of nearly $1,000,000 invested there in the 1920s. This was because the company had ceased lending in Oregon after discovering the potentialities of irrigation in the semi-arid desert of southern Idaho and the improved methods of dry wheat farming in eastern Washington. In the mid-thirties approximately $160,000 was lent in eastern Washington and $640,000 in Idaho. The company had financial interest in twenty-nine different canal companies and irrigation districts in Idaho. There were thirty-four different properties on the salvage list in the Portland agency. Five of these were irrigated properties in Idaho; the bulk were dry wheat farms on marginal or abandoned lands in Oregon, Idaho, and Washington.[94]

A WORLD AT WAR

In 1939 shareholders of the Alliance Trust were reminded that Britain was in a state of grave emergency and tension. Great concern was expressed over the uncertain prospect for peace. Although business had improved in the United States and there was a definite recovery in world trade in 1938, signs of wavering prosperity were seen because of the unsettling effect of events in Europe.[95] The Second Alliance Company held its annual meeting early in September in the immediate shadow of war, and all agreed they could do nothing but await events and be prepared to adapt to changing conditions.[96]

At the outbreak of war, the Scottish companies were forced by the Defence Acts to put all their American investments at the disposal of His Majesty's Treasury. Financial participation in the war effort was no longer on an optional basis as it had been in the World War of 1914-18. When dollars were necessary for national requirements, securities were requisitioned and the companies received the sterling equivalent of the market prices of the stocks handed over. The Scottish-American Mortgage Company announced 'In accordance . . . with the wishes of His Majesty's Treasury the Directors have continued to bring home all available collections in the United States of America.'[97] Directors of the Alliance Trust expected the process to continue until virtually all American stocks and bonds were taken. Shareholders were informed that no one challenged the right of the Government to acquire assets that could contribute so materially to the national effort and few could criticize the procedure adopted for the requisitions. At the same time, they were assured that in parting with the American securities the company was making a contribution that involved sacrifice. The portfolio of dollar securities represented over twenty per cent of the total funds. These had been obtained not in a haphazard manner in a few months, but over the years as the result of experienced management. Those companies that had had the foresight to invest in the United States field years earlier were being penalized, but no one saw a satisfactory alternative. While requisitions were recognized as inevitable, resentment did arise against the inequalities of an excess profits tax which bore heavily upon the current earnings of investment trusts resulting from earlier enterprise.[98]

In April 1941 the Alliance Trust Company reported that the British government had taken $4,000,000 in dollar securities. In addition, the company had realized from sales, interest, dividends, and collections from the mortgage business another $5,000,000 that had been handed over to the Treasury. The investment companies made a contribution of considerable national importance when purchases of war material in the United States could be effected only on a cash basis. Although the passage of Lend-Lease legislation eliminated the urgent necessity to obtain dollars, the Scottish capitalists did not think this agreement relieved Britain of its obligation to pay to the limit of capacity for purchases in the United States. The Alliance Trust prepared to sacrifice all its American investments with the exception of the remaining mortgage business, now only five and one-half per cent of its funds.[99]

Although many Scots regarded the company's mortgage business as moribund for some years and as an unwanted legacy from the early days, they were rewarded in 1940–1 for the care and management of these properties. Negotiations were concluded for the sale of several large plantations in the southern states, including the properties of the Deltic Investment Company. When the opportunity came to sell there was no hesitancy, and the income was sufficient to institute winding-up proceedings for the Deltic Investment Company in which the Alliance Trust held a major interest.[100] Another sale of importance was the Chavez Land Grant in New Mexico, held since 1881. Early in 1940 the United States government expressed an interest in the land, ostensibly to expand the Pueblo Indian Reservation. The 47,000 acres remaining in the grant were sold to the United States for $67,350 with the Scots reserving the oil rights to this property for the next fifty years, as was their custom in parting with all real estate.[101]

Anxiety mounted for the various Scottish companies as the World War spread into the Pacific. The Scottish-American Mortgage Company reassured its investors, 'our direct interest in the territories brought into the war zone by the entry of Japan do not bear a large proportion to the total of the company's investments'. Those few securities held would produce no revenue, however, and the annual income of the company was destined to decrease. The Scottish-American Investment Company expressed the same views.[102]

The close of the world-wide conflict did not solve the many problems faced by the Scottish investment trusts. The chairman of the Scottish-American Investment Company remarked at the end of 1945:

> While the war lasted it was relatively easy to forecast the trend of financial events for everything was controlled with one end in view. Now that we have entered the transition period, the future is much more obscure. Under any Government the difficulties would have been immense; under a Government which appears determined to nationalize substantial sections of our basic industries at the same time that the whole is being converted from a war to a peace basis, there has been added to the inevitable difficulties a new element of uncertainty.[103]

Directors of the American Trust Company sounded a note of discouragement in 1947 by saying 'the possibility of the imposition of further taxation or restrictive measures by the present Government, preclude the making of a forecast'. The trend of earnings could not be foretold the next year 'as the free play of economic forces is meantime overridden by controls and restrictions'.[104]

Frustrated by the Labour regime in Britain, many companies concluded, in 1948, that profits from investments in the United States were great enough to justify paying the premium on the purchase of American dollars to re-enter the field. In July 1949 shareholders of the Second Alliance Trust Company were notified that the company holdings in the United States represented 11·52 per cent of the whole compared with 5·23 per cent the previous year. Chairman W.D. MacDougall mentioned 'we have for some time been at pains to restore some part of our pre-war American investments and part of the rise represents new purchases'. The British Investment Trust in January 1950 reported fifteen per cent in United States holdings as compared with 1·2 per cent the previous year. The Scottish-American Mortgage Company, which had completely liquidated its mortgage and real-estate business in 1945, dealt chiefly with British securities until 1948. In the next three years its holdings in the United States market increased from ten to twenty per cent. The United States Trust Company had sold all but 0·9 per cent of its United States securities in 1948, but following the general trend of Scottish investment, had increased the amount to over twenty per cent by 1950. The American Trust Company report for 1951 explained the development both tersely and bluntly: 'The restriction and discouragement of private enterprise in this country have induced your Directors to increase the company's investments outside the United Kingdom and more particularly in North America.'[105]

Prosperity returned to the Scottish capitalist in the late 1940s. The Alliance Trust Company reported in 1947 that it was in a stronger financial position than at any time in its history. The bond and stock investments which absorbed over ninety-eight per cent of the invested funds showed an appreciation of 65·42 per cent over the valuation in the balance sheet. The annual dividend on ordinary stock was twenty-eight per cent, the highest of all time. The Second Alliance Company was also breaking dividend records, paying twenty-four per cent in 1949. Between 1944 and 1948 the British Investment Trust had increased the annual dividend from eleven and one-half to fifteen per cent; between 1942 and 1947 the United States Investment Corporation went from six to twelve per cent. In Dundee the Scottish American Trust Companies were regaining the prosperity known in the 1920s. The First Company earned thirty-six per cent on its ordinary stock in 1949 and paid a dividend of twenty-two per cent; the Third Company earned thirty-four per cent and paid twenty-one per cent.[106]

All the Scottish-American companies had played a vital role in the dollar mobilization drives in Britain during both world wars. Their aid in bolstering the British economy in the years of crisis was considerable. Moreover, through the remarks of company chairmen, the businessman's viewpoint toward the Great Depression and the New Deal becomes apparent. Perhaps one should not be startled to learn that there appears to have been more unanimity of opinion among capitalists of both the United States and Scotland than among the diplomats and the politicians. Yet in spite of their harshness in criticizing Franklin D. Roosevelt, we find the Scots in the same position in the end as in the beginning—investing in the United States to take advantage of the expanding economy and the comparatively unrestricted position of private enterprise so dear to the Scottish capitalist.

Chapter Twelve

A Summation

A shrewd Forfarshire manufacturer, reflecting on the economic position of Scotland in 1885, observed 'Thirty years syne we were all sma' bodies here. . . . The Juteocracy of Dundee, the Ironocracy of Lanarkshire and Ayrshire, the Shipocracy of the Clyde, and the Tweedocracy of the Border—all date alike from the Crimean War, as the fine old English gentleman traces his pedigree from the Conquest.'[1] In the decades of mid-century, heavy industries displaced textiles as the basis of Scotland's greatness. Iron manufacture was in the ascendancy. Marine engineering had established the glory of the Clyde and made many jobs for iron shipwrights. As an adjunct to the iron and shipbuilding industries, coal-mining had been greatly extended. Although the American Civil War had dealt a blow to the declining cotton industry, printing and dyeing still flourished, and by the 1880s thread-making in Paisley had gone far on the road to monopoly in the hands of the Coats family. Other textile trades still remained profitable, and wool, linen, and jute ran a close race for supremacy.

At the time of the Crimean War, 1853–6, three-fourths of Scotland was predominantly agricultural, but farming was undergoing technical changes to meet the demands of the Industrial Revolution. Cultivation of arable land was replaced by cattle and sheep raising. In the Lowlands the production of wheat declined to make way for dairy and fruit farming. Rents continued to rise on rural lands until 1880, when large-scale importation of wheat and cattle from America provoked a general depression in Scottish agriculture.

The Industrial Revolution did not mean a change in the centre of economic activity in Scotland as it had in England. The Midland Belt, or Forth and Clyde Valley, maintained its pre-eminence. With the increasing importance of shipbuilding, however, there was a tendency for industry and commerce to be concentrated more in the West of Scotland around Glasgow. Lanarkshire became the most populous area in Scotland. By 1891 the total population of Scotland had reached over four million, with approximately two-thirds residing in towns.[2]

The total taxed income in Scotland in 1854–5 was approximately twenty-eight million pounds sterling, almost equally divided between income from real estate and from the trades and professions. In 1885 the tax assessment was made on an aggregate income of about fifty-six millions sterling. This evidence suggests that Scotland, as a nation, had almost doubled its income in one generation. Equally important was a shift in Scottish attitude toward overseas investment, particularly in the eastern shires.

> Scotchmen, when they discovered new sources of wealth in their jute factories, their tweed mills, their iron works, and their shipbuilding yards, shed the penurious habits of their youth, and assumed a character more in keeping with their full purses. Not only are they free spenders on themselves and their families, but have become active investors, and in many cases keen speculators. There are investors and speculators of a sort in all communities, but as a rule they are exceptional beings. In Scotland, however, they form so large a per-centage of the well-to-do class as to be rather the rule than the exception. In Edinburgh, Dundee, and Aberdeen it would be perfectly safe to bet on any man you pass in the street with an income of over three hundred a year being familiar with the fluctuations of Grand Trunks, and having quite as much as he can afford staked on . . . Prairies, or some kindred gamble. A dividend of twenty per cent, or more is to a Scotchman of this class a bait which he cannot resist.[3]

A writer for *Blackwood's Edinburgh Magazine* thought that 'Scotland herself is but dimly conscious of the revolution she has undergone . . . it is much less generally known how much she contributes to the great stream of British capital which is continually flowing out to foreign countries. Whether this vast exportation of our surplus wealth be wise or unwise, Scotland is to a large extent responsible for it. In proportion to her size and the number of her population, she furnishes far more of it than either of the sister kingdoms. England gives sparingly, and Ireland hardly any, but Scotland revels in foreign investment.'[4]

The first 'notable craze' of the Scottish overseas investor was in the mortgage and investment companies organized during the economic depression starting in 1873 in the United States. Taking advantage of the exceptionally low prices for securities on the New York Stock Exchange, the Scots made wholesale investments in the railroads of the United States. With the encouragement of Chicago bankers, Scottish capitalists from Edinburgh lent sterling to rebuild that blackened city following the great fire. This endeavour led to other real estate promotions and, with time, into a mortgage business centred in the agricultural sections of Illinois. Dundee capitalists started lending money at the same time on the security of real estate in the Pacific Northwest. Because of the comparatively weak position of the American dollar in this decade, channelling of gold and sterling to the United States was a profitable business on the monetary exchanges. With the resumption of specie payment at the beginning of 1879 the cheap dollar regained its lost standing, in part, and investments everywhere in the United States appreciated.

By 1880 four Edinburgh companies, one interested in marketable securities and three in mortgages, had invested £1,250,000 in the United States. Dundee companies had lent between £800,000 and £900,000 on mortgages. The investment trusts of this town had a paid-up capital of £1,100,000 invested in stocks and bonds through the New York Exchange. Thus, these better-known organizations had transferred at least £4,150,000 to the United States. The seventies brought great prosperity for the Scottish investor. The two pioneer limited companies of Edinburgh, the Scottish-American Investment Company and the Scottish-American Mortgage Company, paid twelve and one-half and fifteen per cent annual dividends to their shareholders, chiefly because they could borrow the difference between their subscribed and paid-up capital at a low rate of interest in Scotland and lend it for almost twice as much in the United States. The Dundee trusts, using only shareholders' funds, earned eight to nine per cent annual net return and declared even smaller dividends, so that the remaining profits could be used to build up reserves.

The exciting financial success of the mortgage and investment companies precipitated an unprecedented flow of capital to the western United States. The Scottish investor became especially interested in the land and cattle companies. Through the financiers of the Scottish-American Mortgage Company the Prairie Cattle Company was launched in 1880. Not to be outdone, the Scottish-American Investment Company invested in the range cattle industry in 1882 by promoting three enterprises: the California Pastoral and Agricultural Company, the Wyoming Cattle Ranche Company, and the Western American Cattle Company. The excitement caused by the enthusiasm for cattle investments by these well-established syndicates caused a rush of lesser men into the business. Scarcely a month passed in Scotland's political and financial centre without the issuance of a new cattle prospectus. Dundee was not far behind and, for her resources, more heavily involved. The Texas Land and Cattle Company was registered in 1881 under the same American sponsorship as the Prairie Cattle Company. Robert Fleming, Founder of the Scottish American trusts, served on the Board of Directors of another Dundee cattle enterprise, the Matador Land and Cattle Company, organized in 1882.

The Scots also made land purchases, chiefly from the land-grant railroads in the West. Large blocks of strategically located real estate were bought and, when the surrounding country built up, were sold to agriculturalists or for town site promotions. The Dundee Land Investment Company led the way into this field of investment in 1878. Timber companies likewise attracted Scottish capital in 1880–2. William J. Menzies, managing director of the Scottish-American Investment Company, sponsored a British Canadian Lumbering and Timber Company in 1880; its initial success led to the founding of the American Timber Company, operating in Ontario and the northern Michigan peninsula. These same Edinburgh capitalists soon had subscribed between two and three million dollars in the California Redwood Company. Dundee residents invested heavily in the timber companies, and because of their concentration at the time on the Pacific Northwest, they also financed the Oregonian Railway Company in 1880 as a potential competitor to Henry Villard's Oregon and California Railroad. Two and a quarter million dollars went into this project.

Speculations in the Mining Kingdom had largely been left to the English prior to 1880; the sporadic activity of the Scots in the 1870s revealed no geographic preference in the West as minimal endeavours were sponsored in California, Colorado, and Utah. In 1881, when a new mining investment boom got under way in England, the Scottish-American Investment Company sponsored the Scottish Pacific Coast Mining Company in Sierra County, California. The next year, the Scottish-American Mortgage Company became involved in a gigantic mining endeavour, the Arizona Copper Company, upon the recommendation of the same bankers who had first interested the company in the range cattle business. One newspaper correspondent remarked:

> . . . in the summer of 1882 hardly a train came into Edinburgh from the West or the South which did not bring a Yankee with a cattle ranche in one pocket, a 'timber limit' in another, and perhaps an embryo Erie Railway up his sleeve. . . .
> The operation, in fact, was often made ridiculously easy for him. The moment he was heard of in Princes Street, a bevy of S.S.C.'s—*Anglice,* Solicitors before the Supreme Courts—would be after him to hunt him down. Every S.S.C. had his own little syndicate at his back—that is, a group of retired drapers, head clerks, and second-rate accountants, who could

> club together money enough for the advertising, printing, and postages needed to float a Company. The Yankee had no doubt given a good profit to the original owner of the property, and he named a figure which left a pleasant margin for himself, even after he had treated the syndicate handsomely in the way of dinners, doucers, and deferred shares.[5]

Profits from the United States returned to Scotland unabated through 1882. The Prairie Cattle Company started off with a dividend of nineteen and one-half per cent in 1881. Shares of £5 par value were quoted on the market at £19. The next year the annual dividend went to twenty-seven per cent. The Scottish-American Mortgage Company had expanded its mortgage operations from Illinois throughout the upper Mississippi Valley, into the northern Great Plains, and distant California. The Dundee Mortgage and Trust Investment Company moved its mortgage interests eastward out of the Pacific Northwest so they overlapped with those of the Edinburgh companies. The resulting competition led to a search for new fields of investment during 1881, and the major Scottish mortgage companies hurriedly turned South and set up agencies in the Mississippi delta and the Southwest, particularly Texas. Prosperity, increased dividends, and expansion of capital were outstanding characteristics of the Scottish-American mortgage companies in these years. In spite of the unsettled railway market, the Scottish-American Investment Company had the largest income in its history during 1881 and 1882.

An adverse trend appeared for the first time in 1883 and pessimistic stockbrokers sought out evidence to prove that Scottish overseas investments had declined in value. In general, securities held by the mortgage and investment companies were equally divided between those that had shown capital gains and those reporting an annual depreciation. Companies of this type investing in the United States had maintained excellent dividend records and the success of American ventures was further reflected in the value of their shares. Eighty per cent of the mortgage and investment companies recorded capital gains that counterbalanced the depreciation elsewhere.[6] All other classes of United States investments had recorded a drop in market values in 1883. The optimistic argued that the decline was transitory; others insisted that some of the loss was known to be permanent and, in the case of some companies, ruinous. According to W. R. Lawson's *The Scottish Investors' Manual* for 1883, the shares of nine timber, land, and cattle companies had depreciated £729,171, with a most alarming collapse taking place in the timber enterprises.[7] Cattle company shares were at a standstill with only three showing a slight capital appreciation. Conditions were not too bad, however, since several cattle companies paid from ten to twenty and one-half per cent dividends and the total annual return was greater than the combined market depreciation of their shares. A dividend was far more tangible to the investor, of course, than a temporary decline in shares. The range cattle industry was still a favoured and profitable field for investment in 1883. Edinburgh capitalists launched the Swan Land and Cattle Company, Limited, this year. The land companies, on the other hand, appeared to be in the doldrums, and the timber promotions were in desperate straits over the land tenure question. A collapse of mining shares also occurred in 1883. Arizona Copper securities alone dropped in value over a half million pounds, a gross depreciation of fully two-thirds of the paid-up capital in the company. Shares of the Scottish Pacific Coast Mining Company had pursued a downward course until their market value had depreciated £27,500. Lawson insisted that within a twelve-month period the securities of all Scottish-American companies had depreciated £1,240,807.[8]

The adverse trend in the stock market made business observers acutely aware of the size of the Scottish overseas investment in 1884. A commentator suggested that three-fourths of the nineteen British foreign and colonial mortgage and investment companies were of Scottish origin.

> If not actually located in Scotland, they have been hatched by Scotchmen and work on Scottish models. Quite as many of them have their headquarters in Edinburgh as in London, and even the English ones find it necessary to come to Scotland for debenture money and the deposits with which high dividends are conjured up . . . without Scotland they could not in fact exist.

Thirty million pounds was the total estimate of 'the golden flood which the old country has poured into America and the colonies' through this form of company.[9]

Better than three-fourths of the money used in the United States was borrowed on debenture. One creditable feature of these companies was the care and perseverance with which reserve funds had been built up. The Scottish-American Investment Company, for example, had a reserve equal to twenty per cent of its borrowed money; the Scottish-American Mortgage Company, sixteen per cent. A major criticism of all the mortgage companies was the percentage of their gross revenue consumed in interest on debentures, management, and working expenses—averaging sixty one per cent. In spite of this, the investment and mortgage companies, as a group, borrowed at four and one-half per cent, lent at from eight to ten per cent, and paid shareholders from twelve to fifteen per cent annually. Scotland's share in the thirty millions sterling taken from the United Kingdom between 1873 and 1883 was estimated by one economic analyst at two-thirds of the total, or £20,000,000. In addition to this sum which had gone abroad for investment in mortgages and stock market securities, through companies registered in England and Scotland, an estimated £20,000,000 more was in mine, cattle, lumber, and land companies registered in Scotland or privately invested in securities, raising the total Scottish capital abroad in 1884 to approximately £40,000,000.

> For a small country like Scotland to be able to spare, even for a time, tens of millions sterling, is one of the most striking paradoxes in the history of commerce. The Scotch, of all people in the world, are supposed to be best able to take care of themselves and their money. Wherever a passable honest penny can be earned they will not be far to seek; and yet it has come to this with them, that they will face almost any risk for the sake of the difference between 4 per cent at home and 4½ per cent across the Atlantic.[10]

When one considers both the shareholders' and the debenture holders' income, the investment and mortgage companies returned an average of six and one-third per cent, land companies four and one-half per cent, and the lumber companies nothing. These profits were deemed inadequate by some Scots, and one contributor to *Blackwood's* complained:

> If Scottish investors abroad were to make hotch-potch of all their promiscuous speculations—mines, cattle, lumber, mortgages, and railway shares—the return on their whole capital might thus, under the most favourable circumstances, reach 6 per cent. . . . The shareholders of the Investment and Mortgage Companies have had their expectations so far fairly realized, but what a succession of *fiascos* and disappointments have most of our foreign mines proved. . . . Last year was no doubt abnormal.[11]

By January 1885 the full impact of the recession of 1884 was apparent. *The Statist* noted that three or four of the largest timber ventures had been terminated or were in the hands of the liquidator. The American Lumber Company collapse represented an estimated loss of £343,000; the British Canadian Lumbering and Timber Company had squandered another £100,000. Shares of the California Redwood Company, nominally worth £5, were being sold at three pence apiece. At least half of the £800,000 invested in northern California was lost, so these three timber companies alone had used up approximately £900,000 of Scottish savings.

Mining was described as 'Scotland's latest and costliest craze'. The Scottish Pacific Coast Mining Company faced liquidation with a loss of £50,000. Further depreciation of the shares in the Arizona copper promotion had reached three-quarters of a million pounds at the end of 1884. Depreciation in land and cattle shares in North American companies was estimated at a million and a quarter sterling. *The Statist* suggested 'It will be a considerably long time before any sensible Scotchman can again be tempted to lay up treasures for posterity on the boundless prairies, whether in Nebraska or Manitoba.'[12]

The mortgage and investment companies also had an anxious year. The aggregate depreciation in their shares quoted on the Edinburgh Stock List was £220,000, and in Dundee £400,000. At this time there was practically no market in Glasgow for this type of share. Scots investing directly in American railways had also been punished. 'What the canny Scot of forty years ago would have said of flinging about the "saxpences" at such a rate, one fears to contemplate', remarked the editor of a financial journal.[13]

The complaints and bitterness over the investment picture in 1884 were perhaps exaggerated. The liquidation of several timber, mining, and land companies meant a permanent loss of approximately £1,000,000 for shareholders. On the other hand, the depreciation in the investment, mortgage, and cattle companies, and some mining and land companies, in the aggregate about £2,000,000, was only a temporary setback for the Scots. The same was true for the estimated £1,000,000 depreciation in railway shares the Scots had purchased directly from British banking houses. But to the pessimistic, who insisted the depreciation would never be regained, £4,000,000 appeared to be gone. In 1884 Scotland's population was less than four million, so these observers could point out that the money value of marketable securities had been reduced by £1 for every man, woman, and child in the nation. Yet this 'depression', as they described it, was only the prelude to additional disaster.

Perhaps the decade's greatest financial crisis was experienced in the range cattle industry. The rush of capital into this business had led to overproduction, and by 1885 lower prices for cattle meant the income of most companies was so unsatisfactory that dividends had to be reduced. Greed in exploiting the public domain had brought forth the wrath of United States government officials who insisted the national land laws be respected. The overstocked range also led to a reduced calf crop, a basic capital asset in the business. The cold winters of 1884–5 and 1885–6 precipitated the collapse of an industry already on the downgrade. With one exception, all the Scottish cattle companies passed their dividends in 1886. The value of most cattle company shares early in 1887 was from one-half to three-fifths of their value twelve months earlier. This depreciation of the share values of the eight largest companies controlled by Scottish funds approximated £980,000. Herd reduction and operational losses pushed the total depreciation well above £1,000,000. Few Scottish cattle companies were forced to liquidate, however. Single purpose endeavours of all types were largely abandoned by the established Scottish syndicates after the disastrous events of the 1880s. This was a far more significant result of the temporary depression of 1884–5 than the amounts of capital thought to be lost.

Meanwhile, mining promoters turned to Glasgow where men with less experience and reputation as financiers provided the funds to bolster three flagging mining enterprises in Colorado in the depression year 1884. Mining promotion in London reached boom proportions again in 1886 and the next three years witnessed an excitement not unlike that of 1870–3. Once again this 'mania' passed Scotland by, because of the disaster or uncertain future of the giant undertakings sponsored in Edinburgh and Dundee. Scots did finance an experiment in California hydraulic mining, somewhat after the height of this type of activity, and concentrated their attention on the introduction of new technical processes for reclaiming precious metals from low grade deposits both in that state and Colorado.

In this 'Great Decade of Investment' the mortgage and investment companies provided a large part of the income to offset the losses and depreciation in other endeavours. Between 1880 and 1885 five new mortgage companies were registered in Edinburgh, hoping to duplicate the success of those started in the 1870s. They had lent £868,000 on land mortgages in the United States by 1890. In addition, older companies had lent western and southern farmers approximately £2,800,000; so these Scots were providing approximately $20,000,000 for the development of American agriculture in the 1880s. The controversy over alien land ownership discouraged organization of new mortgage companies for the remainder of the decade. The most significant development in these years was the amalgamation of the land and mortgage companies of the 'Mackenzie group' in Dundee into the Alliance Trust Company, capitalized at £2,000,000, with £1,100,000 invested in 1888.

At the close of 1885 American railway securities advanced on the stock exchange and the next year prosperity returned. For the first time in fourteen years, Edinburgh's Scottish-American Investment Company had to meet competition in that city. Between 1887 and 1889 four new investment trusts were organized, and by 1890 they had invested slightly more than £2,000,000 in American securities. These new trusts had a more modern capital structure, with each subscribed share divided into preferred and deferred stock. In most cases, these companies no longer limited their borrowing to the difference between paid-up and subscribed capital. Some issued debentures equal to the *entire* amount of their subscribed capital. A conservative estimate of the capital placed in the United States stock markets by this type of Scottish company by 1890 would be £5,700,000. Thus, through the leading mortgage and investment companies registered in Scotland alone, the 'financial stake' of the Scots in the economy of the United States was approximately $50,000,000. Millions more were tied up in land, cattle, and timber companies, and there is no way to estimate adequately the extent of funds privately invested by Scots through channels other than the limited company and the trusts. Nor do we know for certain how much Scottish capital came to the United States through English limited companies. Scotland, a nation of little more than four millions, may well have had as much as $200,000,000 in the United States in 1890.

The failure of Baring Brothers caused a great deal of financial embarrassment for the new investment companies of Edinburgh in their first years. The depressing effects of the Baring crisis were accentuated because United States railway securities had been abnormally high a few months before, owing to the speculative activity following the Sherman Silver Purchase Act. The three Scottish American Trusts of Dundee weathered the storm without any apparent difficulty, and the prosperous Scottish-American Investment Company seized the opportunity to buy extensively on the depressed market at the close of 1890. For the first time since 1885, the wealthiest directors of the investment trusts thought the time opportune to start two new companies capitalized at £1,250,000. Mortgage companies, unaffected by stock fluctuations, were in a comparatively advantageous position between 1890 and 1892.

Then the Panic of 1893 came, with its destruction and chaos. None of the Scottish-American companies was able to escape its devastating effects. The Dundee trusts and the Scottish-American Investment Company maintained their dividends but had to cut deeply into their reserves to do so. Elsewhere the investment companies were forced to reduce their annual dividends, and their declining incomes were not reversed until 1896. Most companies refused to report on the depreciation of their securities. The mortgage companies were now harder hit than those dealing on the stock exchange, for agricultural staples dropped to a price level not known since the 1840s. Even the great Alliance Company was forced to lower its dividend from twelve and one-half to ten per cent; the Scottish-American Mortgage Company followed close behind. The pattern was soon nation-wide.

In the midst of the depression, the tension growing out of the Venezuela crisis became so acute that the Scottish-American Mortgage Company temporarily ceased lending in the United States. The directors of Dundee's Alliance Trust remained optimistic throughout, insisting that the foreign commerce and movement of capital between the United Kingdom and the United States were too mutually beneficial to be jeopardized by a dispute in Hispanic America. The controversy over the monetary policy of the United States was also a source of anxiety to the Scottish investors in these years, and men in Edinburgh, Dundee, and Glasgow watched the Bryan-McKinley campaign of 1896 with rapt attention, and rejoiced in the outcome.

At the close of the nineteenth century the United States was experiencing another great wave of prosperity. The investment companies of Scotland began purchasing industrial and utility, as well as railway, securities. As early as 1893 the Scottish-American Investment Company had increased its capital to £2,500,000. The British Investment Trust had £2,100,000 invested. The smaller Edinburgh investment companies also increased their capitalization and immediately called-up funds from those who purchased the new shares. In Dundee, the Scottish American Trusts organized a new company, the North American Trust Company, to take advantage of the more modern form of limited company organization and thereby increase borrowing power. All told, the Scots must have had approximately ten millions sterling invested in United State securities through these limited companies registered in the homeland. The ten largest Scottish-American mortgage companies had lent approximately six and one-half million pounds, but they did not share in the prosperity of the later 1890s. When the funds that Scots had invested through London mortgage and investment companies are added to the total, they undoubtedly equalled, if not surpassed, the estimated £20,000,000 invested in the United States by this type of company in the mid-eighties. Any reduction in the Scottish stake in the United States economy had been in the estimated £20,000,000 placed in single purpose ventures during the 1880s, such as the timber, cattle, and land companies. While the flow of capital into the United States slackened somewhat in the 1890s, the value of investment holdings was probably no lower than in the 1880s.

Although the mortgage and investment companies continued to represent the bulk of Scottish investment in the United States, the cattle companies still had sizeable assets. The cattlemen, along with the farmers, struggled for survival throughout the 1890s. The depreciation following 1886 was recognized as permanent and the six largest cattle companies of Edinburgh and Dundee, going through capital reorganizations to wipe out unavailable assets, wrote off approximately £1,200,000. Only one Scottish company ceased operations, but many of the London companies agreed upon immediate liquidations. These English failures cost £940,000 during the 1890s. Shareholders had already lost £470,000 immediately following the collapse of 1886. In all, £1,410,000 had been lost in the American Cattle Kingdom by the English enterprises. Although it is difficult to prove, Scots probably had supplied from forty to fifty per cent of these funds, increasing their losses in the cattle industry to £2,000,000. In spite of this financial tragedy, the major companies registered in Scotland had lands and cattle still appraised at £1,500,000, and by 1895 improvements in the cattle trade were discernible.

The Scots continued to make mining investments in California and Colorado between 1890 and 1893. A half-dozen ventures begun in this period risked £250,000. Emphasis was still placed upon the introduction of new types of machinery and new processes for extracting precious metal, and properties were no longer obtained from individuals but from American syndicates like the Tabor Investment Company of Colorado. After 1893 the Scots moved into new areas of the Mining Kingdom—Idaho, Montana, Arizona, South Dakota, and even the lead mines of Missouri. Glaswegians continued to take the lead in promoting mines. The search for mining wealth at last became a systematic process through the work of organizations like the Glasgow and Western Exploration Company, largely financed by the Coats family of Paisley. Interest in California was revived in 1895 with emphasis upon partially-developed gold mining properties that might, with sufficient capital for development, pay dividends. The favourable position of gold on the money market also made such investments more likely to succeed. A Scottish mining enterprise finally experienced success through a chance discovery during 1896 of an unusually rich ore body in the Jumper Mine in Tuolumne County, California. Gross output of this mine was $3,000,000. For the next five years, Scots concentrated their mining search in this county, trying to duplicate the success of the Jumper Gold Syndicate, California. At least £100,000 was spent in the search, with most of the funds coming from the same Glaswegians who had profited so handsomely from the Jumper. Although the capital expended in the county was but a fraction of the total income from the Jumper, the Scots had spent approximately £730,000 throughout the Mining Kingdom during the decade with no return.

The outstanding characteristic of the years 1900 to 1914 was prosperity. The capital of the Scottish-American investment companies alone passed the £15,000,000 mark. In spite of the recessions of 1904 and 1907, dividend records were unimpaired. After modernizing its capital structure whereby each share was divided into preference stock with a fixed return and an ordinary share with earnings dependent on profits, the Scottish-American Investment Company was able to pay a dividend on ordinary shares as high as sixteen per cent in 1911 and eighteen per cent in 1912; the British Investment Trust went from ten to fourteen per cent between 1910 and 1913. The Edinburgh Investment Trust organized a second company more heavily capitalized than the first. For the first time, Glasgow capitalists took their place alongside those in the east of Scotland by investing £1,000,000 in United States securities and mortgages.

The mortgage companies did not share the prosperity of the early years of the twentieth century on equal terms with the investment companies. While the latter were paying from twelve to eighteen per cent on common stock, the mortgage companies distributed only five to ten per cent. The Alliance Trust Company led the way in transferring funds from the land mortgage business to the stock market. Certain trends in the movement of capital were pronounced just before World War I: the Scots were experiencing very serious competition from domestic capital and interest rates were declining rapidly; profits in the United States were not so easily made. Most investment companies were placing an increasingly larger percentage of their funds in Latin America, South Africa, and Australia; those remaining in the United States concentrated more and more upon industrials.

The Scottish-American cattle companies provided leadership in the early twentieth century for an industry preoccupied with blaming many of its economic troubles upon the conspiracies of the Chicago Beef Trust and the railroad carriers. The cattlemen's campaigns for political action led to national regulatory legislation for both. The weather and the market continued to conspire against the cattlemen; and one major company, the Swan, transferred its interest to sheep, but without any improvement in income. The Scots owning the Matador, Swan, Prairie, and Western Ranches held on tenaciously to what they had. Success varied, with the Matador paying a maximum of three and three-fourths per cent and Western Ranches, twenty per cent. Four operations —the Missouri Land and Livestock Company and the California Pastoral and Agricultural Company of Edinburgh, and the Texas and Hansford companies of Dundee—wound-up their business before World War I. Shareholders in each company reaped a worthy reward from the sale of real estate that had gained in value through the years. The Prairie Cattle Company remained in business until 1915. Earnings in the twentieth century repaid the total losses of the depression years, 1886–94, more than two and a half times. From the sale of their lands and cattle, the Scots who held shares in the company to the end probably received a profit one and one-half times the amount of their investment.

The Scottish enthusiasm for western mining ventures appears to have been on the wane in the twentieth century. The search for gold moved into the Cripple Creek area of Colorado, but the Scottish activity there was in no way comparable to that of the English. A single venture was made in the Tonopah region of southwestern Nevada. More important than gold and silver was the renewed search for copper resources in the Southwest when the price of that metal jumped in the world market. Three Arizona syndicates proved unsuccessful, and the most ambitious project of all, the Fresno Copper Company of California, ended in a fiasco with the loss of at least £100,000. The Arizona Copper Company, on the other hand, was rewarded for perseverance. Between 1901 and 1911 this enterprise distributed £2,933,811 in dividends, almost three times the total capitalization of both the copper company and the Scottish mortgage company that had underwritten its losses in troublesome times.

When the World War broke out in 1914, investments of the Scottish-American companies became a major British asset in the dollar mobilization drive. Three of the larger investment companies, for example, brought home $33,000,000. The mortgage companies were unable to co-operate so extensively, for their assets were not easily convertible. Long before the war was over, the Scots realized the United States would emerge a creditor nation and European investors would find it expedient to withdraw. The mortgage companies, feeling the impact of the severe post-war agricultural depression, continued to liquidate this type of finance and assigned the capital set free to securities. Meanwhile, many mortgage companies consolidated in an attempt to protect their shareholders. Capital expansion characterized all security investment companies in the 1920s, but the percentage of their holdings in the United States declined in indirect ratio. New investment funds were being channelled to other geographic areas, but the total amount of Scottish money in the United States did not greatly diminish, due in part to the appreciation of their real estate.

Several of the larger Scottish mining and cattle companies sold out during the 1920s. After paying annual dividends of sixty to eighty per cent on ordinary stock during the war years, the Arizona Copper Company shareholders agreed to sell their property to the Phelps Dodge Corporation in 1921. Since 1895 the Scots had received a tenfold return on their investment. Western

Ranches and Investment Company also drew its business to a close at the war's end. After averaging a nine per cent annual dividend for thirty-seven years, shareholders were given £9 for every £5 share. The Swan Land and Cattle Company experienced brief prosperity during the war years because of the high price of wool. When the market collapsed after the war, the company was transferred to an American Board and the Scots withdrew, realizing it was unlikely they would regain their capital investment.

In the depression years of 1930–6 the Scottish investors, like those everywhere, once again experienced reversals. The annual reports of companies told a story of depreciation, decline in annual income, smaller dividends, and general withdrawal from the United States. The old-established companies survived, but two newly-established Glasgow investment companies were forced to liquidate. The depression was particularly severe on companies, like the Oregon Mortgage Company, which had failed to reduce their mortgage business in the 1920s. Yet in spite of their misfortunes, the Scottish businessmen would not bring themselves to approve the measures for recovery and reform proposed by the New Dealers under Franklin Roosevelt.

When the world went to war again in 1939, practically every asset of the Scottish-American companies in the United States that could be liquidated had to be sacrificed. In 1941 the Alliance Trust Company revealed that $9,000,000 obtained from mortgage collections and dollar securities had gone to the British Treasury. Yet when the conflict was over, the Scots renewed their interest in the United States as an area for investment. The advantages of free enterprise in an expanding economy justified the payment of a premium on American dollars to continue their investment business. The last of the great cattle companies, the Matador Land and Cattle Company, sold its estate and lands in Texas to the English in 1951. The shareholders who had subscribed for stock nominally worth £200,000 had an equity in the company of £1,274,000. At the time of sale each five shilling share was worth £9 6s. 6d. This was more than a thirtyfold return on capital.

Using the records of limited companies as one standard of measurement, scholars interested in the Scottish contribution to the development of the American West encounter no difficulty in determining the ebb and flow of capital back and forth across the Atlantic in the period after 1873; nor is there any problem encountered in arriving at the relative amounts of capital invested in various types of enterprise: securities, mortgages, cattle, mines, and timber. The popularity of certain geographic areas for each of these types of endeavour at a specified period is also apparent.

The determination of financial rewards or sacrifices both to the

Scottish nation and to individual Scots is more uncertain. In attempting to present a balance sheet on Scottish investments in the United States, care must be exercised not to overemphasize the dramatic profits of the companies liquidated after 1920. When calculating the total capital return to Scotland, as a nation, the comparatively weak position of the pound sterling on the international monetary exchange and the general inflation of prices through the years become vital factors. A pound taken home in 1920 or 1950 was not nearly so valuable as one invested in 1880. Short term profit and loss, for a decade or possibly even a generation, can be more closely estimated than long range profits.

The success or failure of the individual investor is a moot question. Almost three generations had elapsed since the initial investment before some of the mining and cattle companies were wound up. Individual Scots witnessing the finish and reaping the profits were undoubtedly often unrelated to those who first invested. Detailed examination of the shareholders' list for each specific company, which has been preserved according to law, including thousands of names, would be necessary to learn what percentage of the investment remained with the descendants of original investors. Moreover, each of the limited companies periodically reorganized their capital structure and the paid-up capital represented by certain classes of stock, or shares, changed greatly. Profits distributed in the form of dividends can only be evaluated with a thorough knowledge of the capital structure of a specific company. In assessing individual profits the Scottish debenture holder becomes as important as the Scottish shareholder. Another factor that makes an assessment of individual profits difficult is the fluctuating market price for securities. Case studies would be necessary to determine whether securities had been purchased by individuals in time of depression and depreciation, or obtained at a premium with a new issue of stock. In short, no final balance sheet can be prepared until the financial history of individual companies has been analysed. Once this is done, studies can be made of the financial success and failure of groups of companies engaged in similar lines of endeavour, such as mining, cattle, and the mortgage business. Once a summation of the financial history for all limited companies in which the Scots invested, whether registered in Edinburgh or London, has been prepared, the scholar must recognize that Scottish capital was channelled into underdeveloped areas by many other organizations such as insurance companies needing to invest their assets.

Although a great deal of investigation remains to be done, this study of Scottish-American companies suggests certain tentative generalizations. In the first place, economic historians have left the impression, in general, that overseas investments of the United Kingdom were exceptionally profitable in the nineteenth century and that the earnings from developing backward areas bolstered the British economy. Then, we have been told, the pattern shifted around 1900, particularly in the United States where home capital began to compete with foreign, and the World War accelerated Britain's withdrawal from the foreign investment field. This is an oversimplified picture of the situation and, at least for the Scots, the pattern is only partially correct where profits are concerned. The Scots experienced some painful losses in the 1880s, because of the depression of 1884, problems of alien land ownership, and several frauds. The 1890s was a decade of crisis and depreciation for Scottish investors, particularly for those dependent upon agricultural prices. Thus, the Scottish experience in the nineteenth century was not universally rewarding, but following these difficulties there was uninterrupted prosperity and financial gain in the twentieth century until the World War of 1914. The greatest bonanzas of all came at the time of the liquidation of the cattle and mining companies between 1912 and 1921. So for Scotland, at least, the capital gains from investments in the United States during the early twentieth century compared favourably with any rewards of the nineteenth. In Edinburgh and Dundee one often hears the assertion that the Arizona Copper Company returned more money home to Scotland, in the form of dividends between 1895–1921, than the nation had invested in the American West since the Civil War in the United States.

There is also sufficient evidence to question the assumption that the average Scot was inherently canny in financial affairs. This adjective is universally used, and no less an authority than Noah Webster's *Dictionary* insists that the word 'canny' has been adopted into literary English as describing a quality of the Scots. During the Industrial Revolution of the early nineteenth century, the English sportsmen who came north constantly referred to the Scots as thrifty, prudent, and wary. The closeness of the Scottish people who visited London became the subject of many jokes. The Scots were pleased and proud that Englishmen thought them canny and frugal and set out to further the idea and live up to their national reputation. In time, the idea was given international credence. The events of the 1880s in the United States require a modification of this concept of Scottish character in general. With imaginations fired by the success of American enterprises between 1873 and 1880, the Scots invested too rapidly and placed their funds into too many divergent types of economic endeavour. Most Scots were in too big a hurry for dividends, and when the first signs of adversity appeared, many too hastily liquidated, taking unnecessary losses in some cases. A nation of four million people who plunged approximately twenty millions sterling into western lands, railroads, mines, ranches, and forests within a three-year period and then saw their investments lose one million pounds and depreciate in value, at least temporarily, another three million pounds within the twelve months of 1884, must certainly have impaired its reputation for canniness. Moreover, one finds it difficult to discover niggardliness, or parsimoniousness, characterizing the Scots in handling their financial investments.

With United States investments, it was the tenacity, equanimity, and forbearance of the more able financiers of Scotland that paid the greatest dividends. The twentieth-century history of the Arizona Copper Company, Western Ranches and Investment Company, and the Matador Land and Cattle Company are excellent cases in point. As with most business enterprises, those who had 'staying power', and the capital reserves to withstand the impact of adversity, reaped the harvest.

As one examines the history of the many mortgage and investment companies, the exceptional success of experienced capitalists working in syndicates, as compared with the efforts of lesser men, is quickly and sometimes painfully apparent. The capitalists who promoted the Scottish-American Investment Company and the Scottish-American Mortgage Company in Edinburgh, and the associates of Robert Fleming and William Mackenzie of Dundee soon established themselves as an aristocracy of the financial world. They proved that the Scottish taste for success and the skill to command could be extended into new fields. Those who ignored or failed to heed their advice were never able to duplicate their record. Moreover, many lesser men failed where they succeeded. The fact that these men who became financial leaders were first in the field does not fully explain the reason for their success, since later companies, like the British Investment Trust and the Scottish Western Investment Company, sponsored by them were also eminently successful. No true picture of Scottish investments in the United States can overlook the importance of organized, continuing leadership of talented individuals.

A detailed examination of the shareholder lists of the Scottish limited companies, prepared through the years, reveals that much of this leadership came from businessmen whose families had made their money as a result of the Industrial Revolution, primarily in the early nineteenth century. They were the company directors who sought out young men of enterprise or vision, like Fleming or Mackenzie, to serve as managers through the years and make a personal fortune in the process. The funds that were invested came from merchants and tradesmen, from manufacturers and bankers, from clerks, cashiers, and accountants, and from professional people—lawyers, doctors, ministers, teachers, and soldiers. Every class and occupation was represented; for this reason the fortunes of these companies, for good or evil, affected the economy and the people of Scotland in an exaggerated way. Virtually no shareholder considered himself a landed proprietor, and only on the rarest occasion did a Scottish investor list his occupation as that of 'gentleman'. When the first Scottish-American companies were launched it was still deemed advisable to secure the services of a man of rank in order to inspire the confidence of the small investors, but this practice did not long survive. In short, there is not a shred of evidence in the Scottish-American investment picture to support the 'landed gentry thesis' which has suggested that the leisured class, living off its income and known as country 'squires', sought advice of businessmen in the investment field and that this relationship culminated in the institution known as the investment trust. This thesis does not apply to Scotland because the money for investment had been made in industry not in land. There is also ample evidence to suggest that this interpretation needs to be re-appraised in its application to England after 1873.

From the first, Scots recognized the basic problems involved in long distance management—the inadequate and time-consuming avenues of communication, the vastness of the American West and its complicated topography. No overseas enterprise, directed by the most able investment financiers, can be more successful than its agents on the scene are loyal and able. In the 1870s company directors in Scotland inaugurated the policy of establishing American Boards for advice on a nation-wide basis. Varying degrees of success were experienced with these agents. Certainly the Scottish-American Investment Company was rightly incensed by Faulkner, Bell and Company's encouragement of investments in the Scottish Pacific Coast Mining Company and the California Pastoral and Agricultural Company. The Underwood syndicate was damned to fire and brimstone in the 1880s for its stranglehold upon the Arizona Copper Company, the Prairie Cattle Company, and the Texas Land and Cattle Company. Directors of the Edinburgh American Land Mortgage Company perhaps justifiably placed the blame for its poor showing in the mortgage business upon Jesup, Paton and Company, supervisor of its local mortgage agencies. Much of the difficulty stemmed from the simple fact that all American bankers and investment brokers expected to share the profits more than the risks of Scottish investment. The Scots naturally placed the emphasis upon the role of their managers in the United States in reverse order. Antagonism did not always prevail and many mutually beneficial arrangements were worked out that stood the test of time. The Scottish-American Mortgage Company appears to have got on well with Guthrie, Balfour and Company, and the relations of the Oregon Mortgage Company with its Portland Board were unusually harmonious.

Local agents and resident managers were often more responsible for success or failure than the national Boards. The mortgage companies preferred to name local agents to handle their funds, usually men with Scottish blood and connections, and periodically to send out from the homeland a trained inspector to check on their activities. Yet the problem of adequate supervision remained difficult in spite of detailed written and oral instructions. The honest agent was usually too optimistic; there was no way to ascertain where and when dishonesty might occur. In the long run, the Scots were more fortunate in the selection of their lending agents in the rural areas than in the choice of advisers in urban centres. Individual Scots of various and sundry types who came to the United States as business managers played a major role in shaping public opinion toward the Scottish capitalist. There were, of course, the good and the bad, but men like John Clay and Murdo MacKenzie far outnumbered those like William Reid. In general, Scottish agents were known as scrupulously honest, forward-looking businessmen.

The Scottish contribution to the total capital investment in the United States was certainly impressive. When this financial stake is thought of in terms of the Scottish economy and the nation's population and resources, it is a major aspect of modern Scottish history. The Scots proved that their horizons were not limited, that they could make plans on a grandiose scale. They grazed cattle over landed estates the size of Ireland; they planned to divert the Feather River of California from its channel to seek gold in the river bed; they expected to monopolize the redwood timber industry of northern California, and to build a railway connecting that state with the Columbia River. But was it economically feasible for the Scots to undertake such projects? They stretched their financial resources to the breaking point. For example, Dundee with an income of a million and one-half pounds each year of the 1880s, and savings of not over a quarter of a million, had invested five millions in the United States. This amount was nine to ten times the value of the town's real estate and equalled the savings of twenty years. Edinburgh's investment was much larger, but the proportion of its total resources invested in the United States was somewhat less.

Perhaps the United States historian should emphasize the contribution of Scottish capital in the development of the West.

Many acres were reclaimed by drainage and irrigation projects so that Scottish immigrants, and others, could be placed upon the land. The Scots contributed a million dollars to the experiments for draining the swampland in the Sacramento-San Joaquin delta of California, and others were to profit handsomely in this productive land as a result of Scottish sacrifice. Not less than twenty-five million dollars went into the range-cattle industry, and the Scots were in the forefront of the ranching interests which learned in a costly and painful way that raising cattle on the open range was not economically or climatically feasible over a long period of years. Millions were lost in the test before cattlemen in the United States learned to buy their lands, fence pasture, and prepare for winter feeding of the herds. In more recent years, the Scots made a significant contribution in the breeding, transportation, and marketing operations essential to the industry.

Scots also provided money to support the explorations of mining engineers seeking to uncover the hidden mineral resources in the western United States. They financed the development of mining properties that were languishing for lack of capital, paid the wages of many miners, and supported the mining districts by purchases from suppliers. The latest managerial, engineering, and technical skills were brought to bear in constructing tramways to bring ore from mine to mill or smelter, to construct railroads connecting the mining community with the processing centre or the market, and to erect stamp mills and smelters with the latest patented improvements. Funds were provided to make a thorough and exhaustive test of the most advanced methods of drift mining by hydraulic processes in California. Equipment was purchased and transported to Colorado, Idaho, and California to experiment with new patented processes for reclaiming gold and silver by chemical means.

Together with their English cousins, the Scots provided a major portion of the funds needed to underwrite the improvement and maintenance of the railway network of the United States, particularly for those lines west of the Mississippi River. Perhaps their greatest contribution was through the uncounted thousands of loans made to farmers in the western and southern states. In this way, Scottish capital played a significant role in the occupation of the farmer's last frontier in the United States, particularly in the Great Plains and in the Pacific Northwest in the last three decades of the nineteenth century.

NOTES AND REFERENCES

BIBLIOGRAPHY

INDEX

Abbreviations

CRO	Companies Registration Office, Edinburgh
BLRP	Bancroft Library Research Program
LSER	London Stock Exchange Records
LC	Library of Congress
WRCIS	Western Range Cattle Industry Study

Notes and References

Introduction

1. Economic historians have suggested many forces and factors responsible for the economic growth of Great Britain during this period. For example, see T. S. Ashton *An Economic History of England in the 18th Century*; William Ashworth *Economic History of England, 1870–1939*; J. D. Chambers *The Workshop of the World: British Economic History from 1820 to 1880*; J. H. Clapham *An Economic History of Modern Britain* (three volumes); W. H. B. Court *A Concise Economic History of Britain*; and W. W. Rostow *British Economy of the Nineteenth Century*.
2. Leland H. Jenks *The Migration of British Capital to 1875*.
3. C. K. Hobson *The Export of Capital*, 238-9.
4. Clapham *An Economic History of Modern Britain: Free Trade and Steel, 1850–1886*, II, 357.
5. Ibid., 238-9.
6. For a full discussion of the pattern of British foreign investment, see A. K. Cairncross *Home and Foreign Investment, 1870–1913: Studies in Capital Accumulation*. Helpful summaries are also found in Jenks, Hobson, and Clapham, Volumes II and III.
7. Hobson, op. cit., 240.
8. Court, op. cit., 326.
9. H. A. Shannon 'The Coming of General Limited Liability', *Economic History*, II (January 1931) 267-8, 279-80.
10. Ibid., 285.
11. Jenks, op. cit., 132.
12. *Statutes at Large*, Vol. 96, 19 and 20 Vict. Cap. 47. The British 'Memorandum of Association' is comparable in many ways to the charter of an American corporation; the 'Articles of Association' is similar to its By-Laws.
13. *Statutes at Large*, Vol. 102, 25 & 26 Vict. Cap. 89. H. A. Shannon 'The Limited Companies of 1866–1883'. *The Economic History Review*, IV (October 1933) 290-316. This detailed legislation designed to protect those investing in joint stock enterprises as well as those doing business with them resulted in the accumulation of extensive public records making possible systematic investigation of exceptional value both to the historians interested in British economic history and overseas investment and to the scholar concerned with the American West in the nineteenth and twentieth centuries.

For a discussion of the procedures for raising capital, issuing stock, and borrowing money once the limited liability company had been registered, see Theodore J. Grayson *Investment Trusts, Their Origin, Development and Operation*, 24-30.

14. Chambers, op. cit., 146.
15. John Reid *Manual of Scottish Stocks and British Funds with a List of Joint Stock Companies in Scotland, 1841*, 170-1.
16. W. H. Marwick *Economic Developments in Victorian Scotland*; Henry Hamilton, 'The Economic Evolution of Scotland in the 18th and 19th Centuries', *Historical Association Leaflet No. 91*.
17. Memorandum of Association and Articles of Association of the Glasgow Port Washington Iron and Coal Company, Ltd. Original copies in Companies Registration Office, Parliament Square, Edinburgh.
18. Marwick has summarized the general pattern of Scottish overseas investment in three publications: *Economic Developments in Victorian Scotland*; 'Scottish Overseas Investment in the Nineteenth Century', *The Scottish Bankers Magazine* (July 1935); 'The Limited Company in Scottish Economic Development', *Economic History*, III (February 1937) 415-29.
19. Francis Edwin Hyde 'British Capital and American Enterprise in the Northwest', *The Economic History Review*, VI (April 1936) 201-8. The author deals primarily with a case where British finance, through a bondholders' committee, freed promoters of the Northern Pacific Railroad from the domination of unprogressive German financial interests. The incident admittedly was an exception to the pattern.
20. Grayson, op. cit., 12-15. For background information, see A. K. Cairncross, editor, *The Scottish Economy: A Statistical Account of Scottish Life*.
21. C. R. Fay *English Economic History Mainly Since 1870*, 202-4.

Chapter I: American West as a Field for Investment

1. Chester W. Wright *Economic History of the United States*, 481-2.
2. Ibid., 865.
3. *The Scotsman* (Edinburgh), 16 October 1905.
4. Minute Books, Board of Directors, Scottish-American Investment Company, I, 14 March 1873.
5. Prospectus, Scottish-American Investment Company, 1873.
6. *The Scotsman*, 21 October 1892.
7. John Clay *My Life on the Range*, 14.

8. Prospectus, Scottish-American Investment Company, 1873.
9. *The Scotsman*, 27 October 1900.
10. Clay, op. cit., 14.
11. *The Scotsman*, 14 June 1901.
12. Clay, op. cit., 14.
13. Memorandum of Association, Scottish-American Investment Company, 1873.
14. Prospectus, Scottish-American Investment Company, 1873.
15. Minute Books, Boards of Directors, I, 9 May 1873. These railroads were the Chicago and Northwestern; the Cincinnati, Hamilton, and Dayton; the International Railroad of Texas; Iowa Falls to Iowa City; Indianapolis and Vincennes; St Louis, Alton, and Terre Haute; St Louis, Jacksonville, and Chicago; Pacific of Missouri; Cleveland and Pittsburg; New Orleans, Jackson, and Great Northern; and the New York Central.
16. Report of the Annual Meeting of the Company, 5 March 1874.
17. Report of the Annual Meeting of the Company, 2 March 1875.
18. Third Annual Meeting Report, 1 March 1876.
19. Fifth Annual Meeting Report, 1 March 1878.
20. Sixth Annual Meeting Report, 4 March 1879.
21. Papers of the Scottish-American Investment Company, Companies Registration Office, Edinburgh, filmed by the Bancroft Library Research Program in Scotland. Hereafter cited, CRO, BLRP.
22. Notes on the early history of the Scottish-American Mortgage Company, by William Williamson, company clerk. Hereafter cited as Williamson Notes.
23. Prospectus, Scottish-American Mortgage Company, 1874.
24. Memorandum of Association, Scottish-American Mortgage Company, 1874.
25. Articles of Association, Scottish-American Mortgage Company.
26. Williamson Notes.
27. Memorandum of Association, Scottish-American Mortgage Company, 1874.
28. Proceedings of the Second Annual Meeting of Shareholders, Scottish-American Mortgage Company, 18 July 1876.
29. Papers of the Scottish-American Mortgage Company, CRO, BLRP.
30. Third Annual Report to the Stockholders, Scottish-American Mortgage Company, 20 July 1877.
31. Papers of the Scottish-American Mortgage Company, CRO, BLRP.
32. Articles of Association, Scottish-American Mortgage Company; Thomas Skinner *The Stock Exchange Year-Book for 1879 containing a careful digest of information relating to*

the origin, history, and present position of the Joint Stock Companies and Public Securities known to the markets of the United Kingdom, 251. Hereafter cited Skinner *The Stock Exchange Year-Book*.

33. Proceedings of an Extraordinary Meeting of the Scottish-American Mortgage Company, 22 September 1879.
34. 'Agency Books' of the Scottish-American Mortgage Company; Williamson Notes.
35. *The Edinburgh Courant*, 24 April 1884.
36. Memorandum of Association, American Mortgage Company of Scotland, Limited, 20 July 1877; Papers of the American Mortgage Company of Scotland, CRO, BLRP; Skinner *The Stock Exchange Year-Book, 1879*, 214; *1883*, 305; *Scottish Banking and Insurance Magazine*, VIII (May 1886), 130-1.
37. Prospectus, Edinburgh American Land Mortgage Company, 1878.
38. Memorandum of Association, Edinburgh American Land Mortgage Company, 1878.
39. Eric Ivory to the author, 8 March 1950.
40. Ibid.; Prospectus, Edinburgh American Land Mortgage Company, 1878.
41. Minute Book of the Board of Directors, Edinburgh American Land Mortgage Company, 27 August, 19 September 1878.
42. First General Meeting of the Proprietors, 7 January 1879.
43. *The Edinburgh Courant*, 27 January 1880; First Annual Report to the Shareholders, Edinburgh American Land Mortgage Company, 26 January 1880.
44. Minute Book of the Board of Directors, Edinburgh American Land Mortgage Company, 7-20 September 1880.
45. *The Times* (London), 2 August 1933.
46. C.H. Marshall 'Dundee as a Centre of Investment', *Handbook and Guide to Dundee and District, 1912*, 347-50.
47. Trust Deed, Scottish American Investment Trust (First Issue), 1873; J.C. Gilbert *A History of Investment Trusts in Dundee, 1873–1938*. This study by Gilbert, Senior Lecturer in Economics at the University of Sheffield, is the standard work on the Dundee companies. The author generously provided me with a copy of his book, impossible to obtain through publishers. I am indebted for his citations to the newspaper sources and company records in Dundee. An abbreviated summary of Gilbert's investigation may be read in 'The Investment Trusts in Dundee', *A Scientific Survey of Dundee and District, 1939*, ed. R.L. Mackie, 87-93. Prospectus, Scottish American Investment Trust, Second Issue, 1873. Prospectus, Scottish American Investment Trust, Third Issue, 1874.
48. Second General Meeting, Scottish American Investment Trust, 21 May 1874.

49. Report of Special Meeting, 11 March 1879.
50. Report of Seventh Annual Meeting, Scottish American Investment Trust, 26 June 1879.
51. Papers of the First Scottish American Investment Trust Company, Limited, CRO, BLRP.
52. Gilbert, op. cit., 33-4.
53. Memorandum of Association, Oregon and Washington Trust Investment Company, 1873.
54. Gilbert, op. cit., 34.
55. Report to the First Half-Yearly Meeting of Stockholders, Oregon and Washington Trust Investment Company, 25 September 1874.
56. Minute Book, I, 20 October 1873.
57. Ibid., 14 January 1874.
58. Hubert Howe Bancroft *History of Oregon, 1848–1888*, II, 181-2, 325n., 418n., 423n., 434n.; Addison C. Gibbs, 'Notes and Incidents of His Life in Connection with the History of Oregon', ms., Bancroft Library.
59. Minute Book, Oregon and Washington Trust Investment Company, I, 12, 24, 28 February 1874.
60. Ibid., 8 April 1874.
61. Ibid., 17, 20 April, 22 August 1874.
62. Report of Proceedings at the Presentation to Mr William Mackenzie, 1920. Newspaper clippings in William Mackenzie's 'Scrap Book'.
63. Newspaper clippings, William Mackenzie's 'Scrap Book'.
64. Report of the Directors, Oregon and Washington Trust Investment Company, 31 March 1875. Report of the Directors to the Half-Yearly Meeting of the Shareholders, 7 March 1876. Minute Book, I, 22 October 1875.
65. Report to General Ordinary Meeting, 5 August 1875.
66. Minute Book, I, 16 June 1875.
67. Prospectus, Oregon and Washington Mortgage Savings Bank, 1876; Report of the Board of Directors, First Ordinary General Meeting, 20 November 1876.
68. Memorandum of Association, Oregon and Washington Mortgage Savings Bank, 1876. This memorandum was signed by several shareholders of the Oregon and Washington Trust Investment Company, but its Board of Directors did not participate at the time of registration.
69. Report to the Stockholders, Oregon and Washington Trust Investment Company, 7 March 1876; Minute Book, II, 25 July 1876.
70. Prospectus and Memorandum of Association, Dundee Mortgage and Trust Investment Company, 1876.
71. Prospectus, 1876; Report by the Directors, Annual Ordinary General Meeting of Shareholders, 19 July 1878.
72. Minute Book, I, 8 June, 3 October 1876.
73. Ibid., 23 November 1876, 21 December 1877.

74. Circular filed in Records of the Alliance Trust Company, Dundee.
75. Gilbert, op. cit., 43-4.
76. Report of Proceedings at the Presentation to Mr William Mackenzie, 1920.
77. Prospectus, Dundee Land Investment Company, 1878.
78. Report by Directors, First Ordinary General Meeting of Shareholders, 3 January 1879.
79. Minute Book, I, 13.
80. Ibid., 46-8.
81. 22 September 1879. William Mackenzie's 'Scrap Book'.
82. Minute Book, Dundee Land Investment Company, I, 90-1.
83. Ibid., 53, 56, 60-1, 70, 72.
84. Ibid., 88.
85. Minute Book, II, Oregon and Washington Trust Investment Company, 22 February, 1 March, 28 June 1878.
86. William Reid 'Progress of Oregon', 6 January 1879, in *Director's Report, etc.*, Oregon and Washington Trust Investment Company, March 1879.
87. Report of the Directors, Annual Ordinary General Meeting, 4 April 1879.
88. 'Proposed Amalgamation of the Oregon and Washington and the Dundee Mortgage Companies', *Dundee Advertiser*, 22 October 1879; 'Amalgamation of the Oregon and Dundee Mortgage Investment Companies', *Dundee Advertiser*, 22 December 1879.
89. 'Appointment of Travelling Superintendent for the Dundee Mortgage Investment Company', Newspaper clipping, William Mackenzie 'Scrap Book.'
90. Proceedings of Annual Meeting, Dundee Mortgage and Trust Investment Company, 6 May 1880.
91. Minute Book, IV, 20 February 1880.
92. 'Foreign and Colonial Investment Companies', *Scottish Banking and Insurance Magazine*, 1 February 1879.
93. A. K. Cairncross 'Did Foreign Investment Pay?', *Review of Economic Studies*, III (October 1935), 67-78.
94. 'Revival of Trade in America', *The Economist*, XXXVII (4 October 1879), 1133.

Chapter II : The Great Decade of Investment

1. Seventh Annual Report, Scottish-American Mortgage Company, 14 July 1881.
2. Report of the Proceedings, Seventh Annual Meeting, 14 July 1881.

3. Ibid.
4. Eighth Annual Report, 26 July 1882.
5. Ninth Annual Report, 25 July 1883.
6. Report of the Proceedings, Annual Meeting, 22 July 1885.
7. Ibid., 23 July 1886.
8. Third Annual Meeting of the Proprietors, Edinburgh American Land Mortgage Company, 3 March 1882; Fourth Annual Meeting of Shareholders for a Report by Directors, 6 March 1883.
9. Minute Book, I, 9 August 1883.
10. Ibid., 4 December 1883.
11. Ibid., 1 April and 1 July 1884; 6 January, 2 February and 22 June 1886.
12. Memorandum of Association, Scottish Mortgage and Land Investment Company of New Mexico, Limited, 24 September 1882.
13. *The Edinburgh Courant*, 23 January 1883.
14. Ibid., 8 April 1885.
15. Skinner *The Stock Exchange Year-Book, 1887*, 437; *1892*, 730; Papers of the Scottish Mortgage and Land Investment Company of New Mexico, CRO, BLRP.
16. Memorandum of Association, Oregon Mortgage Company, Limited, 20 April 1883.
17. Prospectus, 5 April 1883.
18. Minute Book, 13 April 1883.
19. For a discussion, see Chapter IX.
20. Minute Book, 24 April, 7 November and 5 December 1883; 25 June 1884.
21. Ibid., 25 July and 24 September 1884.
22. Second and Third Annual Reports to the Shareholders, 23 July 1885 and 27 July 1886; Papers of the Oregon Mortgage Company, CRO, BLRP.
23. Minute Book, United States Mortgage of Scotland, Limited, 1 February 1884; Memorandum of Association, 19 March 1884.
24. Minute Book, 14 April 1884.
25. Ibid., 12 May, 4, 23 June, 29 September, 1 and 22 December 1884.
26. Report to Second Annual General Meeting of Shareholders, 16 July 1885.
27. Report to Third General Meeting of Shareholders, 22 July 1886.
28. Third Annual Meeting of Shareholders, 20 July 1887.
29. Papers of the American Trust and Agency Company, Limited, CRO, BLRP.
30. *The Edinburgh Courant*, 23 November 1883.
31. *Scottish Banking and Insurance Magazine*, VI (3 November 1884), 250-1.
32. *The Edinburgh Courant*, 28 October 1884.

33. Memorandum and Articles of Association, Florida Mortgage and Investment Company, Limited, 24 November 1884.
34. *The Edinburgh Courant*, 18 October 1884; *Scottish Banking and Insurance Magazine*, VI (3 November 1884), 265.
35. *The Edinburgh Courant*, 7 February 1885.
36. Note for the shareholders of the Florida Mortgage and Investment Company, Limited, and sole-survivors of the Committee of Advice for the Shareholders and Debenture-holders of the Company relative to Appointment of a Liquidator, 5 April 1905.
37. Papers of the Edinburgh Lombard Investment Company, Limited, CRO, BLRP.
38. Papers of the Scottish & Trans-Atlantic Mortgage Company, Limited, CRO, BLRP.
39. W. R. Lawson *The Scottish Investors' Manual, a Review of the Leading Scottish Securities in 1883*, 11. This Volume is a reprint of Lawson's leading editorials in *The Edinburgh Courant.*
40. 'Scottish Investors in the Dumps,' *The Statist*, XV (17 January 1885), 64.
41. Allan G. Bogue *Money at Interest: The Farm Mortgage on the Middle Border*, 265-6, 272. Professor Bogue's generalizations are based upon a detailed record analysis of typical investors in the eastern United States, John and Ira Davenport; of the J. B. Watkins Land Mortgage Company, as Midwestern middlemen; and of land credit in two western townships, one in Nebraska and another in Kansas. His expanding investigation of Midwestern agriculture is reflected in *From Prairie to Corn Belt*: *Farming on the Illinois and Iowa Prairies in the Nineteenth Century.*
42. Bogue *Money at Interest*, 272-3.
43. Eighth Annual Meeting Report, Scottish-American Investment Company, 1 March 1881.
44. Ninth Annual Meeting Report, 2 March 1882.
45. *The Edinburgh Courant*, 24 December 1880. A report of the receiver of the Philadelphia and Reading Railroad to British share and bond-holders was printed here.
46. *Scottish Banking and Insurance Magazine*, II (1 June 1880), 146.
47. *The Statist*, VIII (24 December 1881), 743.
48. *The Economist*, XL (4 February 1882), 130-1.
49. *The Statist*, IX (18 March 1882), 309.
50. Lawson, op. cit., 38. A full account of the stock market manipulations of Jay Gould can be read in Julius Grodinsky *Jay Gould, His Business Career, 1876–1892.*
51. Annual reports of this railroad were printed, with analysis and comment. See *The Edinburgh Courant*, 2 March 1882; *The Statist*, XI (30 June 1883), 716. For background on

the Denver and Rio Grande Railway, see Herbert O. Brayer *William Blackmore: A Case Study in the Economic Development of the West.* Volume II on 'Early Financing of the Denver and Rio Grande Railway' presents the history to 1878.

52. Quoted in *The Edinburgh Courant*, 22 January 1883.
53. Lawson, op. cit., 40-6. The career of Henry Villard as a railroad financier is ably analyzed in James B. Hedges *Henry Villard and the Railways of the Northwest.* Villard tells his own story at the end of Volume two of his *Memoirs of Henry Villard, Journalist and Financier, 1835–1900.*
54. 'A Black Year for Investors', *Blackwood's Edinburgh Magazine*, 137 (February 1885), 272.
55. Lawson, op. cit., 35-7.
56. Ibid., 11.
57. Eleventh Annual Meeting Report, Scottish-American Investment Company, 7 March 1884.
58. Tenth Annual Meeting Report, 8 March 1883.
59. Eleventh Annual Meeting Report, 7 March 1884.
60. Twelfth Annual Meeting Report, 5 March 1885.
61. 'The Present Position of American Railway Securities', *The Economist*, XLII (26 January 1884), 97-8; 'American Railway Stocks', *The Statist*, XIII (1 March 1884), 238.
62. *The Statist*, XIV (30 August 1884), 239; (6 September 1884), 263-4; (11 October 1884), 407.
63. *Scottish Banking and Insurance Magazine*, VI (5 June 1884), 137.
64. *The Statist*, XIV (4 October 1884), 380; (6 December 1884), 630.
65. 'A Black Year for Investors', *Blackwood's Edinburgh Magazine*, 137 (February 1885), 271-2.
66. Ibid., 277-8.
67. Twelfth Annual Meeting Report, 5 March 1885.
68. 'Scottish Investors in the Dumps', *The Statist*, XV (17 January 1885), 64.
69. *The Edinburgh Courant*, 27 December 1884.
70. Thirteenth Annual Meeting Report, 1 March 1886.
71. J. R. McLaren, Secretary, Scottish-American Investment Company, to the author, 14 December 1949.
72. Valuation of Securities, Scottish-American Investment Company, 31 December 1885.
73. 'The Great Rise in American Railway Securities', *The Economist*, XLIII (24 October 1885), 1289-90.
74. 'United States Railroad Prospects', *The Statist*, XVII (26 June 1886), 696-7.
75. Fifteenth through Eighteenth Annual Meeting Reports, Scottish-American Investment Company, 1888–91.

76. 'British Investments in American Railways', *The Economist*, XLVI (7 January 1888), 5.
77. 'The Great London Houses and the American Railroads', *The Statist*, XXII (15 December 1888), 684-5.
78. 'American Railway Shares', *The Statist*, XXI (7 January 1888), 12.
79. Minute Book, Scottish Investment Trust Company, Limited, 27 July 1887.
80. First Annual Report to the Proprietors, 1 November 1888.
81. Memorandum prepared for the author by R. J. Edgar, Secretary, Scottish Investment Trust Company, January 1950.
82. Minute Book, Second Scottish Investment Trust Company, Limited, 10 June 1889–1 October 1890; Memorandum prepared for the author by R. J. Edgar, Secretary, January 1950.
83. Prospectus, British Investment Trust, Limited.
84. Register of Purchases, British Investment Trust, Volume I, 1889–1929.
85. First Annual Report by the Directors, British Investment Trust; Report of Proceedings of the First Annual Meeting, 14 February 1890.
86. Skinner *The Stock Exchange Year-Book, 1890*, 552; First Annual Report, Edinburgh Investment Trust Company, Limited, 16 April 1890.
87. *The Edinburgh Courant*, 2 January 1884.
88. 'Scottish Capital Abroad', *Blackwood's Edinburgh Magazine*, 136 (October 1884), 476.
89. 'The Boom in Trust Companies', *The Economist*, XLVII (6 April 1889), 433-4.
90. At this time the only other company loaning money on the security of mortgages outside the 'Mackenzie group' was the Dundee American Real Property Company, Limited. This was a private enterprise with a small capital.
91. Report of the Directors, Fifth Annual Ordinary General Meeting of Shareholders, Dundee Mortgage and Trust Investment Company, Limited, 30 March 1881.
92. Report of Proceedings at the Presentation to Mr William Mackenzie of his Portrait, 11 March 1920.
93. Balance Sheet, 1880–1, Minute Book, IV, 81-2.
94. Report of the Directors, Seventh Annual Ordinary General Meeting of Shareholders, 27 April 1883.
95. For a discussion, see Chapter IX.
96. Minute Book, IV, 1 August 1882; Minute Book, V, 12 December 1882.
97. Report of the Directors, Eighth Annual Ordinary General Meeting of Shareholders, 29 April 1884. A summary of the report appeared in the *Aberdeen Free Press*, the *Glasgow Herald*, and *The Scotsman* (Edinburgh) on

25 April and in the Dundee *Courier and Argus* on 26 April.

98. Report of the Directors, Ninth, Tenth, and Eleventh Annual Ordinary General Meeting of Shareholders, 25 April 1885; 30 April 1886; and 29 April 1887; Dundee *Courier and Argus*, 21 April 1887.
99. Report of the Annual Meeting, 27 April 1888; *Dundee Advertiser*, 28 April 1888. This newspaper's accounts always included proceedings of the meetings and sometimes the chairman's remarks as well as the directors' official annual report and are therefore often more revealing than the company records.
100. *Dundee Advertiser*, 28 April 1888.
101. Report of the Directors, Twelfth Annual Ordinary General Meeting of Shareholders, 27 April 1888.
102. 'Death of Lord Airlie', *Kansas City Journal*, 27 September 1881. Clipping in Mackenzie Scrapbook; Report by the Directors, Ordinary General Meeting of Shareholders, Dundee Land Investment Company, Limited, 30 December 1881.
103. Minute Book, I, 136, 139, 146, 158, 165, 172-3, 312, periodic entries during 1880 and 1881.
104. W. Turrentine Jackson 'The Chavez Land Grant: A Scottish Investment in New Mexico, 1881–1940', *Pacific Historical Review*, XXI (November 1952), 349-66.
105. Minute Book, II, 20, 23-4, 17 and 23 June 1881. For a discussion of the Scottish American Land Company, see Chapter IX.
106. Minute Book, II, 12, 51, 152, 154, 162, 164, 13 May, 1 September 1881, and 5 May, 2 June 1882.
107. Report by the Directors, Annual Ordinary General Meeting of Shareholders, 30 March 1883; Dundee *Courier and Argus*, 31 March 1883.
108. Minute Book, 10, 41-2, 60, 93.
109. Ibid., 95, 106, 142-4. For a discussion of the American Lumber Company, see Chapter IX.
110. Report by the Directors, 28 March 1884; Report of Proceedings at the Annual General Meeting, 28 March 1884; *Dundee Advertiser*, 29 March 1884; Report by the Directors, 7 April 1885.
111. Report of Proceedings at the Annual General Meeting, 7 April 1885; *Dundee Advertiser*, 8 April 1885.
112. *The Edinburgh Courant*, 27 June 1884.
113. Report by the Directors, 9 April 1886; Minute Book, 231.
114. Report by the Directors, 15 April 1887; *Dundee Advertiser*, 16 April 1887.
115. Jackson 'The Chavez Land Grant: A Scottish Investment in New Mexico, 1881–1940', loc. cit.
116. Report by the Directors, 30 April 1889.

117. Report of Proceedings at General Meetings, Dundee Mortgage and Trust Investment Company and Dundee Investment Company, 30 April 1889.
118. Circular to the Shareholders, Dundee Mortgage and Trust Investment Company, Limited, and of Dundee Investment Company, Limited, 18 July 1889; Provisional Agreement between the Dundee Investment Company, Limited, and the Alliance Trust Company, Limited, 27 September 1889; Notice of Extraordinary General Meeting of the Dundee Investment Company, Limited, 27 September 1889; 'Amalgamation of Public Companies', *Dundee Advertiser*, 9 October 1889.
119. Report of Proceedings at Annual Meeting, The Alliance Trust Company, Limited, 29 April 1890; *Dundee Advertiser*, 30 April 1890.
120. Report of Proceedings at the Presentation to Mr William Mackenzie of his Portrait, 11 March 1920, 13.
121. Report by the Directors, First Annual Ordinary General Meeting, Hawaiian Investment and Agency Company, Limited, 12 September 1882.
122. Report by the Directors, Second Annual Ordinary General Meeting, 14 September 1883.
123. Report of Directors to the Annual Meetings, 1886–9.
124. First Annual Meeting, First Scottish American Investment Trust Company, 27 May 1880.
125. Second and Third Annual General Meetings, 24 May 1881, and 25 May 1882; *Dundee Advertiser*, 27 May 1881, and 26 May 1882.
126. *Dundee Advertiser*, 25 May 1883.
127. Ibid., 23 May 1884, and 29 May 1885.
128. Ibid., 28 May 1886.
129. Annual Reports of the Second and Third Scottish American Investment Trusts, 1880–90; Skinner *The Stock Exchange Year-Book, 1892*, 728.
130. Gilbert, op. cit., 29-32.
131. Remarks of Robert Fleming, Annual Meeting of Scottish American Investment Trusts, 22 June 1923.
132. 'Scottish Investors in the Dumps', *The Statist*, XV (17 January 1885), 64.

Chapter III : The Cattle Company Boom

1. The material in this chapter has been published in a more detailed fashion in my monograph 'British Interests in the Range Cattle Industry' in *When Grass Was King*, co-authored with Maurice Frink and Agnes Wright Spring. This summary of Scottish-American cattle investments

is essential, however, to present a comprehensive and balanced picture of Scottish financial activity in the American West.

2. The history of the cattleman's frontier has been thoroughly told in three books: Ernest S. Osgood *The Day of the Cattleman*, Edward E. Dale *The Range Cattle Industry*, and Louis Pelzer *The Cattlemen's Frontier*. Moreover, no phase of Scottish investment in the western United States is so well known as that of the land and cattle companies. Brief accounts are even included in most textbooks on western America: e.g., Dan E. Clark *The West in American History*, 596-7; LeRoy R. Hafen and Carl C. Rister *Western America*, 578-80; Ray A. Billington *Westward Expansion*, 683-4.
3. Herbert O. Brayer 'The Influence of British Capital on the Western Range Cattle Industry', *Westerners' Brand Book*, Denver, May 1948, 3-4.
4. George B. Loring 'Report of the Commissioner of Agriculture, 1883–1884', *House Ex. Doc. 33*, 48 Cong., 1 sess. (1883–4), 452-3.
5. Final Report of Her Majesty's Commissioners Appointed to Inquire into the Subject of the Agricultural Depression, 1897. Copy in the Western Range Cattle Industry Study Headquarters, Denver.
6. William Trimble 'Historical Aspects of Surplus Food Production of the United States, 1862–1902', *Annual Report of the American Historical Association for 1918*, I, 231-2; *Agricultural Gazette* (London), 29 January 1877, quoted in Davilla Bright 'Foreigners and Foreign Capital in the Cattle Industry of the United States', M.A. Thesis, University of Oklahoma, 1935, 36n.
7. James Macdonald *Food from the Far West*.
8. Clare Read and Albert Pell 'Further Reports of Assistant Commissioners, Ministry of Agriculture and Fisheries', *Royal Commission on Agriculture, 1879–1882*, 7-16. For an unofficial but equally enthusiastic source, W. Baillie Grohman 'Cattle Ranches in the Far West', *The Fortnightly Review*, XXVIII (New series, July to December 1880), 438-57.
9. Earl of Airlie 'The United States as a Field for Agricultural Settlers', *The Nineteenth Century* (February 1881), 292-301.
10. Skinner *The Stock Exchange Year-Book, 1882*, 287.
11. Reports and Financial Papers of the Colorado Mortgage and Investment Company of London, Limited, and the Colorado Ranche Company, Limited, London Stock Exchange Records filmed by the Library of Congress: The Western Range Cattle Industry Study—Co-operative Project for Micro-filming Western Americana in Europe. Hereafter cited, LSER, LC:WRCIS.

12. Memorandum of Association, Prairie Cattle Company, Limited, 1880. Papers of the Prairie Cattle Company, Limited, CRO, LC:WRCIS; Clay, op. cit., 129-30.
13. Skinner *The Stock Exchange Year-Book, 1885*, 546.
14. M. Riordan 'Murdo MacKenzie, Ranch King', *The Westerner*, November 1943.
15. *The Edinburgh Courant*, 1 January 1883.
16. The meetings of this pioneer cattle company were reported in the columns of the *Courant*. For example, see issues of 8 and 24 December 1881 and 23 December 1882. The first annual report to stockholders of the Prairie Cattle Company is printed in full on 8 December 1881.
17. Clay, op. cit., 131.
18. Memorandum of Association and other Papers of the Texas Land and Cattle Company, Limited. CRO, LC:WRCIS.
19. Edward E. Dale *Cow Country*, 202-11, has an excellent discussion on the leasing of the Cherokee Strip, Cheyenne and Arapaho reservations in the Indian Territory by the cattlemen. For Scottish comment, see 'The Cattle Ranch Country—The Indian Territory', *The Edinburgh Courant*, 28 February 1884.
20. Special Resolutions of the Texas Land and Cattle Company, Limited, passed 19 September 1882; *The Edinburgh Courant*, 16 August, 20 September 1882.
21. William M. Pearce *The Matador Land and Cattle Company* is the definitive study on this enterprise. His primary source of information was the 'Matador Collection', Library of Texas Technological College, Lubbock, that contains records of the company retained in Texas. The author has made an independent examination of company records still in Dundee, including such items as the Memorandum of Agreement between the Vendors and Purchasers, the Memorandum of Association, Articles of Association, Prospectus, and Reports of the Annual Meetings of the company.
22. Prospectus, Reports and Financial Papers of the Hansford Land and Cattle Company, CRO and LSER, LC:WRCIS.
23. Memorandum of Association, 7 June 1882, and Papers of the California Pastoral and Agricultural Company, Limited, CRO, BLRP; Clay, op. cit., 16-17.
24. *The Edinburgh Courant*, 4 January 1883.
25. Memorandum of Association, 26 August 1882, and Papers of the Wyoming Cattle Ranche Company, Limited, CRO, LC: WRCIS; Skinner *The Stock Exchange Year-Book, 1887*, 595; Clay, op. cit., 33-8, 64, 160-1.
26. Prospectus, Memorandum of Association, 12 September 1882, and Articles of Association, Western American Cattle Company, LSER, LC:WRCIS; Clay, op. cit., 41-2.

27. Minute of Agreement between Dorr Clark, of Deadwood . . . and Sir George Warrender of Lochend, Baronet . . . 11 December 1882, Papers of Western Ranches, CRO, LC:WRCIS; Prospectus, Western Ranches, LSER, WRCIS; *The Edinburgh Courant*, 20 and 30 January 1883.
28. Memorandum of Association and Articles of Association, Missouri Land and Livestock Company, Limited, March 1882; *The Edinburgh Courant*, 7 and 22 February 1883.
29. *Scottish Banking and Insurance Magazine*, v (3 November 1883), 241.
30. *The Edinburgh Courant*, 17 October 1883 quoting the *Texas Live Stock Journal*.
31. Ibid., 14 and 24 November 1882.
32. Prospectus, Reports and Financial Papers of the Cattle Ranche and Land Company, Limited, LSER, LC:WRCIS; Clay, op. cit., 20-5, 168; *The Edinburgh Courant*, 2 February 1883 and 28 January 1884.
33. Prospectus, Western Land and Cattle Company, LSER, LC:WRCIS.
34. Prospectus, Reports and Financial Papers of the Arkansas Valley Land and Cattle Company, Limited, LSER, LC:WRCIS.
35. Prospectus, Powder River Cattle Company, Limited, LSER, WRCIS. Herbert O. Brayer has used the extensive Frewen manuscripts collected by the Western Range Cattle Industry Study to write several articles on the career of Moreton Frewen. 'Moreton Frewen, Cattleman', *The Westerners' Brand Book* (Denver, July 1949), 1-21. This article is reprinted under the title 'Moreton Frewen, British Cattleman', *Western Live Stock* (October 1949), 12ff. A revision may be found as 'The 76 Ranch on the Powder River', *Westerners' Brand Book* (Chicago, December 1950), 1 ff.
36. Debenture Prospectus, Maxwell Cattle Company, Limited, WRCIS.
37. Skinner *The Stock Exchange Year-Book, 1884*, 508.
38. Western Ranches, Limited has not been included in these calculations because it was not registered until 1883. However, it was an outgrowth of an earlier promotion begun in 1882 and has been discussed for the sake of continuity.
39. Quoted in *The Edinburgh Courant*, 5 February 1883.
40. 'Cattle Ranches and Land Companies in the States', *Scottish Banking and Insurance Magazine*, v (14 February 1883).
41. 'Cattle Ranching and Cattle Companies', ibid., v (7 April 1883), 71, 80.
42. 'Land and Cattle Companies', *The Economist*, XLI (17 February 1883), 190-1.

43. *The Edinburgh Courant*, 9 February, 14 June and 11 September 1883.
44. Ibid., 21 June 1883.
45. *Scottish Banking and Insurance Magazine*, V (1 May 1883), 96-7. With the exception of a portion of the 1882 annual report and those of 1886 and 1888, official reports of the Prairie Cattle Company have not been located. Fortunately, the Scottish press published these reports in full, usually with editorial comment.
46. For a discussion of this situation, see *The Edinburgh Courant*, 25 June and 20 and 24 August 1883, and *Scottish Banking and Insurance Magazine*, V (2 July 1883), 142-3, (4 September 1883), 192, (4 October 1883), 213, 216.
47. *Money Market Review*, 15 September 1883; *The Edinburgh Courant*, 7 October 1883; *Scottish Banking and Insurance Magazine*, V (3 November 1883), 238.
48. *The Edinburgh Courant*, 10 November 1883.
49. *Scottish Banking and Insurance Magazine*, VI (7 February 1884), 34-5.
50. *The Edinburgh Courant*, 16 January and 24 February 1884.
51. Report of the Board of Directors, Second Annual General Meeting, Missouri Land and Live Stock Company, 15 October 1884, WRCIS.
52. Clay, op. cit., 64-5. For comment, see *The Statist*, XV (7 February 1885), 150.
53. Clay, op. cit., 52.
54. *The Edinburgh Courant*, 17 March 1884.
55. Ibid., 19 February 1884.
56. Ibid. The reports of the Texas Land and Cattle Company were printed in full with analysis and comment. See also Reports and Financial Papers of the Texas Land and Cattle Company, LSER, WRCIS.
57. Clay, op. cit., 88-93.
58. Prospectus, Deer Trail Land and Cattle Company, Limited, LSER, WRCIS.
59. Prospectus, Minutes of the First General Meeting, Swan Land and Cattle Company, 30 July 1883; Report to the Directors by the Chairman, Colin J. Mackenzie, 3 August 1883; Report of the First Annual Meeting, 2 April 1884, WRCIS. See also *The Edinburgh Courant*, 17 March 1884.
60. Prospectus, Dakota Stock and Grazing Company, Limited, LSER, WRCIS.
61. Prospectus, Nevada Land and Cattle Company, Limited, LSER, WRCIS.
62. Memorandum and Articles of Association, Kansas and New Mexico Cattle Company, Limited, WRCIS.
63. Memorandum of Association, Sand Creek Land and Cattle Company, Limited, WRCIS.

64. Memorandum of Association, Rocking Chair Ranche, Limited, WRCIS; Clay, op. cit., 172. For additional information, see Estelle D. Tinkler 'History of the Rocking Chair Ranch', *Panhandle-Plains Historical Review*, XV (1942), 1-88.
65. *The Edinburgh Courant*, 16 April 1883; Skinner *The Stock Exchange Year-Book, 1887*, 573; Papers of the New United States Cattle Ranche Company, Limited, LSER, WRCIS.
66. Compiled Table on 'Wyoming Incorporated Companies, 1870–1900', prepared by Virgil Peterson for WRCIS. Similar tables are available on Montana, Colorado, and New Mexico.
67. *Scottish Banking and Insurance Magazine*, VI (5 July 1884), 260.
68. *The Economist*, XLII (16 February 1884), 197.
69. Loring 'Report of the Commissioner of Agriculture, 1883–84,' loc. cit.; Final Report of Her Majesty's Commissioners Appointed to Inquire into the Subject of the Agricultural Depression, 1897, WRCIS.
70. Negotiations were reported in *The Edinburgh Courant*, 6 and 27 February, 18 March 1884.
71. *Scottish Banking and Insurance Magazine*, VI (5 April 1884), 85-6.
72. Ibid., VI (5 July 1884), 158-9.
73. Affairs reached a chaotic state at this time and dozens of shareholders published opinions on the Underwood business. See *The Edinburgh Courant*, 10, 21 April, 15, 21, 23, 26 May, 2, 3, 14, 19, 21 June 1884.
74. *Dundee Advertiser*, 13 June 1884.
75. For complete information see *The Edinburgh Courant*, 9 September, 1, 5, 20 November, 24 December 1884, and 7, 10, 30, January 1885.
76. Reports and Financial Papers of the Texas Land and Cattle Company, LSER, WRCIS.
77. Clay, op. cit., 163-6.
78. Report by the Directors to the Third Annual General Meeting, Missouri Land and Live Stock Company, 28 October 1884, WRCIS.
79. Complete information on the year's developments can be read in two private reports to the directors: 'Report to the Directors, Swan Land and Cattle Company, Limited, by the Chairman, Mr Colin J. Mackenzie, November 4, 1884'; and 'Report to the Directors by the Secretary, Finlay Dun, November 5, 1884', WRCIS.
80. 'The Dundee Cattle Companies', *The Statist*, XV (7 March 1885), 260-1.
81. 'Scottish-American Cattle Companies', *The Statist*, XV (14 February 1885), 179; Clay, op. cit., 169.

82. For a thoroughgoing statement of this problem, see Osgood, op. cit., 108-12.
83. *The Edinburgh Courant*, 15 May 1884.
84. Correspondence with the Canadian Government over Operation of Clause 3 of the Contagious Diseases (Animals) Act, 1884. Records of the Privy Council, Great Britain, WRCIS. For contemporary comment, see *The Edinburgh Courant*, 26 November 1884. Reopening of the British market became a crusade with Frewen. See Brayer 'Moreton Frewen, Cattleman', loc. cit., 13-16. The problem was first summarized by Frewen in 'The Transatlantic Cattle Trade', *The Fortnightly Review*, XLIX (New Series, January to June 1891), 713-24.
85. This subject has been presented from many viewpoints: e.g. Dale *The Range Cattle Industry*, 105; Osgood, op. cit., 139-40, 180-1; Ora B. Peake *The Colorado Range Cattle Industry*, 31-2.
86. Clay, op. cit., 182-5; *The Edinburgh Courant*, 11 December 1884.
87. J. S. Tait *The Cattle Fields of the Far West*.
88. Prospectus, American Pastoral Company, Limited, LSER, WRCIS; Skinner, *The Stock Exchange Year-Book, 1887*, 390.
89. Prospectus, Espuela Land and Cattle Company, Limited, LSER, WRCIS; *The Edinburgh Courant*, 15 December 1884.
90. Ibid., 6 and 15 December 1884.
91. Prospectus, Carrizozo Cattle Ranch Company, Limited, WRCIS.
92. Prospectus, Consolidated Land and Cattle Company, Limited, LSER, WRCIS; *Scottish Banking and Insurance Magazine*, VII (5 April 1884), 87.
93. Reports and Financial Papers, Cattle Ranche and Freehold Land Company of Texas, Limited, LSER, WRCIS.
94. Papers of the Cresswell Ranche and Cattle Company, CRO, WRCIS; Clay, op. cit., 104-5.
95. Prospectus, Chama Cattle Company, Limited, LSER, WRCIS.
96. Prospectus, Wyoming Hereford Cattle and Land Association, Limited, LSER, WRCIS.
97. Papers of the Montana Sheep and Cattle Company, Limited, CRO, WRCIS.
98. Papers of the Chalk Buttes Ranche and Cattle Company, Limited, CRO, WRCIS; *Scottish Banking and Insurance Magazine*, VII (May 1885), 120.
99. Papers of the Deervale Ranche Company, Limited, CRO, WRCIS.
100. Memorandum and Articles of Association, Rio Arriba Land and Cattle Company, Limited, WRCIS; Memorandum and Articles of Association, Denver Ranching Company, Limited, WRCIS.

101. J. Fred Rippy 'British Investments in Texas Land and Livestock', *The Southwestern Historical Quarterly*, LVIII (January 1955), 331-41.

Chapter IV : Alien Land Tenure and Legislation

1. Roger V. Clements 'British Investment and American Legislative Restrictions in the Trans-Mississippi West, 1880–1900', *Mississippi Valley Historical Review*, XLII (September 1955), 207-28; see also Clements 'British-Controlled Enterprise in the West between 1870 and 1900, and Some Agrarian Reactions', *Agricultural History*, XXVII (October 1953), 132-41.
2. 'Report from the Commissioner of the General Land Office concerning Entries of Public Lands by the Estes Park Company and Other Foreign Corporations', *Senate Executive Doc. 181*, 48 Cong., 1 sess. (1883–4).
3. *Cong. Record*, 48 Cong., 1 sess. (1883–4), 3689-90.
4. *The Edinburgh Courant*, 10 July 1884.
5. 'The Cattle Ranch Country—The Indian Territory', *The Edinburgh Courant*, 28 February 1884. Dale *Cow Country*, 202-11, has an excellent discussion.
6. 'The Land Question in America', *The Edinburgh Courant*, 23 June 1884.
7. Clements 'British Investment and American Legislative Restrictions in the Trans-Mississippi West, 1880–1900', loc. cit., 210-11.
8. Dunham, op. cit., 296-7.
9. *The Edinburgh Courant*, 23 June 1884.
10. Ibid., 31 August 1885. Dale discusses the significances of the removal of ranchmen from the Indian Territory in two somewhat different interpretations: *The Range Cattle Industry*, 106-7; *Cow Country*, 184-5.
11. Quoted in 'The Appropriation of Public Lands in the United States', *The Economist*, XLIII (25 April 1885), 505.
12. An able summary of the effects of Cleveland's proclamation is found in Pelzer *The Cattlemen's Frontier*, 184-90. An important study dealing with a related problem in the Cleveland administration is told by John B. Rae 'Commissioner Sparks and the Railroad Land Grants', *Mississippi Valley Historical Review*, XXV (September 1938), 211-30.
13. Quoted in *The Economist*, XLIII (22 August 1885), 1028. See also 'Awkward for Cattle Companies', *The Edinburgh Courant*, 25 August 1885. No newspaper in the West carried on a more active crusade against the fences of syndicates than *The Daily Boomerang* of Laramie, Wyoming. Its battlecry was 'The Fences Must Go'.

14. *The Galveston News*, 5 August 1885.
15. *The Economist*, XLVIII (29 August 1885), 1052-3.
16. Reports and Financial Papers of the Prairie Cattle Company LSER, LC:WRCIS. For an analysis of the report of 1885, see *The Edinburgh Courant*, 5 February 1886.
17. Third Annual Report, Swan Land and Cattle Company, 12 March 1886.
18. *House Report 2308*, 48 Cong., 2 sess. (1884–5).
19. *New York Times*, 22 and 24 January 1885.
20. *The Economist*, XLIII (29 August 1885), 1052-3.
21. *Cong. Record*, 49 Cong., 1 sess. (1885–6), 3883.
22. *House Report 3455*, 49 Cong., 1 sess. (1885–6).
23. *Cong. Record*, 49 Cong., 1 sess. (1885–6), 7830-2.
24. Ibid., 5108.
25. Ibid., 7954-6.
26. *Cong. Record*, 49 Cong., 2 sess. (1886–7), 2319, 2435.
27. *U.S. Statutes at Large*, XXIV, 476-7.
28. Thirteenth Annual Report, Scottish-American Mortgage Company, 22 July 1887.
29. Report of the Proceedings at Annual Meeting, 22 July 1887.
30. Minute Book, Edinburgh American Land Mortgage Company, 2 May 1887.
31. Minute Book, Oregon Mortgage Company, 28 April and 23 June 1887.
32. Dunham, op. cit., 299.
33. *New York Times*, 11 April 1887.
34. Quoted in *The Humboldt Standard*, 25 June 1885.
35. 'Sparks and the Sharks', *The Humboldt Standard*, 30 January 1886.
36. *Laws, Joint Resolutions and Memorials of the Legislative Assembly of Nebraska, 1887*, 563, 567-8.
37. *Laws of the State of Illinois, 1887*, 5-8.
38. *General Laws of the State of Minnesota, 1887*, 323-4.
39. Thirteenth Annual Report, Scottish-American Mortgage Company, 22 July 1887; Report of Proceedings at the Annual Meeting, 22 July 1887.
40. *General Laws of Texas, 1891*, 82-3.
41. Report of the Directors to the Eighteenth Annual Meeting, Scottish-American Mortgage Company, 25 July 1892.
42. *Laws, Joint Resolutions and Memorials of the Legislature of the State of Nebraska, 1889*, 483-6.
43. *General Laws of the State of Minnesota, 1889*, 219-21.
44. *General Laws of Texas, 1892*, 608.
45. Minute Book, Oregon Mortgage Company, 10 February 1887.
46. Minute Book, Edinburgh American Land Mortgage Company, 6 March 1888.
47. Report of Proceedings at the Annual Meeting, Scottish-American Mortgage Company, 17 July 1890.

48. Clements 'British Investment and American Legislative Restrictions in the Trans-Mississippi West, 1880-1900', loc. cit., 224-8.

Chapter V : The Cattle Companies : Crisis

1. *The Edinburgh Courant*, 13 June 1885.
2. *The Statist*, XVI (10 October 1885), 403-5.
3. This comment referred to the 'Comparative Statements' for 1883 and 1884 appearing in Chapter III. These separates were often printed in Scottish publications with editorial comment. See *Scottish Banking and Insurance Magazine*, VI (5 July 1884).
4. *The Statist*, XVI (10 October 1885), 403-5.
5. Comparative Statement of Cattle Companies' Balance Sheets for the Year 1885, Compiled by Andrew Ogilvie & Company, Stockbrokers, Dundee, WRCIS.
6. *The Statist*, XVII (13 February 1886), 176-8.
7. Third Annual Report, Matador Land and Cattle Company, 2 February 1886; *The Edinburgh Courant*, 3 February 1886.
8. Reports and Financial Papers of the Western Ranches, LSER, WRCIS.
9. Reports and Financial Papers of the Texas Land and Cattle Company, LSER, WRCIS.
10. Comparative Statement of Cattle Companies' Balance Sheets for the Year, 1885, WRCIS.
11. *The Economist*, XLIV (20 March 1886), 364-5. The statistics in *The Economist* had been compiled by Andrew Ogilvie & Company, Stockbrokers, Dundee. The London journal selected only a portion of the information. Other sections were republished in *The Mark Lane Express*, 27 May 1886. The following additional information was available:

	herd : value per head	*land : cost per acre freehold*	*rent per acre*
	$	$	c
Prairie	16·66	3·22	6
Swan	25·97	1·81	
Texas	14·87	1·64	3¼
Matador	17·88	1·64	8⅜
Hansford	24·74	2·32	2½
Arkansas	27·34	19·40	7
Pastoral	25·00	2·53	7
Powder River	28·37		
Western Land	26·46	2·80	
Cattle Ranche	24·99		2½
Western Ranches	27·39		

12. Reports and Financial Papers of the California Pastoral Company, LSER, Bancroft Library, University of California.
13. Report of the Directors of the Third Annual General Meeting of the Missouri Land and Live Stock Company, 28 October 1885, WRCIS; Skinner *The Stock Exchange Year-Book, 1887*, 423-4, 595.
14. Reports and Financial Papers of the Prairie Cattle Company, LSER, WRCIS. For an analysis of the report, see *The Edinburgh Courant*, 5 February 1886.
15. 'Joint Report to the Directors, Swan Land and Cattle Company, by George Prentice and Finlay Dun, October 16 1885': Report of the Third Annual Meeting, Swan Land and Cattle Company, 12 March 1886, WRCIS. The figures do not coincide with those published by Andrew Ogilvie and Company, but the trend is the same.
16. Herbert O. Brayer 'Range Country Troubles, 1885', *The Westerners' Brand Book* (Denver), VIII (March 1952). The federal government had sent out experienced interviewers into the range country in 1884–5 to get a statement of opinion from cattlemen concerning the principal problems facing the cattle industry. Brayer has analysed these reports.
17. W. Turrentine Jackson 'Railroad Relations of the Wyoming Stock Growers Association, 1873–90', *Annals of Wyoming*, XIX (January 1947), 3-23.
18. 'Cattle Company Accounts', *The Statist*, XIX (12 March 1887), 283.
19. Reports and Financial Papers of the Prairie Land and Cattle Company, LSER, WRCIS.
20. Skinner *The Stock Exchange Year-Book, 1888*, 585, 650.
21. Ibid., 593, 630; *1887*, 547.
22. Fourth Annual Report, Matador Land and Cattle Company, 1 February 1887.
23. Report of the Fourth Annual Meeting, Swan Land and Cattle Company, 17 March 1887, WRCIS.
24. *The Scotsman* (Edinburgh), 19 May 1887.
25. Report of the Directors and Minutes of the Fifth Annual General Meeting, Swan Land and Cattle Company, 29 March 1888.
26. Clay, op. cit., 177-9.
27. W. Turrentine Jackson 'The Wyoming Stockgrowers' Association, Its Years of Temporary Decline, 1886–1890', *Agricultural History*, XXII (October 1948), 260-71.
28. Clay, op. cit., 177-9.
29. T. A. Larson 'The Winter of 1886–1887 in Wyoming', *Annals of Wyoming*, XIV (January 1942), 5-17. Osgood, op. cit., 220-2; Pelzer, op. cit., 113-14.
30. Original statement compiled by Macrorie & Thomson, Stockbrokers, 41 George Street, Edinburgh, WRCIS.
31. *The Economist*, XLVI (12 May 1888), 594-5.

32. Ibid.
33. *The Statist*, XXII (22 September 1888), 338-9.
34. Papers of the Prairie Cattle Company, CRO, WRCIS; Reports and Financial Papers of the Prairie Cattle Company, LSER, WRCIS.
35. Papers of the Missouri Land and Live Stock Company, CRO, WRCIS; Reports and Financial Papers of the Missouri Land and Live Stock Company, LSER, WRCIS. An extensive file of the original papers of this company is also available in WRCIS. For more information see 'Diary of George D. Ballingall on his American Trip for the Missouri Land and Live Stock Company', and his 'Memorandum on the "Silver Question" in the United States as affecting the Missouri Land and Live Stock Co., Ltd., October, 1891,' WRCIS.
36. Skinner *The Stock Exchange Year-Book, 1892*, 933; *1895*, 1065; Papers of the California Pastoral and Agricultural Company, CRO, BLRP.
37. Reports of the General Annual Meeting, Swan Land and Cattle Company, Sixth through Thirteenth, 1889–96; Petition of the Swan Land and Cattle Company to the Lords of Council and Session, 17 May 1892; Clay, op. cit., 214.
38. Papers of the Western Ranches, CRO, WRCIS; Reports and Financial Papers of the Western Ranches, LSER, WRCIS.
39. Papers of the Texas Land and Cattle Company, CRO, WRCIS; Reports and Financial Papers of the Texas Land and Cattle Company, LSER, WRCIS.
40. Pearce, op. cit., 38-77. The role of Murdo Mackenzie as manager of the Matador Company in the 1890s is thoroughly handled in this study.
41. Jackson, op. cit., 291-7.
42. Reports and Financial Papers of the American Pastoral Company, Espuela Land and Cattle Company, and the Cedar Valley Land and Cattle Company, LSER, WRCIS.
43. J.R.F.S. 'The American Ranchman', *Longman's Magazine*, XXX (May 1897 to October 1897), 444-60.
44. Records of the Missouri Land and Live Stock Company, and the Missouri Land Company, WRCIS.
45. Skinner *The Stock Exchange Year-Book, 1901*, 1432; *1904*, 1565; *1912*, 1640; *1913*, 1707; Papers of the California Pastoral and Agricultural Company, CRO, BLRP.
46. Papers of the Texas Land and Cattle Company, CRO, WRCIS; Reports and Financial Papers of the Texas Land and Cattle Company, LSER, WRCIS.
47. Papers of the Hansford Land and Cattle Company, CRO, WRCIS.
48. Skinner *The Stock Exchange Year-Book*, 1915, 2096; 1916, 2108; Reports and Financial Papers of the Prairie Cattle

Company, LSER, WRCIS; Reports of the Prairie Cattle Company, CRO, WRCIS.

49. Skinner *The Stock Exchange Year-Book, 1911*, 2543; *1920*, 960; Papers of the Western Ranches and Investment Company, CRO, WRCIS; Reports and Financial Papers of the Western Ranches and Investment Company, LSER, WRCIS.
50. Richard Gibson, of Pringle and Clay, Edinburgh, in a letter to the author, 28 October 1949.
51. The twentieth century activities of the Swan Land and Cattle Company are revealed in the Reports of Annual Meetings, Fourteenth through Thirty-Seventh, 1897-1920; Papers of the Swan Land and Cattle Company, CRO, WRCIS; Records of the Swan Land and Cattle Company, Edinburgh Stock Exchange File. WRCIS.
52. Pearce, op. cit., 78-210. My sources of information on the twentieth century history of the Matador Land and Cattle Company are the records located in the company office in Dundee, now in London.
53. W. D. MacDougall 'Statement of the Chairman', 4 April 1950.
54. 'Scottish Bargain,' *Time* (6 August 1951), 78, 80.
55. Minutes of the Annual Meeting, Matador Land and Cattle Company, 17 July 1942.

Chapter VI : Adventures in the Mining Kingdom

1. Richard E. Towney 'British Investment in California, 1849–60'. Unpublished M.A. Thesis, University of California, Berkeley, 1957.
2. J. D. Whitney *The Metallic Wealth of the United States, Described and Compared with that of Other Countries*, 142.
3. *Scientific Press* (San Francisco), XXIII (2 December 1871).
4. Ibid.; Rodman W. Paul *California Gold, the Beginning of Mining in the Far West*, 301.
5. Albin Joachim Dahl 'British Investment in California Mining, 1870–90.' Unpublished Ph. D. Dissertation, University of California, Berkeley, 1961.
6. These calculations on the total investment of the British in western American mines, 1870–3, are based on two earlier compilations: Clark C. Spence *British Investments in the American Mining Frontier, 1860–1901*, Appendix II, 261, and Dahl, op. cit., 49, 71.
7. Skinner *The Stock Exchange Year-Book, 1879*, 179-89.
8. For a discussion of 'The Emma Silver Mining Company, Limited: A Case Study' see Spence, op. cit., Chapter VIII, 164-5, 174-8. See also, W. Turrentine Jackson 'The

Infamous Emma Mine: A British Interest in the Little Cottonwood District, Utah Territory', *Utah Historical Quarterly*, XXIII (October 1955), 339-62.

9. 'The Most Risky of All Investments', *The Economist*, XXXIX (18 July 1881), 756. The casual reference to one hundred enterprises in a single year was to world-wide participation, not just the United States.
10. 'The Speculation in Mining Shares', *The Economist*, XLVI (28 January 1888), 105-6.
11. Spence discusses 'Individual Promoters' in detail, op. cit., Chapter II. Dahl also summarizes procedures in his dissertation, 23-5, 29-30.
12. Dahl has traced the legal status of the prospectus, as reflected in court decisions, with great care, 25-9. See also Frederick E. Farrer *The Law Relating to Prospectuses*.
13. The procedures whereby promoters manipulated the market and secretly shared in the purchase money has been described by Dahl as the *modus operandi* of 1870–3, 29-38.
14. *The Law Reports, Statutes*, Vol. 2, 30 & 31 Vict. Cap. 131. The Companies Act, 1867, Sec. 38.
15. Dahl discusses *Twycross* v. *Grant. Com. Pleas Div.*, Vol. 2, 530 to illustrate the position of the court, 38-42.
16. *Mining Journal* (London), XLVII (26 May 1877), 556.
17. *New Sombrero Phosphate Company* v. *Erlander, Chancery Division*, Vol. 5, 1877, 73-126. Dahl also discusses this case, 42-3.
18. *Scientific Press* (San Francisco), XX (1 January 1870).
19 Ibid., XXIII (2 December 1871).
20. *The Times* (London), 14 June 1872. Spence discusses the role of this periodical thoroughly, op. cit., 15-18, 22.
21. Editorial comment in the English papers was republished in every issue of the *Scientific Press* during the summer of 1871. See, for example, the issues of 22 July and 19 August 1871.
22. Spence, op. cit., Appendix II, 261.
23. Dahl, op. cit., 71.
24. Information compiled from financial reports and stock exchange quotations in the *Glasgow Herald* and *The Edinburgh Courant*.
25. Papers of the Utah Cotton Wood Mining and Smelting Company, Ltd., CRO, BLRP.
26. Papers of the Kirkland Gold and Silver Mining Company of California, Limited, CRO, BLRP; 'Gold Mines of Placer County', *Thirty-Second Report of the State Mineralogist of California, 1936*, 26.
27. Papers of the Atchison Mining Company, Limited, CRO, BLRP; Thomas P. Corbett *The Colorado Directory of Mines, 1879*, 73.

28. The pattern of British overseas investment, 1880–93, can be traced in infinite detail by using the annual compilations of information on mining companies prepared by Edward Ashmead and published in a January issue each year by the *Mining Journal* (London).
29. Information compiled from Skinner *The Stock Exchange Year-Book, 1879, 1882* and *1884*. For a valuable statistical summary, see Alfred P. Tischendorf 'British Investments in Colorado Mines', *The Colorado Magazine*, XXX (October 1953), 241-6.
30. 'The Most Risky of All Investments', loc. cit., 756.
31. 'New Joint Stock Schemes', *Scottish Banking and Insurance Magazine*, III (April 1881), 119-20.
32. Papers of the Scottish Pacific Coast Mining Company, Limited, CRO, BLRP; *Scottish Banking and Insurance Magazine*, VI (6 August 1884), 183.
33. Memorandum of Association, Scottish Pacific Coast Mining Company, Limited, 5 March 1881.
34. Skinner *The Stock Exchange Year-Book, 1884*, 328-9.
35. *Scottish Banking and Insurance Magazine*, VI (6 August 1884), 183; *The Engineering and Mining Journal*, XXXIX (5 April 1885), 231.
36. 'Note for Francis More, Liquidator of the Scottish Pacific Coast Mining Company, Ltd., to Approve of Accounts, Discharge Liquidator, and Dissolve Company, October 28, 1889', Companies Registration Office, Edinburgh.
37. Prospectus, The Arizona Copper Company, Limited, 1882; Skinner *The Stock Exchange Year-Book, 1884*, 302. Papers of the Arizona Copper Company, Limited, CRO, BLRP.
38. John J. Gosper 'Report of the Acting Governor of Arizona Territory,' in *Report of the Secretary of the Interior, 1881*, II, *House Executive Document 1*, Part 5, 47 Cong., 1 sess. (1881–2), 932.
39. The history of the Arizona Copper Company is told in full in Chapter VII.
40. 'The Outbreak of Speculation in the Mining Market', *The Economist*, XLVIII (19 December 1885), 1537.
41. 'Mining Share Speculation,' *The Statist*, XVI (7 November 1885), 564.
42. 'Mining and Mining Sharks,' ibid., XVI (18 July 1885), 65.
43. Papers of the Scottish Colorado Mining and Smelting Company, Limited, CRO, LC:WRCIS.
44. Papers of the Richardson Gold and Silver Mining Company, Limited, CRO, BLRP. Robert A. Corregan and David F. Lingane *Colorado Mining Directory, 1883*, 302-3. The liquidation of this company proved so troublesome that it was not removed from the Register of Companies until 1933.
45. *The Edinburgh Courant*, 3 February 1885; *La Plata Miner* (Silverton, Colorado), 18 October 1884, quoted in *The*

Edinburgh Courant, 9 February 1885; *Scottish Banking and Insurance Magazine*, VII (February 1885), 32; 'Pride of the West', *The Engineering and Mining Journal*, XXXIX (6 June 1885), 392. For additional facts on this mining property, see Corbett, op. cit., 390 and Corregan and Lingane, op. cit., 665.

46. Robert L. Kelley *Gold vs. Grain: The Hydraulic Mining Controversy in California's Sacramento Valley*. This study is authoritative on all phases of hydraulic mining operations. See also Kelley 'Forgotten Giant: The Hydraulic Gold Mining Industry in California', *The Pacific Historical Review*, XXIII (November 1954), 343-56 and 'The Mining Debris Controversy in the Sacramento Valley', *The Pacific Historical Review*, XXV (November 1956), 331-46.
47. Two valuable contemporary sources of information on deep gravel mining are W. A. Skidmore 'Deep Placer Mining in California', in Rossiter W. Raymond *Mineral Resources* . . . (for 1868), *House Executive Document 54*, 40 Cong., 3 sess., 30ff. and H. G. Hanks 'Placer, Hydraulic and Drift Mining', *California State Mineralogist's Report*, II (1882), 44-118.
48. Papers of the Feather-Fork Gold Gravel Company, Limited, CRO, BLRP. *Eleventh Annual Report of the State Mineralogist of California, 1892*, 330, 419; *Twelfth Report, 1894*, 265-6; *Thirteenth Report, 1896*, 376.
49. Papers of the Scottish California Gold Quartz Mining Company, Limited, Papers of the Leechman Prospecting Company, Limited, CRO, BLRP.
50. Papers of the Crestone Gold Mining Company, Limited, CRO, LC:WRCIS.
51. *Tenth Report of the State Mineralogist of California, 1890*, 397.
52. Papers of the Grass Valley California Gold Extracting Company (Pollock Patents), Limited, CRO, BLRP.
53. Papers of the Mining Development Syndicate (of Colorado), Limited, CRO, LC:WRCIS.
54. Charles W. Henderson *Mining in Colorado, A History of Discovery, Development and Production*, 38-9; Corbett, op. cit., 110; Corregan and Lingane, op. cit., 71.
55. Duane Allan Smith 'Silver Camp Called Caribou', Unpublished M.A. Thesis, University of Colorado, 1961, 107-8. See also Smith 'The Caribou-A Forgotten Mine', *The Colorado Magazine*, XXXIX (January 1962), 47-54. Smith notes that Peter McCourt, brother of Baby Doe Tabor, was Vice President of the Poorman Mining Company, 1888–91
56. Papers of the Poorman Silver Mines (of Colorado), Limited, CRO, BLRP.
57. 24 August 1892, quoted in Smith Thesis, 108.

58. G. A. Wahlgreen *Colorado Mining Directory and Buyer's Guide, 1901*, 24.
59. Papers of the Poorman Silver Mines (of Colorado), Limited, CRO, BLRP.
60. Papers of the Gold and Silver Extraction Company of America, Limited, CRO, LC:WRCIS.
61. 'The Mining Mania', *The Statist*, XVIII (30 October 1886), 483-4.
62. 'Anglo-American Mines', ibid., XX (3 December 1887), 625-6.

Chapter VII : The Arizona Copper Company

1. Papers of the Arizona Copper Company, Limited, 1882, CRO, BLRP; Skinner *The Stock Exchange Year-Book, 1884*, 302.
2. James Colquhoun *The Early History of the Clifton-Morenci District*, 20-58. This account contains many interesting stories too detailed to record. Robert G. Cleland *A History of Phelps Dodge, 1834–1950*, 80.
3. James N. McClintock *Arizona*, II, 421.
4. Ibid.
5. 'The Great Copper Deposits of New Mexico and Arizona', *The Engineering and Mining Journal*, XIX (16 January 1875), 37-8; 'Clifton, New Mexico [*sic*]—Its Copper Mines and Furnaces', ibid., XXXIV (2 September 1882), 121-2. Hubert Howe Bancroft *History of Arizona and New Mexico*, 591 n. does not agree with these details. The confusion arises because there were several discoveries other than the 'Longfellow' in the Clifton area during the 1870s.
6. Richard J. Hinton *The Hand-Book to Arizona, 1878*, 103.
7. McClintock, op. cit., II, 422.
8. Patrick Hamilton *The Resources of Arizona, 1884*, 191.
9. McClintock, op. cit., II, 422.
10. 'The Longfellow Copper Mines', *The Engineering and Mining Journal*, XXIX (14 February 1880), 121; 'The Clifton Copper Mines, Arizona,' ibid. (21 February 1880), 133. The first account is chiefly a reprint from the *Globe Silver Belt*, 31 January 1880. Calculations on the basis of a copper price at twenty-three cents a pound were too optimistic, for the average world price in 1880 was twenty-one and a half cents a pound, and at that a high price.
11. Bancroft *History of Arizona and New Mexico, 1530–1888*, 590, 591 n; Colquhoun, op. cit., 54-5, 79. Ward early displayed an interest in doing business with Phelps Dodge Corporation and by 1895 this company controlled his copper interests.

12. Bancroft *History of Arizona and New Mexico, 1530–1888,* 627.
13. McClintock, op. cit., II, 422.
14. *Mining Journal* (London), LII (16 December 1882), 1515; *The Edinburgh Courant,* 8, 9 December 1882; *The Engineering and Mining Journal,* XXXIV (30 December 1882), 349-50.
15. *The Edinburgh Courant,* 1 June 1883.
16. Ibid., 29 May, 1, 9 June 1883; *Mining Journal* (London), LIII (9 June 1883), 664, (16 June 1883), 692.
17. *Scottish Banking and Insurance Magazine,* V (14 February 1883), 37-8.
18. 2 July 1883, 143-4.
19. 13 July 1883.
20. *The Edinburgh Courant,* 14 July 1883.
21. 19 July 1883.
22. *The Edinburgh Courant,* 31 July 1883.
23. 4 September 1883, 189-91, 200-7.
24. Clifton *Clarion,* 1 August 1883.
25. 'Is Clifton in Arizona?', ibid., 17 October 1883.
26. *The Edinburgh Courant,* 20 October 1883. The full report was printed in the *Scottish Banking and Insurance Magazine,* V (3 November 1883), 247-50.
27. 3 November 1883, 239.
28. Memorandum of Association, Arizona Trust and Mortgage Company, Limited, 30 November 1883; *The Edinburgh Courant,* 20 October 1883; *Mining Journal* (London), LIII (24 November 1883), 1343.
29. *Scottish Banking and Insurance Magazine,* V (3 December 1883), 261-5.
30. Memorandum of Association, Arizona Trust and Mortgage Company, Limited, 30 November 1883.
31. 22, 27 November 1883.
32. 3 December 1883.
33. *Scottish Banking and Insurance Magazine,* VI (10 January 1884), 8. Shareholder lists of both the Copper Company and the Trust Company were published for comparisons to be made by the public, 18-26.
34. *The Edinburgh Courant,* 29 January, 4 March, 4 April 1884.
35. *Scottish Banking and Insurance Magazine,* VI (5 April 1884), 86.
36. 7 April 1884.
37. *Mining Journal* (London), LIV (21 April 1884), 480; *The Edinburgh Courant,* 16, 24 April 1884; *Scottish Banking and Insurance Magazine,* VI (3 May 1884), 108.
38. 'Mines and Mining Sharks', *The Statist,* XVI (18 July 1885), 65. For the history of The Emma Silver Mining Company, see Spence, op. cit., Chapter VIII or Jackson 'The Infamous Emma Mine: A British Investment in the Little Cottonwood District, Utah Territory', loc. cit., 339-62.

39. Agreement between the Arizona Copper Company, Limited, (hereinafter called the Old Company) . . . and The Arizona Copper Company, Limited, (hereinafter called the New Company) . . . 6 August 1884; Memorandum of Association, The Arizona Copper Company, Limited, August 1884; *The Edinburgh Courant*, 29 May, 2 July 1884; *Scottish Banking and Insurance Magazine*, VI (5 July 1884), 158.
40. 'British Enterprise in Arizona—A Model Smelting Works', *Mining Journal* (London), LIV (2 August 1884), 910; Hamilton, op. cit., 192-7.
41. *The Edinburgh Courant*, 22 December 1884, quoting *The Engineering and Mining Journal* of New York.
42. *Scottish Banking and Insurance Magazine*, VII (February 1885), 30.
43. *The Edinburgh Courant*, 22 July 1885.
44. Ibid., 7 January 1886; *Scottish Banking and Insurance Magazine*, VIII (January 1886), 20.
45. *The Edinburgh Courant*, 31 December 1886; *Scottish Banking and Insurance Magazine*, VIII (January 1886), 8, 20-1.
46. XXII (15 September 1888), 305.
47. For details, see Horace J. Stevens *The Copper Handbook, A Manual of the Copper Industry of the World*, X, 1910–11, 1879
48. 'Neglected Copper Shares—The Arizona', *The Statist*, XXII (8 and 15 September 1888), 297, 305.
49. *The Engineering and Mining Journal*, XLV (28 January 1888), 79.
50. Ibid., XLVI (15 September 1888), 212-13.
51. 'Neglected Copper Shares—The Arizona', loc. cit., 297, 305.
52. Papers of the Arizona Copper Company, Limited, 1884, CRO, BLRP; *The Engineering and Mining Journal*, XLVII (5 January 1889), 17.
53. Stevens, op. cit., 1879.
54. *The Engineering and Mining Journal*, LV (15 April 1893), 349.
55. Ibid., LI (14 March 1891), 331.
56. Ibid., LVI (25 November 1893), 651; LVII (13 January 1894), 45.
57. Skinner *The Stock Exchange Year-Book, 1895*, 569-71; *Mining Journal* (London), LXVIII (12 February 1898), 192.
58. *The Engineering and Mining Journal*, LXV (28 May 1898), 644.
59. Skinner *The Stock Exchange Year-Book, 1900*, 600-1. Annual reports are summarized in *The Engineering and Mining Journal*, LXI (22 February 1896), 188, LXIII (13 February 1897), 167.
60. LXVIII (12 February 1898), 192.
61. *The Engineering and Mining Journal*, LXX (1 September 1900), 252.

62. *Mining Journal*, (London), LXIX (11 February 1899), 165.
63. Ibid., LXX (8 September 1900), 1093; *The Engineering and Mining Journal*, LXX (6 October 1900), 402.
64. Papers of the Arizona Copper Company, Limited, 1884, CRO, BLRP.
65. Skinner *The Stock Exchange Year-Book, 1906*, 1202.
66. Papers of the Arizona Copper Company, Limited, 1884, CRO, BLRP.
67. Skinner *The Stock Exchange Year-Book, 1916*, 1405.
68. McClintock, op. cit., 423-4.
69. Ibid.
70. Ibid.; Skinner *The Stock Exchange Year-Book, 1920*, 1561.
71. Cleland, op. cit., 210.
72. Ibid.; Skinner *The Stock Exchange Year-Book, 1922*, 1665-6.
73. Quoted in Cleland, op. cit., 211-12.
74. Skinner *The Stock Exchange Year-Book, 1923*, 1845-6.
75. Ibid., *1929*, 2039-40.

Chapter VIII : Widening Horizons in the Mining Industry

1. Cairncross *Home and Foreign Investments, 1870–1913*, 180.
2. The pattern of mining development for the decade, 1890–1900, is based on figures compiled by Edward Ashmead and published in the January issue each year by the *Mining Journal* (London).
3. *The Law Reports, Statutes*, Vol. 27, 1890. 53 & 54 Vict. Ch. 62-3.
4. *The Engineering and Mining Journal*, LVII (27 January 1894), 93.
5. Papers of the Bear Creek Alluvial Gold Company, Limited, CRO, BLRP.
6. Papers of the Diamond Hill Syndicate, Limited, CRO, BLRP.
7. Papers of the Diamond Hill Gold Mines, Limited, CRO, BLRP.
8. *Sixth Annual Report of the Bureau of Agriculture, Labor and Industry of the State of Montana, 1898*, 173.
9. Liquidation of this company was a long, drawn-out process. The courts took action in 1937 to have the company dissolved and ten years later proceeds from the property had reached $4,655 making possible 'the first and final dividend' on the first ranking preference shares issued at the time of the 1898 reorganization.
10. Papers of the Prescott Development Syndicate, Limited, CRO, BLRP.
11. Papers of the Gold Basin Mining Company, Limited, CRO, BLRP.

12. Papers of the Smelting and Development Company, Limited, CRO, BLRP.
13. Papers of the Bull Creek Mineral Estates, Limited, CRO, BLRP.
14. *The Engineering and Mining Journal,* LXV (14 May 1898), 592.
15. Ibid., LXVI (12 November 1898), 587.
16. Papers of the Meldrum Tunnel and Mining Syndicate, CRO, BLRP.
17. Papers of the Glasgow and Western Exploration Company, Limited, CRO, BLRP.
18. 'Mining and Investment in California', *The Economist,* LIII (13 July 1895), 913. The consul's report is summarized.
19. *Thirteenth Report of the State Mineralogist of California, 1896.* Summaries of the report appeared in *The Engineering and Mining Journal,* LXVII (15 April 1896), 150, and in the *Mining Journal* (London), LXVI (30 May 1896), 693.
20. *The Engineering and Mining Journal,* LXII (26 September 1896), 289.
21. Ibid., LXII (24 October 1896), 385-6.
22. *The Economist,* LIII (13 July 1895), 913.
23. Papers of the California Gold Production Syndicate, Limited, CRO, BLRP; *Thirteenth Report of the State Mineralogist of California, 1896,* 373-4.
24. The papers of these companies may be examined at the Bancroft Library, University of California, Berkeley, where they are on microfilm as a part of the material collected by the Research Program in Scotland.
25. Papers of the Alaska (Glasgow) Gold Mine, Limited, and Papers of Redhill, Limited, CRO, BLRP. The Alaska mine had a long history. For additional information see *Register of Mines and Minerals in California. Nevada County. Quartz Mines,* 4; *Thirty-Seventh Report of the State Mineralogist of California, 1941,* 380-1.
26. Report of the Secretary, Seine River Syndicate, Limited, CRO, BLRP.
27. For the conflicting evidence see Rossiter W. Raymond *Statistics of Mines and Mining in the States and Territories West of the Rocky Mountains, 1872,* 62, and Clarence A. Logan 'Mother Lode Gold Belt of California', *Bulletin No. 108,* California State Division of Mines (November 1934), 167.
28. W. H. Storms 'The Mother Lode Region of California', *Bulletin No. 18,* California State Mining Bureau (October 1900), 131.
29. Logan 'Mother Lode Gold Belt of California', loc. cit., 167.
30. Papers of the Jumper Gold Syndicate of California, Limited, CRO, BLRP.
31. *Thirteenth Report of the State Mineralogist of California, 1896,*

482; Logan 'Mother Lode Gold Belt of California', loc. cit., 167-8; Storms 'The Mother Lode Region of California', loc. cit. 131-2.

32. Papers of the Jumper Gold Syndicate of California, Limited, CRO, BLRP.
33. *Fourteenth Report of the State Mineralogist of California, 1913–1914,* 152-3; Logan 'Mother Lode Gold Belt of California', loc. cit., 168.
34. *Eighth Report of the State Mineralogist of California, 1888,* 672; *Eleventh Report, 1892,* 494; Storms 'The Mother Lode Region of California', loc. cit., 139; Papers of the Longfellow Gold Syndicate, Limited, CRO, BLRP.
35. Papers of the Nonpareil Gold Syndicate, Limited, CRO, BLRP.
36. Papers of California Consols, Limited, CRO, BLRP.
37. Papers of the Atlas Mines Syndicate, Limited, Atlas Development & Mining Company, Limited, and the Atlas Gold Mine, California, Limited, CRO, BLRP; *Thirteenth and Fourteenth Reports of the State Mineralogist of California, 1896,* 473-4, *1913–1914,* 137-8.
38. Papers of the Crystalline Gold Mines, Limited, and Crystalline Mining Company, Limited, CRO, BLRP; *Thirteenth and Fourteenth Reports of the State Mineralogist of California, 1896,* 477, *1913–1914,* 143.
39. Papers of the Herman Mining Company, Limited, CRO, BLRP; *Fifteenth Report of the State Mineralogist of California, 1915–1916,* 341-2; *Thirty-second Report, 1936,* 26.
40. *Mining and Scientific Press,* LXXIII (10 October 1896).
41. Ibid., LXXI (21 September 1895).
42. *Mining Journal* (London), LXVII (9 January 1897), 49-50.
43. Ibid., LXVIII (8 January 1898), 40.
44. Cairncross *Home and Foreign Investments, 1870–1913,* 180-4.
45. *Mining Journal* (London), LXXXIV (23 January 1909), 105.
46. *The Law Reports, Statutes,* Vol. 38, 1900, 63 & 64 Vict., Ch. 48, 96-110.
47. Dahl Dissertation, 56-9, 61.
48. *The Law Reports, Statutes,* Vol. 45, 1907, 7 Edw. VII, Ch. 50, 218-43.
49. Percy S. Fritz *Colorado, the Centennial State,* 310-12; Colin B. Goodykoontz 'The Settlement of Colorado', in James H. Baker and LeRoy R. Hafen *History of Colorado,* III, 468-71.
50. See, for example, the following discussion in *The Economist*: 'Gold Mining Investments—American Mines', LX (27 December 1902), 2023-4; 'American Gold Mines', LXIII (3 June 1905), 909-10. *The Engineering and Mining Journal* reported periodically on the mine during 1899 and in the next two years scarcely an issue appeared without an

account of the activities at Stratton's Independence. Information on the overall British investment at Copper Creek has been compiled from Spence, op. cit., Appendix 1.

51. Spence, op. cit., 28, 107-8, 118, 132-3.
52. Papers of the St Patrick Gold Mine Syndicate, Limited, CRO, LC: WRCIS.
53. Papers of the St Patrick Gold Mine, Limited, CRO, LC:WRCIS and BLRP.
54. W.H. Shearer *Atlas of the Goldfield, Tonopah and Bullfrog Mining District of Nevada, 1905*, 23-5.
55. Richard G. Lillard *Desert Challenge, An Interpretation of Nevada*, 181-2. Lillard's book is an outstanding work on Nevada's history and lore and contains many interesting pages about the Tonopah-Goldfield area.
56. Shearer, op. cit., 25-31.
57. Papers of the Scottish Tonopah Gold Mining Company, Limited, CRO, BLRP.
58. Russell R. Elliott 'The Tonopah-Goldfield-Bullfrog Mining District, 1900–1915: History of a Twentieth Century Mining Boom.' Unpublished Ph.D. Dissertation, University of California, 1946. Elliott has published an article on one aspect of his study 'Labor Troubles in the Mining Camp at Goldfield, Nevada, 1906–1908', *Pacific Historical Review*, XIX (November 1950), 369-84.
59. The story of this enterprise can be followed in the *Scientific Press*, XX (23 April 1870), 268, (30 April 1870), 284, XXI (27 August 1870), 140, (17 September 1870), 202.
60. M.M. O'Shaughnessy 'The Copper Resources of California', *California Mines and Minerals*, California Miners' Association, San Francisco, 1899, 206-7.
61. *The Statist*, XXXVI (19 October 1895), 476-7.
62. *The Economist*, LIX (7 December 1901), 1804–5.
63. Stevens, op. cit.
64. *The Engineering and Mining Journal*, LXVII (25 February 1899), 241.
65. Prescott *Daily Citizen*, 6 May 1899, quoted in ibid., LXVII (20 May 1899), 591.
66. Ibid.
67. Papers of the Mineral Hill Copper Syndicate, Limited, CRO, BLRP. A somewhat similar promotion was the New London Mining Company, Limited, which obtained several silver-lead properties eleven miles northwest of Kingman, Mojave County, Arizona, in the Wallapai Mining District. The sale had been pushed by Dr Samuel Blair, an El Paso, Texas, minister, and a Dr L.D. Godshall, a mining surveyor of Needles, California. The company was capitalized at £20,000, £17,500 of which went for the properties, £10,000 in shares and £7,500 in cash. The venture came to nothing. Blair left for Mexico, Godshall moved to Los Angeles, and

the final legal termination of the company was confirmed in 1941. Papers of the New London Mining Company, Limited, CRO, BLRP.

68. Papers of the British Arizona Copper Company, Limited, CRO, BLRP.
69. 'The Copper Resources of California', *Bulletin No. 50*, California State Mining Bureau (September 1908), 30-8.
70. *Mining Journal* (London), LIX (28 January 1899), 96, (29 April 1899), 486, LX (22 December 1900), 1549; *The Engineering and Mining Journal* LXVII (4 February 1899), 161, (15 April 1899), 448.
71. Prospectus, Papers of the Fresno Copper Company, Limited, CRO, BLRP.
72. Papers of the Glasgow Copper Syndicate, Limited, CRO, BLRP.
73. Papers of the Fresno Copper Company, Limited, CRO, BLRP.
74. 'The Copper Resources of California', loc. cit., 279-81.
75. *Fourteenth Report of the State Mineralogist of California, 1913–1914*, 437.
76. Papers of the Fresno Copper Company, Limited, 1907, CRO, BLRP.

Chapter IX : Single Purpose Ventures

1. Papers of the Glasgow Californian Land Company, Limited, CRO, BLRP.
2. George H. Tinkham *History of San Joaquin County California with Biographical Sketches*, 322-3.
3. *Daily Alta Californian* (San Francisco), 17 May 1870. Great confidence was expressed in Captain Walker. His company had recently reclaimed a nearby island in the delta and he had gained experience as superintendent of the Sauselito Land and Ferry Company and as a construction superintendent on the Western Union Telegraph Company in Asia.
4. *History of San Joaquin County, California, with Illustrations Descriptive of Its Scenery*, [*1879*], 43.
5. Papers of the Glasgow Californian Land Company, CRO, BLRP.
6. *History of San Joaquin County, California, with Illustrations Descriptive of Its Scenery*, [*1879*], 43; *An Illustrated History of San Joaquin County California*, [*1890*], 108-10.
7. *Stockton Daily Independent*, 22 May 1879.
8. Ibid. The criticism against San Franciscans was directed toward the Workingmen's Party led by Denis Kearney.
9. Papers of the Glasgow Californian Land Company, CRO, BLRP.

10. *Sacramento Daily Record-Union*, 19 March 1884.
11. *Stockton Daily Independent*, 18 March 1884.
12. Ibid., 21 March 1884.
13. *Sacramento Daily Record-Union*, 5 April 1884.
14. *Daily Alta Californian*, 4 December 1884.
15. *An Illustrated History of San Joaquin County California*, [*1890*], 110.
16. Tinkham, op. cit., 323.
17. Papers of the Glasgow Californian Land Company, CRO, BLRP.
18. Papers of the Dundee Land Investment Company, CRO, BLRP. For a discussion of the activities of this company, see Chapter II.
19. Memorandum of Association, Scottish American Land Company, Limited, 23 April 1880.
20. Papers of the Scottish American Land Company, CRO, BLRP; Skinner *The Stock Exchange Year-Book, 1887*, 435.
21. *The Edinburgh Courant*, 26 March 1884.
22. Skinner *The Stock Exchange Year-Book, 1887*, 435; *1892*, 728.
23. Papers of the Missouri Land Company of Scotland, Limited, CRO, BLRP.
24. Skinner *The Stock Exchange Year-Book, 1890*, 583; *1895*, 805.
25. Papers of the Missouri Land Company of Scotland, CRO, BLRP.
26. *Scottish Banking and Insurance Magazine*, VIII (5 October 1886), 230; Papers of the American Land and Colonization Company of Scotland, Limited, CRO, BLRP.
27. *The Edinburgh Courant*, 30 June and 14 July 1883.
28. Skinner *The Stock Exchange Year-Book, 1886*, 372.
29. *Scottish Banking and Insurance Magazine*, VIII (5 October 1886), 230.
30. Papers of the Texas and New Mexico Land Syndicate, Limited, CRO, BLRP.
31. Lawson, op. cit., 12.
32. 'Scottish Capital Abroad', loc. cit., 468-80.
33. Papers of the Park Red River Valley Land Company, Limited, CRO, BLRP.
34. Glenn S. Dumke 'Early Las Vegas', *Pacific Historical Review*, XXII, (August 1953), 268. Dumke's information comes from the Las Vegas *Age*, 13 June 1914.
35. Papers of the South Nevada Land and Development Company, CRO, BLRP.
36. Papers of the British Canadian Lumbering and Timber Company, Limited, CRO, BLRP.
37. Memorandum of Association, American Lumber Company, Limited, 20 April 1882.
38. Papers of the American Lumber Company, CRO, BLRP.

39. *The Edinburgh Courant*, 4 January 1884.
40. Minute Book, Dundee Investment Company, 16 March 1883.
41. *The Edinburgh Courant*, 8 and 22 January 1884.
42. *Scottish Banking and Insurance Magazine*, VI (7 February 1884), 41.
43. *The Edinburgh Courant*, 29 January 1884.
44. Ibid., 1 November 1884.
45. 19 September 1885, quoted in *Scottish Banking and Insurance Magazine*, VII (October 1885), 258.
46. *The Edinburgh Courant*, 8 July 1883. The company prospectus was published in this issue.
47. Papers of the California Redwood Company, Limited, CRO, BLRP.
48. *The Humboldt Standard*, 31 December 1883.
49. *Scottish Banking and Insurance Magazine*, V (4 October 1883), 227.
50. *The Edinburgh Courant*, 1 April 1884.
51. *U.S. Statutes at Large*, XX, 113.
52. 'Land Grabbers Brought up with a Round Turn', *San Francisco News Letter and Advertiser*, XXXIV (15 March 1884), 9.
53. Dunham, op. cit., 265.
54. N.C. McFarland, Commissioner of the General Land Office, to H.M. Teller, Secretary of the Interior, 15 May 1884, *Senate Executive Document 181*, 48 Cong., 1 sess. (1883–4).
55. *San Francisco Chronicle*, 25 February 1884.
56. 25 February 1884.
57. 28 February 1884.
58. 'Land Grabbers Brought up with a Round Turn', loc. cit., 9.
59. *Scottish Banking and Insurance Magazine*, VI (3 May 1884), 109, 121.
60. Ibid.
61. *Senate Executive Document 181*, 48 Cong., 1 sess. (1883–4).
62. 'Report of the Commissioner of the General Land Office, October 7, 1886,' *House Executive Document 1*, Part 5, 49 Cong., 2 sess. (1885–6), 94.
63. Ibid.
64. 'The California Redwood Company', *House Executive Document 282*, 50 Cong., 1 sess. (1887–8). This is a report of William F. Vilas, 25 April 1888, answering a House resolution inquiring into the activities of the company. For editorial comment, see the *New York Times*, 28 April 1888.
65. 'Report of the Commissioner of the General Land Office, October 7, 1886.' loc. cit., 95.
66. *House Executive Document 282*, 50 Cong., 1 sess. (1887–8); 'Report of the Commissioner of the General Land Office, September 28, 1887', *House Executive Document 1*, 50 Cong., 1 sess. (1887–8), 162-3.

67. *New York Times*, 5 May 1886 and 16 April 1887.
68. L.Q.C.Lamar to A.H.Garland, 18 November 1886, *House Executive Document 282*, 50 Cong., 1 sess. (1887–8).
69. Ibid., 135-6.
70. *Scottish Banking and Insurance Magazine*, VII (May 1885), 114-15.
71. *The Edinburgh Courant*, 8 May 1885.
72. Ibid., 11 May 1885.
73. Papers of the Humboldt Redwood Company, Limited, CRO, BLRP.
74. *House Executive Document 282*, 50 Cong., 1 sess. (1887–8).
75. Agreement between the California Redwood Company, Limited, and Joseph Russ and David Evans, 11 December 1885; Memorandum of Agreement between The Humboldt Logging Railway Company and Joseph Russ and David Evans, 1 October 1885.
76. *Scottish Banking and Insurance Magazine*, VII (December 1885), 294; VIII (January 1886), 14-15; *The Humboldt Standard*, 6 February 1886, quoting an article on the court proceedings from the Edinburgh *Scotsman*.
77. Memorandum of Association, Edinburgh and San Francisco Redwood Company, Limited, 30 November 1885.
78. *The Humboldt Weekly Standard*, 21 March 1885.
79. Skinner *The Stock Exchange Year-Book, 1892*, 954; *1895*, 1090.
80. *California Redwood Co.* v. *Litle*, 79 Fed. 854. (C.C.N.D Calif. 1897).
81. For example, see *The Morning Call* (San Francisco), 2 February 1895 and 15 December 1896, and *The Herald* (Los Angeles), 15 April 1897.
82. *California Redwood Co.* v. *Mahan* (mem), 80 Fed. 1004 (C.C.N.D.Calif. 1897); *California Redwood Co.* v. *Litle*, 87 Fed. 1004 (C.C.A. 9th, 1898); *California Redwood Co.* v. *Johnson*, 179 U. S. 681 (1900).
83. Papers of the Edinburgh and San Francisco Redwood Company, CRO, BLRP.
84. Memorandum of Association, Scottish Carolina Timber and Land Company, Limited, 22 February 1884; Papers of the Scottish Carolina Timber and Land Company, CRO, BLRP.
85. Skinner *The Stock Exchange Year-Book, 1887*, 585; *1888*, 472; *1889*, 526; *1890*, 599.
86. Papers of the Woodruff Land and Timber Company, Limited, CRO, BLRP.
87. Memorandum of Association, Scottish Californian Orange and Vineyard Company, Limited, 25 September 1884.
88. *Scottish Banking and Insurance Magazine*, VI (4 October 1884), 234-5.
89. Papers of the Scottish Californian Orange and Vineyard Company, CRO, BLRP.

90. Papers of the St Mungo Fruit Growing Company of California, Limited, CRO, BLRP. St Mungo is the patron saint of the City of Glasgow.
91. Papers of the California Vineyards Association, Limited, and the California and Australian Vineyards Union, Limited, CRO, BLRP.
92. Papers of the Barton Vineyard Company, Limited, CRO, BLRP.
93. Ibid.
94. Papers of the Almendros Land Company, Limited, CRO, BLRP.
95. The literature on problems of early Oregon transportation is extensive; e.g., James B. Hedges *Henry Villard and the Railways of the Northwest*; Oswald Garrison Villard (ed.) *The Early History of Transportation in Oregon*; R. C. Clark *History of the Willamette Valley, Oregon*; Joseph L. Gaston 'The Genesis of the Oregon Railway System', *Quarterly of the Oregon Historical Society*, VII (June 1906), 105-32; John T. Ganoe 'The History of the Oregon and California Railroad', *Quarterly of the Oregon Historical Society*, XXV (September 1924), 239-40; Dorothy O. Johansen 'The Oregon Steam Navigation Company: An example of Capitalism on the Frontier', *Pacific Historical Review*, X (June 1941), 234-44. A good summary is found in Oscar O. Winther *The Old Oregon Country*, Chapter XX.
96. Memorandum of Association, Oregonian Railway Company, 4 May 1880; *Dundee Advertiser*, 14 May 1880.
97. Petition to the Court of Sessions for the winding-up of the Oregonian Railway Company and the appointment of a liquidator by the court, 19 March 1889.
98. *The Edinburgh Courant*, 29 September 1881.
99. Ibid., 1 August 1883.
100. Ibid., 21 November 1883.
101. Ibid., 14, 16, 19 May 1884.
102. *Dundee Advertiser*, 14 May 1884.
103. *The Edinburgh Courant*, 24, 27 May 1884.
104. Ibid., 29 May, 2, 4, 5 June 1884.
105. *Scottish Banking and Insurance Magazine*, VI (5 June 1884), 150-1; VI (5 July 1884), 159-60.
106. Ibid., VI (4 October 1884), 243-4.
107. *Oregonian Ry. Co. Ltd.* v. *Oregon Ry. & Nav. Co.*, 22 Fed. 245 (C.C.D.Oreg. 1884).
108. *Oregonian Ry. Co. Ltd.* v. *Oregon Ry. & Nav. Co.*, 23 Fed. 232 (C.C.D.Oreg. 1885).
109. *The Edinburgh Courant*, 20 March 1885.
110. *The Oregonian* (Portland), 19 March 1885.
111. *Scottish Banking and Insurance Magazine*, VII (June 1885), 144-5.

112. *Oregonian Ry. Co. Ltd.* v. *Oregon Ry. & Nav. Co.*, 37 Fed. 733 (C.C.D.Oreg. 1885).
113. *The Edinburgh Courant*, 28 July 1885; Skinner *The Stock Exchange Year-Book, 1887*, 167.
114. *Oregonian Ry. Co. Ltd.* v. *Oregon Ry. & Nav. Co.*, 27 Fed. 277 (C.C.D.Oreg. 1886).
115. *Scottish Banking and Insurance Magazine*, VIII (5 October 1886), 238-9.
116. *Oregon Ry. & Nav. Co.* v. *Oregonian Ry. Co. Ltd.*, 130 U.S. 1. (1889).
117. Petition to the Court of Sessions, 19 March 1889.
118. Winther, op. cit., 299-300; Bancroft *History of Oregon, 1848–1888*, II, 747-8.
119. Report of Proceedings at the Presentation to Mr William Mackenzie of His Portrait, 11 March 1920, 7.
120. Memorandum of Association, The Salem (Oregon) Capitol Flour Mills Company, Limited, 1 May 1884; *The Edinburgh Courant*, 24 November and 1 December 1883; *Scottish Banking and Insurance Magazine*, V (3 December 1883), 260, 271.
121. Papers of the Salem (Oregon) Capitol Mills Company, CRO, BLRP.
122. Papers of the Scoto-American Sugar Syndicate, Limited, CRO, BLRP.

Chapter X: Patterns and Problems

1. Bogue *Money at Interest*, 267.
2. *The Economist*, XLVII (6 July 1889), 861-2.
3. Ibid., (31 August 1889), 1115-16.
4. Fifteenth and Sixteenth Annual Reports, Scottish-American Mortgage Company, 26 July 1889 and 17 July 1890.
5. *The Edinburgh Courant*, 2 January 1884.
6. Bogue *Money at Interest*, 267.
7. Report of the Directors to the Eighteenth and Nineteenth Annual Meetings of the Shareholders, 25 July 1892 and 28 July 1893.
8. 'Notes by William Williamson', Clerk of the Scottish-American Mortgage Company.
9. Report of the Directors to the Fourteenth and Fifteenth Annual Meetings of Shareholders, Edinburgh American Land Mortgage Company, 28 March 1893 and 20 March 1894.
10. Gilbert, op. cit., 28-9; John D. Hicks *The American Nation*, 255-6.

11. 'To What Extent British Investors Have Over-Committed Themselves', *The Economist*, XLVIII (11 January 1890), 36-7; 'The "Boom" in American Rails', ibid., (3 May 1890), 550.
12. 'Our Investments in 1890', ibid., (27 December 1890), 1627–8. The history of the Insurance Trust and Agency, Limited, of Glasgow is perhaps the best example of a company launched in 1890 that came to grief during the first years of the decade and, unable to raise cash, had to go into liquidation. *See* Papers of the Insurance Trust and Agency, Limited, CRO, BLRP.
13. Detailed information is available in the following: Second and Third Annual Reports to the Stockholders, British Investment Trust Company, Limited, 5 February 1891 and 15 February 1892 and Proceedings at the Second Annual Meeting, 15 February 1892; Fourth Annual Report and Statement, Scottish Investment Trust Company, 1 November 1891; Minute Book, Second Scottish Investment Trust Company, I, 192-4, December 1891. R. J. Edgar, Secretary of the Scottish Investment Trust Company, also provided information in a memorandum prepared for the author in January 1950.
14. Eighteenth, Nineteenth, and Twentieth Annual Meetings, Scottish-American Investment Company, 10 March 1891, 26 February 1892, and 27 February 1893.
15. Menzies *America as a Field for Investment*, 1-24.
16. Report of the Directors to the Twelfth and Thirteenth Annual Meetings, First Scottish American Trust Company, 1 May 1891 and 23 May 1892 in the *Dundee Advertiser*, 22 May 1891 and 24 May 1892.
17. Prospectus, United States Investment Corporation, Limited, 1891.
18. Remarks of the Chairman, Statutory Meeting, United States Investment Corporation, 2 March 1891; First and Second Reports to the General Meeting, 22 February 1892 and 10 February 1893.
19. Statutory Meeting, Investors' Mortgage Security Company, Limited, 6 November 1891.
20. Directors' Reports to the Eighth, Ninth, and Tenth Meetings of Shareholders, Oregon Mortgage Company, 23 July 1891, 21 July 1892, and 20 July 1893.
21. Minute Book, United States Investment Corporation, Limited, I, 29 January 1891 and 28 November 1892.
22. Minute Book, Investors' Mortgage Security Company, entries from 22 July 1891 to 4 July 1892.
23. Memorandum prepared for the author by company secretaries, 24 February 1950.
24. Fred A. Shannon *Economic History of the People of the United States*, 481-2; Wright, op. cit., 873-6.

25. 'Depreciation in American Securities', *The Statist*, XXXII (22 July 1893), 97-8.
26. 'Unprofitable Investments—American Railway Shares.' *The Economist*, LII (15 September 1894), 1126-7.
27. Directors' Reports to the Fifteenth and Sixteenth Annual Meetings, First Scottish American Trust Company, 17 May 1894 and 23 May 1895 in the *Dundee Advertiser*, 19 July 1895; Proceedings of Annual Meetings, Second and Third Scottish American Trust Companies, 1894–6, reported in the *Dundee Advertiser*.
28. Directors' Reports to the Twenty-First, Twenty-Second and Twenty-Third Annual Meetings, Scottish-American Investment Company, 28 February 1894, 28 February 1895, and 27 February 1896.
29. Fifth, Sixth and Seventh Annual Reports of the Directors, British Investment Trust Company, 22 January 1894, 15 February 1895, and 24 February 1896.
30. Dividend Record from 'Private Memoranda for the Directors, 1902,' Edinburgh Investment Trust Company; Memoranda to the author from R. J. Edgar, January 1950.
31. Hicks, op. cit., 255-6; Shannon, op. cit., 480; Wright, op. cit., 875.
32. Report of the Directors to the Annual Ordinary General Meeting of Shareholders, Alliance Trust Company, 25 April 1893, 30 April 1894, and 30 April 1895. Proceedings of the annual meetings on the same dates.
33. Directors' Reports to the Eleventh and Twelfth Annual Meetings of Shareholders, United States Mortgage Company of Scotland, 25 July 1895 and 27 July 1896.
34. Report of the Directors to the Annual Ordinary General Meeting of Shareholders, Alliance Trust Company, 30 April 1894.
35. Report of the Directors to the Sixteenth Annual Meeting, Edinburgh American Land Mortgage Company, 30 March 1895.
36. Directors' Reports to the Eleventh, Twelfth, and Thirteenth Annual Meetings, Oregon Mortgage Company, 22 July 1894, 23 July 1895, and 23 July 1896.
37. Minute Book, United States Investment Corporation, I, Entries for 20 March, 1 May, 12 June and 7 August 1893; 5 February 1895; and 13 January 1896.
38. Memorandum of Agreement between Messrs Caldwell and Judah and the Alliance Trust Company of Dundee, Minute Book, I, Scottish Investment Trust Company, 424.
39. Minute Book, Deltic Investment Company, Limited, I, 28 November 1894; 30 January, 11 March and 14 December 1895.
40. 'Some American Land Mortgage Companies: The Experience of the "Friends," ' *The Statist*, XXXI (24 June 1893), 691-2.

41. *The Statist*, XXXIV (17 November 1894), 591.
42. Ibid., XXXI (24 June 1893), 691-2.
43. Ibid., XXXII (16, 23, 30 September 1893), 322, 348-9, 379-80.
44. Ibid., XXXIII (14 April 1894), 477.
45. Bogue *Money at Interest*, 275.
46. Ibid., 276.
47. For a discussion and analysis of the Venezuelan Crisis, see Samuel Flagg Bemis *A Diplomatic History of the United States*, 415-19 and Thomas A Bailey *A Diplomatic History of the American People*, 477-88.
48. Directors' Report, Twenty-Fourth Annual Meeting, Scottish-American Investment Company, 1 March 1897.
49. *Dundee Advertiser*, 29 May 1896.
50. Directors' Report to the Shareholders at the Twenty-Second Annual Meeting, Scottish-American Mortgage Company, 24 July 1896.
51. Directors' Report to the Shareholders, Alliance Trust Company, 28 April 1896.
52. Bailey, op. cit., 488-92; Bemis, op.cit., 419-22.
53. Directors' Report to the Shareholders, Investors' Mortgage Security Company, 9 December 1896.
54. *The Economist*, LIV (25 January 1896), 99.
55. Manuscript, Records of the Alliance Trust Company.
56. Chairman's Remarks, Fourteenth Annual Meeting of the First Scottish American Trust Company, 19 May 1893, in the *Dundee Advertiser*, 19 May 1893.
57. Directors' Report to the Shareholders, Annual Ordinary General Meeting of the Shareholders, Alliance Trust Company, 30 April 1894.
58. Ibid., 28 April 1896.
59. *The Statist*, XXV (3 June 1895), 722-3.
60. Chairman's Speech, Annual Meeting of Shareholders, Investors' Mortgage Security Company, 9 December 1896.
61. *The Economist*, LIV (7 November 1896), 1452.
62. Prospectus, North American Trust Company, Limited, 1896; Directors' Reports, Second and Third Annual General Meetings, 1 December 1898 and 7 December 1899; *Dundee Advertiser*, 3 December 1897 and 8 December 1899.
63. Minute Book, (old) American Trust Company, Limited, 29 September, 14 November, and 5 December 1899; 15 March and 9 November 1900. Minutes of the First Annual Ordinary Meeting, American Trust Company, 4 January 1901.
64. Chairman's Remarks, Eighteenth Annual Meeting, First Scottish American Trust Company, in *Dundee Advertiser*, 28 May 1897.
65. Directors' Report, Twenty-Fifth Annual Meeting, Scottish-American Investment Company, 25 February 1898.
66. *The Statist*, XLI (8 January 1898), 61-2.

67. Chairman's Remarks, Nineteenth and Twentieth Annual Meetings, First Scottish American Trust Company, in the *Dundee Advertiser*, 27 May 1898 and 2 June 1899.
68. *The Economist*, LV (11 September 1897), 1289-90.
69. *The Statist*, XL (18 September 1897), 435-6.
70. Directors' Reports, Twenty-Sixth and Twenty-Seventh Annual Meetings, Scottish-American Investment Company, 24 February 1899 and 23 February 1900.
71. *The Statist*, XXXIX (17 April 1897), 612.
72. Directors' Report, Eighth, Tenth, and Eleventh Annual Meeting of Shareholders, British Investment Trust Company, 15 February 1897, 16 February 1899 and 19 February 1900.
73. The Edinburgh Investment Trust Company paid two per cent in 1896, three per cent for 1897 and 1898, five per cent for 1899 and 1900. The Scottish Investment Trust Company paid one and one-half per cent annually between 1895 and 1898, two per cent annually for 1899-1900. The Second Scottish Investment Trust Company paid one and one-half per cent for 1896, two per cent for 1897, two and one-half per cent for 1898, and three per cent for 1899 and 1900.
74. *The Statist*, XXXIX (17 April 1897), 612.
75. Directors' Report to the Shareholders, Twenty-Third Annual Meeting, Scottish-American Mortgage Company, 23 July 1897.
76. Directors' Report to the Shareholders, Thirteenth Annual Meeting, United States Mortgage Company of Scotland, 26 July 1897.
77. Directors' Report to the Shareholders, Ninth Annual Meeting, United States Investment Corporation, 26 March 1900.
78. Directors' Report to the Shareholders, Fourteenth Annual Meeting, United States Mortgage Company of Scotland, 25 July 1898.
79. Directors' Report to the Shareholders, Twenty-Sixth Annual Meeting, Scottish-American Mortgage Company, 30 July 1900.
80. Reports by Directors to the Annual Ordinary General Meeting of Shareholders, Alliance Trust Company, 30 April 1897 and 28 April, 1899; Chairman's Remarks at the Annual Meeting, 28 April 1899, in the *Dundee Advertiser*, 28 April 1899.
81. Chairman's Remarks at the Annual Meeting, 27 April 1900, in the *Dundee Advertiser*, 28 April 1900.
82. Directors' Reports to the Shareholders, Fourteenth through Sixteenth Annual Meetings, United States Mortgage Company of Scotland, 25 July 1898, 21 July 1899, and 23 July 1900.
83. Directors' Reports to the Shareholders, Fourteenth through

Seventeenth Annual Meetings, Oregon Mortgage Company, 22 July 1897, 21 July 1898, 25 July 1899, and 25 July 1900.

84. Papers of the West of Scotland American Investment Company, Limited, CRO, BLRP. For a discussion of the history of the American Land and Colonization Company of Scotland, see Chapter IX.
85. *The Statist*, XLIII (29 April 1899), 605-6.

Chapter XI : Twentieth-Century Trends

1. Directors' Report, Twenty-Ninth Annual Meeting, Scottish-American Investment Company, 24 February 1902.
2. Circular to the Shareholders, Scottish American Trust Company, in the *Dundee Advertiser*, 5 March 1905.
3. Skinner *The Stock Exchange Year-Book, 1911*, 905-6.
4. Directors' Reports to Annual Meetings of Shareholders, British Investment Trust Company, February 1900-February 1914.
5. Book of Private Memoranda for the Directors, 1902–6, Edinburgh Investment Trust Company; Memorandum for the Directors, 6 February 1907.
6. The capital reorganization of the Scottish-American Investment Company is succinctly summarized in Skinner *The Stock Exchange Year-Book, 1911*, 905-6.
7. The *Dundee Advertiser*, 9 June 1911.
8. Book of Private Memoranda for the Directors, 1902–6, Edinburgh Investment Trust Company, Note for March 1902.
9. Ibid.
10. Directors' Report to the Annual Meeting of Shareholders, British Investment Trust Company, February 1914.
11. Minute Book of (old) American Trust Company, 21 January 1901.
12. Reports of the Directors to the Thirty-Third and Thirty-Fifth Annual Meetings of Shareholders, First Scottish American Trust Company, 6 June 1912 and 5 June 1914.
13. Gilbert, op. cit., 80-1.
14. Minute Book of (old) American Trust Company, 9 May, 17 and 29 June, 2 August 1901.
15. Book of Private Memoranda for the Directors, 1902–6, Edinburgh Investment Trust Company, Notes on Realisations from Securities, 15 September 1903; Private Memorandum, 4 March 1904; Memorandum for Directors, March 1906.

16. Directors' Report to the Annual Meeting of Shareholders, British Investment Trust Company, February 1914.
17. Statement of New Income, 15 March 1904, Edinburgh Investment Trust Company.
18. Wright, op. cit., 877.
19. *Dundee Advertiser*, 20 December 1907.
20. Chairman's Remarks, Fifth Ordinary General Meeting of Shareholders, American Trust Company, 3 April 1908.
21. Report of the Directors to the Thirty-Fifth Annual Meeting of Shareholders, First Scottish American Trust Company, 5 June 1914.
22. Papers of the Scottish North American Trust, Limited, CRO, BLRP.
23. Papers of the Scottish Western Investment Company, Limited, CRO, BLRP.
24. Papers of the Scottish Colonial Investment Company, Limited, CRO, BLRP.
25. Papers of the Scottish American Development Corporation, Limited, CRO, BLRP.
26. Papers of the Glasgow American Trust Company, Limited, CRO, BLRP.
27. Wright, op. cit., 876.
28. Proceedings of the Annual Meeting, Scottish-American Mortgage Company, 25 July 1901.
29. Proceedings of Extraordinary Meeting of Shareholders, 1906.
30. Ibid., 18 July 1907.
31. Directors' Reports to the Thirty-First Annual Meeting of Shareholders, Edinburgh American Land Mortgage Company, April 1910.
32. Proceedings of the Eleventh, Sixteenth, Nineteenth and Twenty-Second Annual Meetings of the Investors' Mortgage Security Company, 23 December 1902, 24 December 1907, 14 December 1910, and 17 December 1913.
33. Directors' Reports, Fifteenth and Nineteenth Annual Meeting of Shareholders, 28 March 1906 and 30 March 1910.
34. Proceedings of the Annual Ordinary General Meeting of Shareholders, Alliance Trust Company, 27 April 1901.
35. Directors' Reports to the Twenty-First and Twenty-Fifth Annual Meetings of Shareholders, Oregon Mortgage Company, 21 July 1904 and 16 July 1908; Chairman's Remarks at the Annual Meetings of Shareholders, 22 July 1909, 29 July 1910, and 18 July 1912.
36. Information compiled from Annual Directors' Reports and Accounts, 1905–15.
37. 'Particulars on Mortgage Loan to the Summit Lake Investment Company, February, 1909', Records of the Alliance Trust Company.

38. Jackson 'The Chavez Land Grant: A Scottish Investment in New Mexico, 1881–1940', loc. cit., 349-66.
39. Statement by the Directors, Deltic Investment Company, 29 August 1902.
40. Minute Book, 11, 6 December 1906, and 17 May 1907.
41. Reports of the Directors, Annual Ordinary General Meetings, 24 November 1909, 22 December 1910, 30 October 1913, and 22 December 1914.
42. Ibid., 8 November 1912 and 30 October 1913.
43. Ibid., 8 November 1912, 30 October 1913, and 22 December 1914.
44. Chairman's Remarks, Twenty-Third Annual Meeting, Investors' Mortgage Security Company, 16 December 1914.
45. Directors' Report, Annual Meeting of Shareholders, British Investment Trust, 5 February 1917.
46. Directors' Report, Annual Meeting of Shareholders, Scottish-American Investment Company, 14 February 1917.
47. Ibid.
48. Directors' Report, Annual Ordinary General Meeting of Shareholders, Alliance Trust Company, 26 April 1918.
49. *Dundee Advertiser*, 19 December 1914, 5 June and 18 December 1915, 16 June 1916, and 16 December 1917.
50. Directors' Report, Fourteenth Annual Meeting of Shareholders, American Trust Company, 1 May 1917.
51. Directors' Report, Annual Ordinary General Meeting of Shareholders, Alliance Trust Company, 26 April 1918; *Dundee Advertiser*, 16 December 1917, and 22 June 1918.
52. Directors' Report, Thirty-Fifth Annual Meeting of Shareholders, United States Mortgage Company of Scotland, 3 August 1918; Directors' Report, Thirty-Fifth Annual Meeting, Oregon Mortgage Company, 25 July 1918.
53. Directors' Reports, Fifty-Fourth and Fifty-Sixth Annual Reports, Scottish-American Mortgage Company, 1 August 1918, and 21 July 1920.
54. Directors' Report, Fortieth Annual Meeting of Shareholders, First Scottish American Trust Company, Limited, 27 June 1919.
55. Directors' Report, Annual Meeting of Shareholders, British Investment Trust Company, 11 February 1918.
56. *Dundee Advertiser*, 27 December 1918.
57. Ibid.
58. Skinner *The Stock Exchange Year-Book, 1921*, 778; *1922*, 839.
59. Directors' Report to the Annual Meeting of Shareholders, Oregon Mortgage Company, 22 July 1920.
60. Skinner *The Stock Exchange Year-Book, 1920*, 954; Papers of the United States Mortgage Company, CRO, BLRP.

61. George Glasgow *The Scottish Investment Trust Companies*, 60.
62. Ibid., 96.
63. Papers of the Scottish-American Mortgage Company, CRO, BLRP.
64. Directors' Report, Annual Meeting of Shareholders, First Scottish American Trust Company, 25 June 1920; Proceedings in the *Dundee Advertiser*, 26 June 1920.
65. Papers of the West of Scotland American Investment Company and Papers of the Scottish Western Investment Company, CRO, BLRP.
66. Papers of the Second American Trust Company and Papers of the Third Scottish Western Investment Trust, CRO, BLRP.
67. The following records of the Alliance Trust Company have been examined in connection with the agricultural depression in the United States and its effect on the mortgage business: Directors' Report to the Annual Ordinary General Meeting of Shareholders, 18 April 1921 and 21 April 1922; Report of Proceedings, Annual Ordinary General Meetings, 21 April 1924, 17 April 1925, 9 April 1926, 20 April 1928.
68. Directors' Reports, Annual Meetings of Shareholders, Oregon Mortgage Company, 1921-30; Chairman's Remarks, Annual Meetings of Shareholders, 22 July 1924 and 18 July 1926.
69. Report of Proceedings, Annual Ordinary General Meeting, Alliance Trust Company, 8 April 1927.
70. *The Times* (London), 1 January 1927.
71. Report of Proceedings, Annual Ordinary General Meeting, Western and Hawaiian Investment Company, 20 September 1918; Prospectus, Second Alliance Trust Company, Limited, 1924; Information compiled from the Reports of Proceedings at the Annual Ordinary General Meetings, Second Alliance Trust Company, 1924–9.
72. Report of Proceedings, Annual Ordinary General Meeting, Alliance Trust Company, 20 April 1928.
73. Annual Report of the Directors, Deltic Investment Company, 19 December 1918, 30 December 1920, 30 December 1921, 5 November 1926, 16 September 1927, 14 September 1928, and 17 September 1929.
74. Report of Proceedings, Annual Ordinary General Meeting, Alliance Trust Company, 16 April 1930.
75. Report of Proceedings, Annual Ordinary General Meeting, Second Alliance Trust Company, 9 September 1930.
76. Ibid., 22 September 1933.
77. Report of Proceedings, Annual Ordinary General Meeting, Alliance Trust Company, 7 April 1933.
78. Directors' Report, Annual General Meeting, First Scottish

American Trust Company, 23 June 1933.

79. Papers of the American Trust Company, CRO, BLRP.
80. Papers of the Second American Trust Company, CRO, BLRP.
81. Report of Proceedings, Annual Ordinary General Meeting, Alliance Trust Company, 7 April 1933.
82. Directors' Reports, Annual Meetings of Shareholders, Oregon Mortgage Company, 17 July 1930; 1944-8.
83. Papers of the Glasgow American Trust Company, CRO, BLRP.
84. Papers of the West of Scotland American Investment Company, CRO, BLRP.
85. Papers of the Scottish Western Investment Company, CRO, BLRP.
86. Report of Proceedings, Annual Ordinary General Meeting, Alliance Trust Company, 13 April 1934.
87. Report of Proceedings, Annual Ordinary General Meeting, Second Alliance Trust Company, 21 September 1934.
88. Report of Proceedings, Annual Ordinary General Meeting, Alliance Trust Company, 18 April 1935.
89. Report of Proceedings, Annual Ordinary General Meeting, Second Alliance Trust Company, 18 September 1936.
90. Reports of Proceedings, Annual Ordinary General Meetings, Alliance Trust Company, 17 April 1936, and 16 April 1937.
91. Report of Proceedings, Annual Ordinary General Meeting, Second Alliance Trust Company, 17 September 1937.
92. Ibid., 16 September 1938; Report of Proceedings, Alliance Trust Company, 12 April 1938.
93. Inspector's Report on B. S. Arnold Loan in Randall and Armstrong counties, Texas, 20 May 1920; Some Historic Notes on the Palo Duro Canyon, May 1937, Alliance Trust Company records.
94. Memorandum on Idaho Irrigated Properties, 30 August 1934, Alliance Trust Company Records.
95. Report of Proceedings, Annual Ordinary General Meeting, Alliance Trust Company, 19 April 1939.
96. Report of Proceedings, Annual Ordinary General Meeting, Second Alliance Trust Company, 8 September 1939.
97. Papers of the Scottish-American Mortgage Company, CRO, BLRP.
98. Report of Proceedings, Annual Ordinary General Meeting, Alliance Trust Company, 26 April 1940.
99. Ibid., 25 April 1941.
100. Directors' Reports and Accounts, Deltic Investment Company, 1930–41.
101. Jackson 'The Chavez Land Grant: A Scottish Investment in New Mexico, 1881–1940', loc. cit.
102. Papers of the Scottish-American Mortgage Company and Papers of the Scottish-American Investment Company, CRO, BLRP.

103. Ibid.
104. Papers of the American Trust Company, CRO, BLRP.
105. Report of Directors and Statement of Accounts, Second Alliance Trust Company, 31 July 1949; Report of Directors and Accounts, British Investment Trust Company, 1 January 1950; Papers of the Scottish-American Mortgage Company; Papers of the United States Trust Company; Papers of the American Trust Company, CRO, BLRP.
106. Directors' Annual Report and Accounts, Alliance Trust Company, 31 January 1947; Sheets of Statistical Information on the British Investment Trust and the United States Investment Corporation compiled from the 'Daily Statistical Service', The Exchange Telegraph Company, Limited, London; Report by the Directors, First Scottish American Trust Company, 3 June 1949; Third Company, 30 July 1949.

Chapter XII : A Summation

1. 'Scottish Investors in the Dumps', *The Statist*, XV (10 January 1885), 36.
2. Marwick, op. cit., 17-25, 223-31.
3. 'Scottish Investors in the Dumps', loc. cit., 36.
4. 'Scottish Capital Abroad', loc. cit., 468.
5. 'Scottish Investors in the Dumps', loc. cit., 37.
6. W. R. Lawson *The Scottish Investors' Manual. A Review of the Leading Scottish Securities in 1883*, 11. As evidence of the comparative success of the mortgage and investment companies and the stability or appreciation of their shares, Lawson presented the following random selection.

Market Value of Shares of the Scottish Mortgage and Investment Companies, 1882 and 1883.

number of shares	*company*	*30 Dec. 1882*	*30 Dec. 1883*	*increased value of capital*
		£ s. d.	*£ s. d.*	*£*
42,800	American Mortgage of Scotland	1 13 6	1 19 0	11,770
70,000	Dundee Mortgage and Trust Investment	3 4 0	3 6 6	8,750
50,000	Edinburgh American Land Mortgage	1 0 0	1 0 0	
170,000	Scottish-American Investment	4 4 0	4 7 6	29,750
				£50,270

7. Ibid., 11-12. The following data indicated, to Lawson, the financial problems of the timber, cattle and land companies:

Market Value of Shares of the Timber, Cattle and Land Companies, 1882 and 1883.

number of shares	*company*	*30 Dec. 1882*	*30 Dec. 1883*	*reduced value of capital*
		£ s. d.	*£ s. d.*	*£*
34,500	American Lumber	6 15 0	0 11 0	£213,900
10,300	British Canadian Lumber	11 10 0	4 10 0	72,100
263,425	Canada North-West	4 2 6	3 6 6	210,740
60,000	Cattle Ranche	5 5 0	5 2 6	7,500
9,075	Missouri Land of Scotland	3 18 6	3 13 6	2,269
12,500	Prairie Cattle I.	13 15 0	8 12 6	67,187
25,000	Prairie Cattle II.	13 10 0	8 12 6	128,125
5,000	Scottish American Land	8 12 6	6 17 6	8,750
5,000	Scottish American Land New	3 0 0	2 0 0	5,000
16,000	Western Land and Cattle Ordinary	7 15 0	7 5 0	8,000
22,400	Western Ranches	5 0 0	4 15 0	5,000
				£729,171

8. Ibid., 1-7, 13.
9. 'Scottish Capital Abroad', loc. cit., 469. In this critic's calculations, only four companies operating in the western United States were included—American Mortgage of Scotland, Edinburgh American Land, Scottish-American Investment, and Scottish-American Mortgage. Their total subscribed capital in 1884 was £2,950,000, with approximately £700,000 paid-up. An equally large investment from Dundee was overlooked in the computation of *Blackwood's* contributor, so apparently his conclusions applied only to Edinburgh.
10. Ibid., 477.
11. Ibid., 480.
12. 'Scottish Investors in the Dumps, No. II', *The Statist*, XV (17 January 1885), 64.
13. Ibid., 65.

Bibliography

Manuscripts and Unpublished Sources

Manuscript Collections

The Bancroft Library Research Program in Scotland:
Records from the Companies Registration Office, Exchequer Chambers, 1 Parliament Square, Edinburgh, Scotland:
Microfilmed public records of Scottish limited companies primarily interested in America as a field for investment. Ninety-two reels of film. One hundred and twenty-seven Scottish companies active in the western United States. These records include the Memoranda of Association, Articles of Association, Annual Summaries of Capital and Shares, Annual Lists of Stockholders, Winding-Up Records, etc.
London Stock Exchange Records:
Reports and Financial Papers of Scottish companies operating in California.
The Library of Congress and Colorado State Historical Society: The Western Range Cattle Industry Study—Co-operative Project for Microfilming Western Americana in Europe:
Records from the Companies Registration Office, Edinburgh, Scotland:
Microfilmed public records of Scottish limited companies primarily interested in the range cattle industry in the western United States. Seventeen reels of film. Fifteen land and cattle companies; nine mining companies primarily interested in Colorado.
Edinburgh Stock Exchange Records:
Confidential correspondence relative to the Swan Land and Cattle Company, 1883–1944, primarily concerned with procedures and progress of liquidation.
London Stock Exchange Records:
Reports and Financial Papers of Western American cattle and land corporations, 1881–1921. Share and Loan Department, Austin Friars, 'The City.'
Prospectuses of seven Scottish companies.
Western Range Cattle Industry Study Headquarters, State Historical Society of Colorado, State Museum, Denver, Colorado:
Reports, operational records, and files of several land and cattle companies:
Swan Land and Cattle Company, Limited. Reports of annual meetings from 1883 to 1925, Annual Reports of the Directors

to the Shareholders, 1883–5, Minutes of the First General Meeting, local land records, etc.
Texas Land Cattle Company, Limited. Scattered annual reports, 1881–1908.
Missouri Land and Live Stock Company, Limited. Annual reports from 1883 to 1907, extensive land purchase and sales records, etc.
Diary of George D. Ballingall on his American Trip for the Missouri Land and Live Stock Company. Memorandum on the 'Silver Question' in the United States as affecting the Missouri Land and Live Stock Company, Limited, October 1891.
Missouri Land Company, Limited. Annual reports and winding up records, etc.
Hansford Land and Cattle Company, Limited. Annual reports and local ranch records.
Prospectus, Memorandum of Association, Articles of Association and/or Certificate of Incorporation obtained from State Officials in charge of registration records for five western American cattle companies.

Limited Company Records. Examined in company offices in Edinburgh, Glasgow, and Dundee, Scotland:
Alliance Trust Company, Limited.
Memoranda on the Chavez Land Grant.
William Mackenzie's Scrap Book of duplicate business transactions, newspaper clippings, etc.
Annual Reports to the Stockholders and Proceedings of the Annual Meetings, 1889–1941.
American Trust Company, Limited (Old).
Minute Books of the Directors' Meetings, including Annual Reports to the Stockholders, 1899–1902.
American Trust Company, Limited.
Directors' Reports and Accounts and Chairman's Speeches at Annual Meetings from the Inception of the Company [1902] to and Including Year Ending January 1923.
British Investment Trust, Limited.
Annual Reports to the Stockholders and Proceedings of the Annual Meetings: Volume 1, 1889–1913; Volume 2, 1914–43.
Register of Purchases, 1889–1929.
Register of Sales, 1889–1923.
Deltic Investment Company, Limited.
Minute Books of the Meetings of the Board of Directors: Volume 1, 1894–1901; Volume 2, 1901–9; Volume 3, 1921–6; Volume 4, 1938–.
Annual Reports to the Stockholders, 1909–38.
Dundee Investment Company, Limited.
Annual Reports to the Stockholders, 1882–9.
Minute Books of the Meetings of the Board of Directors, 1882–7.

Dundee Land Investment Company, Limited.
Annual Reports to the Stockholders and Proceedings of the Annual Meetings, 1879–82.
Minute Books of the Meetings of the Board of Directors: Volume 1, 1878–81; Volume 2, 1881–2.
Dundee Mortgage and Trust Investment Company, Limited.
Prospectus and Memorandum of Association, 1876.
Annual Reports to the Shareholders, 1876–89.
Minute Books: Volumes 1-4, 1876–80.
Balance Sheet, 1880.
General Abstract of Loans, 1881.
Edinburgh American Land Mortgage Company, Limited.
Annual Reports to the Stockholders, 1879–1919.
Minute Books of the Directors' Meetings; Volume 1, 1878–83; Volume 2, 1884–8.
Edinburgh Investment Trust, Limited.
Minute Books.
Annual Reports to the Stockholders.
Private Memoranda for the Directors, 1889–1926.
Investors' Mortgage Security Company, Limited.
Directors' Reports and Accounts and Annual Speeches at Annual Meetings from the Inception of the Company [1891] to and including the Year Ending 30 September 1915.
Minute Books: Volume 1, 1891–8; Volume 2, 1898–1906; Volume 3, 1906–11; Volume 4, 1912–16.
Matador Land and Cattle Company, Limited.
Annual Reports to the Stockholders and Proceedings of the Annual Meetings, 1883–1934.
North American Trust Company, Limited.
Annual Reports to the Stockholders, 1897–1922.
Oregon and Washington Mortgage Savings Bank, Limited.
Prospectus.
Annual Reports to the Stockholders.
Minutes of the Meetings of the Board of Directors, 1876–82.
Oregon and Washington Trust Investment Company, Limited.
Minute Books of the Meetings of the Board of Directors, including Annual Reports to the Stockholders: Volume 1, 1873–5; Volume 2, 1876–8; Volume 3, 1878–9.
Oregon Mortgage Company, Limited.
Annual Reports to the Stockholders and Accounts: Volume 1, 1883–1908; Volume 2, 1909–30.
Minute Books of Directors' Meetings: Volume 1, 1883–91; Volume 2, 1891–1900.
Scottish–American Investment Company, Limited.
Prospectus.
Minute Book of the Meetings of Board of Directors, 1873–4.
Annual Reports to the Stockholders and Proceedings of the Annual Meetings, 1874–1917.
Minute Book of the New York Advisory Board, 1880–96.

Scottish–American Mortgage Company, Limited.
Prospectus and Annual Reports to the Stockholders, 1874–1920.
Proceedings of the Annual Meetings including Remarks of the Chairman of the Board: Volume 1, 1874–99, Volume 2, 1900–8; Volume 3, 1909–26.
'Agency Books' with reports from local agencies in Kansas, Missouri, Georgia, Illinois, Nebraska, Iowa, Washington, Minnesota, Texas, South Carolina, Tennessee, Alabama, North and South Dakota.
Confidential Notes on the Early History of the Company by William Williamson.
Scottish Investment Trust Company, Limited.
Minute Books of Directors' Meetings, 1887–1900, including Annual Reports to the Stockholders.
Second Alliance Trust Company, Limited.
Reports of Proceedings at Annual Ordinary General Meetings, 1924–49.
Second Scottish Investment Trust, Limited.
Minute Books of Directors' Meetings including Annual Reports to the Stockholders, 1889–1909.
Swan Land and Cattle Company, Limited.
Annual Reports to the Stockholders, 1883–1912.
United States Investment Corporation, Limited.
Minute Books of the Board of Directors, 1890–1912.
Annual Reports to the Stockholders, 1891–1947.
United States Mortgage Company of Scotland, Limited.
Minute Books, 1884–92.
Western and Hawaiian Investment Company, Limited.
Directors' Reports and Accounts, Proceedings of the Annual Meetings, 1904–22.
Bancroft Library, University of California, Berkeley:
Gibbs, Addison C., Notes and Incidents of His Life in Connection with the History of Oregon, MS., Bancroft Library, University of California, Berkeley.

Unpublished Theses and Dissertations

Bright, Davilla, Foreigners and Foreign Capital in the Cattle Industry of the United States. M.A. Thesis, University of Oklahoma, 1935.

Dahl, Albin Joachim, British Investment in California Mining, 1870–1890. PH.D. Dissertation, University of California, Berkeley, 1961.

Elliott, Russell Richard, The Tonopah-Goldfield-Bullfrog Mining District, 1900–1915: History of a Twentieth-Century Mining Boom. PH.D. Dissertation, University of California, Berkeley, 1946.

Smith, Duane Allan, Silver Camp Called Caribou. M.A. Thesis, University of Colorado, Boulder, 1961.

Towney, Richard E., British Investment in California, 1849–1860. M.A. Thesis, University of California, Berkeley, 1957.

Printed Government Records

British

Statutes at Large, Vol. 96 (19 & 20 Vict.); Vol. 102 (25 & 26 Vict.).
The Law Reports, Statutes, Vol. 2 (30 & 31 Vict.); Vol. 27 (53 & 54 Vict.); Vol. 38 (63 & 64 Vict.); Vol. 45 (7 Edw. VII).
Common Pleas Division, Vol. 2.
Chancery Division, Vol. 5.
Read, Clare and Albert Pell, Further Reports of Assistant Commissioners, 1880, *Royal Commission on Agriculture, 1879–1882*. Vol. 71, Ministry of Agriculture and Fisheries.
Final Report of Her Majesty's Commissioners Appointed to Inquire into the Subject of the Agricultural Depression, 1897. WRCIS.

United States, Federal

U.S. Statutes at Large, Vol. XX, 45 Congress, 1877–9; Vol. XXIV, 49 Congress, 1885–7.
Congressional Record, Vols. XV, XVII, XVIII, 48-9 Congress, 1883–7.
Federal Reporter
California Redwood Co. *v.* Litle, LXXIX, 854; LXXXVII, 1004.
California Redwood Co. *v.* Mahan, LXXX, 1004.
Oregonian Ry. Co. Ltd. *v.* Oregon Ry. & Nav. Co., XXII, 245; XXIII, 232; XXVII, 277; XXXVII, 733.
United States Reports
California Redwood Co. *v.* Johnson, CLXXIX, 681.
Oregon Ry. & Nav. Co. *v.* Oregonian Ry. Co., CXXX, 1.
Senate:
Senate Executive Document 181, (Serial 2167), 48 Congress, 1 Session, 1883–4.
House:
Skidmore, W. A., Deep Placer Mining in California, in Rossiter W. Raymond, *Mineral Resources* . . . [for 1868], *House Executive Document 54*, 30ff., 40 Congress, 3 Session, 1868.
Gosper, John J., Report of the Acting Governor of Arizona Territory, in *Report of the Secretary of the Interior, 1881*, II, *House Executive Document 1*, Part 5 (serial 1028), 932, 47 Congress, 1 Session, 1881–2.
Loring, George B., Report of the Commissioner of Agriculture, 1883–4, *House Executive Document 33* (serial 2198), 48 Congress, 1 Session, 1883–4.
House Report 2308 (serial 2328), 48 Congress, 2 Session, 1884–5.
House Report 3455 (serial 2445), 49 Congress, 1 Session, 1885–6.

Report of the Commissioner of the General Land Office, October 7, 1886, *House Executive Document 1*, Part 5 (serial 2468), 94, 49 Congress, 2 Session, 1885–6.

Report of the Commissioner of the General Land Office, September 28, 1887, *House Executive Document 1* (serial 2547), 50 Congress, 1 Session, 1887–8.

The California Redwood Company, *House Executive Document 282* (serial 2561), 50 Congress, 1 Session, 1887–8.

UNITED STATES, STATE

California:

Reports of the State Mineralogist. The California Mining Bureau. Second, II (1882); Eighth (1888); Tenth-Fifteenth (1890–1916); Thirty-second (1936); Thirty-seventh (1941).

Register of Mines and Minerals in California. Nevada County. Quartz Mines.

Bulletins of the California State Mining Bureau. San Francisco.

Bulletin No. 18. Storms, W.H., The Mother Lode Region of California. October 1900.

Bulletin No. 50. The Copper Resources of California. September 1908.

Bulletin No. 108. Logan, Clarence A., The Mother Lode Gold Belt of California. November 1934.

Laws of the State of Illinois, 1887.

General Laws of the State of Minnesota, 1887, 1889.

Sixth Annual Report of the Bureau of Agriculture, Labor, and Industry of the State of Montana, 1898 (Helena, Montana, 1898).

Laws, Joint Resolutions and Memorials of the Legislative Assembly of Nebraska, 1887; Laws, Joint Resolutions and Memorials of the Legislature of the State of Nebraska, 1889.

General Laws of Texas, 1891, 1892.

Messages of the Governors of Wyoming to the Territorial Legislatures, 1873–88, Message of Governor Thomas Moonlight, 10 January 1888. Wyoming Corporation Law of 1887, WRCIS.

Secondary Works

NEWSPAPERS. Great Britain

Aberdeen Free Press (Aberdeen, Scotland).

Courier and Argus (Dundee, Scotland).

Dundee Advertiser. Broken files from May 1876, to July 1920.

The Edinburgh Courant. Files from January 1874, to March 1886.

Glasgow Herald. Files from January 1880, to January 1887.

The Scotsman (Edinburgh). Scattered file from January 1872, to June 1887, and from October 1892, to October 1905.

The Times (London). 1870–

NEWSPAPERS. United States*

The Bulletin (San Francisco).
Clifton *Clarion* (Clifton, Arizona).
Daily Alta Californian (San Francisco).
The Galveston News (Galveston, Texas).
The Herald (Los Angeles).
The Humboldt Standard (Eureka, California).
The Morning Call (San Francisco).
New York Times.
The Oregonian (Portland, Oregon).
Sacramento Daily Record-Union.
San Francisco Chronicle.
Stockton Daily Independent.
Scrap Book of William Mackenzie. Newspaper clippings from dozens of United States newspapers, chiefly western, are included.

* The periods covered by each newspaper are omitted here. Definite citations appear in the notes.

PERIODICALS

The Economist, Weekly Commercial Times, Bankers' Gazette, and Railway Monitor: A Political, Literary, and General Newspaper. Vols. 35–72, January 1877–June 1914.
The Engineering and Mining Journal, Vols. 1-70, 1866–1900.
The Mining Journal (London), Vols. 38-74, 1868–1905.
Mining and Scientific Press, Vols. 1-80, 1860–1900.
Scottish Banking and Insurance Magazine, Financial Record, Economist & Railway Review, Vols. 1-8, 1879–86.
The Statist, A Weekly Journal for Economists and Men of Business. Vols. VII-XLIV, January 1881 10 December 1899.

MAGAZINE ARTICLES, PAMPHLETS, AND CHARTS

Airlie, Earl of, The United States as a Field for Agricultural Settlers, *The Nineteenth Century* (February 1881), 292-301.
Brayer, Herbert O., The Influence of British Capital on the Western Range Cattle Industry, *The Westerners' Brand Book* (Denver), IV (May 1948), 1-19.
Moreton Frewen, Cattleman, *The Westerners' Brand Book* (Denver), V (July 1949), 1-21.
Moreton Frewen, British Cattleman, *Western Live Stock* (October 1949), 12ff.
The 76 Ranch on the Powder River, *The Westerners,* VII (December 1950).
Range Country Troubles, 1885, *The Westerners' Brand Book* (Denver), VIII (March 1952).
Cairncross, A. K., Did Foreign Investments Pay? *Review of Economic Studies,* III (October 1935), 67-78.

Clements, Roger V., British-Controlled Enterprise in the West Between 1870 and 1900, and Some Agrarian Reactions, *Agricultural History*, XXVII (October 1953), 132-41.

British Investment and American Legislative Restrictions in the Trans-Mississippi West, 1880–1900, *Mississippi Valley Historical Review*, XLII (September 1955), 207-28.

Comparative Statement of Cattle Companies Balance Sheets, 1883, 1884, 1885, 1886, and 1888, WRCIS.

Dumke, Glenn S., Early Las Vegas, *The Pacific Historical Review*, XXII (August 1953), 257-70.

Elliott, Russell R., Labor Troubles in the Mining Camp at Goldfield, Nevada, 1906–1908, *The Pacific Historical Review*, XIX (November 1950), 369-84.

Frewen, Moreton, The Transatlantic Cattle Trade, *The Fortnightly Review*, XLIX (New Series, January to June 1891), 713-24.

Ganoe, John T., The History of the Oregon and California Railroad, *Quarterly of the Oregon Historical Society*, XXV (September 1924), 239-40.

Gaston, Joseph L., The Genesis of the Oregon Railway System, *Quarterly of the Oregon Historical Society*, VII (June 1906), 105-32.

Gilbert, J. C., The Investment Trusts in Dundee, in *A Scientific Survey of Dundee and District* (1939) 87-93, edited by R. L. Mackie. Published by the British Association for the Advancement of Science, London.

Grohman, W. Baillie, Cattle Ranches in the Far West, *The Fortnightly Review*, XXVIII (New Series, July to December 1880), 438-57.

Hamilton, Henry, The Economic Evolution of Scotland in the 18th and 19th Centuries, *Historical Association Leaflet 91*. Published for The Historical Association by G. Bell and Sons, Limited, London, 1933.

Hyde, Francis Edwin, British Capital and American Enterprise in the Northwest, *The Economic History Review*, VI (April 1936), 201-8. Published for the Economic History Society by A & C Black, Limited, London.

J.R.F.S., The American Ranchman, *Longman's Magazine*, XXX (May 1897 to October 1897), 444-60.

Jackson, W. Turrentine, Railroad Relations of the Wyoming Stock Growers Association, 1873–1890, *Annals of Wyoming*, XIX (January 1947), 3-23.

The Wyoming Stock Growers' Association, Its Years of Temporary Decline, 1886–1890, *Agricultural History*, XXII (October 1948), 260-71.

The Infamous Emma Mine: A British Interest in the Little Cottonwood District, Utah Territory, *Utah Historical Review*, XXIII (October 1955), 339-62.

The Chavez Land Grant: A Scottish Investment in New Mexico, 1881–1940, *The Pacific Historical Review*, XXI (November 1952), 349-66.

Johansen, Dorothy O., The Oregon Steam Navigation Company: An Example of Capitalism on the Frontier, *The Pacific Historical Review*, x (June 1941), 234-44.

Kelley, Robert L., The Mining Debris Controversy in the Sacramento Valley, *The Pacific Historical Review*, XXV (November 1956), 331-46.

Forgotten Giant: The Hydraulic Gold Mining Industry in California, *The Pacific Historical Review*, XXIII (November 1954), 343-56.

Larson, T. A., The Winter of 1886–1887 in Wyoming, *Annals of Wyoming*, XIV (January 1942), 5-17.

Marshall, C.H., Dundee as a Centre of Investment, in *Handbook and Guide to Dundee and District, 1912*, edited by A.W. Paton and A.H. Millar. Published by David Winter and Son, Dundee.

Marwick, W.H., Scottish Overseas Investment in the Nineteenth Century, *The Scottish Bankers Magazine*, (July 1935). Separate printed by William Blackwood and Sons, Limited, Edinburgh, 1935.

The Limited Company in Scottish Economic Development, *Economic History* (Supplement), III (February 1937).

Menzies, William John, *America as a Field for Investment*. Lecture delivered 18 February 1892. Published by William Blackwood and Sons, Limited, Edinburgh and London, 1892.

Nef, John U., The Industrial Revolution Reconsidered, *Journal of Economic History*, III (May 1943), 1-31.

Rae, John B., Commissioner Sparks and the Railroad Land Grants, *Mississippi Valley Historical Review*, XXV (September 1938), 211-30.

Riordan, M., Murdo Mackenzie, Ranch King, *The Westerner* (October 1943, to March 1944).

Rippy, J. Fred, British Investments in Texas Lands and Livestock, *The Southwestern Historical Quarterly*, LVIII (January 1955), 331-41.

Saul, S.B., Britain and World Trade, 1870–1914, *Economic History Review*, Second Series, VII (August 1954), 49-66.

Shannon, H.A., The Coming of General Limited Liability, *Economic History* (Supplement to the *Economic Journal*), II (January 1931), 267-91.

The Limited Companies of 1866–1883, *The Economic History Review*, IV (October 1933), 290-307.

Smith, Duane Allan, The Caribou—A Forgotten Mine, *The Colorado Magazine*, XXX (October 1953), 241-6.

Tinkler, Estelle D., History of the Rocking Chair Ranch, *Panhandle-Plains Historical Review*, XV (1942), 1-88.

Tischendorf, Alfred P., British Investments in Colorado Mines, *The Colorado Magazine*, XXX (October 1953), 241-6.

Trimble, William, Historical Aspects of the Surplus Food Production of the United States, 1862–1902, *Annual Report of the American Historical Association for 1918*, I, 231-2.

* * *

A Black Year for Investors, *Blackwood's Edinburgh Magazine*, CXXXVII (February 1885), 269-84.
The Alliance Trust Company, Limited, Presentation of Portrait to William Mackenzie, Esq., 11th March, 1920, Privately printed.
Land Grabbers Brought up with a Round Turn, *San Francisco News Letter and California Advertiser*, XXXIV (15 March 1884).
The Matador Land and Cattle Company, Limited, One Day on the Alamositas Ranch, 25th April, 1949. Privately printed.
Scottish Bargain, *Time* (6 August 1951), 78, 80.
Scottish Capital Abroad, *Blackwood's Edinburgh Magazine*, CXXXVI (October 1884), 468-80.

BOOKS

An Illustrated History of San Joaquin County, California. Chicago: The Lewis Publishing Company, 1890.
Ashton, T. S. *An Economic History of England in the 18th Century*. London: Methuen and Company, Limited, 1955.
Ashworth, William *Economic History of England, 1870–1939*. London: Methuen; New York: Barnes and Noble, 1960.
Bailey, Thomas A. *A Diplomatic History of the American People*. New York: F.S.Crofts and Company, 1947.
Baker, James H. and LeRoy R.Hafen *History of Colorado*. Three volumes Denver: Linderman Company, 1927.
Bancroft, Hubert Howe *History of Arizona and New Mexico, 1530–1880*. San Francisco: The History Company, 1889.
History of Oregon, 1848–1888. Two volumes. San Francisco: The History Company, 1888.
Bemis, Samuel Flagg *A Diplomatic History of the United States*. New York: Henry Holt and Company, 1942.
Billington, Ray Allen *Westward Expansion: A History of the American Frontier*. New York: The Macmillan Company, 1949.
Bogue, Allen G. *From Prairie to Corn Belt: Farming on the Illinois and Iowa Prairies in the Nineteenth Century*. Chicago and London: The University of Chicago Press, 1963.
Money at Interest: The Farm Mortgage on the Middle Border. Ithaca, New York: Cornell University Press, 1955.
Brayer, Herbert O. *William Blackmore: A Case Study in the Economic Development of the West*. Two volumes. Denver: Bradford-Robinson, 1949.
Cairncross, A. K. *Home and Foreign Investments 1870–1913. Studies in Capital Accumulation*. Cambridge: Cambridge University Press, 1953.
editor, *The Scottish Economy: A Statistical Account of Scottish Life*. Cambridge: Cambridge University Press, 1954.
Chambers, J.D. *The Workshop of the World: British Economic History from 1820 to 1880*. London, New York and Toronto: Oxford University Press, 1961.
Clapham, J.H. *An Economic History of Modern Britain*. Three volumes. Cambridge: Cambridge University Press, 1953.

Clark, Dan Elbert *The West in American History*. New York: Thomas Y. Crowell Company, 1937.

Clark, Robert Carlton *History of the Willamette Valley, Oregon*. Indianapolis: S. J. Clarke Publishing Company, 1927.

Clay, John *My Life on the Range*. Chicago: Privately printed, 1924.

Cleland, Robert Glass *A History of Phelps Dodge, 1834–1950*. New York: Alfred A. Knopf, 1952.

Colquhoun, James *The Early History of the Clifton-Morenci District*. London and Beccles: William Clowes and Sons, Limited, n.d.

Corbett, Thomas B. *The Colorado Directory of Mines containing a description of the mines and mills, and the mining and milling corporations of Colorado arranged alphabetically by counties*. Denver: Rocky Mountain News Printing Company, 1879.

Corregan, Robert A. and David F. Lingane *Colorado Mining Directory, 1883*. Denver: Colorado Mining Directory Company, 1883.

Court, W. H. B. *A Concise Economic History of Britain*. Cambridge: Cambridge University Press, 1954.

Dale, Edward Everett *Cow Country*. Norman: University of Oklahoma Press, 1942.

The Range Cattle Industry. Norman: University of Oklahoma Press, 1942.

Dunham, Harold Hathaway *Government Handout, A Study in the Administration of the Public Lands, 1875–1891*. Ann Arbor, Michigan: Edwards Brothers, Inc., 1941.

Farrer, Frederick E. *The Law Relating to Prospectuses*. London: Effingham Wilson, 1913.

Fay, C. R. *English Economic History Mainly Since 1870*. Cambridge: W. Heffer & Sons, Ltd., 1940.

Frink, Maurice, W. Turrentine Jackson, and Agnes W. Spring *When Grass Was King*. Boulder: University of Colorado Press, 1956.

Fritz, Percy Stanley *Colorado, The Centennial State*. New York: Prentice-Hall, 1941.

Gilbert, J. E. *A History of Investment Trusts in Dundee, 1873–1938*. London: P. S. King and Son, Limited, 1939.

Glasgow, George *The Scottish Investment Trust Companies*. London: Eyre and Spottiswoode, Limited, 1932.

Grant, Isabel F. *The Economic History of Scotland*. London: Longmans, Green and Company, Limited, 1934.

Grayson, Theodore J. *Investment Trusts, Their Origin, Development and Operation*. New York: John Wiley and Sons, 1928.

Grodinsky, Julius *Jay Gould, His Business Career, 1867–1892*. Philadelphia: University of Pennsylvania Press, 1957.

Hafen, LeRoy R. and Carl Coke Rister *Western America: The Exploration, Settlement, and Development of the Region Beyond the Mississippi*. New York: Prentice-Hall, 1941.

Hamilton, Henry *The Industrial Revolution in Scotland*. Oxford: The Clarendon Press, 1932.

Hamilton, Patrick *The Resources of Arizona, 1884*. San Francisco: A.L. Bancroft & Company, Printers, 1884.

Heaton, Herbert *Economic History of Europe*. New York: Harper and Brothers, 1948.

Hedges, James B. *Henry Villard and the Railways of the Northwest*. New Haven: Yale University Press; London: H. Milford, Oxford University Press, 1930.

Henderson, Charles W. *Mining in Colorado, A History of Discovery, Development and Production*. U.S. Department of the Interior, Geological Survey, No. 138. Washington: Government Printing Office, 1926.

Hicks, John D. *The American Nation*. Boston: Houghton Mifflin Company, 1941.

Hinton, Richard J. *The Hand-Book to Arizona, 1878*. San Francisco: Payot, Upham and Company; New York: American News Company, 1878.

History of San Joaquin County, California, With Illustrations Descriptive of Its Scenery. Oakland: Thompson and West, 1879.

Hobson, C.K. *The Export of Capital*. London: Constable and Company, Limited, 1914.

Jenks, Leland Hamilton *The Migration of British Capital to 1875*. London: Jonathan Cape, Limited, 1938.

Kelley, Robert L. *Gold vs. Grain: The Hydraulic Mining Controversy in California's Sacramento Valley*. Glendale: The Arthur H. Clark Company, 1959.

Lawson, W. R. *The Scottish Investors' Manual, A Review of the Leading Scottish Securities in 1883*. Edinburgh and London: William Blackwood and Sons, Limited, 1884.

Lillard, Richard G. *Desert Challenge, An Interpretation of Nevada*. New York: Alfred A. Knopf, 1942.

McClintock, James H. *Arizona*. Two volumes. Chicago: The S. J. Clarke Publishing Company, 1916.

MacDonald, James *Food from the Far West*. Edinburgh: W.P. Nimmo, 1878.

Mackenzie, Agnes Mure *Scotland in Modern Times, 1720–1939*. London and Edinburgh: W. & R. Chambers, Limited, 1941.

Mackie, R.L. *A Short History of Scotland*. New York: Frederick A. Praeger, 1963.

Mackinnon, James *The Social and Industrial History of Scotland*. London and New York: Longmans, Green and Company, Limited, 1921.

Marwick, W.H. *Economic Developments in Victorian Scotland*. London: George Allen and Unwin, Limited, 1936.

Notestein, Wallace *The Scot in History: A Study of the Interplay of Character and History*. New Haven: Yale University Press, 1947.

Osgood, Ernest Staples *The Day of the Cattleman*. Minneapolis: University of Minnesota Press, 1929.

O'Shaughnessy, M.M., The Copper Resources of California, *California Mines and Minerals*, San Francisco: California Miners' Association, 1899.

Paul, Rodman W. *California Gold, the Beginning of Mining in the Far West*. Cambridge: Harvard University Press, 1947.

Peake, Ora B. *The Colorado Range Cattle Industry*. Glendale: The Arthur H. Clark Company, 1937.

Pearce, William Martin *The Matador Land and Cattle Company*. Norman: University of Oklahoma Press, 1964.

Pelzer, Louis *The Cattlemen's Frontier*. Glendale: The Arthur H. Clark Company, 1936.

Pryde, George S. *Scotland from 1603 to the Present Day*. Edinburgh: Thomas Nelson and Sons, Limited, 1962.

Raymond, Rossiter W. *Statistics of Mines and Mining in the States and Territories West of the Rocky Mountains, 1872*. Washington: Government Printing Office, 1872.

Reid, John *Manual of the Scottish Stocks and British Funds with a List of the Joint Stock Companies in Scotland, 1841*. Edinburgh, 1841.

Rostow, W. W. *British Economy of the Nineteenth Century*. Oxford: University Press, 1953.

Shannon, Fred A. *Economic History of the People of the United States*. New York: The Macmillan Company, 1936.

Shearer, W.H. *Atlas of the Goldfield, Tonopah and Bullfrog Mining Districts of Nevada, 1905*. Chicago: Rand, McNally and Company, 1905.

Skinner, Thomas *The Stock Exchange Year-Book, containing a careful digest of information relative to the origin, history, and present position of the Joint Stock Companies and Public Securities known to the markets of the United Kingdom*. Annual editions, 1879 to 1904. London, Paris, and New York: Cassell Petter and Galpin.

Spence, Clark C. *British Investments in the American Mining Frontier, 1860–1901*. Ithaca: Cornell University Press, 1958.

Stevens, Horace J. *The Copper Handbook, A Manual of the Copper Industry of the World*, x. Houghton, Michigan: Horace J. Stevens, 1911.

Tait, J.S. *The Cattle Fields of the Far West*. Edinburgh and London: William Blackwood and Sons, 1884.

Tinkham, George H. *History of San Joaquin County, California, with Biographical Sketches*. Los Angeles Historical Record Company, 1923.

Villard, Henry *Memoirs of Henry Villard, Journalist and Financier, 1835–1900*. Boston and New York: Houghton, Mifflin & Co., 1904.

The Early History of Transportation in Oregon. Edited by Oswald Garrison Villard. Eugene, Oregon, 1944.

Wahlgreen, G.A. *Colorado Mining Directory and Buyer's Guide, 1901*. Denver, 1901.

Whitney, J. D. *The Metallic Wealth of the United States, Described and Compared with that of Other Countries*. Philadelphia: Lippincott, Granbo and Company, 1854.

Winther, Oscar Osburn *The Old Oregon Country: A History of Frontier Trade, Transportation, and Travel.* Stanford: Stanford University Press, 1950.

Wright, Chester W. *Economic History of the United States*. New York: McGraw-Hill Book Company, 1941.

Index